SHOUT IT OUT LOUD

SHOUT IT OUT LOUD

THE STORY OF KISS's
DESTROYER
and the Making of an American Icon

JAMES CAMPION

Backbeat Books

AN IMPRINT OF HAL LEONARD CORPORATION

Copyright © 2015 by James Campion

All rights reserved. No part of this book may be reproduced in any form, without written permission, except by a newspaper or magazine reviewer who wishes to quote brief passages in connection with a review.

Published in 2015 by Backbeat Books
An Imprint of Hal Leonard Corporation
7777 West Bluemound Road
Milwaukee, WI 53213

Trade Book Division Editorial Offices
33 Plymouth St., Montclair, NJ 07042

Printed in the United States of America

Book design by Michael Kellner

Every reasonable effort has been made to contact copyright holders and secure permissions. Omissions can be remedied in future editions.

Acknowledgments of permission to reprint previously published materials are on page 381, which constitutes an extension of this copyright page.

Library of Congress Cataloging-in-Publication Data is available upon request.

ISBN 978-1-61713-618-4

www.backbeatbooks.com

For Scarlet,
my little rock-and-roller

"I dream my painting and I paint my dream."
—Vincent van Gogh

Contents

Preface ix
Introduction xiii

SIDE ONE — 1

"Detroit Rock City" — 3

CHAPTER 1 The Act — 7
CHAPTER 2 Zeitgeist — 17
CHAPTER 3 Wilderness — 29

"King of the Night Time World" — 41

CHAPTER 4 The Show — 45
CHAPTER 5 School's Out — 55

"God of Thunder" — 65

CHAPTER 6 The Meeting — 69
CHAPTER 7 Boot Camp — 77

"Great Expectations" — 91

CHAPTER 8 Four Dimensions — 95

SIDE TWO — 105

"Flaming Youth" — 107

CHAPTER 9 The Songs, Part One: Origins — 109
CHAPTER 10 The Songs, Part Two: Collaborations — 121

CHAPTER 11 And Suddenly... "Beth"	133
CHAPTER 12 The Palette	141
"Sweet Pain"	**155**
CHAPTER 13 All Right, Campers!	159
CHAPTER 14 Sessions	171
CHAPTER 15 Games	185
CHAPTER 16 Exit Ace—Enter Maestro and the Kids	199
"Shout It Out Loud"	**213**
CHAPTER 17 Black Ties and Tales	217
CHAPTER 18 The Cover	231
CHAPTER 19 Finishing Touches	247
"Beth"	**263**
CHAPTER 20 Aftermath	267
CHAPTER 21 Stratosphere	283
CHAPTER 22 Legacy	299
"Do You Love Me?"	**319**
Afterword	*323*
Acknowledgments	*331*
Notes	*335*
Selected Bibliography	*357*
Index	*359*
Permissions	*381*

Preface

It is the sweltering summer of my thirteenth year. A freshly minted, freckle-faced, greasy suburban teen is sequestered in his upstairs bedroom. This is the special time: the opening of a new record album, fueled, as ever, with unrivaled anticipation. Sweet vinyl salvation—a sacred ritual.

Hallelujah!

Ah, the tingles, as I carefully run a fingernail across the shrink-wrap on the sleeve opening—a hallowed prelude to the unveiling of the disc itself. The unsheathing of a mystical siren set aloft by strange creatures resembling men, but so much more somehow.

Suddenly the intoxicating aroma of freshly pressed wax fills my head. I am ready to be delivered.

Next comes a scrupulous perusing of the cover: four cartoon figures in near-flight from atop a ragged mountain, the smoldering blue haze of a razed city behind them. Their faces emblazoned with a stark white: the Demon, the Star Child, the Space Ace, and the Cat Man. A collective visage of heroism. Or is it villainy? Perhaps both.

Once the sleeve is freed from its wrapping and slipped from its casing, it is hard not to be transfixed by the shiny black exterior, grainy to the touch with an exhilarating lure of having come from another realm. A blazing hot red, yellow, and white KISS Army shield rests above four words written boldly across the top: "SHOUT IT OUT LOUD."

Ooooh, yeah. This is gonna be good.

On the back, the deep black is assaulted by a glorious logo: the balanced fulcrum of the mighty *K*, which expands out from left to right as puckered lips to the single monolithic *I*, as insolent as a single index finger poised to the sky or a middle one mocking the world. The twin lightning-bolt *S*'s summarize its intent. The burned-orange/yellow mélange gives way to lyrics below the title, "Detroit Rock City." They begin defiantly, an impatient exaltation for life to commence anew, far beyond the walls of my secret den of masquerades, by clutching the wheel of a car cruising at incredible speeds across an infinite blacktop into night. I want to read on, but there is the music to consider. Yes, the blessed sacrament beckons.

As I pull the disc from its sleek protection and let it shimmer in the light of the late afternoon, the grooves reveal several shades of ebony casting a glow beneath the blue-and-white Casablanca Records logo spread across the label. Spinning it several times in my hands, as one would examine the details of a rare stone, I place it reverently onto the tiny turntable of a child's portable record player—a cheap mono thing made for sing-along tunes and Disney soundtracks, as so many had been played before. These would eventually give way to the Jackson 5 and then Elton John and various 45s from a glut of one-hit wonders. Later, my first hard-rock record, the Who's *Tommy*, and then *Jesus Christ Superstar*, and on to Alice Cooper's *Welcome to My Nightmare* and Queen's *A Night at the Opera*.

Not long into my last weeks of grade eight, I was talking to a friend about our mutual admiration for George Carlin. Our initial conversation about our favorite comedian turned into a discussion of comic books and rock music and then, ultimately, inevitably, this rock band called KISS. As we yammered on, I could not help but notice a copy of *Alive!* held tightly under his arm. I had to know who or what were these costumed creatures striking spastic poses amid the smoky glare of the stage. From that moment on, I had never wanted a record more—and, to my parents' lasting credit, it would soon be wrapped for my graduation festivities, freed as I was to pursue higher education and all its waiting tremors of teenage-hood: zits, masturbation, booze, drugs, sex, cars, and sure . . . well . . . my studies.

And did I play the damn thing. Day and night, night and day throughout the steamy summer of 1976, our nation's bicentennial, dissecting every liner note and studying each photograph, reveling in the distinctive KISS magic: the face paint, the blood, the fire and explosions, the costumes and the mayhem hijacking every inch of my rabid imagination.

For me, KISS represented my own declaration of independence—a crude but enticing slice of liberation, but not as defined or revelatory as I had embraced in music to that point. Films, books, and comics may have scratched an itch, but this . . . this was weirdly dissimilar. There was a tangible and cathartic release prevalent in its power and a mischievous smirk in its message. Mostly, it lent a voice to an id I had not yet discovered in early adolescence but knew was hiding there, ever so unhinged in pristine youth, while also remaining mysterious . . . until now. It was as if KISS would stand as the last exhale of my waning innocence, a distant call from uncharted recesses where one day the fantasies of invincible adventurers performed for my pleasure.

Soon a rock magazine revealed a new KISS record had been released in March, and how could I not own it? Chores, odd jobs, and shameless begging preceded a quick bicycle ride to the record store, and soon *Destroyer* was mine.

And so the time has come.

The needle is released from its crude moorings and lifted ever so precisely above the spinning black sphere. The slightest drawing of a breath and the faintest wry smile as I await the moment of truth.

Introduction

Destroyer is the most compelling and influential musical statement in the highly provocative if not distinguished career of a hard-rock band from New York City whose name was an afterthought to the original vulgarity proffered at the band's inception in the year 1973. Instead of going with FUCK, clearer heads prevailed—namely that of the band's promotionally savvy twenty-three-year-old bass player, previously known as Gene Klein, and his partner, the former Stanley Eisen, a fellow Queens native and twenty-one-year-old rhythm guitarist, who suggested the more acceptable but no less bombastic KISS. By then, the perpetually forward-thinking Klein had been anointed Gene Simmons, and the singularly driven Eisen had become Paul Stanley. The drummer, Peter Criscuola, more famously known as Peter Criss, a twenty-eight-year-old Italian tough from the mean streets of Brooklyn, had been a veteran of several half-cocked bands trolling the Gotham club circuit when Simmons answered his desperate plea looking for steady work in the East Coast edition of *Rolling Stone*.

The last member to join, after answering a *Village Voice* ad calling for a "flashy guitarist," was twenty-two-year-old Bronx-bred Paul Frehley, who was never one to contemplate matters beyond the next laugh—which, coming from him, was something of a high-pitched cackle. There was already another Paul in the band, so Ace was born. It was the kind of sparkling moniker that would make Stanley's innate sense of the rock idiom tingle and Simmons's keen marketing acumen shimmer. It didn't hurt that Frehley designed the iconic double-lightning-bolt design, which turned a watered down ode to physical bliss into the ultimate rock-and-roll symbol of gory spectacle.

Destroyer would be the band's fourth studio effort and its Holy Grail. For over twenty-four road-weary months, KISS had transformed four masked and costumed characters into a militant tontine to notoriety, yet its members knew mostly poverty, ridicule, and frustration. Despite KISS's best efforts to shock, cajole, and amuse, the music industry mostly ignored the band's rather stupefying effect on what was soon becoming a religiously loyal army of fans. That the band survived long enough to realize *Destroyer* was itself nothing short of miraculous.

This incredible fortitude in the face of every possible obstacle was primarily due to The Act: a perfectly constructed amalgam of illogical but determined illusions peddled tirelessly in mass volume and glitz. From its inception, KISS held a singular, unwavering belief in The Act's mystical cocktail of pure image, celebrated bravado, and unabashed machismo wrapped neatly inside a relentlessly unapologetic torrent of narcissism. By painting their faces clown-white with black and silver designs, dying their hair a uniformed blue-black, and donning black leather and high-heeled boots, The Act became a cohesive and individual visual statement, providing KISS the ample armor to combat the gnawing strains of reality. Thus shielded, The Act's only mission was fame and fortune, and its desired effect was mass hallucination: a hypnotizing assault on the senses that never failed to ignite an orgasmic emotional release, performance as spectacle further insulating the impenetrable façade.

On the very precipice of this grand vision, in the spring of 1976, KISS unleashed its testimonial.

Destroyer is not merely the philosophical, spiritual, and musical culmination of The Act in all its hyperbolic glory. There may not be a better symbol of the entire over-stimulated, affluent, suburban, white, male, long-haired, fist-pumping zeitgeist that represented the living, breathing backbone of '70s rock. Scores of social misfits lapped up every unapologetic sensation the "Me" Decade could dream up. These were the freshly minted faces of rock and roll's third generation; the mutated offspring of the 1950s teen-consumer monster that shed the postwar dirge for a sock-hop, greasy stroll on the sexual side of the Caucasian blues, and the direct descendants of the 1960s' acid-crazed fade of the Woodstock echo. Theirs was music not haunted by outer demons of oppression or the threat of war but best reflected in the bedroom mirror. And here were creatures devoid of fear and brazen enough to paint a new facade.

Thus *Destroyer* is the indisputable KISS mission statement—the realization of a dream that stridently reflects the extraordinary time from which it was fashioned. *Destroyer* is '70s rock: loud, yes, and decadent, you bet, but mostly it is pompous, weird, and fantastical. It rocks, it chants, and it sure as hell bellows, growls, pulses, and panders like a motherfucker. It is a cartoon fantasy's parody of excess. Its message is fun and doom all rolled up in a thunderous package of melodramatic farce. *Destroyer* is to The Act what the Declaration of Independence is to the American Revolution. And isn't it fitting that it was conceived and fashioned during the nation's bicentennial celebration? KISS launched its gargantuan Spirit of '76 tour to support *Destroyer* one day before the Fourth of July; a more capitalistic ode to unfettered liberty is hard to top.

However, it would be unfair to infer that *Destroyer* is an anachronism. In fact, it manages to transcend its wildly ludicrous era with universally impassioned themes of youth—sex, fantasy, and volume—which converge to form a united front of inestimable rebellion. Its chest-thumping, feel-good elixir still prompts *Destroyer* to roll off the tongue of even the most casual observer of the band.

Destroyer is certainly KISS's seminal album, standing beside its immediate predecessor, the legendary *Alive!*, if not realizing its mammoth potential. It is arguably KISS's only true music-as-image opus, encapsulating everything the band stands for in the pantheon of hard rock. *Destroyer* is a singular event, as unique to its creators as it was to those who absorbed it. Certainly, nothing KISS recorded before or after *Destroyer* is comparable in any way—an achievement that may be impossible to state about any other long-running rock-and-roll outfit. Thus, many hardcore fans of the band at first gasped at the album and then railed against it. Newcomers seduced by its promise would sadly get no viable follow-up.

Beyond being a career-defining moment for its creators and its cultural impact, *Destroyer* has a sound all its own, exploding from its grooves as a tank division rumbling into battle. It is also ironically tender and playful, richly displaying the best overindulgent claptrap of the period—art in the guise of schlock and schlock impersonating art. There is a guiltless, way-over-the-top flavor to *Destroyer* that is enviable. The listener may feel ambushed and condescended but never cheated, for *Destroyer* is pure entertainment from start to finish. It unfurls as a KISS novella, from its radio-theater prologue to the oddly tapered looping conclusion, ornately colored in between with villains and heroes, melancholia and triumph, recklessness and solidarity. All of it filtered through a vortex of unbounded youth.

Destroyer is also the story of its producer, Bob Ezrin, who at the age of twenty-six had already become a force in the rock world. His work writing for, arranging, producing, coercing, motivating, and defining the bizarre aura of superstar Alice Cooper introduced full-out camp and melodrama to the trade. An unflinching perfectionist and tireless taskmaster, Ezrin left just enough room for madness in his method. By 1976, he was at the height of his musical powers and a highly sought-after commodity, and one who chose to seek out the challenge of entering the myopic cauldron of KISS to put his stamp on its legacy.

The nine songs on *Destroyer*—seven of which Ezrin co-authored—cover an impressive range of subject matter, from flashback fantasy to teenage lust, Greek myth to gleeful sadomasochism, while celebrating the most sordid tried and true elements of rock and roll inspiration: speed, greed, and sex, sex, sex. Nearly all of the songs deal in some way with power, be it personal or cultural, each flowing into the next as a seamless gospel to defying the ho-hum. The mischief-making is ornately adorned by a symphony of guitars, chimes, pipe organs, calliopes, lush orchestration, and the Brooklyn Boys Choir—a circus extravaganza beyond scope or restraint.

Ultimately, what KISS envisioned and Bob Ezrin molded in *Destroyer* is a tribute to the ceaseless energy of rock and roll: more of an ideal than a musical idea, an unstoppable force that fueled four hungry New York City kids to turn the genre into an impenitent spectacle and rouse a fan base resembling more devoted congregation than mere audience. *Destroyer* is its tribal call, as ancient an art form as the race of humanity has conjured.

For KISS, *Destroyer* became, in essence, both an artistic triumph and a personal Waterloo. It marks time as a line of defiance between the garage-tinged thrash of the band's assault on the disjointed post-'60s rock scene and the well-oiled marketing monolith that was to come. *Destroyer* single-handedly turned KISS from a fledgling underground sensation—perhaps otherwise destined to be a one-trick oddity—to another thing entirely: a vehicle so completely and shamelessly commercial that it left plain "rock group" status far behind. Artist Ken Kelly's famous cover painting of the band as cartoon marauders leaping from a charred mountain, leaving a wake of destruction in its path, says it all. *Destroyer* transformed KISS forever.

The band and its four unique characters would soon enter an uncharted pop-culture stratosphere of showbiz marketing, product licensing, and overindulgent multimedia sensationalism, all with no assistance from radio, major national press coverage, or a #1 hit. This unprecedented achievement irreparably altered its participants, transforming management, record label, and most assuredly Simmons, Stanley, Criss, and Frehley from corny daydreamers into invincible egos inhabiting an ivory tower from which none would emerge unscathed.

In the sordid, bizarre, and glorious history of rock and roll, KISS is an enduring symbol of defiance. Mocked by critics and summarily dismissed by "serious" musicologists—while being fanatically celebrated as deity among its faithful—the band is a unique creation that stands alone, and *Destroyer* is its triumph. Before it, KISS is a curious heavy-rock act with burlesque appeal. Afterward, it is an image-driven international multi-million-dollar juggernaut.

Making *Destroyer* unquestionably challenged the band's creative resolve. Outside influences, musicians, and songwriters infiltrated the delicate balance of The Act's inner sanctum, causing fractions that would never again heal. Nevertheless, its success saved its record label and expanded its producer's career from one of Svengali translator of icons like Alice Cooper and Lou Reed to unprecedented chart master, leading to his jumpstarting of Peter Gabriel's solo career and realizing of Pink Floyd's *The Wall*. There was no going back after *Destroyer*. As with all great creative statements, it changed everything.

*Destroye*r is the central theme in an improbable story of one of the most successful, provocative, and underrated (overrated?) bands in rock history.

This is how it all went down.

SIDE ONE

"Detroit Rock City"

Get up, everybody's gonna move their feet!
Get down, everybody's gonna leave their seat!

Fade in...

The early morning sounds of dishes being meticulously washed in a cozy suburban kitchen setting. A distended monotone echoes steadily from a nearby transistor radio. *In Detroit, a Pontiac, Michigan youth was reported dead at the scene of a head-on collision on Grand Avenue this morning. He was reportedly driving on the wrong side of the boulevard when he struck a delivery truck and was catapulted through the windshield of his car. The driver of the truck is reported to be uninjured. Identities of both men are being withheld by local police.*

As effortlessly and casually as if spitting out random barometer readings, the patrician voice shifts inflection, but its tone remains ever stoic and detached.

County legislators today are expected to rally to the aid of striking longshoremen with hopes to end the nine-month deadlock...

The voice fades into the ether, as dispensable as its gruesome dissemination. It is on to the next chapter—or, in this case, a drift backward in time. A door slams shut, the shifting of weight into a car seat. Keys jingle before one is inserted into the ignition. Two pumps on the clutch and *revv-revv*, the engine roars to life. Within seconds, a familiar guitar riff pumps through the dashboard speakers, the rumble of the engine a counter-rhythm to the manic wail of a scolding solo. This too disappears into the ether, leaving only the hum of the engine beneath its hood, tires whirring across the blacktop below.

Back inside, the music plays on, the tribal thump of drums, a walloping bass, and a distinct and rousing refrain now more than familiar: "I wanna rock and roll all night! And party every day!" The driver cannot help but to sing along joyfully. He knows the lyric. He feels the message. It is loud and it is clear. "I wanna rock and roll all night! And party every day!"

Then it is gone. Again. All that remains is the ascending grind of an accelerating engine. We've taken flight.

Speed.
Freedom.
Rock and roll.

The pulse of a single electric guitar rises from this *mise en scène*—*da-a-na-a-na-a-na-a-na-a-na-a*. Its hypnotic tempo, born of the churning pistons, preludes another harmonious guitar—*da-a-na-a-na-a-na-a-na-a-na*—raising the intensity and the stakes. They build together in blessed volume with a promise of speed and freedom, impeded only for an instant by the thunderous *rat-a-tat-tat* of a canon-fire drum roll, the hammering intro for two concussive power chords: *BA-BAM!* And for good measure, this time on the downbeat, the notes power again: *BA-BAM!* Now the drums have a place to land, right into the eternal drive. It is rock and roll personified, the restless heartbeat of the double-time blues burning fuel, ever threatening to explode upon re-entry. Not the *train a-rollin'* or *the giddy-up 409* but a supernatural rocket blast blowing holes in infinity.

As the song gains momentum, the booming burrow of bass joins the fray: chugging, chugging, laying down the chassis framework for the rumbling engine block. Is it speeding up? How fast? How far? Can it be stopped?

BA-BAM!

The singer, invincibly guiltless, comes alive.

I feel uptight on a Saturday night!
Nine o'clock, the radio's the only light!

His words are accented by choral guitars and a funky bass run, all powered relentlessly by the concussive *thunk-ta-wack, thunk-ta-wack* of the backbeat assault.

I hear my song and it pulls me through!

This is wild abandon, no return, the stuff of American folklore: the open road leading to endless night.

Tells me what I've got to do, I've got to . . .

An invisible congregation chants, "Get up!" The hedonistic, amped-up, testosterone-addled preacher testifies. "Everybody's gonna move their feet!"

"Get down!" the faithful retort.

"Everybody's gonna leave their seat!" is the willful refrain.

The guitars suddenly turn on themselves across the divide and begin a melodic riff, as if defying the downhill rumble of the drums.

You gotta loose your mind in Detroit . . . rock city!

Then back to the power chords, resonating mischief again.

Get up . . . Everybody's gonna move their feet!
Get down . . . Everybody's gonna leave their seat!

The second verse repeats the musical tour de force. The singer (driver) tells us it's getting late and he just can't wait: it's ten o'clock and he's gotta hit the road, and the listener has no choice. We're along for the ride. We know that first he drinks and then he smokes, because he proudly announces it, frantically starting up the car in the dire need *to make the midnight show.*

Get up . . . Everybody's gonna move their feet!
Get down . . . Everybody's gonna leave their seat!

The backdrop melodic riff now leaves the vocals behind and takes center stage, as contagious a boogie-woogie groove as can be imagined at ear-splitting levels. The stampede of drums is not merely driving the thing but crushing chunks of terra in its thundering wake, burring car sounds rumbling along beneath it. It is the noise-inducing equivalent of a speed-crazed delinquent pounding his fist on the dashboard until it cracks in two.

The elasticity point of the riff lifts a step as a hard-charging slam on midrange piano keys ushers in those skull-cracking power chords once more, lending an operatic melancholia to the wild proceedings. It is the perfect undercurrent to the singer's third verse, replete with anguished hosannas to acceleration, hitting ninety-five on the speedometer but still moving *much too slow.* "I feel so good, I'm so alive!" he shouts, with mad glee. The song, *his* song, pounds a mantra in his spinning brain:

Get up . . . Everybody's gonna move their feet!
Get down . . . Everybody's gonna leave their seat!

Suddenly the guitars disappear, allowing the drums to heighten the mood, bass drum to snare: *thunk-ta-wack, thunk-ta-wack,* an unstoppable four-to-the-floor testimony to the driver at the wheel of his careening chariot. *Thunk-*

ta-wack, thunk-ta-wack. A rattling snare assails a beautifully melodious guitar interlude, which soon turns into a forlornly decadent symphony of guitars, a final musical lullaby from helpless angels hovering above, before the stirring denouement:

> *Twelve o'clock, I gotta rock.*
> *There's a truck ahead, lights staring at my eyes.*
> *Oh my God, no time to turn.*
> *I've got to laugh 'cause I know I'm gonna die!*

We know from the gory prologue that our hero is doomed. *Michigan youth was reported dead at the scene of a head-on collision on Grand Avenue.* He is young, recklessly determined, and high as a kite, speeding through the darkness like a banshee. The ultimate example of immortality soon to be cut down. It is abundantly clear that at the crescendo of this incredible rock opener—chock full of naïve faith in seducing omniscience—death is nigh. It is foretold in an almost biblical tones before the volume and rhythm ever kick in. It is a suicide mission torn from the playbook of rock and roll's greatest vehicular tragedies: "Leader of the Pack" (Shangri-Las), "Dead Man's Curve" (Jan & Dean), "Tell Laura I Love Her" (Ray Peterson), "Teen Angel" (Mark Dinning), "Wreck on the Highway" (Bruce Springsteen), and the list goes on . . .

Yet in our timeless tale of auto-destruction as rebellious, sexual, youthful release, for a fleeting moment this ode to reckless abandon—set in the teeming Midwestern metropolis where the American automobile was born, bred, and sold to a generation of gear-heads and hot-rod addicts—is given an unexpected reprieve. Our euphoric narrator's final utterance is his Hamlet moment:

> *I've got to laugh 'cause I know I'm gonna die! WHY??*

The distended Greek chorus wraps it all up in a final climax as the horrific sounds of tires shriek across a blacktop—the prelude of deadly impact.

> *Get up . . . Everybody's gonna move their feet!*
> *Get down . . . Everybody's gonna leave their seat!*

Screeeeeeeeeeeeeeecccchhhhhhhh . . . rrrrrrrrrraaaahhhh . . . . CRASH!

1
The Act

I'll never forget the first review we got was from a New Jersey paper and it tore us to bits. But it attacked us in such a way that made us look like stars. It said, "Four wild men from Borneo." I mean, that's the greatest way to put someone down. Everyone wants to see four wild men from Borneo.
—GENE SIMMONS[1]

Perhaps more so than any rock-and-roll band in history, KISS proudly wore the "do anything to make it and stay there" attitude as a badge of courage. The Act could never languish too long in dingy clubs filling sets with bland cover material, nor could it slowly attract audiences by acquiring a theme or style over the usual incubation period of a burgeoning rock band. The primary commitment to concept allowed little room for the tedium of gradual development.

From its ingeniously structured origins, KISS was conceived to aim for the stars or bust, ignoring poverty, rejection, and ridicule to craft a living myth each member cultivated with zealot belligerence. "From the time that the group became a foursome, there was something special about what we were doing," Paul Stanley boasts to David Leaf and Ken Sharp, in their eminently readable *KISS: Behind the Mask: The Official Authorized Biography*. "It was all really magical. It wasn't something you could create artificially or buy. It was *there*."[2]

The idea that even in the early 1970s—when David Bowie, Alice Cooper, and a host of cross-dressing, glam-bam androgynous posers ran the gamut of queer taste to outright absurdity—four rather homely New Yorkers would paint their faces in kabuki style and clad themselves in cheap leather, while balancing precariously on seven-inch, spike-heeled boots, seemed ludicrous. Never mind the empty stack of Marshall amplifier cabinets lined dramatically across the back of stages fogged in dry ice and adorned with eerie accouterment. The music, it would seem, was an afterthought.

"I *want* notoriety," Simmons told his biographers. "And I don't want just rock-and-roll notoriety. I want fifty years from now to be the musical group of the '70s, just like the Beatles are the '60s, and Elvis is the '50s. And I don't care if people remember a single song. I don't have any hang-ups about musicianship. By its very nature rock and roll is not complex music. It's throwaway art. The only thing I hope is to entertain my audience."[3]

When KISS began to muscle its way onto the big city stages—at a time when New York was the grungy cesspool best depicted in Martin Scorsese's *Taxi Driver*, released a month before *Destroyer*—it was not so much to volunteer its services than to conquer and bludgeon. As Simmons explains in *KISS: Behind the Mask*, "When we came out for the show in makeup, we scared the living daylights out of everybody. Nobody knew what the hell was going on. And we were playing real, real loud."[4] Most of all, KISS created an otherworldly alternative to the harsh realities of a broke and corrupt metropolis, ravaged by violence, crime, and apathy, not unlike contemporaries the New York Dolls but with an all-out blitz of showmanship and unwavering dedication to The Act.

"KISS was influenced by the New York Dolls in a sense that they went to see the Dolls after rehearsal and realized that the Dolls were the best-looking band out there and they couldn't compete with them as far as trying to look good. The best way to compete with them was to the look like monsters, because nobody was doing that," says the legendary rock photographer Bob Gruen, whose early work photographing KISS began to build the carefully crafted myth of The Act. "In fact, the first time any of them wore what became the KISS makeup was when Ace Frehley dressed up to go to the New York Dolls Halloween Ball at the Waldorf Astoria."[5]

Kim Fowley, rock impresario and co-author of two songs that appear on *Destroyer*, agreed. "KISS was smart because they took what was going on at Mercer Art Center and expanded it tenfold. It evolved from Max's Kansas City, where the New York Dolls came out of, and then you had CBGB's with the Tuff Darts and Mink DeVille, which developed all the makeup and theatrics within the confines of club bands, but KISS put a big sound to it and made it arena and stadium."[6]

"KISS really took it to another level," Gruen adds. "The image was very much based on the Japanese kabuki ideas of exaggerated wild monsters, dressing the part of cartoon characters rather than using the makeup or costumes as enhancement, the way some men would put on makeup to look like women. KISS put on makeup to look like monsters."[7]

Frank Rose's 1976 *Circus* magazine cover story, "Invasion of the Glitter Goths," frames The Act's intention to reach far beyond the seductive grip of Manhattan's glitzy underground. "While other groups were sitting in Max's running up bar bills they couldn't pay, KISS was in their loft plotting how to become a supergroup. Aside from the Dolls, the problem with the glitter groups was they couldn't see beyond the Manhattan skyline. Most of them realized their life's ambitions the night they got to sit in the back room at Max's. Not KISS. They had smarts enough to realize that the New York thing had limited appeal and that if they were going to go anywhere they would have to build an image which defined itself."[8]

In the same feature, Paul Stanley expounds, "We used New York as a springboard, and we took advantage of the situation. But we were never really accepted by the New York people. We were never part of the crowd that hung out at Max's. We tried to keep away from that. It was really important for us to maintain our individuality, because we didn't want to live and die with the New York scene. And ultimately it died."[9]

KISS's first manager, Lew Linet, who prepared the band for the abuse it was sure to suffer in the crosshairs of hard-bitten New York audiences, put it best in Curt Gooch and Jeff Suhs's comprehensive performance compendium, *KISS Alive Forever*. "The funny thing was that all four of them, especially Gene and Paul, would say to me over and over again, 'Lew don't worry about a thing. Doesn't matter what they say or what they write, we don't care because we are going to be the biggest band in the world.' Understand that this is coming from two guys who were recently playing songs on the corner in Greenwich Village with their guitar cases open collecting quarters, a guy who was a refugee from a bar band in Queens and was ready to give up music entirely, and this crazy Ace Frehley guy from Mars."[10]

From the very start, with no fan base, unknown to the press, and working on a zero-sum budget, KISS perpetuated the rock-god fantasy with pinpoint aggression. As near-deaf rock legend Pete Townshend once mused on the success of the Who, "Power and volume . . . power and volume!"[11] KISS mauled audiences with almost laughably simplistic rock fodder presented as horror-sci-fi-burlesque-fiasco. Culling inspiration from another P. T., as in Barnum, the band concentrated its collective energy on performance as spectacle and suspense, effecting an electrified rock homage to carnival thrills and spook house chills. The accompanying music was a well-worn mixture of lurid wet-dream lyrics caterwauled over distorted barre chords and crude rhythms unleashed by four cartoon characters straight out of Lon Chaney's grab-bag of trickery.

The most visibly delighted by all this was the supremely confident Gene Simmons, an Israeli immigrant whose Hungarian-born mother had escaped the Holocaust and an absentee husband to spirit her son to America, where the mostly isolated preteen Chaim Witz gorged on television heroes and comic-book lore. Simmons's Demon character came complete with an artfully protruding tongue that not only defied logic in length (purportedly nearly six inches or seven inches, depending on who's measuring) but in his ability to make it curl. Looking like a curious cross between a high-class hooker and Dante's chief tormentor, the Demon's extended papillae both teased and revolted. His face makeup, black bat-wings running from his prominent cheekbones to his considerable forehead—accentuated by pulling his dark, curly locks back into a Samurai warrior coif—was only the beginning of Simmons's high-wire act. KISS's stage-stomping bass player wore a leather bat-wing costume with skull and crossbones emblazoned across the chest, hoisting his already lengthy frame onto seven-inch heeled boots, looming from the stage as Godzilla to an already freaked audience. And, of course, the Demon could breathe fire (a neat trick tutored by someone called Presto the Magician, wherein a mouth filled with kerosene is dramatically ignited by a torch) and spit blood (a boiled concoction of eggs, cottage cheese, maple syrup, and yogurt with red dye), all in the name of showbiz.

Simmons's KISS co-founder, Paul Stanley, the youngest of two children born to Jewish-American parents—his father a furniture salesman, his mother a teacher—whom he describes in his memoir as "not happy people,"[12] was the Star Child, and as such wore the symbol of his youthful ambitions over his right eye. A single black star and ruby-red lipstick would adorn his alabaster face, which spent the majority of the time pursed in an eternal smooch and the rest bellowing out stridently raw vocals. An otherwise soft-spoken philosophical type with a formal education in music and art, Stanley may have possessed less ballsy charisma than Simmons—who didn't?—but was nonetheless a stirring front man. As he sashayed luridly on his own seven-inch heeled boots, a bare-chested sequined jumpsuit dominating the spotlight, his razor-sharp voice coerced raucous chants and impassioned sing-alongs with a religious fervor rarely exhibited beyond gospel and soul revues. Yet Stanley's star-trip was not that of the traditional lead vocalist—which the KISS model of four-equals-one rejected anyway—but that of the shaman leading willing minions into his daydream world of fast women and hot guitar licks.

With Stanley as the effeminately romantic preacher man and Simmons the gruesome beast patrolling the darker and deeper sides of KISS, Ace Frehley and Peter Criss provided the wildly off-kilter balance.

Frehley, the youngest of three offspring to his working-class parents, was a carefree, booze-addled jokester and reluctant spotlight grabber—specifically in the considerable stage shadows cast by Simmons and Stanley. The Space Ace, adorned in streamlined futuristic jumpsuit with knee-high flying-saucer boots, would become the intergalactic alien presence in the harlequin quartet, the only member to allow a color (silver) other than traditional minstrel blacks and reds into his makeup. (Criss would later add some green and a spot of silver into his Cat Man mask.) Frehley's slender frame and languid stage moves helped shape the Ace persona, which he fulfilled with the rapid-fire fret-fingering that made him the most famously aped lead guitarist of his time. With Stanley's relentless dedication to laying down solid rhythms that he rarely strayed from allowing for extemporaneous digit calisthenics by his fellow guitarist, Ace was the flash to Stanley's postures and Simmons's machinations. It was a formidable stage-presence trio, each clearly defined and easily identifiable.

The hardcore backbone was provided by drummer Peter Criss, whose background in street doo-wop and '50s-style rhythm and blues did not hurt the painfully Caucasian middle-class threesome out front. The most soulful of the band's voices, Criss further added to the KISS philosophy that all four members share the spotlight. Although the band was made up of city kids, Criss, the eldest of four in a traditional Italian-American family, was the street-savvy troubled urchin, having spent his youth in roving gangs, barely surviving street fights. Significantly, he was the band's senior member by five years—an eternity in the realm of influences, both in pop culture and music. While the other three found their chops in the '60s rock stable—Cream, the Rolling Stones, Jimi Hendrix—Criss was weaned on Gene Krupa, Frank Sinatra, and the 1940s big band sound, thus adding a kind of swing that would have been sorely missed had KISS gone with a more traditional rock drummer. An affinity for and embracing of the nine lives mystery of cats perfectly suited his smoldering back-alley manner, so Criss chose to be the Cat Man, which lent a literal sensibility to his makeup and character.

Like Frehley, Criss was a veteran of several squabbling bands that could not get over the hump, and thus he did not initially mind being on board for anything. Only later did he openly bristle at being in a band made up of Halloween parade floats and forced to duck the odd explosion or blood spat. Having already drummed for numerous flops, most notably a New York band called Chelsea, Criss was as primed for the big time as Stanley and Simmons, both of whom had similarly tasted minor success and major disappointment with the short-lived Wicked Lester (Criss entered as it splintered), which recorded a forgettable album that was dumped upon completion by Epic Records. After absorbing Frehley, who showed up to his audition already half in the bag and wearing two different colored sneakers in late 1972, it took KISS only a handful of lukewarm club gigs and a quickly patchworked demo, fortuitously produced by Eddie Kramer of Electric Lady Studios fame, to be on its way.

Wasting even less time, the band put together several self-promoted showcases in the summer of 1973 for label executives and potential management, many of them trumped up by cleverly-worded "press releases" followed by a crudely cobbled version of what would be the KISS model: the Star Child's bellowed prancing, the Space Ace's wobbly bending of riotous notes, the Demon stomping about menacingly, and the ferocious pounding of the skins by the Cat Man. It was at one of these well-rehearsed previews of The Act that KISS's ear-splitting theatrics caught the attention of a thirty-year-old television producer named Bill Aucoin.

Aucoin, a slickly dressed smooth-talker with an overly enthusiastic streak, shared much of The Act's irrepressible lust for fame and fortune, harboring all the what-the-hell sense of gambling needed for the coming deluge. With an extensive background in television advertising, directing, and editing commercials for Reeves Teletape and later his own company, Direction Plus, his best known contribution to rock and roll was his MTV antecedent *Flipside*, a syndicated popular music interview/performance show. A television man through and through—which meant he was no stranger to the peddling of illusion for mass hypnotizing—Aucoin did not have a reticent bone in his body and welcomed embarrassment and ridicule as clear signs that boatloads of cash were soon to follow. Almost immediately, he began to huddle with the band on its image and presentation, further increasing KISS's hunger to become outlandishly notorious.

"To put it bluntly, the four of us created the makeup, the logo, the tunes, and the look and feel of KISS, but it was Bill who took it all the way," Gene Simmons admits, in *Behind the Mask*. "It was Bill who said, 'Let's take this to the nth degree. Let's breathe fire. Let's have explosions and all sorts of things.' We didn't have the technical expertise and/or the money to do any of that. But Bill did."[13]

To that end, Aucoin introduced his lover, showbiz impresario Sean Delaney, to the band. Delaney, a transvestite with professional dance, theater, and stage chops, was well versed in alter-ego costume performance and ushered KISS through New York's underground S&M fashion scene of studded leather, chains, corsets, dog collars, elaborate cod pieces, and high-heeled boots. He dyed all of their hair a sinister blue-black, creating an alien solidarity, accented by costumes dominated by a singular color scheme of deep blacks and metallic silvers. Most importantly, Delaney, with the assistance of Aucoin's videotape equipment, began molding the band's live personas, demanding they never break character before, during, or after performances. Hours of reviews and refinements quickly transformed gimmick into conceptual art.

"Sean Delaney was, in my estimation, the fifth member of KISS," writes Peter Criss in his engrossing memoir, *Makeup to Breakup: My Life in and Out of KISS*. "He was a tremendously talented force. Sean worked 24/7 with us. He was like an obsessed drill sergeant. When we'd get in that rehearsal room and were all up there together on that stage, he would get in front of us and it was like he was leading the largest orchestra in the world, he was so into it. I was nobody then, but when I was around Sean, I felt like royalty, like I was the greatest drummer in the world. Both Sean and Bill knew instinctively that it was important to treat us all like stars, and they absolutely did."[14]

Dennis Woloch, who would eventually head up the design team behind *Destroyer*, was the art director/creative director at Howard Marks Advertising, which shared space on Madison Avenue with Bill Aucoin. He recalled a bizarre daily ritual during an interview for this book. "I remember when Gene was learning how to blow fire and he was doing it right up in the office. He had some circus guy up there teaching him. He was this little brown guy who looked exotic. He was teaching Gene how to make a good mist. Gene was just blowing water out of his mouth, going through the choreographed move where he would hold the torch up and stand a certain way. He just kept spitting water all over Bill Aucoin's office. When it was time to use the fuel, he was blowing flames right in the office. You could smell kerosene all over the place."[15]

Aucoin also sought the expertise of the Jules Fischer Organization to assist in the band's original staging. With its extensive resume of Broadway sets, the group was led by Fischer's distinct eye for the dramatic. To focus in on the youth/rock market, Fischer tapped a recent graduate of NYU's School of the Arts for Theatrical Design, Mark Ravitz, who was a student in his lighting-design class and had done some work staging rock shows at Bill Graham's famed Fillmore East. Ravitz immediately sized up the personalities before him: "Bill Aucoin was an alchemist; he could turn shit into gold. Sean Delaney was sort of an older rock-and-roller living out some of his dreams through the band. Peter Criss was the oldest and for him this was 'make or break'—it was his life, and so he was a little more serious about it. Ace seemed to be blasted most of the time, although the logo was his idea. Paul kept mostly to himself. Gene was the one pretty much running the show."[16]

Ravitz helped design the set for the first official KISS show under Aucoin's steady hand at Manhattan's Academy of Music, building the now iconic four-foot-high KISS logo that would be suspended at center stage above the band, along with the original flash pots and other minor stage effects that would later evolve into ear-splitting explosions. Alongside Delaney in acting as a key member of the inner sanctum at the launch of the band's live persona, Ravitz would later play a major role in the immense expanse of the KISS live model set alight by the conceiving of *Destroyer*.

Come autumn, Aucoin offered KISS a management contract, which the band agreed to sign when he boldly promised to procure them a record deal within the month. True to his signature, Aucoin came through, thanks in no small part to his company Direction Plus (later to become Rock Steady) and its relationship with Buddah Records' top man, Neil Bogart, who would soon leave to start his own label and needed to make a splash.

On November 1, 1973, KISS became the first act to join what would become Casablanca Records. Its chairman, the thirty-year-old Bogart, was best known in the industry for his creation, promotion, and massaging of such bubblegum acts as the Ohio Express, the 1910 Fruitgum Company, and Melanie, among others. He jumped at the chance of a showbiz-ready product. In his extensive inside history of the scandalously outrageous and hugely successful Casablanca Records, *And Party Every Day*, executive vice president (and Bogart's cousin) Larry Harris remembers the label's reaction to KISS vividly. "KISS was an incredibly compelling band. These guys commanded your attention, and there was no way you could walk away from them feeling apathetic. Love them or hate them, you were going to have a strong reaction, and Neil and I both knew that anyone capable of provoking this type of visceral response was the stuff of future superstardom."[17]

It was no coincidence that Bogart, who had had a brief run as a pop performer following the release of a minor teen hit "Bobby" (credited to Neil Scott) in 1961, and Aucoin, the producer of a visual representation of rock performance, would join forces to build on the core philosophy of The Act. In his exhaustive overview of the 1970s KISS machine, *KISS and Sell—The Making of a Supergroup*, C. K. Lendt, the former vice president of KISS's business management team, summarizes this collective philosophy within Aucoin's singular methodology. "Bill's earliest sermons to KISS was to promote themselves at all times. Talk big, act big, project success—it'll pay dividends. That was the whole point—not just making KISS big, but making it bigger than it really was."[18]

KISS biographer Ken Sharp, whose prodigious research for *Nothin' to Lose—The Making of KISS 1972–1975* involved interviewing hundreds of people in and around the band, came away with an unflinchingly absurd picture of The Act's invincibility. "Listening to every story, you can really feel the devotion and naiveté surrounding the band then. They needed it to overcome the barriers they faced and the doors that were shut in their face. These guys were adorned with a supernatural sense of belief in themselves, and the people that surrounded them were the perfect dreamers. Put all together, it formed a pretty spectacular force."[19]

In less than one year, Simmons, Stanley, Frehley, and Criss had formed a band, created a four-point, fully realized image and its accompanying act, whipped together a crude but functioning list of original songs, settled on simpatico management, and signed a record deal with a burgeoning hype-crazed label. It is no wonder that, within two years, they would be on the cusp of conquering the rock world.

2
Zeitgeist

Everyone used to laugh at me. Everybody did. Even all my friends when they were playing Grateful Dead music. I'd say, "Don't you know you're not going to make any money, you're not going to get anywhere copying the Grateful Dead?" I said, "If you wanna make it in rock you have to do something spectacular."
—Ace Frehley[1]

To the band's most ardent fans, the true KISS charm is its unapologetic, unyielding, irresistible dedication to full-out, bloodletting showmanship. Even as they formed the band, culled management, and secured a label, Simmons, Stanley, Criss, and Frehley craved a different space in the rock idiom. They wanted to be stars and they wanted to be rich, and they made no bones about it. But they also wanted to create a band that they would pay to see. Stanley: "We understood the audience, because, in a sense, we *are* the audience. We know what looks good and we do it. I know that I would enjoy seeing us if I were sitting down in the crowd."[2]

Alternate reasons for scores of young men to take up an instrument beyond escaping a soul-crushing nine-to-five subsistence or to get pussy were always lost on KISS. The concept behind The Act—even more so than the band itself—was rooted in its rejection of rock's seminal methods of angst posturing that had begun in the late 1960s. Unlike the spate of socially conscious counterculture acts and the newly minted self-important "prog rock" that dominated the early 1970s music scene, The Act had no political agenda nor felt the need to front or ride a movement. It would offer no counterculture pitch, would not herald the wonders of recreational substances, and would never dare display the slightest interest in subtle subtext. There would be no ulterior motive or artistic sentiment beyond grabbing an audience whether that audience loved or despised it. Simmons: "The premise behind KISS is we are there to give people a couple of hours of pure escapism. We're not here to tell you how bad things are. Everybody's aware of that. We want to make you forget, give you a good time."[3]

KISS was the quintessence of the tried-and-true American spirit in the business called show, creating a product brimming with transparent pretense. If being cool and artsy meant feigning detachment or appearing as though it were a chore to entertain, then KISS would be none of that. If anything, it would exist to expunge the very notion of the tortured artist and replace it with the idea that rock and roll "beats the hell out of digging ditches." KISS celebrated fun, volume, self-parody, and good times, and it certainly didn't solicit the approval from an invisible imprimatur of rock-and-roll purity. Stanley: "It's fantasy, escape, and power. It is no different for the audience than it is for me."[4]

At its artistic root, The Act was a postmodern howitzer blast through the heart of 1960s existentialism. Such lofty mantles were reserved for the late-'70s punk and new wave movements, whose ironic apathy as trash art played around with gender-bending, senseless violence, and anti-social narcissism. KISS laid waste to those and future preconceptions by quite obviously—in presentation and ambition—mass-producing pointless diversion as statement. This was shameless exhibitionism for a singular purpose: to create shameless exhibition. This would not only blaze a new path for KISS but alter the expectations of the rock audience forever. It was, ultimately, the audience that would give The Act its *raison d'être*: the celebration of band and fandom sharing an inside joke, that fun for fun's sake as a quasi-religious vow to hedonism is in itself a righteous practice.

In a 1991 interview, chameleon rocker David Bowie deconstructed the period during which he fashioned several bizarre personas to pave his road to stardom. "Whatever came out of early '70s music that had any longevity to it generally had a sense of humor underlying it. There was a real sense of irony about what we were doing. I remember saying at the time that rock must prostitute itself, and I'll stand by that. If you're going to work in a whorehouse, you'd better be the best whore in it."[5]

In a 2003 review of retro-'70s styles taken to cinematic art form by Quentin Tarantino in his film *Pulp Fiction* (itself rife with the kind of post-modern pop culture miasma that unleashed KISS), Dana Polan, professor in the critical studies program of the School of Cinema-TV at USC, writes, "The primary goal for the spectator is not to look for meanings, but have an experience, to luxuriate in sensations. Commentators on post-modernity have seen it in a culture of surfaces, 'what you see is what you get.' In some cases, the idea that post-modernity has no depths—and indeed may be opposed to notions of profundity—has led critics to regard its play of experiences as a lacking in intensity. But in another way, it might well be that post-modernity also has to do with an intensification of sensory experience—rendering of a viscerality so intense that it substitutes for all concern with deep meaning. A roller-coaster ride, an explosion in a movie, a virtuoso camera movement are not interpreted so much as enjoyed, absorbed as further bits of the society of the spectacle we're immersed in."[6]

In a 1978 *Trouser Press* piece, journalist Dave Schulps frames the gut-level impulse of The Act: "Simply, KISS were on one hand larger than life, totally unapproachable and unreal, and on the other hand spoke the audience's language in terms *anyone* could understand. You didn't have to be *cool* to dig KISS; they were merely four distinct images up there acting out *your* fantasies of stardom and superherodom—there was nothing to understand, no secret meanings to grasp. They didn't even exist as people, not really, and if whatever was under that makeup and costume was any smarter or any better in any way than you were, they sure weren't letting on to it."[7]

"We've often been accused of being pretentious, but in actuality our concept of what we're doing is an effort to shy away from pretentiousness," Paul Stanley told *Punk Rock* magazine in 1978. "The thing we do is very surface, for there are no built in subtleties in our music or what we do on stage. We feel our whole image is based on the use of imagination."[8]

KISS represented a new generation of rock-and-rollers born not of country twang or downhome blues, rockabilly or New Orleans bebop, William Blake or lysergic acid, all-day festivals or ponderous jazzed-up jams. As the 1970s progressed, rock's drug-fueled, protest-happy anti-establishment rank and file gave way to the outrageous and the androgynous—the tits-and-confetti set. After the Living Theater, *Hair*, Andy Warhol's Factory, the Manson Family, and *Jesus Christ Superstar*, the *show* had definitely been hurled back into the *business*. Shock as fame and noise over matter began to transform a movement that would coagulate into the "Me" Decade: an age of one-off decadence packaged to dazzle. The drugs no longer represented enlightenment so much as escape; the sex became less about liberation than libation; and the music was an unhinged assault of pop, power, and cabaret. Suddenly, making an obscene fortune playing three-chords with a smirk and a scowl was welcome behavior. Changing the world and sparking a generational shift gave way to making hay and cashing in. It would soon be a decade awash in overkill or bust; posters, decals, and pastel designs—the groovy, goofy cash-in of blockbusters, platinum lifts, arena, laser, three-ring fusion of lights, camera, play time!

In his lurid memoir of a rock-and-roll life, *No Regrets*, Ace Frehley plainly observes, with some agony and mildly feigned trepidation, "It was always about money, expanding and enhancing the brand. It was never about art. Never about music. Never."[9]

As Kathi Stein expounded in *Circus* magazine in 1976, "Comic books have been successfully selling Armageddon tales to all of us since the Manhattan Project's A-bomb began tinkering with the real fate of the planet since the '40s and '50s. Quasi-mythological end-of-the-world scenarios tend to relieve Hydrogen Age anxieties in the young and whip up furious passions. KISS knows all about it. But the real effort KISS put behind their enactment of the spectacle is fueled by a passionate need to entertain and the desire to make money. They don't deny it, either."[10]

Indeed, the showbiz model built into the KISS idiom was hardly the product of the flash-and-dash '70s. The essence of The Act—specifically its clever use of makeup as illusionary tool to form a barrier between reality and fantasy, sheltering KISS's four egos as if behind an impenetrable personality fortress—harkened back to a time long before rock and roll, television, or the post–World War II duck-and-cover fears of Cold War madness, deep into the American psyche: exploitive times of black-faced minstrel shows, trick-a-minute, joke-a-line song-and-dance vaudevillian slapstick characters and bawdy songsters; traveling caravan troubadours selling snake oil and dark promises of shocking freaks behind velvet curtains; the ancient craft of carnival farce and old-time gospel hour spiritual tent revivals offering brimstone and fire and performing ritual healings.

As C. K. Lendt—a representative of the mid-'70s KISS marketing ethos—philosophizes in *KISS and Sell*, "You could read anything you wanted into KISS—partying, pleasure seeking, rebelling, aggression. KISS's attitude sent out a signal to fans that it was okay to cut loose and let it all out for a few hours in a jam-packed arena, immersed in a frenzy of blinding lights, crushing sounds, and ear-splitting explosions, before returning to the drudgery and dreariness of their lives."[11]

The societal shift into a schizophrenic embrace of psychic individualism—whether cultural, generational, spiritual, or racial—coupled with a similar rush to find group identification in the collective consciousness was also a psyche specific to 1970s America. And it was this organically created canvas of intense self-awareness intertwined with an awakened urge to form a subculture of solidarity that perfectly suited The Act. A rock band completely identifiable as one with costumes and face paint, as if uniforms, in a singular visual experience that within it also revealed each member to be its own entity in self-expression—which was quite literally painted on their faces and played out upon the stage as spectacle—was a visceral expression of the period's cultural landscape.

And with its pompous exceptionalism, rugged individualistic spirit, and outlandish egoism celebrating the very core of the free spirit of rebellion and expression as if a cult, KISS was nothing if not an American band. Its impetus came not from the twelve-bar or the British invasion, the coffeehouse troubadour or the art house drop-out, but from horror films, comic books, B-movies, *Playboy*, strip clubs, glamour magazines, and Disneyland—in other words, modern Americana. Philosophically, the band is a rush to celebrity, a blatant swipe at not only hording a piece of the pie but devouring the whole damned thing. Get noticed, get rich: rock and roll as ladder-climbing salvation, a way to not only circumvent the trappings of a lower-middle-class stranglehold but also transform into the beautiful people with little more than a shtick and a song. "I'm in it to make money," Gene Simmons told *Melody Maker* magazine in 1975. "I'd like to make that perfectly clear."[12]

When asked by Roy Carr in the September 1974 issue of British pop/rock magazine *New Musical Express* about the mercenary aspect of "new bands" (of which KISS was certainly one), '60s counterculture icon turned '70s jet-setting idol Mick Jagger could see the writing on the wall—and praised it. "I think that's a good attitude. You should want to go out and make it with the first record. It's much harder to make it now than it ever was. Everyone has seen everything—wait, maybe that's not quite true, because the very young kids haven't seen anything, so you're really starting all over again. And that's why there's a Donny Osmond."[13]

Although it is accepted theory to judge harshly the "mercenary" aspect of the era—and KISS in particular—it is patently unfair. Truth is, even venerated pioneers of rock and roll, American or otherwise, from Elvis Presley to Bob Dylan and even the almighty Beatles—all ostensibly driven by genuine creative pursuits bathed in the light of truth and justice—merely yearned for riches and fame. And each of those acts—along with the entire roll call of the rock chronology, including those in the genuflecting eminence of the punk movement—created characters as fabricated and theatrical as KISS. The characters may not have been face-painted costumed *übermen*—and perhaps they evolved through professional survival, personal creativity, or to simply move with the times—but they were characters just the same. Elvis, the wild country sexual dynamo cum gold-plated hit machine cum black-haired movie star cum Vegas showman. Dylan, the vagabond troubadour cum street-voice protester cum electrified hipster cum Woodstock auteur. The Beatles, lovable mop-tops cum psychedelic shamans cum solitary studio gurus cum hippie individualists. Pick any rock act over the sixty-plus years of its history and it's difficult to deny any performer did not create a character, image, or persona that expanded its brand.

Even so, by the time KISS was relevant to the culture, an entire generation of rock bands who competed beneath the formidable shadow of the Beatles had passed. The new age had no such albatross. All four members of KISS could look to the Beatles as something from another time, and certainly another place, just as the Beatles, on the opposite end of the Pond, had worshipped Elvis Presley a generation earlier. To KISS, the Beatles were the Greek gods of Mount Olympus—not something to compete with or expand on, but something to emulate. In his 2001 autobiography, *KISS and Make-Up*, Gene Simmons describes lasting effect of the Fab Four for the then fifteen-year-old, beyond even the inspiring nature of the historic *Ed Sullivan* performance that launched a generation of star-gazers just like him. "The first thing that struck me wasn't the music. It was the way they looked: perfectly coordinated, cooler than cool. They looked like a band."[14]

More than any other band in the '70s, KISS was the reality-obliterating conglomerate the Beatles had become in the '60s. The Beatles' alien appearance in dress, grooming, speech, and good humor seemed to explode from nowhere out of the dreary vacuum of Elvis Presley's soulless movie career and the horrors of the Kennedy assassination to emerge as a fantasy of joy, youth, and bravado. To the early '70s—with its harbinger of a counterculture obliterated by drug abuse and failed political uprisings exacerbated by a crippling energy crisis, economic and urban downturns, and a pop culture obsessed with disaster films and doomsayer literature best depicted in the evangelist Hal Lindsey's wildly popular *The Late Great Planet Earth*—KISS represented a similar fantasy escape that if nothing else acted as a welcomed distraction.

Ultimately, like the Beatles a decade earlier, KISS understood the initial seduction of rock and roll as an exploitive soundtrack of hormonal overload in an insatiable youth culture. Simply put, kids loved it. But by the early '70s, the kids occupying the first two generations of its existence had grown up, and the burgeoning third generation was not ready or willing to embrace the seriousness of that maturity. David Bowie, whose intergalactic narcissus Ziggy Stardust catapulted him to superstardom in 1972, told *Playboy* magazine in September of 1976, "Most people still want their idols and gods to be shallow, like cheap toys. Why do you think teenagers are the way they are? They run around like ants, chewing gum and flitting onto a certain style of dressing for a day; that's as deep as they wish to go. It's no surprise that Ziggy was a huge success."[15]

Somewhere between the ass-shaking exploits of a Memphis trucker and the gutter glam of KISS, rock, as Gene Simmons once mused, lost its roll. By 1973 there was a gaping chasm between AM pop, filled with everything and anything that could be tossed up the charts by fad, payola, and dumb luck—with the occasional talent thrown in—and FM AOR (album oriented rock), with its "serious artist" set of concepts, concerts, and extended, self-indulgent solos, mixed with patched jeans, ragged T-shirts, and heavily bearded types that ran the spectrum from California cool to Southern drawl.

Armed with a television mind for managerial expertise in Bill Aucoin, along with his partner, Sean Delaney, a showbiz stalwart whose choreographic contributions to The Act are universally accepted to have been instrumental, and working for a label run by a ballsy pop kingmaker in Neil Bogart, KISS had the brain trust it needed to set its own course—and not that of the fading '60s standard, or, as rock's most outspoken critic of the time, Lester Bangs, dubbed it, "the death rattle." That was a mantle taken up and repackaged by Bruce Springsteen, who, from the opposite end of the '70s rock-and-roll matrix, was anointed "the future of rock and roll," just as the critics, most of them aging hippies, scripted it.

The noisy mess coming out of Detroit—the MC5, Grand Funk Railroad, the Stooges, and Ted Nugent—was the antithesis of a flower-power youth movement. It was a rancorous celebration of raw, unflinching individualism that reveled in mocking convention. "There was a new generation of young whites around Detroit and Ann Arbor who had finally decided that, much as they dug reproducing, they did not want to *produce* one more hubcap!" Bangs proclaimed, in the December 1972 issue of *Phonograph Record*. "And all their lives they had been hearing metallic, mechanical rhythms in the din from the factories that destroys the hearing of everyone in this city just as the pollution of the water in the Detroit River forces them all, much as they might resist, into drinking alcoholic beverages every day and night. So the young white kids picked up this sheet-metal din, hearing how close it was to the rattly clankings of rock 'n' roll, and turned it into a *new* brand of rock 'n' roll which was more metallic, heavy, crazed, and mechanical than anything heard on the face of the earth in 6,000 years of Western history."[16]

Bangs's metaphoric reference to what was soon to be officially coined heavy metal was but a minor blip in the exploding hard-rock movement of 1972. The term was first written into the fringe of pop culture by Beat writer William Burroughs in his 1962 novel *The Soft Machine*, which features Uralian Willy, the Heavy Metal Kid later used to describe the thunderous roar of a motorcycle in Steppenwolf's 1968 hit, "Born to Be Wild," and still later sharpened as a pejorative term to eviscerate loud, violent, or macho rock in the harrumphing pages of *Rolling Stone*. And while KISS would eventually be penciled in as forerunners of heavy metal, if not predated as originators by Deep Purple and Black Sabbath, then certainly metal's precepts, ideologies, and effusive badge-of-honor attitudes underlined The Act's most persuasive quality: a sense of conquest in the face of insurmountable odds.

Journalist Chuck Klosterman made this very point in VH1's miniseries on the origins, effect, and lasting legacy of heavy metal music, *Metal: A Headbanger's Journey*. "If you listen to the Smiths or the Replacements or something when you're young what it's sort of says is that you feel weird, you feel different, but that's because you're smart. You are different than these other people, but you should be happy with that. But metal really seemed to tell people that you feel weird, but you're not! That's why I was so interested in the idea of the KISS Army. It was this idea that if you like KISS that means actually you are part of this massive coven of people that have the same values that you have. KISS songs always seem to imply that as KISS fans we're being somewhat persecuted for it. Like if you listen to the song 'Crazy Crazy Nights' [from *Crazy, Crazy Nights*, 1987] it somehow implies people are trying to stop us from liking KISS. I think that's a really brilliant idea, and I think that's part of the draw to metal. It makes people feel like it's not a way to understand your loneliness; it's sort of a way to feel as though you are part of something that's larger than yourself, because everything about metal is larger than it is in life."[17]

Detroit's "rattly clankings" was just another head-banging undercurrent to what Britain was offering up in the pop/glam showbiz role of Elton John, T. Rex, Roxy Music, Slade, Gary Glitter, and David Bowie or America's softer equivalent of the singer/songwriter class: James Taylor, Jim Croce, Joni Mitchell, and Carole King. All of this, from pop to pulp, competed for the limited space on the early-'70s charts with a myriad of one-hit wonders, novelty acts, and kid groups, a funky, sing-song, bubblegum potion designed to capture trends, fashion, and ultimately dollars. It was the perfect stew into which to add the soon-to-come disco broth and later spike with a lethal dose of vitriolic punk.

On the outskirts of this pop/rock/folk hodgepodge, KISS jump-started its recording career in October of 1973. A little over ten months after the band became whole, and some thirty days before it signed an official record deal, KISS entered Bell Sound Studios on West Fifty-Fourth Street in Manhattan to record its self-titled debut. With no more than a handful of local gigs behind it, the music was raw, relatively unimaginative, and hardly representative of an explosive, big-time rock show. Its most defining feature begins and ends with the cover photograph by Joel Brodsky, whose previous works included the Doors' *Strange Days* (1967), Van Morrison's *Astral Weeks* (1968), and the Nazz's *Nazz* (1968). It is here the legend of KISS begins: four clown-white faces set starkly against a pitch black backdrop, unabashedly reminiscent of the iconic *With the Beatles* cover, each member trying too hard to stand out, make the mark, pull the weight. Gene Simmons, mouth agape and eyes ablaze, showing teeth and hinting at a growl; Paul Stanley, pursed lips, a come-hither stare, stoic but commanding; Ace Frehley, weirdly distant and overtly feminine; and the most outlandish of all, Peter Criss, painted and coiffed like something out of a Japanese kabuki nightmare. It was hard to ignore, music or no music.

If the cover is the statement, then perhaps somewhere on the vinyl there is the makings of a hard-rock foundation; "Strutter," "Firehouse," "Deuce," "Cold Gin," and the dynamic "Black Diamond," quickly-fused snippets of disparate styles and derivative chord progressions echoing much of what inhabited the heavy, white, pre-punk era: Black Sabbath, Mountain, Deep Purple, Grand Funk, and especially Slade, the British precursor to the science fiction cum glam rock fashioned by KISS in New York and from which both Simmons and Stanley admittedly borrowed heavily in style and comportment. Yet the songs also boasted a keen sense of hooks and riffs reminiscent in the best pop-rock elements of bands like the Sweet, Brownsville Station, and even the Bay City Rollers.

Lyrically, *KISS* reeked of the city: streetwalkers and cheap alcoholics; horny, hard-working males thirsty for some action, fueled by sweat, grit, booze, and sex. Simple driving rhythms and memorable youth tropes helped many of the *KISS* songs to remain perennial stage numbers across countless reunion tours, cranked out of state-of-the-art twenty-first-century arena sound systems for years. But in the sealed compression of a studio played by newly adorned professionals, whose sole purpose for barely ten months was to create a theme, a look, and an image, it is a fairly nondescript showing.

With the band having had only a ridiculously condensed time to truly gel as a unit, most of the songs presented to Casablanca for *KISS* were Wicked Lester survivors or pieces of reworked compositions from earlier aborted attempts. Simmons contributed two, Stanley three, with two songs credited to Simmons/Stanley and one instrumental credited to all four members. Frehley chipped in with one of his own but refused to take the lead vocal due to a lack of confidence. Rushed into a later session and coupled with a cross-promoted national kissing contest radio gimmick, "Kissin' Time" was later forced onto a second pressing. Neil Bogart's desperate swipe at giving his new charges a hit with a piece of fluff originally recorded in 1959 by Bobby Rydell and lyrically manipulated by the band is a glaring example of how the old bubblegum king's habits were not only hard to break but would also provide a constant source of friction between his overtly pop-orientated sensibilities and the hard rocking KISS brand. Bogart found it increasingly difficult to accept that, in rock circles, the album had long eclipsed the single, even for a band formed to attract as many paying customers as humanly possible.

One last possible drawback to a less than stellar opening statement by KISS was the choice of producers, Kenny Kerner and Richie Wise, both friends and colleagues of Bogart and Aucoin. Former members of a pop/rock band called Dust, the duo had come to prominence behind the board working with the syrupy Beatles-esque knockoff Badfinger. In other words, they were not the perfect pair to translate the raw combative emotion of The Act.

During an interview for this book, famed radio disc jockey Scott Shannon—who in his capacity as station manager for Atlanta's #1 pop station, WQXI, had originally suggested to Neil Bogart that KISS re-record "Kissin' Time" and tie it to the kissing contest idea—expressed a theory about Casablanca's president that might explain the ill-suited choice of Kerner and Wise. "Neil was so confident of himself he didn't need anybody else, so he hired family members. Larry [Harris—Casablanca Vice President] was related to him. Buck Reingold, the first promotion director, whose place I eventually took, was married to his wife's sister. He worked at a deli in New York. The guy that ran Chocolate City [a subsidiary of Casablanca] wasn't related to Neil, but he was a friend of his. He had no respect in the business. Nice guy, Cecil Holmes, but had no juice whatsoever. Neil was so self-confident he didn't care."[18]

All four members of the band retrospectively expressed their frustration for having missed the mark with *KISS*. In his memoir, Peter Criss recalls his distress at hearing the "pedestrian" mixes. "There were no balls between those grooves. They were making us sound like a pop band."[19] Ace Frehley bemoans, "I'd love to redo some of those songs today using state-of-the-art equipment."[20]

In their wonderfully detailed account of the early days of the band, *Nothin' to Lose: The Making of KISS 1972–1975*, Simmons and Stanley pull no punches. Simmons describes the producing team of Kerner and Wise as "disappointing," adding that they did not "get a handle on our sound."[21] Stanley is more effusive: "I don't think it's a competitive-sounding album in terms of our contemporaries at that point. That became a familiar story every time we went into the studio. We didn't have the experience or the knowledge to articulate what we were looking for or what was lacking in terms of the sound. I always thought that the material we had was much better than the recordings that represented them. I always felt we missed the boat in terms of being competitive on a world level with some of the other bands who had albums out. I thought our songs were every bit as good if not better than many but that sonically our albums were pretty tame."[22]

In the same account, even co-producer Richie Wise expresses regret: "In hindsight, I thought it sounded wimpy. I didn't think the album was aggressive enough."[23]

Regardless of its limitations, *KISS* was released in late February of 1974, heralded by a huge Los Angeles launch party and an ensuing tour, wherein KISS would truly earn its stripes and begin to seduce a rabid and loyal audience, one pyrotechnic exploding blood-puke at a time. Just two months earlier, during a New Year's Eve gig in New York opening for the recently minted Long Island rockers Blue Öyster Cult, Gene Simmons lit his hair on fire during the flame-breathing bit, something of an unexpected band staple in the years to come. Inauspicious as it was, it had a far more lasting effect on keeping KISS alive in the public imagination than anything found on *KISS*.

Reviews of *KISS* were lukewarmly curious. The general sentiment revolved around, "What the . . . ?" Unable to fathom what to make of the whole thing, *Billboard* tossed off a "new energy group with strong ensemble singing" that provided some "dance cuts."[24] Leading hard-rock monthly *Circus* magazine actually used the word "Phew!" after labeling the music "non-existent" and spending most of the review on the band's image: "They dress like Walt Disney out-takes (one of them looks like a mutated Mickey Mouse)."[25] *Rolling Stone*'s Gordon Fletcher served up the usual backhanded aplomb, providing bemused descriptions of the work as having an "all-enveloping forcefulness" that produced "fine music for crushing skulls," with a special notice to Stanley's rhythm guitar playing as "the star of the proceedings, barking out the coarse chord patterns that comprise the foundation of the band's material" and Simmons's "fluid bass patterns" being "an extra dimension to the band's music." He added that Frehley's "frenetic fretting" could have been used to greater effect. But the review also noted what would become something of an Achilles heel for the band's succeeding studio output: "*KISS* is an exceptional album, but could have been even better had the group incorporated more of their concert sound into the recording studio."[26]

Usually, for a band with so much riding on a "Ta-da!" entrance, desperate to create a mood in which to unfold a lasting narrative, a debut album is everything. Think of similar bands with an antithetical style to that of their contemporaries, with the visual essence laid upon the tracks as a road map to where it will take you and what the listener can expect from here on out. One centers on the opening salvo by the Doors, another self-titled first effort. *The Doors* (1967) is rock's quintessential opening statement: dark, foreboding, strange, and threateningly sexual, it sounded like nothing else around at the time, and its messages, torn from Greek tragedy to Beat poetry, are sung in a unique manner by a charismatic figure whose baritone crooning demands attention. The trouble for Jim Morrison and the Doors was that it peaked right there. Nothing the band would create in the following four years of its brief existence compares to "Break on Through," "Light My Fire," or, let's face it,

"The End," a cataclysmic eleven-minute opus that closes out the record with screeching Oedipal madness. It was almost too perfect, if that is possible, for although there were glimpses of this kind of brilliance again, it was all downhill for the Doors. The rock and roll equivalent of "It was the best of times, it was the worst of times"—an opening line that clearly states what the story is all about—it signaled both the overture and the encore of its promise all at once.

If nothing else, *KISS* is a serviceable early-'70s hard-rock record. It poses neither that kind of perfection nor curse; to achieve that measure of statement, the band would have to labor on floorboards across America, which it did with fervor unmatched for such a rough-edged unit still learning the ropes of stage presence and musical dynamics.

"In our first gigs, everybody just sat there in total shock," Peter Criss revealed to KISS biographers Leaf and Sharp. "It wasn't until the middle of the show when they started to get into it and really believing that we meant it. Gene would go out and look into their faces, like, 'We're not kidding. We want to rock.' Finally, they'd realize we were okay, that we weren't put-ons and we weren't gay and we weren't from another planet."[27]

3

Wilderness

Didn't you hear, we're the clowns of rock and roll.
—Paul Stanley[1]

For months on end, KISS toured relentlessly, opening for whichever band would allow its bombardment of explosions, a crude but effective elevating drum riser, and Gene Simmons's shenanigans. These included first-time appearances on television during late night (Dick Clark's *In Concert*, for which the band stunned the director and camera crew by rehearsing in jeans and T-shirts and then arriving for the taping in full maniacal regalia) and mid-afternoon (*The Mike Douglas Show*, during which Simmons was literally pushed onto the set to trade a series of uncomfortable barbs with veteran comedienne Totie Fields).

Curt Gooch and Jeff Suhs provide an excellent overview of The Act on parade in *KISS Alive Forever*. "The band's commitment to nonstop touring was so stringent that its early itinerary made almost no geographical sense whatsoever, especially considering it traveled via station wagon. The road crew dubbed the early dates 'The Star of David Tour,' jesting that if you were to draw lines on a map linking the sites of the concerts, the result would be a Star of David. Some billings were laughably mismatched, with KISS paired up with the likes of tranquil art-rockers Renaissance, folk singer Kathi McDonald, and Billy Preston. All of this is testimony that KISS would play anywhere, at any time, with anyone who would have them."[2]

Still, after nearly one year on the road, *KISS* had sold just 75,000 copies, spending an uneventful sixteen weeks on the charts and peaking at #87. Its only charting single (the first, "Nothin' to Lose," and last, "Strutter" vanished without a peep) was Neil Bogart's ill-conceived "Kissin' Time" experiment, which dipped into the *Billboard* 100 at #83 and stalled at #79 in *Cash Box* before disappearing altogether.

To exacerbate the issue, the newly formed Casablanca Records was showing signs of being unable to absorb any measure of loss. According to Larry Harris's published account in *And Party Every Day*, as part of an initial distribution deal with Warner Bros., the label was expected to show a profit almost immediately or run the risk of being absorbed into the parent label. This edict came on the heels of a strong request from Warner Bros. that KISS bag the makeup and circus hijinks—something Bogart reluctantly ran by Aucoin, who in no uncertain terms flatly refused to consider it. After all, it was Aucoin who'd initiated the outlandish notion that the band—the members of which were nobodies—conceal their identities from the public, disallowing KISS to be photographed by the media and fans and instructing its security to confiscate the offending film or buy-off would-be paparazzi. Aucoin's ritual paid off, as many in the media loved perpetuating the KISS myth-making in exchange for the promise of exclusive interviews and backstories.

"We gave them a lot of coverage when everybody else was treating them like a joke," recalls rock journalist Jaan Uhelszki of *Creem* magazine. Uhelszki was the first and only photographer to take candid shots of the band sans makeup, outside the *Creem* offices in 1975, but never released a single one during KISS's heyday. "To me, it was a campy, bizarre, death-of-art, Warholian kind of thing. Why would you ruin their superhero kind of appeal by printing those photos of them without their makeup? It never really entered our minds to do that. Okay, maybe it entered our minds, but ..."[3]

"KISS only existed as a band when they were in makeup," renowned rock photographer Bob Gruen explained, during an interview for this book. "It made the job harder *and* easier, in the sense that we didn't have to work all night. When the show was over, the photography was over. We didn't have to go in the dressing room or go to the after-party. On the other hand, if you wanted to get pictures of KISS off-stage you only had a ten minute window after the makeup was on and before they went onstage when they were *actually* KISS."[4]

To his credit, Bogart stood his ground for The Act, but although Warner Bros. backed down, a chilly relationship ensued. There was also growing evidence that Warner Bros.' shipping department—and, even more crucially, its promotions department—had abandoned the cause. "I had to do the *KISS* album promotion and marketing almost all by myself," writes Harris. "The Warner Bros. staff was no help at all, providing little more than delivery service. The head of promotions, Gary Davis, told his field staff to ignore the product of the custom labels and only work the Warner-owned artists."[5]

And so, in October of '74, with the pressure cooker turned up during a nonstop touring grind bouncing as opening act from one headliner to the next, the band swung in to Village Recorder Studios in West Los Angeles to record a follow-up. Within a day of arriving, Paul Stanley had his favorite custom Flying V guitar stolen. This was followed by what Gene Simmons would later mockingly dub "another of Ace Frehley's famous car wrecks that smashed up his face."[6] Meanwhile, Peter Criss began to show his claws, threatening to quit over the removal of a lengthy drum solo no one but he seemed to want. Things didn't improve as producers Kerner and Wise, who had also helmed *KISS*, took its lack of chart success upon themselves and vowed to erase the overall bland, plodding sound from the first New York sessions for a glitzier, more polished one in sunny L.A. Instead, the sessions left the guitars sounding as if they'd been sifted through a rinse cycle Wurlitzer flange-device, a drum sound akin to Tupperware filled with wet sand (which is too bad, since Criss's work is inspired here), and the bass nowhere to be found. Stanley's vocals, a shredding snarl of bluesy affectation on *KISS*, are reduced to a flimsy, singsong falsetto. Simmons's animalistic phrasings, fed through a compressed echo chamber, fall flat.

Being gritty New Yorkers smack dab in the middle of plastic land began to cause fractions within KISS that would last until the pieces completely came apart six years later. Frehley and Criss, the band's two reckless imbibers, reveled in Hollywood's fast-lane party atmosphere, while straight-and-narrow Stanley and Simmons bemoaned their homesickness. Constantly hovering over the entire proceedings was the dreary air of hand-to-mouth living and the increasing burden to break out of it. Despite all of their tireless performing efforts, money was tight (struggling Casablanca had yet to pay them any royalties) and the studio work directionless. Paul Stanley admitted as much to *Circus* magazine in 1976: "I can remember going into our manager's office and saying, 'I really need a new pair of shoes.' Then I would look at his shoes and they had holes in them. That's what keeps you going, when you know that everybody's going hungry together."[7] It was a bad experience for everyone, and the sessions' results—neither plodding, polished, or otherwise—pushed the band's now well-oiled live sound further from listeners.

The album's ironic working title, *The Harder They Come*, eventually became *Hotter Than Hell*, taken from arguably its best and most lasting selection, one of five Paul Stanley compositions. Stanley not only once again shared writing duties with Simmons on "Let Me Go Rock and Roll" but also with Frehley on "Comin' Home," a fairly pop-oriented effort for Ace, who chipped in three of his own this time around, including a soon-to-be KISS perennial, "Parasite." As was the case with *KISS*'s "Cold Gin," Frehley, still admittedly feeling intimidated, declined to provide a lead vocal. Gene Simmons's contribution totaled four songs—on all of which he took the lead, of course—including the one penned with Paul and "Goin' Blind," a strange tale of nonagenarian love co-written with longtime friend and former Wicked Lester bandmate Stephen Coronel. The songs—some beloved KISS staples like "Got to Choose," "Hotter Than Hell," and "Watchin' You"—had been cobbled together in hotel rooms and bumpy conveyances across the U.S. and paled by comparison to much of what was on *KISS*. The cover—a cheaply presented, indistinguishable black-and-white cutout photo of the band surrounded by Japanese script, shot and designed by the sought-after Norman Seef, who had once toiled for Andy Warhol and recently contributed photos for the Rolling Stones' legendary *Exile on Main St.*—was certainly worse. The entire effort sounded and looked like a sinking ship on its last submergence rather than a brand new rock group building the type of momentum needed to sustain the platinum career to come.

Once again, in retrospect, all the band members expressed frustration with the results of their second studio effort. "We were spending our days in the studio working on an album that we hoped would remedy the sonic deficiencies we found in the first album," Stanley explains in 2013's *Nothin' to Lose*. "We were never as rock-and-rolly or good timey as we sounded on that album [*KISS*]. We were much heavier live. So we tried to capture sonically how we sounded live. Unfortunately, the people that we were working with were probably not the right people to be doing it with."[8] Gene Simmons expounds on what he deemed a lack of effort from the band in *Behind the Mask*: "We didn't have the temperament to stick it out and record a proper studio album. That takes time. We weren't experienced. The production values of the record had more to do with, 'Gee, I like that song more than that song.' It didn't have to do with real engineering styles. We were all like blind men walking through the dark."[9] Ace Frehley writes, in his memoir that the *Hotter Than Hell* sessions "lacked spontaneity,"[10] while Peter Criss admits, in *Behind the Mask*, "We were still green."[11]

In the same account, co-producer Kenny Wise, whom Simmons credits with being the main hands-on musical force behind both *KISS* and *Hotter Than Hell*, detailed the studio failures that vexed them. "I hated the sound of that album. I swear to God, every two days there would be new speakers in the room. They were changing them on us all the time because they were having problems. We couldn't get it to sound right, the vibe was really bad. It's the worst-sounding album I ever recorded. It was overly compressed and overdriven. We couldn't get a mix to sound right. I knew I was in trouble with that record after the mix. I would have loved to have remixed that whole album in a different studio but it was too late. So I spent every waking minute trying to master the record and get the bottom to sound better, the high end to sound better. But it was too late. I knew that there was a sonic problem. I think we came out with a very brittle-sounding album that was very unpleasant, very harsh and just disgusting. The intent was to make a Black Sabbath kind of sounding record, but it just didn't pan out sonically."[12]

Predictably, reviews for *Hotter Than Hell* were not kind. Ed Naha wrote in *Rolling Stone* that the record "spews forth a deceptively controlled type of thunderous hysteria closely akin to the sound once popularized by the German panzer tank division," half-mockingly stating that the band had achieved some level of success "churning out quite a bit of high-energy instrumentation and cheerful, nonsensical vocalizing."[13]

Still, *Hotter Than Hell* improved on the debut's sales, moving 125,000 units, but did nothing to improve KISS's image, sound, or standing in the rock world. To make matters worse, Casablanca finally lost its distribution deal just before the album's release. Warner Bros. could no longer ignore its accountants' cries about how Bogart had gone mad by dumping his entire venture into a single non-bankable product that received no airplay and seemed incapable of shaking the "novelty" tag. As a result, Casablanca could no longer abide the conflict-of-interest game Warner Bros. was playing and took on the unenviable task of going it alone. As Larry Harris recalls in his book, "The circumstances for a neophyte label (just months old, really) that had its corporate umbrella suddenly yanked away were dire."[14]

Faced with this new challenge and mounting debt serious enough that Bogart had to take credit at a Las Vegas casino just to pay his staff, Casablanca did less to promote *Hotter Than Hell* than it did for *KISS*. The album's only single, "Let Me Go Rock and Roll," crashed upon entry. Neither the single nor the album charted. It is one of the great feats in music history that KISS, Casablanca, and Bill Aucoin—who had by now sunk tens of thousands of his own cash into The Act—survived at all, much less hung around to see the lofty heights and millions of dollars that were to be enjoyed when they did.

"They weren't getting money because we didn't have any for sales and we were pumping so much money into them that wasn't recoupable," explains Larry Harris. "You know, normally if you put money into a band, the record company can recoup most of it, like if you put up money for their show or something like that in advance, you usually get that back in royalties before they pay the band. But we were spending money that had nothing to do with the normal contractual relationship with the band. We were just spending money hand over fist trying to get them to happen. Instead of the promoters advertising the band, we were advertising the band, because nobody wanted them to open for them, so we had to have them headline. So we were spending a fortune on them, and plus not too much before that we had left Warner Bros., so we had no money to pay them. They weren't thrilled with us because Bill Aucoin, their manager, is putting everything on his credit card. He had American Express chasing him all around the country trying to get paid."[15]

Having struggled for over a year to make it on the road with no record sales and a floundering label, KISS was summarily pulled from the *Hotter Than Hell* tour in February 1975 and summoned to New York to record something else. With no money for a proper producer, and motivated by a possible end-around to keep KISS and Bill Aucoin from skipping to another label—which coincidently led to the dismissal of producer team Kerner and Wise for allegedly encouraging KISS to leave—Neil Bogart acted ostensibly as producer for what would become the band's third album, *Dressed to Kill*.

Larry Harris describes Bogart's mood and his reasoning for taking over the studio reins: "The bottom line is, Neil was pissed at them [Kerner and Wise]. He felt that they were being disloyal to him, who gave them their shot, and if Neil felt you were disloyal to him, you were dead to him. So number one, during the first record they were telling the band not to do 'Kissin' Time,' which Neil was pushing, and number two, they were the ones who suggested that [the band] go looking for a new record deal. That ended it for them. Neil would never hire them again to produce an album."[16]

Everything about *Dressed to Kill* reeks of desperation, time-constraints, and limited creativity in both length and packaging (the Bob Gruen black-and-white cover shot of the band on a Manhattan street corner dressed in street clothes, the back cover simply a negative of the same photograph). Stanley, Simmons, and Frehley were all pushed into songwriting duties with even less time than had been allotted for the previous record, which everyone had to admit was hardly ample. Discarded segments of previous material—some from the Wicked Lester days and others half-imagined riffs grafted to fragmented melodies—along with a slapdash of new material whipped off in a frenzy of pressurized authorship had to fit the bill.

Bogart's creative influence, allegedly provided through a haze of marijuana smoke, appears to be in the lack of guitar solos or interesting instrumental breaks, so prominent on the previous two albums. A paucity of quality material and the streamlined arrangements are the primary reasons the finished recording runs to a mere thirty minutes, prompting Casablanca to extend the blank grooves between each track, even then barely broadening it to long-player status. However, unlike the two prior attempts, *Dressed to Kill* actually unfolds as a slick, tight, and passionate rock-and-roll recording. The guitars are crisp and raunchy; the vocals, complete with some harmony flourishes, are up front, confident, and punchy. Simmons's thudding bass is back, and the drums have a New York *in-yo-face* feel.

Another spate of KISS perennials emerged, including "Rock Bottom," "She," and "C'mon and Love Me." Stanley had a hand in penning six of the ten tracks; Simmons co-wrote two with Stanley and added two of his own, while Frehley added the haunting acoustic guitar opening to "Rock Bottom" and another vocal vehicle for Criss, "Get Away." Perhaps it was the nearly two years onstage, a maturing musicality, or a seething desperation that translated into a superior performance from the band, for if *Dressed to Kill* did nothing else, it unleashed onto the unsuspecting world "Rock and Roll All Nite," one of the finest rock songs of its or any time—although it would take another seven months for that idea to take hold.

An infectiously basic rocker with tribal drums and a chanting chorus, "Rock and Roll All Nite" was not only a classic 1970s New York track but also the template for the ultimate Simmons/Stanley collaboration, with Simmons's lurid verses sung with a lascivious growl heading into Stanley's raucous, Slade-like chorus. It was something new for KISS: a little pop melded into a stadium anthem, hinting at what a musical soundtrack for The Act could be.

Predictably, reviews for KISS's third album were mostly dismal. *Rolling Stone* declared, "KISS does not play music—it makes very high-volume noise."[17] *Billboard*, still unsure what KISS had in mind, thought the record revealed "a more refined technique" with "commercial potential."[18]

Bogart's foray into record producing came and went much in the manner of the first two KISS records. Two singles were released: "C'mon and Love Me" did nothing, but the budding rock anthem par excellence "Rock and Roll All Nite" charted at #68 in *Billboard*'s Top 100 and #57 on *Cash Box*, unexpectedly getting rare if not sparse airplay on the staunchly pedestrian AM stations. Maybe it was the fuel of "Rock and Roll All Nite" that provided the only glimmer of hope for *Dressed to Kill*, as it managed to outsell its commercially barren predecessors, eventually reaching 175,000 units. In times of professional misery, this was taken as something of a victory for KISS and an embattled Bill Aucoin. As for Casablanca, the shadows of bankruptcy were descending, as an ill-conceived and over-shipped album tribute to Johnny Carson and *The Tonight Show* had recently tanked. For all involved, it was three up, three down, and nowhere else to turn but to the one thing that was not failing KISS: The Act.

"We had to tour constantly," Bill Aucoin recounted in *Behind the Mask*. "It was our only way of reaching the public, because KISS didn't get any airplay. The DJs complained about our image and didn't take us seriously. We were hardcore rock and roll when all the talk was about the death of rock."[19]

The hypnotic nature of KISS's performances—which *Circus* magazine dubbed "Count Dracula Meets the Normandy Invasion"[20]—replete with bludgeoning volume, smoke bombs, lasers, pyrotechnics, and stage antics, may have been conspicuously absent on vinyl, but was beginning to take hold in person. In his exposé on the band, *KISS and Sell*, C. K. Lendt describes his first experience seeing KISS at Roosevelt Stadium in 1976. "The volume had become painful for me, so loud I couldn't hear anything except a maddening ringing noise in my ears that wouldn't stop. But I couldn't turn away, either. It was like witnessing a bizarre ritual, where thousands of faithful followers congregated to experience a spectacle of overwhelming power, leaving them in a trancelike state of ecstasy and delirium."[21]

"It's almost like Hitler-rock," Detroit concert promoter Steve Glantz, a loyal supporter of KISS from the early days, noted irreverently to *Circus* in 1976. "I mean, they have that audience hypnotized. They could say, 'We're going out there and lifting up this building,' and they'd just go lift it up. That's the kind of control they have. That's why their following is so strong and so indestructible. That's why there's no question in my mind that they have something I've never seen any other group have."[22]

Photographer Fin Costello, a Brit who had only been in the United States a few days when a colleague took him to KISS's first headlining show at the famous Beacon Theater in New York City, could not fully comprehend what he was about witness. "I had been shooting the Brecker Bros at Todd Rundgren's studio that afternoon, so I had the cameras with me," he told www.blabbermouth.net in 2005. "I have often described it as being akin to the Gates of Hell or Dante's Inferno. They were doing the first number when we came into the back of the theater and I had never seen anything like it. Smoke, flames, etc., and the audience going ballistic."[23]

The Act—a powerful mindset Simmons, Stanley, Criss, and Frehley had used to frenzy-whip the singular notion of star power—was now fully imbued into KISS, its fans, its management, and its destiny. Bill Aucoin's immovable faith in the costumes, makeup, stagecraft, and the promotional value of myth-making, Sean Delaney's creation of a four-part cult-of-performance instinct, and the band's relentless pursuit of entertainment at all costs was now a juggernaut—a living, breathing amalgam of its resplendent logo, which some interpreted as a transparent homage to the Nazi S.S. lightning-bolt insignia. Beneath the surface, it could also have stood as the Tarot's lightning-bolt symbol of the Tower, wherein the subject has "a revelation of truth behind the fabrication of everyday life emerging reinvented into something far more significant and mesmerizing."

Peter Criss: "The night I knew we made it, we were backstage and I could hear from a distance, 'KISS! KISS! KISS!' And we went down the stairs to the stage and it kept getting louder and louder, 'till it was like thunder, 'KISS! KISS! KISS!' And when we hit the stage the kids were going crazy, rushing the stage, jumping up on the seats. This is when I said, 'This is it! We made it! We did it! There's something about us that's different!'"[24]

Casablanca took notice of the feedback KISS had been getting on the road through 1974 and early '75. The Act had legs. Despite offering little more than primitive pyrotechnics plus the Herculean efforts of four young men packaged as a traveling freak show, KISS was a live band of repute with a growing fan base—the notable exception being grumpy promoters who griped about KISS's always sloppy and mostly dangerous stage effects. Then there were the headlining acts for which the band had been hired to open. It became something of a joke that any "normal" rock group having to follow over seven-foot tall costumed thespians blowing up half the arena would be in for a long night. As a result, KISS was booted off tours supporting Argent, Savoy Brown, and Black Sabbath, among others. Many bands flat out refused to allow the six-foot-high KISS logo in bright flashing lights the band insisted on hanging above the stage or the knife-brandishing roadies paid to erect it. In Aerosmith's *Walk This Way*, Joe Perry says the KISS crew "terrorized everyone."[25] In his autobiography, *Kiss and Make-Up*, Gene Simmons recounts an incident when opening for Argent wherein the crowd was chanting for an encore and the headliner's road manager pulled the plug, only to be crammed into a road case by KISS's burly road manager, J. R. Smalling, until the band had concluded its set.

In cities like Detroit (the birthplace of "rattly clankings"), KISS fans began to chant the band's name before the house lights were dimmed, which was quite odd for a struggling recording act with overdrawn management, badly marketed material, and a cash-hemorrhaging record company. But then that was the model from day one: The Act created illusion, playing the part of the rock star and master showman no matter how ill equipped, underfunded, or inexperienced the product. The mere fact that KISS came out blasting without so much as a care for who might be prepared to endure it was the primary reason it survived what by rights would have felled any mortal band.

The Act existed to obliterate reality, and to its ultimate credit, KISS had succeeded in feeding its illusions to the audience. Next up would have to be those directly responsible for their careers; management and the record label, both of whom were about to prove their undying devotion. Crazier than starting a band on the premise that attitude and grit would see it through to fame and fortune, and crazier still than signing a nine-month-old rock group with no foreseeable hit single or any real performance background to a representation contract, and even crazier than leaving a prominent executive position at a major record company to start a label from scratch and as its first act launch KISS may well be the half-baked plan to release a double live album by a band that had failed to move any studio-recorded one.

Against all odds and nearly dead broke, Casablanca agreed to release a live recording of a KISS show. This perfectly fit the *modus operandi* of Neil Bogart, a man who had intrepidly made his own way in a shark-infested business of music, rising as a young executive for two major labels and starting his own out of nowhere. "Neil was a gambler," Larry Harris stresses in *And Party Every Day*, "the kind of guy who would bet a hundred dollars on when the cheese in the fridge was going to get moldy."[26] Moreover, the label was desperate to showcase The Act in sonic form with a kind of souvenir of what everyone had mostly ignored on three hit-or-miss studio attempts. In pure economic terms, it would have been natural for Bogart to seriously contemplate cutting ties with KISS after the original four-album contract expired. Putting out a set of live tapes, mostly free of studio expenses, would seem like the most cost-effective way out.

"The only reason there was a live album at that point and time—because nobody has ever come out with a live album who doesn't have some hits before it, or at least one hit—was because we had no money and we felt it was a cheaper way to go and we needed the product out as soon as possible," says Larry Harris. "It really had nothing to do with 'Hey, they do a great live show and it's not being captured on disc!' That was never the thought. The thought was we need product to generate revenue to keep the company alive."[27]

With KISS vindictively denied soundchecks by headliners and told by promoters to "tone down" its stage antics and quell special effects to allow the featured artists to shine, the long road from struggling opening act to a significant hard rock gate attraction had the band convinced that its studio sound had been a career detriment. In his unauthorized biography of KISS, *Black Diamond*, Dale Sherman encapsulates the overall mood. "The band's argument was that the crowds at the shows did not correspond with the album sales, and upon asking some of the audience why this was, discovered that people were coming to see the band simply on word of mouth about the spectacular show they put on and nothing more. In fact, some people did not realize that KISS had three albums out on a national label, much less that they had anything out on vinyl."[28] If all else failed, the logic went, a live recording would serve as a time capsule for those who wanted to relive The Act the way it had been designed in that cramped, roach-infested rehearsal loft on East Twenty-Third Street, where Gene Simmons and Paul Stanley welcomed Peter Criss and Ace Frehley into their dreamscape.

The "show" was recorded over several performances spanning five crucial months of 1975 for the KISS camp, all the while manager Bill Aucoin bankrolling the harried proceedings on his American Express card, living meal to meal and hotel to hotel. Casablanca was running on the last shred of a shoestring budget, still failing to pay even the miniscule allotment of royalties KISS was registering. Aucoin had little choice but to agree that producing live tapes beat the hell out of busting ass writing and recording another studio album for no pay.

Legend insists that the most memorable cuts were taken from the May 16 show at the hallowed Cobo Hall in Detroit, Michigan—made manifest in Fin Costello's incredibly serendipitous back-cover photo of two young KISS fans holding up a homemade banner, the one to the right of the frame smiling hazily with a congratulatory fist in the air. Behind them is an absolutely jam-packed arena poised to be rocked by KISS, as you, the listener are about to be, if you are astute enough to purchase and then enjoy these hot little discs in your grubby paws. Yet other venues mentioned from several sources over the years point to complete or partial recordings later meshed together: from the Music Hall in Cleveland, Ohio (June 21), from two performances at the RKO Orpheum Theatre in Davenport, Iowa (July 20), and from the Wildwoods Convention Center in Wildwood, New Jersey (July 23).

Eddie Kramer, who in his storied career had already crossed paths with KISS when recording the band's first demos, was employed to make heads or tails of it all. Retiring to his hub at Electric Lady Studios to pore over the tapes, the famed producer made the key decision to call the band in to heavily overdub and manipulate studio revisions to the original concert recordings. Over the years, many in the KISS inner circle, the band members, and even Kramer himself have openly confessed to these machinations, especially since most live albums from the period featured a preponderance of copious overdubbing for a cleaner audio experience. And in the case of KISS—a band more focused on performance than musicianship—it is hard to argue with it. The limitations of stage monitors of the time, coupled with the massive volume and lousy acoustics of big arenas, and whatever heavy artillery was being spewed forth from the stage, demanded Kramer's steady hand. Whichever way it is digested, the "live" experiment was too important not to complete as near to perfection as humanly or electronically possible. Livelihoods, fortunes, and futures were on the line.

As the band and Eddie Kramer were settling in to choose a listenable set list from the hours of live recordings that would soon change their fortunes forever, the plans for KISS to conquer the mysteries of the studio were being formed without Casablanca. With his band entering a new phase of its career and a buyout of his former partner, Joyce Biawitz, who had now become Mrs.

Neil Bogart, Aucoin moved aggressively on to the next studio album, a key part of which involved finding a proper producer. For the embattled manager, deep in debt and soon to be entangled in a lawsuit with his band's current label, there was only one man fit for the job.

"King of the Night Time World"

Come live your secret dream.

CRASH!

The terrible aftermath of a head-on collision: gnarled metal, exploding gasoline, and the billowing black cinders of certain death.

Floating from up out of the ghastly din, a single bending note feeds back into the night sky. Joining the wailing refrain, a galloping snare drum evokes the deadly speed once again, but it is far more joyful now, almost beatific. Two introductory electric guitar chords call out. The drums increase in momentum, as if rising out of the smoldering heap behind us. We're on to something new, resurrected in their entwined ecstasy. To be damn sure, we're now fully engaged—the chords resound again, but this time they evolve into a rolling, tumbling progression. Each riff tails off as invisible hands slide languidly down maple necks, undulating into the ether. Momentum builds with each double crash on the cymbals. Until . . .

The double time strangely disappears, along with the thundering bass and the in-your-face guitars, which now settle back into a half-time echo chamber that forms a cloudy bed for the singer's lament:

> *It's so sad livin' at home*
> *Far from the city, and the midnight fun*
> *It's so bad goin' to school*
> *So far from me and the dirty things that we do*

The singer/driver is the same one killed in a frenzy of booze, speed, and fire during the rousing opener. We know this from the initial news report, as well as from experiencing every skin-tingling note of his trip as it unfolded. But now, here is that voice again—proud, invincible, impenetrable, and still unmistakably defiant. He's imprisoned in his home, another dime-a-dozen suburban kid trapped in a world not of his making, parents, school, and night after night without any far-off promise of *midnight fun*. Turns out, fair listener, he has not been wiped out, and nor, more to the point, has his indomitable spirit. Not yet, my friends, maybe not ever. One causality of rebellion cannot quell the eternal yearn to breathe free.

Now, just as before, the drums begin their double-time rumble anew; the chords crash ahead as the singer, our hero reborn, beckons his fantasy alter-ego, like Clark Kent emerging triumphantly from the cramped phone booth to take to the skies or Nietzsche's *Übermensch* becoming the American Superman.

> *I'm the king of the night time world*
> *And you're my headlight queen*
> *I'm the king of the night time world*
> *Come live your secret dream*

As darkness descends, dreary daytime teenagers transmogrify into gleaming royalty, emancipated this time not by rock and roll, a speeding automobile, or the infinite escape to the midnight show, but by a woman, *the* woman, who shares the plight of kept youth—so much to conquer and so little time.

> *It's so fine lovin' with ease*
> *Far from the house and the family fights*
> *It's so fine bein' with you*
> *Bein' with me makes everything alright*

To love and be loved, to understand and be understood, is the ultimate rock-and-roll manifesto. It breathes in the desires of youth, deranged with raging hormones and awkward expressions (livin', goin', lovin', bein'), a furious need to find the comfort zone when all about is an intimidating dose of reality: no money, no place of my own, no fucking freedom! The chorus shouts out the alternative: to rule the night with my girl by my side making everything *all right*!

The music agrees. A single guitar breaks free into a funky, raunchy riff, riding the unstoppable wave of drums, finally giving way to an orgasmic lead descending into its own mellifluence. It repeats the choral dreamscape of the king in his nocturnal dominion. When the music coalesces again, our hero puts the finishing touches to his elegy to youthful imagination:

> *It's so sad you're not content*
> *Far from the music and the neon glow*

> *Ain't you glad we got the time*
> *Far from our folks, they'll never ever know*

Now the tale reaches its core truth: the young couple creates its own slice of boundless heaven. Never mind its tangible, earthly locale, limited by brick, mortar, and damnable reality, *there's a place for us*—a place for the misunderstood wanderers of *West Side Story*, an elixir once hinted at in Brian Wilson's "Wouldn't It Be Nice?" or the insular sanctuary of another Beach Boys youthful fairytale, "In My Room." It is, after all, Dorothy's siren song to a better world, "Somewhere Over the Rainbow."

A final refrain: *King of the night time world!* The drums break into a staccato *Thump-bam*! *Thump-bam*! *You're my headlight queen!* The guitars wail along approvingly, laying out the yellow brick road to teenaged nirvana. *I'm the king of the night time world! Come live your secret dream!*

Unable to contain the excitement any longer, the drums are unleashed as a runaway stallion, rushing to the place of secret dreams. The singer, infused with unbridled delight, runs away with them: *I'm the king! I'm the king! I'm the king! I'm the king!*

This is the mantra: the clicking of the ruby slippers transporting our hero and his girl from shunned zit-faced, clumsy prisoners of suburbia to masters of a faraway realm.

4

The Show

I was just a nice hippie kid from Toronto. I'd never seen anything like this. We felt like we had been dropped into an alien planet. The place was filled with people wearing spandex and spider eyes. They all had black fingernails and black lipstick. And they all had deathly white complexions.
—Bob Ezrin[1]

Predating The Act by half a decade was The Show, presented in deplorable splendor by the godfathers of foot-stomping, ear-splitting macabre, Alice Cooper.

Fronted by an emaciated, dark-haired, beer-swilling Detroit son of a preacher named Vincent Furnier, who legally changed his name to that of the band (an intriguing moniker pulled out of thin air but gleefully rumored to be that of a nineteenth-century witch summoned from a Ouija board), the Alice Cooper group plunged stage theatrics to their lowest brow. Mixing antisocial humor and an endless grab bag of repulsive props (mutilated baby dolls, guillotines, straitjackets, and a live boa constrictor), Furnier's wickedly ironic persona turned the rock zeitgeist on its head.

"You couldn't have a rock-and-roll drama without a villain," Cooper explained, when I interviewed him for a 2009 *East Coast Rocker* cover story. "There needs to be heroes, villains, and victims, and Alice needed to be a visual villain. There wasn't one personified villain in rock and roll, so I said, 'Well, I will gladly be that!' And the great thing about being the villain is usually the villain has a great sense of humor."[2]

The villain, fully realized and patently unrepentant, was truly a character in every sense of the word, so much so that Furnier began almost immediately referring to his wicked alter ego in the third person, as in "Alice wouldn't do that!" or "Alice would love that!"—or, in darker times, "Alice is killing me."

The Alice Cooper group hit the ground running in the late '60s, hot on the heels of the California flower-power/acid craze. One night in 1969, the band that would one day be credited with "driving a stake through the heart of the peace and love generation" cleared the hip Cheetah Club in Hollywood halfway through its first set, inspiring an offer of management from Shep Gordon, a twenty-one-year-old former L.A. probation cop whose only brush with rock and roll up to that point was being punched in the face by a soused Janis Joplin. "It seemed like the bottom line of being an entertainer was to evoke emotion, whether hate or love," Gordon told Steve Demorest for his early paperback bio of the band. "What struck me about Alice Cooper was their negative energy."[3]

With designs on being a hard-rock outfit worthy of Yardbirds status, the band opened for such top acts as the Doors on the Sunset Strip, duly impressing the Mothers of Invention's main man, Frank Zappa. Having immediately signed the band to his Straight Records label after the hungover members mistakenly showed up at his house dressed in bizarre regalia at 7:00 a.m. instead of the scheduled *p.m.* for an audition, Zappa—himself no stranger to concept-driven farce—encouraged Alice Cooper to go as far out of the mainstream as it could stand.

Ninety percent of the Alice Cooper image was created from whole cloth before being massaged through a willing press and gladly passed on through the fan channels by Gordon: Cooper screwing in coffins, his giant pet snake being allowed to slither free in hotel lobbies, the band becoming wrapped up in a satanic cult. There were tales of orgies, ritualistic sacrifices of every conceivable animal, and one serious misstep when a rumor the singer had died was reported by a British tabloid before someone in the Cooper camp got around to denying it.

When gory innuendo couldn't do the trick, there was always the more direct, manipulative approach. Prior to headlining an important gig at London's Wembley Empire Pool, a truck driver was paid to purposely stall a vehicle in the middle of jammed Piccadilly Square during rush hour. His cargo? A twenty-by-nine-foot billboard of Alice in the buff, save for a boa constrictor crawling between his legs. Oh, and by the way, the location, date, and time for the show were all prominently displayed in bold lettering above the image. The result? Commuters furious, authorities summoned, press assembled, show sold out.

Finally, when all else tanked, there was the eminently successful infamous happenstance, which was quickly exploited by the luminous Alice Cooper publicity machine. It began at a Toronto festival headlined by soon-to-be ex-Beatle John Lennon. Cooper, unbeknown to his urban roots, heaved a live chicken into the audience, thinking it could fly—which of course it couldn't. The bird was torn apart by the frantic crowd, the mangled pieces hurled back onstage. The entire incident—a hideous mistake—was blown into "Alice Cooper Bites Head Off Chicken and Sucks Blood Out."

The oddity route could only take Alice Cooper so far, however. Soon after Warner Bros. absorbed Frank Zappa's label and the "anything goes" '70s kicked in, hit songs began to push the label's freak show to the forefront. "I'm Eighteen," "Under My Wheels," and finally the teen-angst rebellious home run of "School's Out" made Alice Cooper a household name, even if inevitably the lead singer's macabre figure and his dynamic stage antics outshone the rest of the band.

By 1973—the year KISS was forming in its roach-infested Manhattan hovel—Alice Cooper was the biggest thing in rock and pop culture. The band's chart-topping *Billion Dollar Babies* (#1 in both the U.S. and U.K.) and the ensuing traveling circus of a world tour (captured for posterity in books and a feature film) not only shattered attendance records set by the Rolling Stones but also produced hits. Four of the record's singles cracked the Top 100, a fairly remarkable feat for any group, much less one hell bent on pissing off the masses. Now, when comedians wanted to reference the sublevel of dirty, dastardly, and dangerous in a quip, Alice Cooper fit the mold. And, of course, the kids loved it, while their parents not only hated it but were confused as all hell by it.

Vincent Furnier and the boys guffawed all the way to fame and fortune. "We're merely the end product of an affluent society," Cooper told *Circus* magazine in 1971. "We enjoy coming on stage and showing the public what their world has come to. Only usually they're shocked."[4]

Hits or no hits, Alice could not merely sing songs: he had to make statements, create moods, and lampoon any social convention thrown his way. The music, the lyrical themes, and the overall recording style and its presentation were designed primarily to feed into The Show, which by extension was the Alice Cooper image. This is why there are very few, if any, traditional Alice Cooper love songs; even those serenading the joys of lust tend to express a deviant slant. The usual roadmap for rock or pop songs—looking for love, finding love, making love, losing love, or a general wonderment of what the hell love is—are laid to waste in the band's best work, from *Love It to Death* (1971) through *Killer* (1971) and *School's Out* (1972), culminating in the epic *Billion Dollar Babies* (1973), each sniffing at "concept"—but only in so much as each song gets weirder and sicker and darker, less inclined to please but rather to disturb.

It was a calculated team effort to creatively prelude each new Alice Cooper staging with an album acting as the libretto to a bizarre opera with material that would translate seamlessly to The Show. Songs with provocative titles like "Dead Babies," "Desperado," "Halo of Flies," "Sick Things," and "I Love the

Dead" delivered the goods in both dramatic arrangement and lyrical content, inspiring ritual beheadings, staged hangings, and general violent outbursts. And as each tour dwarfed previous attendance records, and each ensuing record sold more and more copies, the formula proved airtight.

As with any formula—especially one steeped in gothic overtones—there must be a mad scientist to concoct it, and for Alice Cooper his name was Bob Ezrin. An infectiously energetic musical prodigy from Toronto, Canada (ironically the birthplace of what would become the infinite showbiz Alice Cooper myth machine), Robert Alan "Bob" Ezrin was a lethal combination in a recording studio. He possessed a keen ear for not only the correct notes, operative keys, and layering of instrumentation, but also for deciding what phrasing best enhanced a performance, including choosing the decisive hooks and the specific musicians to bring it all home. Crucially, Ezrin had a knack for homing in on what would be most serviceable to the song being recorded and how it fit within the overall project it would eventually complete. And, most pressingly, Ezrin was always quite sure of the exact way to go about this process, which usually centered on *his* process: a no-nonsense hybrid of sustained effort mixed with fun-loving experimentation.

"My primary responsibility is to make the recording experience as productive and constructive as possible for the people involved," Ezrin explained to *Electronic Musician* in 1996. "My secondary responsibility is to ensure that there is some empirical quality level in the product. If all you care about is the product and you don't care about the people, the product will suffer, because the people are what make it great."[5]

Classically trained (as a boy he studied piano and composition at the Royal Conservatory in Toronto) with an encyclopedic knowledge of music theory plus a firm grasp of orchestration techniques and creative recording trickery, Bob Ezrin is a riddle wrapped inside a paradox: less producer than artist (his first professional experience was as a composer and folksinger in a duo called the Messengers), he was the strict taskmaster with a bent slant, the by-the-books realist and a cockeyed optimist. The legend of Bob Ezrin at the helm of a recording session is that his fingerprints will not only be all over the music, they'll be inside, across, underneath, and hovering all around.

"Bob was an accomplished musician and certainly knew what he was talking about when he was trying to describe any musical ideas he had to the band," recalls highly acclaimed engineer Jay Messina, whose role as lead board-man on *Destroyer* complimented Ezrin's manic, experimental, shoot-from-the-hip style. "I got to appreciate his level of musicianship. He's a really fine musician."[6]

Legendary session drummer Allan Schwartzberg, who played on hits for

Melissa Manchester, Tony Orlando & Dawn, and Gloria Gaynor, and later worked with Ezrin on the Alice Cooper projects *Goes To Hell* and *Lace & Whiskey*, described Ezrin's uniquely hands-on approach to Mitch Lafon of www.bravewords.com. "I worked with a lot of different producers at the time and my first session with Bob the engineer gets sick and has to go home. So, he engineers the tape himself. Then he comes out and says, 'Allan get up for a second. I'm hearing the drums like this.' Then sits down at the drums and plays something. Then he goes over to the bass and says, 'How about something like this?' He goes around the room and plays every instrument. For the takes, he's sitting at the piano and singing the songs. That was after he had the assistant engineer press 'record.' He's now singing the reference vocal. Bob Ezrin is the only guy that before that day and since, have I ever seen do that. You have producers who show up in the studio once a month, sit back, and say, 'I don't know why, but I just don't like it.'"[7]

"I really enjoyed working with Bob," recalls engineer Rod O'Brien, who assisted Ezrin on several projects. "Bob was one of those producers who came in and he would say, 'Let's do this,' and he would describe something either to a musician or something and you would kind of look at him like, 'Why are we doing it this way?'—and three or four overdubs later, everything started to make sense and you realized Bob had thought this out like a chess master four steps ahead of everybody else."[8]

Perhaps Ezrin's greatest talent for getting down a representative rock-and-roll experience is an innate, almost clairvoyant ability to tap into the root expression of the artist and apply those observations to the documenting of his or her composition. He would hear something inherent in the piece from its very inception that even the composer may have missed or had added subconsciously but glossed over by being too close to it. Then, when translating the discovery, he would do so with the enthusiasm of someone forcefully committed to the song's most cherished aspects.

"I prefer to take a raw talent, a personality rather than a technician, and go in and teach the technique myself," Ezrin explained to *Circus* magazine in 1976. "I'll take the raw talent every time, because if the brilliance is there it can be molded into just about anything. If you've got a great craftsman with no personality there is no way you're gonna make a great record."[9]

In a televised review of the Alice Cooper phenomenon, Cooper explained Ezrin's impact on the band's signature sound to interviewer Nick Sahakian. "We became so close creatively that I would think of what Bob might think of an idea. I would write a lyric and I would go, 'Bob's gonna hate this lyric,' so I'd write another one and say, 'Bob's gonna love this lyric.' We wouldn't just write the thing; we would talk about it for hours until it was just sick enough, twisted in the right little mold. What I thought was really sick could be sicker if we just twisted it a little more or the chord he'd put on top of it would make it more demented."[10]

This hands-on approach is the primary reason Ezrin's writing credits festoon the backs of records he's chosen to produce: his musical ideas not only invoke a collaborative environment but also instill a renewed confidence in the material being presented for a project and ultimately its recording for posterity. (Even when omitted, as on those classic Alice Cooper albums, the evidence of his involvement is irrefutable.) "From having some folk music in my background and having played folk music for so long, I understood what a really great song felt like. I had played a lot of them," Ezrin explained to Larry LeBlanc of *Celebrity Access Mediawire*.[11]

"The beauty of working with a producer like Bob Ezrin, who is classically trained, is he knows music inside and out," says Corky Stasiak, who worked with Ezrin on several projects, including as assistant engineer on *Destroyer*. "When we'd record jingles, I would sometimes work with Paul Shaffer, who would write out all the parts for everybody and arrange the music and conduct the musicians. Inevitably, somebody from the advertising agency, who we called 'the suits,' would huddle with him and say, 'Gee, that sounds nice, but I don't know how to describe it, but I really wanted that section of the music to *smile*!' Now a person like Ezrin or Paul Shaffer or Barry Manilow, when he was doing commercials, can say, 'I know what you mean, give me five minutes.' Then he would take a paper and pencil and go off to each musician and rewrite the parts: 'Make this a C-flat, make this an augmented seven,' and he'd make sure they had it and then command, 'Okay, let's run it down, one, two, three . . .' and then the advertising people, who didn't really know music, would shout, 'That's it!' So you can tell when you're working with someone who really knows music. They can get a *sneer* in music or a *laugh* or a *smile*, or play a range of songs to provide the listener an emotional link. It's like what George Martin used to say about music being mathematical, if you had a grasp of its frequencies, you could make music *wink* at you."[12]

"When I first worked with Bob, I formed an impression of him as a very visual, theatrical guy," recalls arranger and composer Allan Macmillan. "He really had a visual conception of what was going on in music at that time. He had demonstrated he could translate this into actual performance values."[13] Macmillan, who would later play a major role in Ezrin's career and eventually collaborate with him on several projects, including *Destroyer*, first asked a teenaged Ezrin to assist in staging the annual Toronto Spring Thaw musical revue in the late '60s. By then, Macmillan was a respected veteran of big bands and jazz clubs and had made his name composing and arranging live musical studio broadcasts for CBC Radio in Vancouver. Already in his late thirties, and thus hailing from a previous musical generation, Macmillan was finding it difficult to incorporate a more contemporary sound in the popular revue when he tapped Ezrin, who was then managing what the arranger describes as "a popular grass band" around Toronto.[14] The young phenom became a conduit between the younger musicians and Macmillan. "Bob acted as the front guy," Macmillan recalls. "He translated my thoughts about what should be done musically into reality and worked up the band; backing the singer and other performers in the show."[15]

"There was always a certain grandiose part of me that loved the theater of everything," Ezrin explained, during interviews for this book. "I came into this from theater. I was working in musical theater when Allan Macmillan recommended that Jack Richardson hire me, and that's when I went to work for Nimbus 9."[16]

Richardson, who had an extensive background in advertising, made his bones in the music business producing hits for the Guess Who and would later guide the recordings of Bob Seger, Poco, and Badfinger. He launched Nimbus 9 in Toronto with Macmillan, who was put in charge of music publishing, Peter Clayton, another successful ad man, and Ben McPeek, who was known across Canada as Mr. Jingle, having produced over 2,000 ad melodies. "I thought we needed somebody to do artist management and music publishing," Macmillan recalls, of recommending the young Ezrin to his colleagues. "Although I was in charge of music publishing, I thought Bob really had the right instincts for this end of the business. So Jack and I decided to bring Bob into the mix and before you knew it Shep Gordon appeared on our doorstep and wanted Jack to get involved with Alice."[17]

It was after Gordon's incessant badgering of Richardson to produce the Alice Cooper group that in the first weeks of 1970 Nimbus 9 dispatched the nineteen-year-old Ezrin to New York City to witness an early incarnation of The Show at the famed Max's Kansas City. Fully prepared to endure another excruciating evening having to watch a struggling band and then inform its members they were not ready for the big time, Ezrin was instead completely blown away. "I have never experienced the range of emotions that I was put through by Alice Cooper that night," he told *Circus* magazine in 1976. "They thrilled me and they scared me. I figured that any group that could affect me like that—I was pretty jaded already—had to be pretty special."[18]

Ezrin later admitted to having difficulty deciphering the band's crudely hammered-out distortion, never mind understanding much of what the lead singer was spouting, but he was specifically intrigued by one song in which he thought Cooper kept screeching, "I'm edgy! I'm edgy!" (It was actually the chorus to a soon-to-be hit record, "I'm Eighteen.") Where many had only witnessed sideshow cacophony, Ezrin saw star quality. Mostly, he intuited real musical potential.

"Bob heard hooks there," Cooper recalled, in an online interview with the Nimbus School of Recording Arts. "He turned us into a monster, this thing that actually had a sound, and from that he created Alice Cooper. We were more of a gang than a band at first, an empty canvas that needed to be painted."[19]

Having already told the group Nimbus 9 would take them on—something he had no authority to do—the feisty Ezrin, fully expecting to be sacked for his insubordination, rushed back to Canada to convince his new boss that Alice Cooper was worth a serious shot. "Richardson told me, 'If you like them so damn much, you do it,'" Ezrin told Michael Butler, on his web-streamed *Rock N' Roll Geek Show* in 2006. "I had no qualifications. There was no way I should have been producing anything."[20] It would be the first of a continuing series of bold but smart moves that would solidify Ezrin's rightful place in rock-and-roll history.

Looking back, decades later, in a 1996 *Electronic Musician* interview, Ezrin recalled his rapt enthusiasm for Alice Cooper. "As far as I was concerned this was more than music. This was the beginning of a cultural movement. I wasn't thinking of it in terms of [radio] frequency bands. I was thinking of it simply in terms of a segment of society, meaning kids and that I felt being one of them, that this was what was happening, which was that we were adopting a more fantastical approach to our entertainment. We were beginning to embrace experimentation with the stretching of boundaries and the bending of norms. We were doing it politically already. We were kind of doing it lyrically in our music, but we hadn't touched on things like how we dressed or what our sexual orientation was through our music."[21]

Alice Cooper represented many things to the nineteen-year-old Bob Ezrin as he assisted Richardson in RCA's Mid American Studios in Chicago for his baptism in the producer's chair (a gig he was handed when literally no one in the company would dare): image, rebellion, artistry, provocation, sexuality, violence, controversy—in a word, America. For the still-impressionable Canadian, it was a slice of the wild side. Mostly it was a chance to work side by side with the man who would be his mentor and get an honest to goodness hard-rock act down on tape, as it deserved to sound. There was much potential to be mined, and Bob Ezrin was not shy in expressing it.

For Alice Cooper, whose singer and namesake has said repeatedly over the years that Ezrin represented what George Martin was for the Beatles—mentor, musical interpreter, technical magician, and sonic Sherpa—this was a chance to get down to business. While the band's first album for Straight Records, *Pretties for You* (1969), had dipped its toes in the shallow end of the rock waters, it strayed more into psychedelic fad than the badass sound the band had envisioned. Moreover, the band was forced to finish the record sans producer when a bored Frank Zappa abandoned the sessions, resulting in a rudderless exercise that yielded bad reviews and abysmal sales. *Easy Action* (1970) was no better, despite the presence behind the console of twenty-six-year-old David Briggs, best known for his work with Neil Young. As Alice Cooper drummer Neal Smith remembers, "David hated our music and us. I recall the term that he used, referring to our music, was 'psychedelic shit.'"[22]

Initially, Ezrin agreed with this assessment. "I hated the record," he explained, in a 1973 *New Musical Express* interview. "We had it lying around the office and I put it on and everyone just broke up laughing. We didn't know if Alice Cooper was a guy or a chick and eventually it became a standing joke that if anyone messed up that week we'd be forced to go and work with Alice Cooper."[23]

The feeling may have been mutual, for certainly no one in the Alice Cooper camp gave a flying hump about Bob Ezrin. He was a midlevel employee with Nimbus 9 who was merely sent as an errand boy to quiet the incessant requests from the band's manager to secure his boss to produce the next record.

Thrown together in a professional detente, Ezrin immediately became a port in a storm for Alice Cooper. As the lead singer remembered, "When Bob came along and told us he could get hits out of the band he confirmed our thinking, so we figured, hell, this guy actually likes us, let's go with him."[24]

5

School's Out

As far as Bob was concerned, he was the artist, he was the creator, and we were just the guys who would let him get on with it.
  —Alice Cooper guitarist, Glen Buxton[1]

Right from the start, Bob Ezrin began running Cooper sessions like a classroom, preaching song structure, stressing performance, and mining attitude. Providing a combination of straightforward rock and roll with string quartets, French horns, and Moog synthesizers—in addition to strange layers of everything from chants and sounds recorded from African exorcisms to weirdly tuned oboes—the young producer fiddled around with key changes and tweaked lyrics. In many ways, he became a part of the band in the studio, playing piano on many tracks and acting as an invaluable sounding board for its lead singer.

The group's bassist and contributor of dark-themed songs, Dennis Dunaway, explained Ezrin's impact on Alice Cooper in Dave Thompson's 2012 book *Welcome to My Nightmare*. "We had a tendency to try and force too many ideas into one song, and as a result it wouldn't have any continuity. Ezrin was able to take those ideas and say, 'Okay, wait a minute, let's focus on this one thing and let that other thing fall by the wayside.' He was like a director, which was extremely important for us. Ezrin came along at a time when we were ready to go in a more acceptable and less abstract direction."[2]

"I use various hand signals in the studio, head signals, hand signals—each one means something, and I sort of dance with the group while they play," Ezrin told *Circus* magazine in 1976. "It evolves to the point where I can take a group Svengali-style and sort of play them like an instrument. Eventually this leaves them free to think about their job of injecting the right emotions at the right time, because they don't have to worry about the technical part, they'd have it down."[3]

Ezrin gathered all of his resources to help realize the raw potential he had seen in New York and bring it to fruition. The result, *Love It to Death*, is as much a debut for what would become the Alice Cooper brand as it was for the Bob Ezrin sound. Its combination of the basic two guitars, bass, and drums combo in songs like "Caught in a Dream" and "Long Way to Go," atmospheric mini-dramas in "Ballard of Dwight Fry" and "Black Juju," and catchy fodder like "Is It My Body" and "I'm Eighteen" (the latter reaching #21 on the *Billboard* Top 100) made for one hell of a rock album, and an amazing baptism of fire for the blossoming Ezrin. The record climbed to #35 on the *Billboard* albums chart and set the formerly "psychedelic shit" Alice Cooper band running. "Ultimately Bob was the cohesion that made Alice Cooper Alice Cooper," raves Cooper today.[4]

Beyond his astute studio techniques and musical brilliance, Ezrin flourished in the one area any artist needs above all: timing. The 1970s album era was perfectly suited to his cinematic approach. Its format, with its two sides, as if two acts in a play with an intermission, allows for a crucial arc in the storytelling. Additionally, turntable technology held the listener in a controlled environment, which would later be expanded with the rollout of portable tape machines, car stereos, boom boxes, the CD Walkman, and eventually iPods, smart phones, and other portable electronic devices. Moreover, headphones dominated the culture's aural experience, wherein the listener, enveloped in intricate stereo panning, atmospheric sounds, and multilayered vocal trickery, had come to expect a sonic thrill ride. Adding to this solitary ambiance were mood lamps, recreational drugs, and comfortable home settings to better absorb the music with no outside distraction. This kept the listener rapt to each song: how one flowed into the other, their connecting lyrical content, and the melding of instrumentation.

The album format was also perfectly suited to '70s kids. Still in the dark ages compared with today's ubiquitous media fluidity, and long before the Internet or social media, many of them were unable to control the family television or even the kitchen radio. This led to the prioritizing of the bedroom or upstairs den: the imagination capsule, locked away inside the headphone dreamscape, studying every corner of the 12-inch artwork and delving deeper into lyrical subtext, whether in ways intended by the artist or not. As if sitting in their own theater of the mind—already hijacked by comic-book fantasy images of horror and science fiction, advertising propaganda, and the American promise of grandeur—they were willing participants in the playful meandering of their rock-and-roll heroes.

"Theater was the primitive and fundamental building block for all entertainment back then," explains Ezrin. "Everything was expressed in scenes and acts, and you would have a story arc: you would start something and end the act with a dramatic event. Films were built that way, television was built that way, theater was experienced that way, books—instead of acts, there were chapters, or book one, book two, book three, and the chapters were the scenes—everything was built in that way, yet with music it was just song, song, song, song, with no through line. It was just a series of two- or three-minute experiences. Nothing wrong with that, but my orientation tended more toward theater, film, and TV, so I brought that sensibility to my producing. And I loved that ritual. To me, that ritual of opening up that record and putting it on the platter and sitting back and letting it wash over you for about twenty minutes—which seemed just about the right amount of time before you needed a break—to me that was the perfect experience for music."[5]

In an interview for this book, artist, Ken Kelly, whose spectacular superhero painting of the four member of KISS for the cover of *Destroyer* would greatly enhance the enraptured listener's imagination, agreed that the boom of the era's cover art provided a landscape for his talents. "Those were the days you had the entire theater in your ears, and the only visual you had was the album cover, and it was a very singular thing you were doing, because you were alone wherever that record player was, and that's what you stared at. As they were screaming out their songs, you just completely bought the entire fantasy, the whole thing; hook, line, and sinker."[6]

"The Beatles had a lot to do with it," Ezrin concludes, "because I think that once they started to become more aware of the album as an art form, they started creating stuff that was literally built for that container. Those were amazing experiences: when you listened from the first beat to the last beat of a side of a Beatles album, you really went on an emotional journey. Then you needed a break, and then you put on the next side and its journey number two! Or it's the end of the story. That whole experience just felt appropriate and fulfilling and really inspiring for me."[7]

For the next four years, save for pit stops with other artists like Lou Reed, on his theatrically eerie and luridly experimental *Berlin*, Ezrin was primarily the exclusive property of the Alice Cooper group. And he did not disappoint. Each ensuing record improved on the one before, both musically and lyrically, all contributing mightily to the Alice Cooper image and most importantly The Show. None was more iconic or seminal in the history of rock and roll than "School's Out," arguably the finest of rock anthems and a sonic tour de force. Its signature guitar opening, voice-shredding vocals, chill-inducing chorus (replete with frenetically serenading children), and hilariously moronic lyric transformed a glam cult outfit from punch line to household name. The single dominated the airwaves throughout the summer of 1972, reaching #7 on the

U.S. *Billboard* chart and sitting at #1 in the U.K. for three solid weeks in August, becoming the largest-selling international single in Warner Bros. history. The album of the same name was an amazing array of dark composition, showbiz parody, nostalgic posturing, and vaudevillian nonsense, juxtaposing an entire generation of pompous studio flirtations with significant musical force.

School's Out was satirical fun and a rock breakthrough, but it only hinted at what was to come. *Billion Dollar Babies* broke the mold, and the bank, and sent the Alice Cooper group into the pop/rock stratosphere. All the while, behind the scenes, the master manipulator—the button-pushing, dial-spinning mad scientist, Bob Ezrin—called the shots, co-writing, arranging, and literally producing what the world would come to know as Alice Cooper. Adding horns, strings, background singers, and bizarre tape and sound effects to vocal manipulations and electric instruments turned back around and upside down, the young producer worked the band ragged, creating a unique netherworld in which it could roam.

The engrossing and infectious single "Elected," with its sixteen horn-section overdubs, took the band weeks to record; Cooper, placed in front of a full-length mirror to watch himself, as if making a political speech to thousands of constituents, days to sing; and Ezrin an astounding eighty hours to mix. It eventually cost Warner Bros. a mind-numbing ten grand (nearly $57,000 today). Many in the industry fell over themselves trying to figure out how the hell this Canadian kid was receiving carte blanche from one of the industry's most powerful labels, turning out startlingly original performances from a rag-tag bunch, and why every one of the albums sounded so distinctively magnificent.

One of those industry insiders was Bill Aucoin, who, as early as 1974 felt justified in directly seeking out a big-time producer for his band. Always connected to the incestuous nature of the music business, Aucoin had instinctively noted the costumed showman/shock-rock connection between his band and Alice Cooper from the very beginning. In the summer of 1973, each member of KISS had stated, mere days after seeing The Show when it rolled through New York City, *just imagine what four Alice Coopers could achieve*? In a serendipitous crossing of paths, Cooper had been in Casablanca's industry-only audience when KISS made its first appearance in L.A. to launch its debut album. Afterward, he famously smirked, "What these guys need is a gimmick." According to Gene Simmons's recollections in his autobiography, the legendary rock fiend was the only one in that audience who truly "got it." Call it a blessing or an initiation in the spectacle brotherhood, but Cooper indeed "got" exactly what Bill Aucoin and eventually Neil Bogart did—which, coincidentally, was what Bob Ezrin had seen in Cooper's own volume-addled Show several years earlier:

the beginning of a cultural movement, a segment of society, meaning kids, adopting a more fantastical approach to entertainment, an embrace of experimentation with the stretching of boundaries and the bending of norms in our music.

Aucoin revealed to journalist Frank Rose his original impetus for corralling KISS: "Alice was really in my mind peaking. He was at the top of the ladder, and I knew that Shep [Gordon] wanted to take him off the road and I knew that Alice wanted to become an actor. And together they went to the coast to effectively start that career. Now that meant that Alice had built up all that audience and no one was really out there to fulfill their needs. I don't think they wanted another Alice Cooper, but they wanted that kind of showmanship."[8]

Like Aucoin, Ezrin had professional reasons to seek new creative horizons. At the conclusion of Alice Cooper's historically lucrative *Billion Dollar Babies* tour, and without first consulting the rest of the band, Vincent Furnier hinted at retiring from the stage to pursue a career in the movies. Shep Gordon had already begun floating the singer's name in Hollywood circles as a potential actor. This did not infuse the studio with positive vibes when Alice Cooper reconvened to record its next album, *Muscle of Love*. Squabbles about Furnier getting all the publicity and the music taking a backseat to the theatrics while musicians were being treated as session puppets in the grand Bob Ezrin scheme inevitably led to Jack Richardson—Ezrin's mentor, and the band's initial choice of producer in 1971—to handle the producing chores. The result was the most unimaginative Cooper record yet, followed by a bummer of a tour, filled with what was now being perceived by fans and press as the band dragging out the same old tired "shock" routines, cashing the resulting sizable checks, and getting back to cushy lives of celebrity. The end appeared nigh.

It was, then, the irony of ironies that the specter of KISS began inching its way into the Alice Cooper transom. As Bill Aucoin was trying to woo Bob Ezrin to achieve the missing ingredient in the KISS model, The Show was feeling the stage heat from The Act.

The success of KISS's full-blitz presentation through late '74 into 1975—which kept the band and its management afloat and eventually led to the idea of a live album—was causing a seismic shift in how theatrical shows would or could be staged. This was territory originally carved out and until then wholly dominated by the Alice Cooper group. Bamboozled by The Act's full-speed-ahead hallucinations, the usually unflinching Cooper camp was unaware of the growing paranoia and cash-strapped situation between Casablanca and KISS. In David Thompson's insightful 2012 biography *Alice Cooper: Welcome to My Nightmare*, Gordon and Cooper are described as being convinced that KISS shows were "devouring twice as much money per show as the Coopers spent on an entire tour."[9] They erroneously believed the KISS show was "financed by the bottomless pockets of Casablanca Records"[10]—mainly because this is what Neil Bogart (like Bill Aucoin and KISS) wanted everyone to believe. The label and Rock Steady, along with booking agency ATI, were dumping tons of cash into the rolling extravaganza that was The Act, but were doing so on deep credit, using shifty distributing deals and tough, grassroots promotion from every angle, profits be damned.

Bob Ezrin, however, denies being as intimidated by KISS's momentum in the shock-rock marketplace as Gordon or Cooper. "We weren't thinking, 'Gee, we gotta compete with this one or that one,'" he argued, when pressed about it for this book. "There was no question in anybody's minds about Alice's importance. We always felt that he was a superstar, and even though I wasn't a huge fan of *Muscle of Love*, it didn't diminish his importance on the scene. I was never feeling anyone's breath on my neck, and I don't think he was either. We were just trying to do something really cool."[11] Nevertheless, as Ezrin told *Rolling Stone* in 1976, "I could hear a rumble from the street, and I've always had a very good sense of that. I knew KISS was having a profound effect on people already and they weren't even home yet. No airplay. No singles. No real big headlining tours."[12]

The brain trust surmised that if Alice Cooper bore the KISS model, then it must not be allowed to outduel the originators. Cooper, especially, thought it was time to up the ante. Thompson's book paints a picture of the Cooper camp being pressed to take back the theatrical ground yielded to KISS by funneling the massive profits from *Billion Dollar Babies* into a highly stylized conceptual studio production, followed by an immense multimedia rollout into film, television, and concerts. However, with the rest of the band already feeling eclipsed by all the stage antics, the real or imagined hoopla, and their singer appearing solo on every magazine cover, they could not be persuaded to hock their financial future to out-spectacle the likes of KISS.

When I interviewed him in 2012 for the *Aquarian Weekly*, Alice Cooper echoed Thompson's scenario by recalling the stakes that may have led to the Cooper group's demise. "Everyone thought *Billion Dollar Babies* was the end-all in shows, because it broke a whole bunch of records and it was pretty theatrical. To me, I was already thinking if we just had the time and the money and the imagination, *Welcome to My Nightmare* could be the most theatrical show of all time. And I think that's where I lost the original band, 'cause what it meant was putting all the money back into the show. And it also meant another two or three or four months, whatever it is, of rehearsing ten hours a day, and I think the original guys went, 'Enough! We've been touring for six, seven years without a break, and now you're talking about doing a show bigger than *Billion Dollar Babies*?' I think that's where I kind of lost them."[13]

The Alice Cooper group, at its absolute zenith, was coming apart. But as the rest of band remained in a holding pattern, fairly certain that some kind of reconciliation was in the offing, Gordon, Ezrin, and Cooper went back to work conceiving a three-tiered rollout of stage performance, film presentation (both dramatic, for television, and concert presentation, for theaters), and a full-length concept album. *Welcome to My Nightmare* was a true collaboration between the hot Canadian producer and his ghoulish ingénue. It was to be everything Bob Ezrin had infused into the Alice Cooper oeuvre, but without the limitation of a predetermined lineup or so it appeared a budget.

Ezrin: "We developed it around the storyline of a rock star who had gone down in a plane crash with somebody he wasn't supposed to be with, and when they finally found him, after this avalanche where he had been trapped for a really long time, he was alone. No one else was there. The entire incident changed him. After that he was rock star by day, monster by night. So we started writing music to go with this, and some of that music is in *Welcome to My Nightmare*, particularly the whole middle section to the song, 'Only Women Bleed,' which comes from the scene where they're picking at the ice to see if there are any survivors under there. The character's name was Steven, and that's where we got our guy for the song 'Steven.' So that was our original idea. At that point all we knew was the only thing we wanted was to do something we hadn't done before and it had to be really amazing and encompass a storyline. When the film didn't work out, we had these bits and pieces, which gave us an idea, and then we starting thinking about, 'Well, what if we did this; what if it was a nightmare?' Because a part of the movie was the question of whether this guy's experience was part of a nightmare or was it real?"[14]

They spent months honing the overall theme, its general mood, and, of course, the songs, attracting the best and brightest studio musicians. These included much of Lou Reed's touring band, which had just completed recording the highly acclaimed live album *Rock n Roll Animal* the previous year; Prakash John (who also played with Casablanca's Parliament/Funkadelic, the wildly theatrical R&B answer to KISS) on bass; guitarist Steve Hunter, who'd worked with Detroit hero Mitch Ryder; and fellow Motown axe man deluxe Dick Wagner, who would not only play a major role in the future of the Alice Cooper show but also become a key cog in Ezrin's future projects, including a major stake in *Destroyer*. Ezrin also booked a bevy of polished background singers and a horn section, delving headlong into his usual bag of sound effects and studio magic, culminating in an eerie mix of pathos and camp. The project even boasted an appearance by the prince of horror films, Vincent Price. Most notably, *Welcome to My Nightmare* marked the unveiling of something that would not only come to be an Alice Cooper specialty but also set the standard for what all hard-rock/heavy-metal bands would emulate for decades: the power ballad. With the magnificently poignant and haunting "Only Women Bleed," Cooper and Ezrin—with enormous assistance from Wagner, who had provided the original song, "Keep Movin' On," with different lyrics—altered the terrain of modern rock.

On the strength of Alice Cooper's already gargantuan notoriety, and the success of "Only Women Bleed," which reached #12 on the *Billboard* Top 100, *Welcome to My Nightmare* was a certified smash hit, spending months rising up the charts to #5 and launching his groundbreaking staging of the performance worldwide. The Show now consisted of an elaborate set replete with a giant nylon spider's web, a working guillotine, an oversized toy chest, a revolving poster bed, and a film screen, which Cooper busted through in the performance's stirring denouement. Dancers, extras, and an enormous, hairy Cyclops joined Wagner, Hunter, and the band, as the singer and star of the show made several costume changes while acting, two-stepping, and playing the fool. Without missing a beat, since his actual name was that of his former band, Alice Cooper seamlessly began a rock solo career rarely if ever duplicated.

At the time of its February 1975 release, the inventive and dramatic *Welcome to My Nightmare* signaled a new era in rock—a self-effacing showbiz '70s melodrama serenaded by a smart-aleck deviant unimpressed by the serious undertones of apocalyptic prophecy à la David Bowie's brilliant but grim *Ziggy Stardust and the Spiders from Mars* (1972), the schizophrenic anti-hero in The Who's *Quadrophenia* (1973), Genesis's lurid melancholia in *The Lamb Lies Down on Broadway* (1974), or Pink Floyd's vivid descent into madness on *Wish You Were Here* (1975). Alice Cooper's villain/jester grinning smarmily from the cover of his masterpiece, respectfully tipping a top hat and dressed in tails with a nifty corsage, gave you all you needed to know about what was to come: carnivorous black widows, crooning lechers, emotionally stunted sociopaths, and an ode to necrophilia. A gravely voiced Henny Youngman meets Salvador Dali starring in a Creature Feature.

Welcome to My Nightmare succeeded in reinventing the hard rock macabre of the Alice Cooper group by lifting its eponymous front man and feeding his many images—the serial killer, the desperado, the delinquent, the satirist, the jester, and the ghoul—into one conceptual package. It was only fitting that the specter of KISS blowing up half of America would partially inspire such a wildly creative spending spree, which accounted for everything Cooper and his manager Shep Gordon had in the world. Cooper admitted as much to me in 2012: "It was a giant roll of the dice. I'm telling you, if it wouldn't have worked . . . it was one of those defining moments of 'I talk the talk, am I gonna walk the walk?' And Shep and I put all of our money and Bob and I put our entire reputations into that show, and if it would have been a failure we would have had to start all over again."[15]

In a fiduciary sense, Cooper and Gordon found themselves at the same creative and professional nexus as Bill Aucoin and KISS, creating a scenario in which to break out of the shackles of a record contract—much to Warner Bros. chagrin, Gordon had smartly wooed Atlantic Records to release *Welcome to My Nightmare*, exploiting a loophole in standard '70s record contracts when dealing with "soundtracks"—and unleash the mad scientist Bob Ezrin to help create the essential fusion of the audio melodrama by tapping into the consciousness of the hard-rock theater of the mind to huge commercial success. Across the divide, with dark legal clouds rolling in on Casablanca, Bill Aucoin knew it was now KISS's turn at a defining moment.

"God of Thunder"

Hear my words and take heed.

It comes from nowhere. Out of the ether again, but this time it is not a distended voice on the radio, nor a single floating note released from the wreckage. It is the voice of a child, pitched high, with a tinge of playful delight. Its delicate but commanding voice echoes as if from a dark place or alight in heavenly repose: *Okay? Now start singing.*

The guitars begin a sinister refrain, ushered in uniformly by a thundering bass clip and the *boom-boom-boom* of a relentless drum beat. Across the stereo divide seep disturbing noises: ghostly wisps beneath crackling hints of electromagnetic aftershock and the foreboding hollow of whistles beyond the darkness. The dreamscape of the previous song quickly fades into distant memory. We are immediately transported to a subterranean realm of molten lava and braying cherubs; the innocent child's cries now crease through the pounding notes with mischievous glee. But none of it could prepare the ears for the voice that emerges triumphant:

You've got something about you.
You've got something I need.

A gruff baritone, growling from the depths of its being. It's only human trait is in the words we comprehend, but their origin is foreign, an unholy swath of gothic arrogance.

Daughter of Aphrodite
Hear my words and take heed.

The imaginary world of nighttime royalty appears to have been made manifest in this demon god. What has our yearning souls wrought? In the zeal to escape our earthly dirge, we have been catapulted into Hades; this thing calling back from its bottomless pit is beyond manageable, and it sounds as if it is not fucking around.

I was born on Olympus
To my father a son
I was raised by the demons
Trained to reign as the one

It is the God of Thunder, a fierce caricature of the rock-and-roll spirit; the grinning devil at Robert Johnson's crossroads, the howl of the heel-nipping hellhound, the boogie-woogie Beelzebub from your Faustian bargain. (Ha! You went too far now, buddy.) It's time to pay the piper, and the piper is an unyielding creature of immense proportions: a fire-breathing, blood-spouting, black-eyed beast with ill humor and gargantuan appetites.

The spell you're under
Will slowly rob you of your virgin soul.

Uh-oh.

Maybe, just maybe, we didn't survive that car ride, or perhaps we're stuck in a purgatory beyond mere parental tyranny and school daze. We wanted a bit of *midnight fun*, so we dared peek into the shadows. Now there's this guy . . .

I'm the lord of the wastelands
A modern day man of steel
I gather darkness to please me
And I command you to kneel before the . . .
God of Thunder and rock and roll!

The wild cherubs mockingly cackle and hiss. Sounds of the netherworld swirl about the crushing chord progression, which rumbles along, undaunted by the din. Suddenly the drums begin pounding out a raucous counter-stampede: *shhhumpth- shhhumpth shhhumpth*, the rolling thunder of the fast-approaching storm. Is this the demon's minions, come to take battle? Hitching a ride on the crest of this eruption is a tortuous wave of distortion, a guitar groaning forth, trailing the *thump-thump-thump* of the low, steady downbeat of the bass drum. The notes break free and begin a whining, grievous melody. They weep for the souls that have come before, once pristine victims of the spell.

Before our trip is complete, the senses are overloaded with clutching shrieks, backward growls, and braying children. The rolling thunder-drums now turn inside out and swoosh their way to the finality of two requiem chords.

Wooooooooo . . .

6

The Meeting

It's hard to say why we let Bob have so much control, yet it's also easy. When somebody has an idea and can communicate that idea as effectively as Bob, they automatically command a certain respect.
—Gene Simmons[1]

As early as 1974, Aucoin's plan to fill the Alice Cooper vacuum provided by the group's implosion was embodied in the enthusiasm of a sixteen-year-old Canadian high-school student by the name of Mike Longman. A teenage boy, the very core of the KISS fan base, clearly deduced that KISS's albums were missing something: imagination, diversity, musicality—all the elements of a Bob Ezrin production. An avid Cooper and Ezrin fan, Longman had begun incessantly bugging the famed producer with phone calls mining information about his heroes.

"Here was this sixteen-year-old kid, who was a rock fan and out there listening," remembers Ezrin. "Somehow he decided to look in the phone book and found my name there. I didn't un-list my number in those days—I probably should have, but he found my name and rang me up and told me what I ought to do, which at the time I thought was really cheeky, but at the same time I was fascinated by what he had to say."[2]

Soon the conversations became less of a strain for the then-twenty-four-year-old Ezrin, who was getting raw and emotional opinions about the current youth vibe. "He *was* the target audience for a lot of the work I was doing, so it was interesting for me to hear from him," admits Ezrin. "Did he teach me about my market in a way that I was unaware? I wasn't *that* much older than Mike Longman then, so I was listening to a lot of what he was listening to, but I did love hearing it from the teen perspective. It kept me connected."[3]

During one of these discussions, Longman asked Ezrin why he hadn't yet produced a KISS album. In a feature article in the March 25, 1976, issue of *Rolling Stone* upon the release of *Destroyer*, author David McGee described the chat. "'Oh man, they're great,' Longman told him [Ezrin]. 'The kids in high school love them. Only problem is their records are *so* shitty.' Ezrin wondered why, if their records were so shitty, he should get involved. 'Because they're so good, we buy their records anyway,' answered Longman."[4]

Ezrin, an astute industry social networker, remembered young Longman's advice during a chance encounter in the stairwell of Toronto's City-TV studios in the spring of 1974. It was most likely on or around September 15, as the band played the city's Victory Theater (aka Massey Hall) the same day. "By sheer coincidence, I ran into them just a few weeks after Longman mentioned it," recalls Ezrin. "So I was pre-sold before I met them. He planted the seed—the thought that maybe I should become their producer."[5]

Accompanying Gary Bonner, the prolific composer of the Turtles' hit "Happy Together," to promote a record titled "Baby, Baby" that he'd recently completed for Ezrin's fledgling label, Migration Records, the young producer was taken with what he describes as "monsters walking down the stairs toward me. I remember distinctly saying, 'Wait a minute; are you guys KISS?' And Paul Stanley said, 'Yeah.' And I said, 'I'm Bob Ezrin.' And he said, 'I know who you are!' which was kind of interesting. And I said, 'I know who *you* are!' And I didn't explain the Mike Longman connection, but I said, 'This may be out of line, but can I ask you: are you happy with your records?' And Stanley said, 'Well, yeah, why?' So I said, 'Well, if you ever decide you're not, I'd love to work with you guys.' And that was that. I went up the stairs, they went down the stairs, and then I got the phone call."[6]

There is very little chance Paul Stanley or any member of KISS would readily admit to anyone, much less an industry titan, that their records were subpar, and by September of 1974, with barely a year of touring under their belts and still a month from the arrival of the follow-up to their debut record, The Act had yet to endure its most devastating professional blows in the studio or on the charts. News of Casablanca's money and distribution woes were in the future, and no one was yet aware of royalties being lost in the shuffle. But by the time Bill Aucoin got around to making his call to Ezrin to take him up on his boldly off-the-cuff stairwell offer, the ensuing *Hotter Than Hell* had tanked, and, with it, Casablanca's relationship with Warner Bros. The band had been yanked from the road to record what would become *Dressed to Kill*, with tensions between Neil Bogart and Aucoin festering during the sessions.

Aucoin's in was KISS's promotion director, Alan Miller, who had not-so-coincidentally previously worked as Ezrin's personal New York representative at Nimbus 9. He placed a call to his former boss, who assured him he had already been "doing my homework" on the band.[7] This is precisely why, upon reaching his man, Aucoin immediately found Ezrin's enthusiasm infectious, which of course was his own avenue of proficiency. The two men spoke as if they realized they were both on the cusp of something special, and they had a dual inclination that the project could very well be the culmination of everyone's careers. In an article on the origins of the *Destroyer* sessions in the June 1, 1976, issue of *Circus* magazine, Ezrin described Aucoin's momentum. "Bill was real cute when we got together," the young producer explained to Gary Kenton. "I thought of KISS as a 150,000-to-200,000-unit group at best and I usually like to do twice that, but Bill kept on treating me like he was giving me the biggest act in the world. He has a real cockiness about him and he radiates a confidence which everybody with KISS picks up on. He plays the game very well—if it isn't the biggest, you've got to make it appear that way."[8]

In *Behind the Mask*, Aucoin described the mutual admiration both heavy-hitters displayed right from the start of negotiations. "Bob got caught up in the excitement. He's very strong. Ace called him the Dictator, but I loved him because he was bright and together and really wanted to make a very successful record. And he was good for them, I thought. It brought them to another level. I wanted to try and cut across a wider range and show people that they could really do something more significant."[9]

Paul Stanley is quoted in the same account as coming to similar conclusions. "The Alice Cooper stuff was so brilliant that we needed a producer. Even though we didn't know half of what we thought we knew, we weren't really ready to listen to anybody. But Ezrin's talent and track record was undeniable."[10]

One major aspect of Ezrin's approach hit a resonant chord when it got back to the band. "Art is the first thing I outlaw," Ezrin told *Circus*. "If you want art there's a whole set of rules you have to follow and a long, drawn-out philosophical approach involved." Ezrin also made it known to the band, and *Circus*, that not only did he understand its ultra-capitalist myopia, he unabashedly shared it. "These guys want to know how much money they're gonna have in the bank when they retire and I've got to respect that. They're not John McLaughlin and they're not going to be able to do what they're doing when they're fifty."[11]

In the spring of 1975—Ezrin surmises that it was within a few months of his initial conversation with Aucoin, in which he suggested seeing the band live—he attended a show on the final leg of the *Dressed to Kill* tour. Ezrin recalls the venue as having been in Saginaw, Michigan, but according to research by Curt Gooch and Jeff Suhs for "Destroyer: Recording and Marketing a Rock and Roll Classic," which appeared in *KISS Magazine* #3 (Spring 2005), he likely attended the Metro Ice Arena show in Lansing, Michigan, on April 29.

Whatever the time and place, one thing is certain: it was while seeing KISS in all its pomp and extravagance that Ezrin's instincts began to percolate and inform the themes that would help make *Destroyer* a defining statement for The Act. Ezrin, who would later tell reporters that he saw KISS as a "caricature of all the urges of youth,"[12] recalled his initial reaction to www.kissonline.com: "I went to see them play in Michigan, in an arena where 9,000 people got up on their feet, and stayed on their feet, through the whole show, for a band who had never sold many records. And I watched the show and I watched what they did, and I came away with a vision that I put forward to the band."[13]

The vision included a reimagining of The Act—or, more to the point, an epiphany for what was at its core. Beneath what KISS had created and exposed to the world, Ezrin saw deeper shades of grey in the black-and-white of the makeup; and he looked beyond the machismo of the stage posturing and songs replete with tortured metaphors for humping.

"They were filling halls of fifteen-year-old pimply boys," Ezrin explains. "And that was good, but I felt that it was a limited universe. I saw something far more sexy and compelling about the band that should appeal to women, but it wasn't getting there because of the kind of material they were writing and how they generally presented themselves. So it was a conscious effort on *Destroyer* to expand the audience by painting them in a more three-dimensional light with a lot more different shades of coloring, not so monochromatic, as I thought they were prior. Before that it was all about who drinks: 'How many people here like whiskey?' There were no songs that talked about one's unrealized aspirations. There were no songs that talked about vulnerability. There was nothing like 'Do You Love Me?' You know, 'You like this, you like that, but . . . do you *love* me? Do *you* love *me*?' There was no KISS song like that; nothing in the band's material that revealed a vulnerable or soft side to the band."[14]

After expressing this to the band in the dressing room immediately after the show, the young producer arranged a meeting back in New York, where he had been living for the past two years. "We sat in a restaurant and I basically said, 'Right now you guys are like paper cutouts. You're superheroes of rock with a singular power, and that's it. There's no depth to you and, by the way, you're also not that attractive to women—in case you haven't noticed.' They were very attractive to women offstage, but there weren't a lot of women in the crowd when they were playing. So what I suggested was I would like to take an approach with them on the next album, if we did it together, where they were less like Lee Marvin in *The Wild One* and more like Marlon Brando. *The Wild One* was a biker movie. In fact, it was the first biker movie ever in the '50s. It was really tame, but Lee Marvin was a one-dimensional, just nasty piece of shit leader of a biker gang that was going to terrorize the town. Marlon Brando was also a leader of a biker gang, but there was something incredibly deep about Marlon Brando, and something slightly broken about him, that made every good American girl in her poodle skirt and tied-up hair want to take him home and fix him. They just wanted to love him, because they felt he would be so much better if only they could."[15]

In truth, the Marlon Brando subtext was already playing out weekly on network television in the form of the nation's most beloved character, Arthur Fonzerelli, aka the Fonz, in the top-rated show *Happy Days*. Actor Henry Winkler—coincidently profiled in the June 1, 1976, issue of *Circus* magazine wherein Bob Ezrin's work with KISS is also featured—would sum up his character's lovable duality by saying, "Fonzie is a hard guy, but a hard guy with a soul. He's spontaneous. He lives hard and he loves hard." With *Happy Days* positioned as a family show airing during prime time on the nation's number one network (ABC), its producers and writers aimed to sanitize the '70s anti-hero trend by expanding on the Fonz's delinquent, wise-guy attitude. He had a tender family side, too, and as Winkler also noted at the time, a moral center usually grounded in heroic figures. "Women want to marry me. People name dogs and birds and cats after Fonzie. I was asked to join the Hell's Angels."[16]

Ezrin: "So I wanted to try and get the KISS guys to that place, where they were dangerous, but in an attractive way where every girl in America wanted to be close to them and wanted to love them and wanted to fix them and wanted to be with them. There was just an undertone of vulnerability, sensuality, sexuality, all sitting underneath this rock-god veneer that they had. I just wanted to add layers, basically. I just wanted there to be layers. I didn't want to peel off the makeup and costume and find that there was nothing there. So they liked that. All of them were very big fans of American cinema and television. They got it. When put in those terms, they got it instantly. They were all in favor. So we decided to go ahead and do it."[17]

Armed with a rousing overture from an acclaimed producer, Bill Aucoin eventually swayed the members of KISS toward Ezrin. His most arduous work lay with Frehley and Criss, who needed some persuading. Both were enamored with Eddie Kramer. After all, he was working his magic turning the band's live tapes into a formidable collection, and everyone agreed that the KISS demos he recorded in 1973 outshone any of the three commercial releases. Yet in their memoirs, Frehley and Criss both write of their excitement at the prospect of working with Ezrin, mainly due to his impressive resume with Alice Cooper. "I could understand the desire for change," Criss admits. "I was getting pretty bored playing the same boom-ba, boom-boom-ba, boom-ba, boom-boom-ba beat song after song."[18]

Stanley and Simmons had already been sold on Ezrin's stellar track record and core strategies long before the producer's philosophical deconstruction of The Act, and they needed little prodding. Stanley admits as much in the double-volume *KISStory*. "We knew that if we didn't play our cards right we were in danger of becoming another fad like the hula-hoop, and Bob was the one to take us to the next level."[19]

Simmons concurs. "Up until we met Bob Ezrin," he writes, in his memoir, "we were leery of letting anybody else have a say as to what we should record. That included management, record companies, producers, anybody. Bob Ezrin was the first and continues to be the only producer who ever really had an effect on the band."[20]

Ezrin began to subtly infuse a sense of pathos into the KISS ethos, remaining cautious not to undo the carefully crafted braggadocio humor and absurd romp the band perfected on the road and to a great extent in its only branded hit, "Rock and Roll All Nite." It would be a delicate balance, but one he'd achieved with Alice Cooper by working out the schizophrenically abstract sides of the ambiguous rock villain from goofy misfit to ragged victim to raging monster, while keeping the band's irony and vitality intact. KISS had momentum, Ezrin presumed, but the songs did not reflect it. He had come to believe—and had proved, with the incredible success of Alice Cooper—that music as image would drive the most blessed tenets of The Act home. Ezrin explained his fervent pitch to KISS to www.kissonline.com: "With a little bit of a different approach to the songs themselves, we could create a relationship between this band and their audience, which was much more emotional and much more broadly appealing. So we could keep the edge and the drama."[21]

In his revealing memoir, *Face the Music*, Paul Stanley adds, "One of the things he did was challenge us not to write 'fuck me suck me' songs. 'No more I'm a rock star, suck my dick,' he insisted. And as we worked on lyrics, he had no problem saying very plainly, 'No, I don't like that.'"[22]

In addition to Ezrin's valuable insights into the KISS aura, Bill Aucoin keenly understood the critical advantages of landing him as a songwriter and musician, even more so than as a successful hands-on studio magician. For one, he added a dynamic missing in the rush-in/bang-out chaos that shackled previous KISS recording sessions. Frank Rose's 1976 *Circus* magazine feature, "Invasion of the Glitter Goths," provides a telling Aucoin quote: "We wanted someone who was not only a strong producer but also could help them arrange their songs and even in some cases help with the final writing of their songs, because when you're on the road so much you're writing but you're not necessarily finishing everything. We decided that Bob was pretty much a key producer in our minds, because he pretty much did the same thing with Alice."[23]

While this was a healthy critique of his band's lack of serious compositional mentality, it was also a shot across the bow at Casablanca's inability to provide his boys with the proper assistance for the material the band was forced to patch together under immense pressure in a few anxious weeks, only to be quickly thrown back into the tour cauldron. It was soon made known to Bogart that, this time, KISS would take its time to realize its massive potential. Then—and only then—Aucoin was certain a KISS studio effort would make its mark.

"When we were ready to make our next studio album," Stanley writes, "Bill Aucoin said, 'You can either use *Alive!* as a springboard to take you to another level, or you can be a one-hit wonder that just goes back to doing what you were doing before.' He had a point. To go back to what we had done earlier did seem stupid. After all, it didn't work before *Alive!*, so why would it work now? The reason our first three albums didn't sell was because listeners didn't like the way they sounded—there was something intrinsically wrong with them, though I still couldn't have put my finger on exactly what it was."[24]

Aucoin's assessment was astute precisely because he had been there from the very beginning of the scramble for immediate notoriety The Act had wrought on the bulk of KISS's material. Musically, the band had barely enough time to work out the kinks between the early days cramped in a rehearsal loft, hurriedly creating a suitable song list, and the ensuing months of staging highly elaborate shows in its wake. In the blink of an eye, KISS had been thrust into tireless self-promotion and hyperbole, forced to learn to ply the craft of songwriting from limited subject matter. The studio production teams were also rushed along, given no time or room to ponder what the songs or the records might engender in the fans' imagination. Get the songs down and move on—that was the order of creative output for KISS for two solid years across three records, all cut in a few harried weeks each, all comprised of songs culled from different stages of the composers' careers, some conjoined under duress, happenstance, or need, others penned by one member and given to another to sing with no thought to the end results. KISS albums sorely lacked cohesion.

Paul Stanley echoed this sentiment in his own clearly defiant statement to *Circus* magazine during the making of *Destroyer*. "When you're a band that's up-and-coming, you can go to your record company and say, 'We need a month to put out a piece of quality,' and the record company will say, 'Hey, your budget is so-and-so and you've got a date in two weeks. You go in and get that album done.' That's the way it had to be. But at this point we can say, 'Hey, this is the way we're doing it."[25]

Time, highly qualified professional assistance, a broader palette, and the chance to put every layer of The Act into a singular musical statement meant that KISS had to put aside all expectations as to what it was to be a recording ensemble. And as hard as KISS worked live and relentlessly sacrificed beneath a torrent of abuse from the competition and lack of airplay credibility, the band would have to be aware of what lay ahead. The days of thrashing through basic live takes with minor overdubbing and quick mixes to be rushed out between tours were over. The members of the original Alice Cooper group would be the first to attest that banging on instruments and riffing all over the joint was not going to cut it for Master Ezrin. Inverting old Stones fodder and twisting well-known heavy-rock fare into three-minute barre-chord foot-stompers would have to be abandoned for a scrupulous dedication to the song: its lyrics, its mood, and its place in the overall theme of the album. Where there was once trite repetition and faint nods to hooks and layers, now there would be hardcore musical structure. Intricate harmonies would replace mere gang-vocal exercises. Steady time-keeping drum tracks would replace wild, free-form pounding. Take after take after take would not only be expected but demanded. Thanks to Bill Aucoin's desperation and Bob Ezrin's teenage phone pal, very soon KISS would enter a self-described "boot camp" to work as hard and as long as they ever did or ever would in a studio.

7

Boot Camp

At the time, I actually went to a primal therapy institute where John Lennon went, because I went so far into it that I totally lost reality.
—Peter Criss[1]

The two parties convened in the late summer of 1975 at Carroll's Rehearsal Studios on West Fifty-Fifth; the likely dates vary from August 11–15 and/or 17–23—the only breaks in KISS's brutal tour schedule—to the first full week of September. (The band would definitely use some of these August dates to complete the overdubs for the proposed live album, while Ezrin is quite certain of a September start.) The young, brash producer understood that he could be an intimidating presence and, fully aware that he was not the band's first choice, allegedly decided to alter the anxious mood by ceremoniously greeting the members, as Aucoin operative Sean Delaney recalled it, "stark-assed naked," save for a bow tie. When asked for this book whether this was another in a long and impressive line of apocryphal KISS tales, Ezrin sat silent for a long moment before letting out a hearty laugh for a good ten seconds and finally answering, "Sure, why not?" Then, after gathering himself, he exhaled. "Well . . . oh, I don't remember. But you know what they say of that era, if you remember then you weren't there."[2]

If it's true, it was a brilliant move. Any preconceptions the band had about the stern Canadian taskmaster would have faded immediately, as KISS was introduced to Ezrin's jester side, his willingness to playfully shock his skeptical charges with no fear of embarrassment—a practice the band had already turned into an art form. Not coincidentally, the self-effacing stunt, while breaking the ice and illustrating how the young producer could be more colleague than overlord, would have registered with the otherwise lukewarm Ace Frehley, KISS's resident wiseass. The other member dubious of Ezrin, Peter Criss, notoriously fond of exposing himself whenever the notion moved him, would also have been sufficiently amused at such a prank.

"I think I may have been aware of a certain tension the band had at the start of the sessions," recalls Ezrin. "I'm not sure I remember exactly, but I did a lot of things during those sessions to relieve tensions. There were all kind of fun things happening, crazy things like practical jokes and pranks on other bands. I pitied anyone who was working in the studio next to us, because we were vicious. When it came to practical jokes, we'd get very elaborate. Of course, those were the days when you could afford to do those things in the studio. So, I did many things to elevate tension, but I don't recall it being so much at the onset of the sessions. It was more as we went along."[3]

Reading the potential for sour moods and bad vibes was another of Ezrin's rare instincts. Only months before, during the uninspired take-after-take of the intense "Only Women Bleed," he had ordered up a mini-circus to swing into the studio and perform for the suddenly shocked and then guffawing musicians. After ten solid minutes of this needed "distraction," Ezrin quickly counted off and the band recorded the keeper take of the legendary ballad.

Fun and games aside, there was still the matter of mining the type of music that fit the new search for injecting pathos into the heart of KISS. Sometime before rehearsals, Paul Stanley and Gene Simmons gathered potential material for Ezrin to dissect or disregard, both keeping in mind the edict on trading in themes from the usual "cock-rock" fare for a more diverse libretto. "They were just playing that straight-ahead rock," says Ezrin. "Now a lot of people really loved that and were very angry with me for changing that. One reviewer said he wanted to punch me in the nose on behalf of KISS fans everywhere for what I did with them on *Destroyer*. And I suppose for the fifteen-year-old fan boy, I had ruined the gang leader. I defiled them by making them a little more Little Lord Fauntleroy. They didn't appreciate what I was doing, but for me, I felt like if they didn't expand their images, their future would be quite limited."[4]

With the idea of approaching a broader sample of composition as a template, the band began auditioning snippets of song ideas. As Aucoin alluded to when discussing the haphazard KISS studio methods, it was not unusual for the band to hash out skeletal frameworks of riffs and unrealized hooks when beginning a new project. Yet where previous producers lent vague suggestions and occasional direction, this was an area of the process Ezrin not only welcomed but thrived in. Musical asides from hither and yon pushed him into the comfortable role of eager collaborator—an approach that eased the band's load and gave birth to a reasoned deconstruction of disparate themes.

"We would all come in with ideas," explains Ezrin. "Sometimes they would come in with a demo for something, and then the three of us would get together and tear it apart and make it better. I would just sit there with them and say, 'Well, instead of going to this chord, why don't we go here?' and 'I've got an idea for a chorus melody, what about this?' or 'I have an idea for a lyric.' It was really collaborative writing."[5]

In his memoir, Paul Stanley recounts, "Bob would have four of us in a circle and he would say, 'Who's got an idea? Anybody have an idea for a verse? Who's got a part?' Someone would play a snippet and he might say no. Then someone else would play something and Bob would shout, 'Okay, that's good. Now who has another part?' A lot of the songs came together like that—pieces of this and that stitched together with input from Bob."[6]

Simmons, who had long filled notebooks with potential song titles, partial lyrics, and chord progressions while on the road, was always bursting with material. According to the liner notes to *The Box Set*, he had demoed ten songs for the new sessions at Magna Graphic Studios in Greenwich Village in the summer of 1975, with Ace Frehley adding lead guitar and Simmons playing basically all the other instruments. Thanks to various bootlegs, an extended list includes "Rock and Rolls Royce" (the bulk of which would become "Love 'Em, Leave 'Em," destined for *Destroyer*'s follow-up, *Rock and Roll Over*, although according to Simmons it would also donate a key undercurrent to the final version of "Sweet Pain"), "Bad Bad Lovin'" (which morphed into "Calling Dr. Love" and also ended up on *Rock and Roll Over*), "Man of a Thousand Faces," and "True Confessions" (both of which wound up on his solo KISS album), "Don't Want No Romance," "Love Is Alright," "Burnin' Up with Fever," "High and Low," "Howlin' for Your Love," and "I'm a Star," as well as another precursor to "Sweet Pain," "Night Fly." Among his mostly finished pieces, one that eventually made it on *Destroyer* was an unusual folksy ballad called "You've Got Nothing to Live For," which later, with major contributions from Ezrin, became the lush "Great Expectations." Also presented during rehearsals was an undistinguished number called "Mad Dog," which only partially made the cut. "When it was time to pick the songs that KISS would record for *Destroyer*, Bob Ezrin went through all the demos and, in a very KISS-like fashion, picked out pieces of songs that he thought were interesting, and discarded the rest," Simmons recalled. "He'd liked the 'Mad Dog' riffs but didn't think much of the song. Eventually the riff became the guitar line that was used throughout 'Flaming Youth.'"[7]

As expected, Stanley too had completed demos for songs, including two funky Slade/Free-style numbers that would have fit well in previous KISS albums: "Dontcha Hesitate" (left over from the *Dressed to Kill* demos) and "It Ain't the Smoke That Burns Ya," or, as it is sometimes referred to in bootleg circles, "Smoke." He also compiled bits of several tunes, but each needed fleshing out, including the framework of the aforementioned "Flaming Youth," titled after the name of an all-girl group the band once shared a bill with in the early days; a rollicking slice of machismo called "God of Thunder"; and an intriguing hard-rocking tribute to the town that propelled KISS toward fame combined with a requiem for a fan who'd allegedly died on the way to a KISS show, "Detroit Rock City." During downtime in touring, Stanley had also recorded complete demos of the songs with Simmons on bass and tour manager J. R. Smalling on drums at the downtown Magna Graphics Studios, likely around the same time of Simmons's extensive demo recordings.

Frehley, who is also credited with a riff that helped along "Flaming Youth," was by now well into his reoccurring role of rock star in extremis, meaning he was either tapped or more likely burned out and contributed no original material for the sessions—something he had done on each of the previous three records. Over the years, a rumor has perpetuated that a song exists titled "Queen for a Day," offered by Frehley and accompanied by a missing demo or perhaps a heretofore unearthed *Destroyer*-era recording, but none has been corroborated by anyone involved with the project, including Ace. It is more likely it surfaced, if at all, later in the year for *Destroyer*'s follow-up, *Rock and Roll Over*.

As for Peter Criss, having long since abandoned hope of getting any of his older ideas into the fray, he simply laid low, as always, and waited for someone to offer him a lead vocal opportunity. That opportunity came sooner than later, for along with pushing the band's musical abilities beyond its expectations, Ezrin wasted no time in testing KISS's already legendary resolve, suggesting it demo "Ain't None of Your Business," a mid-tempo country-rock number heavy on rancor, and compelling Criss to use his soulful vocal attack to full force. Introducing the Becky Hobbs/Lew Anderson composition, more country honk than rocker, not only allowed Ezrin to witness the band tackle a song outside its immediate comfort zone but also echoed the producer's recent success on the chart topping *Billion Dollar Babies*, wherein the Alice Cooper group reworked a Judy Collins folk tune written by Canadian singer Rolf Kempf called "Hello Hooray" into a heavy, show-opening epic. But while an inspired vocal by the streetwise Criss reverberates with pugilistic glee, the rest of the band's effort on "Ain't None of Your Business" is fairly listless. Ezrin, who eventually scrapped it, later described the song as "not as sophisticated as the other tracks," adding that it "didn't belong in the package."[8]

Nonetheless, the experiment proved the willingness of KISS to allow the producer full rein not only to expand its sphere of material but also to bring in established songs while introducing additional writing talent to work alongside the group. Soon, a discarded song by a failed Los Angeles rock band would yield the rollicking "King of the Night Time World," as would Ezrin's strongly suggested plea for Paul Stanley to bare his more vulnerable side on "Do You Love Me?" But it was the strange coalescing of a song out of the three riffs provided by Stanley, Simmons, and Frehley, respectively, that appears to have triggered what has become known in KISS legend as the Boot Camp.

After deftly grafting together the detailed pieces of "Flaming Youth," Ezrin began instructing the band to play the song in 7/4 time, to which each member looked as if he were speaking another language—which, of course he was: the secret language of music. Later, when Ezrin began suggesting harmony guitar parts and eighths and ninths of chords, he could clearly see the band wasn't getting it.

"We started messing around with ideas, and I said, 'Well, okay, why don't we try this in half time?'" Ezrin later told biographers David Leaf and Ken Sharp. "I asked Peter if he knew what half time was and he said, 'Not really.' I said, 'Well, that's okay. It's when we are playing 4/4, do you know what 4/4/ is?' And he said, 'Well, not really.' So I said, 'Instruments down, we are going to school.'"[9]

Ezrin detected right away that he would need to hone each band member's skills by convincing them they could achieve a more stylized method of attacking a song by ignoring their immediate inclination that they were incapable of accomplishing anything he threw at them by shifting time signatures, augmenting chords on top of basic progressions, harmonizing two or even three and four guitar parts with the vocals, and adding bass lines that would both infuse the groove and provide counter melodies to basic chord structures.

"Bob was not only a catalyst but an organizer," Frehley explained to *Circus* magazine in 1976. "He got us into really disciplining ourselves and our practices. He's also taught us different ways of writing songs, piecing songs together. He's a great teacher."[10]

Ezrin: "They're really, really bright guys. I think that anything that was challenging but sounded sensible would catch their interest in those days and probably still does today. It wasn't a hard sell. Everyone was interested in trying stuff out. At first, they'd be skeptical about their ability—not about the idea, but rather their ability to carry it off. When we worked at it in rehearsal and I showed them that they could do it, they were thrilled with themselves. They loved it. They were very proud of that 7/4 stuff and the fact that they could play it live."[11]

Gene Simmons: "Other bands have stories about meeting up with producers who teach them how to be professionals—before these producers came along, they were noble savages, beating on their guitars and just hoping for the best. It wasn't like that with KISS. We had known what we were doing from the beginning. Bob didn't make us go faster. In fact, he slowed the process down considerably."[12]

"Ezrin would take everything apart, like a scientist, and start from ground zero," Peter Criss told *Modern Drummer* magazine in 1999. "He would come up with all these ideas and say, 'Try it this way.' One thing about him is that he can play every instrument in the band and he had a great ear."[13]

Ezrin: "I had a routine based on my experience with the Alice Cooper group to set the material with the band I was working with and repeat it over and over and over until it was great. So the idea was, 'Let's not just work out the songs and play it three or four times and then we can go home.' This was, 'Arrange the song and routine it until it was perfect, and play it over and over and over again until we can play it without making any mistakes.' To me, that was the 'boot camp' part. That we can actually execute without making mistakes. Because then, what that allowed us to do was to go into the studio and not worry about the boredom of execution, but simply worry about getting great performances and making interesting new sounds and creating and coming up with new ideas and strange little additions and accouterments to the music that gave it that extra salt, that extra sparkle."[14]

Bill Aucoin's dream of his band taking its time to get it right this time is described in detail by Simmons, Criss, Frehley, and Stanley in their memoirs. They admit that Ezrin went so far as to show the band how to tune their instruments and play off one another in less of a power struggle to achieve maximum volume and more a musical ensemble supporting the song.

"For a bunch of guys who thought they were hot shit, it was initially jarring to go into a studio with somebody who treated us like children," Stanley writes, in *Face the Music*.[15] To their lasting credit, all four members bought into the process, grinding through each session willing to learn any technique that would improve on their previous studio efforts.

Ace Frehley remembers it this way: "It was like he was conducting the class—he was the teacher and we were his students. The funny thing is, Bob wasn't a whole lot older than any of us. He was only in his late twenties when we recorded *Destroyer*, so it wasn't like he was the grown-up and we were the children. But it sort of felt that way. Bob carried himself with an air of maturity and importance. He believed in himself, which is half the battle if you want to be a record producer, and we wanted to believe in him."[16]

"Bob Ezrin was like a boy genius. He knew exactly what to do," Peter Criss is quoted as saying in *KISS: Behind the Mask*, with Stanley adding, "We went in there green and came out a lot smarter for it."[17]

Setting the scene that Criss describes in his memoir as "musical summer camp,"¹⁸ and which stretched out for a solid week, Ezrin recalls, "We absolutely pulled out a blackboard and started introducing them to the very basics of music theory, just enough so we were speaking the same language. We had to do it. For instance, there was that section in 'Flaming Youth' that changes time signature into seven over four, and I was trying to explain it using numbers. Of course, everyone's eyes kind of glazed over, and they looked at me like I was speaking Martian. So, first I explained what the numbers meant and then showed them what the music was. But once they had seen it and heard it and saw the numbers on a blackboard, then it sort of clicked in and everybody understood what I was talking about. So, yes, we did do a little bit of music theory. It wasn't as if I took them back to basics and went all the way up to grade-ten piano. That wasn't happening. But, yeah, there was a bit of a 'boot camp.'"¹⁹

KISS left Carroll's Rehearsal Studios after August 23 to play six shows that finally concluded the *Dressed to Kill* tour before reconvening and then going back on the road for five more shows (September 10–14) that marked the release of the anticipated live album everyone had bet their hides on. This would leave a full two weeks (September 15–October 1) open for the band to continue composing, rehearse material, and even, according to Ezrin, begin recording. The stated locations for these follow-up sessions vary, however. Firstly, there is the late Jimi Hendrix's Electric Lady Studios on West Eighth Street in Greenwich Village, where the original KISS demos had been recorded by proprietor, Eddie Kramer, and where the famed producer was cobbling together the tapes that would become *Alive!*, which was slated to be released on September 10. Although no official records remain of KISS's time there during these dates, Bob Ezrin is quite adamant that a first round of serious rehearsals and possible recordings were completed there. "Once we started the project, we practically lived together, seeing each other every day, all day, until we got half of the album done." he writes, in the liner notes to the remastered 2012 version of the album, *Destroyer Resurrected*.²⁰ However, when interviewed for this book, the other credited members of what would be Ezrin's *Destroyer* recording team—Jay Messina (lead engineer) and Corky Stasiak (assistant engineer)—had no recollection of these sessions. To add to the confusion, the professionally recorded and fully mixed "Ain't None of Your Business" was also a mystery to both Messina and Stasiak. Even Ezrin does not recall the song being part of the "official" *Destroyer* sessions. "I don't even remember that song, honestly," he admits, when pressed.²¹

What Ezrin *does* recall is the ensuing September sessions. "I distinctly remember we cut the album in two halves," he insists, when confronted with the copious studio journals kept by Stasiak that list only one month of *Destroyer* sessions, beginning in January of 1976. "If any recording was done in September, it might have been at Electric Lady, where the guys had done their Wicked Lester stuff."[22]

According to print sources—primarily the well-researched *KISS Magazine* article "Destroyer: Recording and Marketing a Rock and Roll Classic" by *KISS Alive! Forever* authors Curt Gooch and Jeff Suhs—there were indeed September sessions, but they took place immediately after the last of the *Dressed to Kill* shows on August 30, and most likely continued until September 9, the day before *Alive!* was released. However, the article also suggests that these took place at the Record Plant uptown. The only quote from either Record Plant engineers that hints at possible earlier sessions there comes from Stasiak, who told me during the initial interviews for this book that when he first met the band, KISS had yet to taste any success from the upcoming *Alive!* release. "During the recording of this album, they shot out of a cannon," he says. "They walked in the studio paupers and left millionaires."[23]

Stanley and Simmons also hint at early sessions for *Destroyer* in a January 20, 1976, article in *Circus* magazine titled "KISS ALIVE!—Sing While You Die" by Peter Crescenti. Stanley: "The real reason we put this album [*Alive!*] out is that we're in the midst of doing a new studio album, which is quite a bit different from what we've done to date as far as music goes. It's a bit more polished. Most of our albums took us about a week to do, but this fifth album so far has taken about a month to finish half of it. The thing about the live album is that it's pretty much a capper for the first phase of KISS. We're going on to something different."[24] Simmons: "We're working on our first studio album, really. Up until now, we've been doing live type recordings in the studio that were hopefully kind of representative of what we were doing live."[25]

Yet another account in *Circus* magazine—this one penned by Frank Rose, the only journalist to have been inside the Record Plant studio while the band recorded *Destroyer*—describes a moment toward the end of the sessions, during the recording of "Shout It Out Loud," that corroborates Stasiak's journal, which clearly lists the dates of the sessions as being from January 2 through February 5. "We're in the Record Plant," writes Rose. "It's 2 a.m. on a sub-freezing night. Loudon Wainwright is in the next studio. An uneasy truce prevails whenever the two camps meet in the halls. KISS and Ezrin have been working on this album for four weeks, and today they've been in the studio since 1 p.m."[26]

A most curious detail emerged when Stasiak mentioned, upon initial contact before official interviews commenced for this book, that the financial crisis and legal wrangling between Rock Steady and Casablanca had yet to be resolved when work began on the album. "I found out later Bill Aucoin put up the cash for the *Destroyer* sessions," he remembers. "I think he mortgaged his house. I know he had plans to pay for the recording of the new KISS album and sell the tapes to another record company. Bob [Ezrin] may have known, but Jay [Messina] and I certainly didn't know this was going on."[27]

However, in another interview for this book, Casablanca vice president Larry Harris refuted this. "Bill didn't even have a house," he laughed. "He lived in an apartment in New York, so he couldn't have put up his house for money. He might've said to Ezrin, 'Oh, I'm going to do this and this,' but that's bullshit. He probably just wanted Ezrin to do it and believe him. Because I'll tell you, Bill was running away from creditors all the time. His American Express card was so fucking drained it was amazing. I don't know how much he put on his American Express card, but it was tens of thousands of dollars, and you know, in those days, not that it isn't today, but that was a fortune. He went through the money. I mean, he'd throw these incredible parties and stuff that cost $100,000. But Bill had the most to lose because he had most to gain. He owned the biggest piece. He owned more than any other member of the band: 25 percent! Plus he owned the merchandising."[28]

Author and KISS historian Ken Sharp concurs with Harris's account, explaining that it is highly unlikely anyone outside of Casablanca would have financed the sessions, specifically since KISS was under contract. "It would be very odd for management to be bankrolling a recording session when it's the record label's professional responsibility. It certainly would be against the principles of a deal. Now, had KISS not been under contract to the label, it could have potentially happened, since there was some animosity building there between Bill and Casablanca. But as of September of 1975, they were still under contract to the label."[29]

Stasiak's reference to Aucoin's desperate foray into independence may or may not provide insight into earlier recording sessions for *Destroyer*, but it does illuminate the ongoing battles over royalties that had come to a head by the first weeks of September 1975. Because the struggling record company had failed to pay its premier act any royalties for its first three albums over two years, it was becoming glaringly obvious to all involved that Casablanca's influence in the KISS camp was waning. The band was livid at not seeing fiduciary returns for any of its record sales; now KISS, backed ably and defiantly by its manager, would be calling the shots.

In *Nothin' to Lose*, Jeff Franklin, owner of the band's booking agency, ATI, argues that the costs of bankrolling the star-studded spectacle embodied in The Act had run all wells dry. "KISS was so far in the red there was nothing to get. There was so much money spent on them, where did they expect royalties to come from? We poured a ton of money into the label and KISS. Neil had mortgaged his house and I was in it for a half a million, million dollars. Our cards were on the table. Neil would call me and say, 'Do you have a hundred grand?' I said, 'For what?' He said, 'They need it.' I said, 'I haven't got it but I'll get it for you in a week.'"[30]

"The biggest problem with KISS was the way Bill ran their touring," adds Larry Harris. "They were losing money, and they had to stop hemorrhaging that touring money because, not unlike Casablanca, they kept making a bigger show and a bigger show and more expensive and more expensive, just like Casablanca did. We kept signing more artists and more artists and hiring more people. We were always struggling for money, which is one of the main reasons that KISS had to put out two albums every year. We simply needed the cash flow."[31]

Aside from the lack of royalties from Casablanca, Aucoin had ulterior business motives for circling the wagons. Since Casablanca signed its original recording contract with KISS, Rock Steady co-owner Joyce Biawitz had become romantically linked to label president Neil Bogart, causing on more than one occasion a conflict of interest. During the recording of *Dressed to Kill*—which Bogart produced, motivated mainly by Biawitz's pillow-talk about producers Kenny Kerner and Richie Wise urging KISS to abandon the failing Casablanca—Aucoin had deftly avoided Bogart's play to get closer to the band. Bogart's alleged goal of either convincing the band to stay at Casablanca and drop legal avenues to claim past royalties or perhaps sacking Rock Steady to allow new girlfriend Biawitz to run the show under the auspices of the record company had failed.

When asked about this possible plot, Harris explains the complications in the foggy mist between business and kinship. "Neil never came out specifically and said, 'I'd love to get rid of Bill.' Not in so many words, but I'm sure in the back of Neil's mind it was there, because he did it with Donna Summer. He had Joyce manage Donna, so he had complete control on every level. He probably would've liked to get rid of Bill, so he would have more control over the band, but the band—and he knew it and I knew it—weren't going to stand for it. Bill was really close to them. Actually, Bill and Neil did get along really well. Neil was bisexual and Bill was gay. I know they never went to bed together because I've spoken to Bill about it and he would've told me, but Neil used to talk about having a three-way with Bill involved, according to what Aucoin told me a few years before he died when we were hanging out. In fact, Neil asked Joyce to ask Bill."[32]

A failed *coup d'état* and a missed *ménage à trois* aside, Casablanca tried to smooth things over upon Biawitz's split with Rock Steady, according to Harris's account in *And Party Every Day*, by tearing up the original 1973 contract and drafting a new one on May 1, 1975. KISS and Aucoin would agree to deliver two new studio albums within a calendar year, with an option for two more over the next eighteen months, for an average of an outrageous sum of one million dollars per record, with a half-million dollars to be allocated for advertising and controlled by KISS, Rock Steady, and the Howard Marks Agency. "If they had trusted us we would have spent the money on advertising anyway," Harris recalled. "But they didn't, and they had decided to take control of their own destiny."[33]

The caveat to the new signing meant that Casablanca did not have to present the band with its first royalty payments—already nearly two years overdue—until September 20, 1975. The potential new deal would be "alleviating our financial crunch," as Harris writes, but it was no boon to Aucoin or KISS.[34] Thus Aucoin had already begun acting on his own accord to separate from Casablanca, which was still very much in the throes of near-bankruptcy. As motions to sue the record company over lack of royalty payments began, both Aucoin and the band—none too happy about the previous choice of producers and their inconsistent results—were convinced that prior album sessions had been sabotaged in one way or the other. According to Larry Harris, upon the release of *Alive!*, Aucoin was already listening to offers from competing record companies. "For two weeks we heard rumors from several sources that Bill was shopping KISS to all the heavy hitters: Warner, Atlantic, and Capitol. On September 15, he [Neil Bogart] showed me a letter of termination from Bill Aucoin. KISS was leaving Casablanca."[35] That letter noted "breach of contract relating to Casablanca's failure to pay KISS their contractual royalties."[36] Aucoin admitted his anguish over the move. "The last thing I wanted to do was leave Neil, but as a manager, I had to take a stand."[37]

Two days later, an incensed Bogart responded by serving his own summons to KISS and Rock Steady, listing "(1) breach of contract; (2) malicious interference with contractual rights; (3) declaratory judgment as to contractual rights; (4) injunctive relief" and claiming "Compensatory damages, $500,000.00; Punitive damages, $500,000.00"—all of which Aucoin duly ignored.[38]

"Neil never wanted to admit that he couldn't pay, even though we all kinda knew we were doing this together," Aucoin explained to *Kissaholics* in 1997. "Except I really needed to know where I stood, where the band stood, and we got into an argument over it and Neil felt a little threatened by it because on the one hand Neil was the type of guy if you had a handshake it was good. So he kinda felt that 'Hey, I told the guys I would take care of this.' And I said that's not the point. The point is we all [need to] have contracts. If something happened it's gonna all fall apart. Anyway, we all went to court on it and at that point Neil already had *Alive!* and he knew something was happening. We all knew we were doing great on the road. In the middle of that I got a call from Atlantic Records saying, 'Hey listen we know you can leave Bogart, come with us.'"[39]

Official court records obtained at the New York Country Clerk's Office in Lower Manhattan reveal that Aucoin not only "listened" but that he aggressively pursued a new label while still under contract to Casablanca. In an affidavit dated October 3, 1975, Neil Bogart's lawyer, Richard S. Trugman, claims that on the morning of September 29, 1975, he received a telephone call from the president of Warner Bros. Records, Mo Ostin, who told Trugman that KISS had been "offered" to the label with the "information that they were offered elsewhere as well."[40] The document goes on to cite that in the attorney's presence, an agitated Bogart was informed by an unidentified Columbia Records representative that KISS was also pitched there. The final blow was a discussion with Atlantic Records' attorney, Mike Mayer, who, according to Trugman, "acknowledged to me that he had met with the President of defendant Rock Steady and Paul Marshall, the attorney for KISS and that active negotiations were in fact in progress for a recording agreement with a record company in direct competition with plaintiff."[41] This was confirmed on October 2, when Marshall admitted to Casablanca that KISS "was in fact in negotiations with Atlantic for a new agreement as recording artists."[42]

Larry Harris: "Because Joyce was Neil's girlfriend and the co-manager of the band, we already knew everything that was going on in their camp, so Neil also put a cease-and-desist against Atlantic Records, who was seriously thinking about signing KISS. It's very interesting that nobody gave a shit about this band: Sony passed on them, CBS at the time, or Epic, whatever. They passed on them after they put them in the studio. No other label in the industry wanted this band, and we stuck our necks out and we almost went belly up trying to make them stars. So it got to be personal."[43]

All of these legal fisticuffs would soon be the primary cause for the making of *Destroyer* to splinter into two halves, as Ezrin remembers it, backed by a signed deposition on October 3, in which Bogart states, "Specifically, through mid-September KISS was at work for the plaintiff recording their fifth album under the Production Agreement at the Record Plant studios in New York City."[44] The abrupt halt to the proceedings put KISS's future in a tailspin. On the cusp of a creative breakthrough, the band was told to shut it down. Ezrin was sure that was it. His work, his vision, his growing rapport with KISS could be dissolved in one fell swoop. Aucoin made a desperate attempt to sidestep Casablanca by trying to convince Ezrin to keep working outside of the label's umbrella, but the young producer felt his professional options limited.

Ezrin: "Bill Aucoin came to me and asked me if I would take the tapes and finish the album for them without giving it to the label, but by that time I'd already signed a contract with the label. I was working for the label, technically. In those days the label hired you, not the group. So, I said, 'I can't. You know, I would love to, but I can't.' And I completely understand the group's frustration with the label, and Aucoin made all kinds of good points about why they should move or why their deal was rotten, but there was no way to legally do what they asked me to do. So the album went on hiatus. I suppose they could have finished it without me, and maybe had our relationship not been as good then they would have thought about that. I was very thankful they didn't, because I really loved working with them and I really enjoyed making that record. It's one of the great experiences of my life. So we waited until they resolved their issues with Neil Bogart."[45]

While Ezrin and KISS were trapped in legal limbo, and the band hit the road again to support a live album that's existence fell somewhere between desperation and financial necessity, something wholly unexpected transpired that would catapult KISS into the rock mainstream and present The Act with a new sense of urgency that added a different kind of pressure to the *Destroyer* sessions.

"Great Expectations"

Do you want to play the role?

The opening strains of Beethoven's Sonata No. 8 ("Pathetique") Second Movement tenderly emerge from the silence. A melodic piano, accompanied languidly by a stylized electric guitar and the faintest hint of classical chimes, preludes a warm acoustic guitar, strummed delicately. The smooth tenor croons wistfully, as if from a marble pulpit before a congregation of angels.

> *You're sittin' in your seat, and then you stand and clutch your breast*
> *Our music drives you wild along with the rest*

A soft bed of piano and acoustic guitar taps out the resolution to this gentle progression. Issuing a signature prologue for an electric rhythm guitar to forcefully make its entrance, the serenade breathlessly devolves into playful seduction.

> *You watch me singing this song, you see what my mouth can do*
> *And you wish you were the one I was doing it to*

The guitar is joined by a second, more aggressive partner, accented triumphantly by a single cymbal splash.

> *You watch me playing guitar, and you feel what my fingers can do*
> *And you wish you were the one I was doing it to*

> *Well listen . . .*

Rumbling drums roll from the deepest toms and crescendo into a heavy chorus of grandly echoed guitars, which herald fanciful carillon in choral splendor. The singer is strangely (if only slightly) reminiscent of the smoldering creature thankfully vanquished with the final chords of the preceding number. He boldly recites above a bellowing choir:

> *You've got great expectations!*
> *You've got great expectations!*

The ensuing verse picks up the tempo as the drums lay a quickening beat. There is more than a sense now that our narrator is speaking directly—not to the congregation, but your id: the one that is transmogrified in celebrity through the sheer power of his talents. The beast may have softened his touch but not his bravado. He knows instinctively that you crave the slimmest measure of his fantasy lifestyle. He is the omniscient creature hinted at by the dreamy-eyed teenagers who craved the elusive "midnight dream," the lurid destination for the kid speeding recklessly to get to that "midnight show," where the shaman will sing his ode to the unreachable star beneath the spotlight, so close but so far out of reach. And so it has chimed midnight, and the chariot has not turned into a pumpkin after all. Instead, it reads your soul.

> *You're dying to be seen, and you wave and call my name*
> *But in the din it seems I'm a million miles away*
>
> *You watch me beatin' my drums and you know what my hands can do*
> *And you wish you were the one I was doing it to*
>
> *Well listen . . .*
>
> *You've got great expectations!*
> *You've got great expectations!*

The Beethoven theme returns in full force as the band grinds away behind the single melodic guitar line. A piano scuttles across the bottom of the sensuous interlude, which glides on a steady drum pattern. It is movement, no doubt, but a slow, languid march beyond the ether. Suddenly the narrator speaks the part of each member of the band, telepathically expressing their inner thoughts beneath the promethium arch. His spirit spirals over the heads of the clamoring hordes, a silent voice now melded into yours as one:

> *Then you feel these eyes from the stage*
> *And you see me staring at you*

And you read between the lines, my voice is calling to you

The heavy feedback of the electric symphony gives way to a full-blown orchestra crashing in. The choir is front and center, repeating the refrain, mocking, beseeching:

You've got great expectations!
You've got great expectations!

The narrator can be heard within it, a distended but still rigorous presence. His voice, hollow and distant, crawls into your subconscious.

Do you want to play the role?
You'd even sell me your soul.

He is the demon, after all; shrouded in the white tie and tails of the seductive redeemer, the dark spirit at the crossroads setting out his Faustian bargain for fame and fortune. Sign on the bottom line. Give up the workaday world of mediocrity and follow his operatic coda into the sunset. You too can inhabit the infinite. Live forever. Everyone has a price.

The Act: A perfectly constructed amalgam of illogical but determined illusions peddled tirelessly in mass volume and glitz. (Fin Costello/Redferns/Getty Images)

Paul Stanley: Vain, driven, and indestructible. The vulnerability and lyrical depth in "Do You Love Me?" and "Detroit Rock City" provided KISS their third dimension. (Lydia Criss/ Sealed With A KISS www.lydiacriss.com)

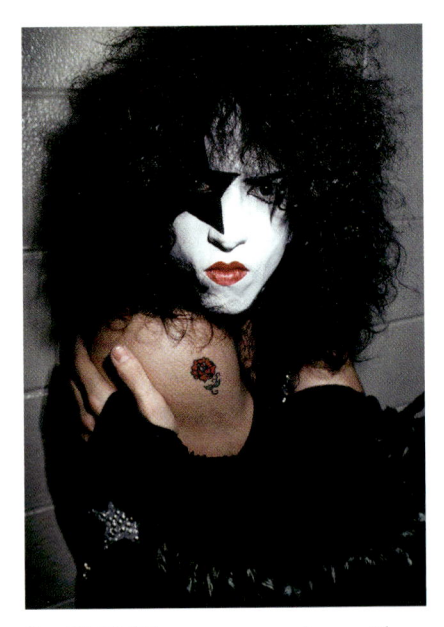

Star Child: "If we attract an audience with the other stuff, wait until everybody hears what we can do." (Fin Costello/Redferns/ Getty Images)

Gene Simmons: Egocentric, fearsome, and tireless. The cinematic growl of "God of Thunder" and the croon of "Great Expectations" pushed the aural boundaries of the band. (Lydia Criss/Sealed With A KISS www.lydiacriss.com)

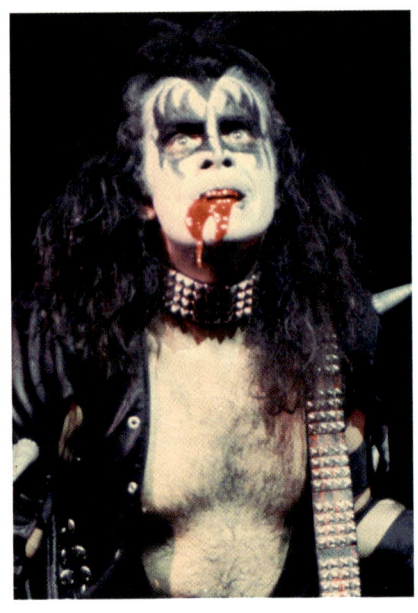

Demon: "We scared the living daylights out of everybody."(Chris Walter/WireImage/ Getty Images)

Ace Frehley: Challenged, paranoid, and stoned. *Destroyer* pushed him to the brink. (Lydia Criss/Sealed With A KISS www.lydiacriss.com)

Space Ace: "The pressure was on—and with a hangover as a frequent distraction, I hit a brick wall occasionally." (Michael Ochs Archives/Getty Images)

Peter Criss: Volatile, passionate, and insecure. His ordeal laying down drum tracks and his emotionally charged contribution of "Beth" made *Destroyer* arguably his finest hour in the band. (Lydia Criss/Sealed With A KISS www.lydiacriss.com)

Cat Man: "It was excruciatingly painful, but the outcome was genius." (Fin Costello/Redferns/Getty Images)

The Visionary: Manager Bill Aucoin, lording over his mid-'70s KISS empire, did not have a reticent bone in his body and welcomed embarrassment and ridicule as clear signs that boatloads of cash were soon to follow. He would cleverly mastermind the production, presentation, and purpose of *Destroyer*. Gene Simmons recalls, "to put it bluntly, the four of us created the make-up, the logo, the tunes, and the look and feel of KISS, but it was Bill who took it all the way." (Brad Elterman/FilmMagic/Getty Images)

The Gambler: Neil Bogart, pictured here with Donna Summer and his lineup of '70s stars, was entrenched in a bitter legal battle with the band throughout *Destroyer*. His upstart Casablanca Records chose KISS as its opening musical and visual statement but would have to survive many financial and creative hurdles before his dream of a mega-hit for the band was realized. Bill Aucoin said of Bogart, "Neil was the only person crazy enough to buy into all the nutty things we came up with; you really need that kind of flamboyant person who shared your enthusiasm." (Michael Ochs Archives/Getty Images)

The Tactician: Larry Harris, vice president of Casablanca Records, poses with KISS and their gold albums for *Alive!* He commandeered the album's unlikely rise to the top of the charts and found himself caught in the vortex of the KISS machine, which would find him delicately balancing the battle between the label and the band's management throughout the making of *Destroyer*. "Neil and I both knew that anyone capable of provoking this type of visceral response was the stuff of future superstardom." (Fin Costello/Redferns/Getty Images)

The Show: Alice Cooper, with his infamous python in 1972. His wickedly ironic villain persona turned the rock zeitgeist on its head. The group he fronted was the godfathers of foot-stomping, ear-splitting macabre that inspired KISS and eventually led to the band seeking out its producer to helm *Destroyer*. "We enjoy coming on stage and showing the public what their world has come to. Only usually they're shocked." (Jan Persson/Getty Images)

The Studio Whiz Kid: Bob Ezrin with the Alice Cooper group in the early 1970s. His unique mastery of cinematic soundscapes filled in the band's shocking imagery while also managing to methodically squeeze out hit after hit. "I'll take the raw talent every time, because if the brilliance is there it can be molded into just about anything." (From the private collection of Bob Ezrin)

Like Musical Minds: The young Bob Ezrin reviews charts with his mentor and arranger Allan Macmillan. Macmillan says today, "Bob really had a visual conception of what was going on in music at that time and had demonstrated he could translate this into actual performance values." (From the private collection of Bob Ezrin)

The Avatar: The iconic image and persona of Marlon Brando in 1953's *The Wild One* would be Bob Ezrin's cultural touchtone for KISS in the context of *Destroyer*. Ezrin: "There was just an undertone of vulnerability and sensuality sitting underneath this rock-god veneer that they had. I just wanted to add layers." (Alain Benainous/Gammo-Rapho/Getty Images)

The Master and his pupils at A&R Studios, January 13, 1976. Gene Simmons notes, "Bob Ezrin was the first and continues to be the only producer to ever really have an effect on the band." (© Bob Gruen/www.bobgruen.com)

The Hollywood Stars: The band that wrote and originally recorded "King of the Night Time World," its members pictured here in 1976, *from left to right*: Ruben de Fuentes, Terry Rae, Mark Anthony, Bobby Drier, and Michael Rummans. The song's co-author, Kim Fowley, recalled, "Right before the band broke up, I called Ezrin, and he said, 'Great, KISS will rewrite the song and you'll make more money with this band breaking up then if the band would have survived.'" (From the private collection of Michael Rummans)

Rock and pop impresario Kim Fowley, co-author of "King of the Night Time World" and "Do You Love Me?," visits KISS backstage at the band's career-altering Anaheim concert, August 20, 1976. Fowley exclaimed in 2012, "KISS was about to be the biggest band in the world, and to land two songs on *Destroyer* would be like today in sales some guy getting two songs on a Lady Gaga record." (© Bob Gruen/www.bobgruen.com)

Crisis: The summons from Casablanca Records, marked September 17, 1975, and delivered to Bill Aucoin (Rock Steady) and KISS, that threatened to implode the intense progress of the *Destroyer* sessions and put the future of the band, on the cusp of success, in jeopardy. Says Larry Harris, "No other label in the industry wanted this band, and we stuck our necks out and we almost went belly up trying to make them stars. So it got to be personal." (New York State Supreme Court County Clerk Records Department)

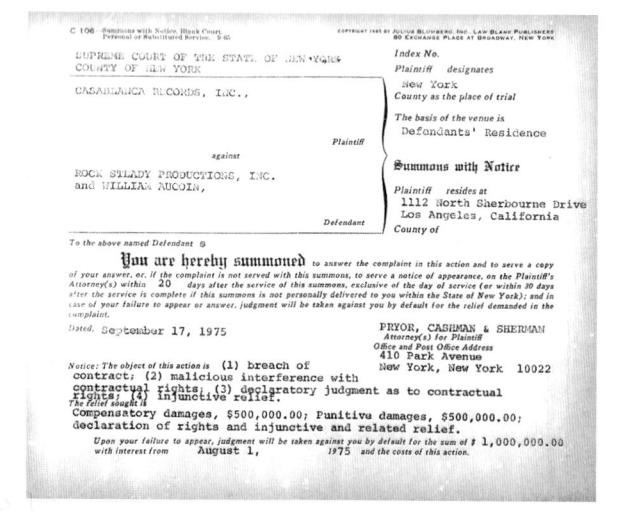

8

Four Dimensions

The masses go with extremes. American tastes are like that; that's why American food is not popular. The stuff that's sweet is real sweet, and stuff that's bitter is REAL bitter. I mean it's extremes.
—Gene Simmons[1]

Alive! hit the shelves on September 10, 1975, and something magical happened. It sold. And it sold. And it sold some more. Subsequently, within the first month of its release, audiences at the autumn KISS shows began to grow exponentially. Now, in reverse, *Alive!* was putting fans on notice: *you must see this in person!* You have to see what those explosions are like; see for real if this lunatic is actually spewing blood and blowing flames from his maw. You have to be there to chant along when the singer begs you to testify to the glory of rock and roll. And when you do—and he says, "Then why don't you stand up for what you believe in!"—you'll be right there standing as one with the faithful. And wouldn't it be cool to witness firsthand that kicking drum solo in the middle of "100,000 Years," or the face-melting guitar run at the end of that wild jam in "She"? Who wouldn't want to be waiting with everyone jacked on crazed anticipation for that booming voice to declare, "You wanted the best, you got the best: the greatest band in the land ... KISS!" And then those four ghoulish figures prance onstage to the rocked-out rhythms of "Deuce," poured straight into the funky "Strutter," and those deafening sirens at the end of "Firehouse." What could we be missing when the band bounds in after a forceful "Hit it!" and is off and running into that kick-ass "Black Diamond," with those raunchy power chords and the *pop, pop, pop* of the pyrotechnics? And, man, I want to be there when they bring the roof down with that rousing "Rock and Roll All Nite," fucker! Hot damn!

If *Alive!* set the stage, "Rock and Roll All Nite" knocked 'em dead.

Beyond the not-so-subtle use of a sped-up live performance, with the amped crowd driving its thunderous drumbeat and hammering rock guitars—

accompanied periodically by Paul Stanley's contagious catcalls of "I can't hear you!"—the success of "Rock and Roll All Nite" was built in. In those dark days of early 1975, during a bitterly cold New York February when Neil Bogart, label chairman turned producer, implored Simmons and Stanley to hand over the "rock anthem" he'd ordered up months before, the duo presented it as penned, a combination of Simmons's lewdly inviting verses from a scrapped song called "Drive Me Wild" and Stanley's ingenious chorus, the perfect antidote to the teenage humdrum: "I wanna rock and roll all night! And party everyday!" Fuckin' A. Who doesn't?

That neither author of this hedonistic mantra partied mattered little. Stanley rarely drank, and when he did, as in the case of the infamous *Hotter Than Hell* photo shoot, he became unhinged; Simmons never imbibed in a single mind-altering substance beyond his relentless pursuit of fame, skirt, and moolah. Once again, on cue, the KISS illusion kicks in. The Act now had its signature tune—what many today rightfully dub the Rock and Roll National Anthem, whipped off in two parts by road-weary troubadours in a hotel in far away Los Angeles during the drag-ass 1975 tour. Long before Electric Lady Studios and Cobo Hall, where *Alive!* made it as famous a rock venue as there is in the continental United States, Stanley stood onstage and proudly announced that "Rock and Roll All Nite" had been written *about* Detroit, *for* Detroit, the city of "rattly clankings," the place where, when everyone else had all-but ignored them, they stood and chanted KISS to victory.

Within a few weeks, *KISS Alive!* became the stuff of American legend. An analogous political experience would be that of Dick Nixon left for road kill after an ignominious defeat in the 1962 California gubernatorial race, in which he all but spat at the national press, only to emerge six years later to claim the presidency he was denied as a candidate eight years earlier. In sports, it is the 1980 U.S. men's hockey team, a collection of green college kids pummeled by the mighty Soviet Union's professional squad months earlier, arriving wide-eyed and skilled enough to defeat the same seemingly unbeatable force on the way to an unimaginable Olympic gold medal. In the realm of entertainment, it is a struggling vaudevillian tossing together a pathetic tramp's outfit and inventing the iconic Charlie Chaplin.

On the surface, *Alive!* makes no damn sense. Everything was stacked against its mere existence, and certainly its chance of success. In actuality, its achievement is a matter of will and the utter determination of those who put it on the line one last time before having no other alternative but to give up the ghost. It is the survival instincts of KISS coupled with a management team, led by the clairvoyant Bill Aucoin and his charges, and a record company that, despite a great deal of wild mismanagement, had never failed to back their whims.

"A little before *Alive!* took off, Neil and I were with his kids during Halloween," recalls Larry Harris. "I wasn't married yet, and I didn't have kids, so I went with him on Halloween, and we were just sitting in the car as his kids would go from house to house to get treats, and we started seeing more and more little kids wearing KISS makeup, and it was at that point we knew that something was up."[2]

The nucleus of *Alive!* was a microcosm of The Act's post-modernist approach: a masquerade of epic proportions—a live album that is only partly live (canned cheering, copious overdubs) and a double-record from a struggling studio band—packaged as a must-see spectacle. Medium as message. If nothing else, KISS, Casablanca, and Bill Aucoin's crazy idea to pull a failing venture out of its recording morass (or ridding all parties of the fallout) by doubling the pleasure, thus raising the price of a heretofore mostly unwanted product, dressing it up with wild crowd noises and adding sound effects, adorning the gatefold with handwritten notes from the band members—each carefully worded to be both personal affections and marketable insights into the characters—and a glossy, full-color insert booklet acting as a de facto tour program with vivid live photos of the boys whooping and menacing it up, signaled a more focused approach to the dogmatic principles of the KISS entity.

What was, in reality, a last-ditch, possibly contract-severing effort had been formed as the band was in the throes of professional upheaval and near financial devastation, when it had yet to prove itself a worthy recording outfit. Its previous representation on vinyl was at best raw and at worst crap, and straining matters further was an increasing divide between KISS music and The Act, which heretofore had wasted the strong personalities that reflected its audacious image—something already built into the product. Onstage, KISS was larger than life, four diverse pieces of a whole: the Demon, Star Child, Cat Man, and Space Ace. Save for the album covers with which an audience could somewhat connect to the band's carefully crafted concept, KISS's records, as pointed out to the band by Bob Ezrin, were not distinct to those incredibly memorable faces and the personalities behind them. Unless you were a loyal fan—still something of a malleable concept at this juncture in the band's career—it was hard to tell the voices apart or guess who might be the author or driving principal of a particular number. This was never a problem for a band with a lead singer, who for the most part fronted the concept and acted as its main lyricist and a resounding voice—Mick Jagger, Jim Morrison, Freddie Mercury, Steven Tyler, and most notably, in the theatrical realm, Alice Cooper, a man who actually changed his name to that of the band he fronted. In the case of the Beatles, the four-headed monster was clearly displayed on record: Paul, cute, sensitive, melodic; John, clever, caustic, solemn; George, quiet, spiritual, experimental; Ringo, lighthearted, funny, approachable. Where were those distinctions within KISS?

Correcting that glaring hole in the KISS model became the marketing aim of *Alive!* Much of it came from Bill Aucoin and his uncanny sense of genuine faith in what The Act had presented to him two years earlier in the dingy Hotel Diplomat in Midtown Manhattan. If music and performance could not equal the band's indestructible illusions—something Aucoin was sure Ezrin's relentless expertise and the band's tireless stage antics would achieve—then, he surmised, *Alive!*'s packaging could and would. The brain trust had bet that the album's full-color booklet, personal messages, and close-up stage-persona shots of the band would bridge the sonic presentation of KISS with the one so perfectly suited for a visual assault.

A major contributor in failing to exploit the fusing of the stage image with a musical one stems from an absence in the KISS camp—although all supportive to the point of ridicule and poverty—of anyone trained in this essential endeavor. Aucoin's assistant and stage guru Sean Delaney may have helped the band create the stage personas that to this day have served the franchise well, but he possessed no talent for creative design. Thus *Alive!*'s crucial impact on the prefiguring of KISS as a character-driven device, so prevalent in its immediate future in the creation of *Destroyer*, was in large part the brainchild and complete conceptual baby of Howard Marks's advertising art/creative director Dennis Woloch.

The thirty-two-year-old Woloch had worked with KISS from the very beginning. Aucoin shared office space with the Howard Marks agency, the company that helped him launch Direction Plus in 1973 and partnered with him through the early '70s, into his foray as the band's manager. From mocking up generic concert posters to gluing the KISS logo on to bass drum heads to hiring the famed graphic designer David Byrd to assist with the band's makeup application for the first KISS album cover, Woloch became Aucoin's designer in residence, which would earn him the inevitable responsibility to realize the *Alive!* package—an assignment he relished down to the smallest detail.

"They gave me a photo for the front cover and a photo for the back cover, so I didn't really have to come up with any concept, I just really had to graphically design it," Woloch recalled, during an interview for this book. "I did the inside, which were concepts with the little handwritten notes from the guys. I don't remember if it was Bill or me who came up with the idea, but the *image* of KISS was just starting to form. We told those guys, 'You're different characters. You each have your own persona. How about writing a little personal note to the fans from each of you?' And they said, 'Yeah, sure, fine.' They just went along with everything in those days, because they weren't hot shit yet. They were in our office all the time, so I sat each one down and told them separately, 'Here, you use this pen and this paper and you use this pen and this paper,' 'cause I wanted it to look like they actually sat there at night and thought about this in their little apartments somewhere. We did the inside book, too: the layout of the photos, et cetera. Concept-wise, Fin Costello had the photograph and handed it to me, and for the back cover we had that great audience shot. It was my idea to write 'One, Two, Three, Four' for the individual sides of the record, kind of like counting down music. Just about any contribution I could think of, I was trying."[3]

Woloch's creativity (best exemplified by his creation of KISS's alter egos for *Alive!*), Aucoin's astuteness (already demonstrated by his corralling of Bob Ezrin), and Howard Marks's professional air would all soon figure prominently in the creation of The Act's most stirring pronouncement, *Destroyer*. By no coincidence, Glickman/Marks, the investment wing of the Howard Marks Advertising agency, which had absorbed Aucoin's Direction Plus years before, and Rock Steady were already operating under one roof: 75 East Fifty-Fifth Street off Madison Avenue, the epicenter of American advertising and marketing. Woloch describes the close-knit interaction of what, for all intents and purposes, was KISS Master Control: "Howard was in that corner, I was in this corner, C. K. Lendt was over there, Carl Glickman was over there, Bill Aucoin was next to Howard, until KISS started getting big then he moved the operation out, but only right down the street to 635 Madison or something, but it was right next door."[4]

Expanding his professional independence after the release of *Alive!*, Aucoin would eventually seek a sizable bridge loan to keep The Act afloat. "KISS needed money and Bill [Aucoin] was willing to consider just about anything," Lendt, the vice president of Glickman/Marks Management, writes in *KISS and Sell*. "In early 1976, Clark Glickman, Howard Marks, and a third partner, a wealthy shopping center developer from Cleveland, reportedly agreed to pony up $100,000 for a stake in Bill's financial interest in KISS."[5] This entrenched, high-powered cabal of marketing admen began to infuse its will on the fortunes of The Act. It was bound from day one, given the singular ambitions of Aucoin and KISS, by total immersion into a multi-tiered media/market saturation machine. This above all else allowed KISS a level of autonomy not previously available. Although the success of *Alive!* would alleviate much of Aucoin's money troubles later in the year, Glickman/Marks Management had by now officially joined Aucoin Management as key players in guiding what would be three of the most lucrative years any rock band would enjoy.

"One of the reasons for a lack of creative direction [in] depicting the band's individual personas is that the albums were being done by the record company," explains Woloch. "The record company designed the first three albums. The record company handled the promotion. KISS was just sharing office space with us, the advertising agency—we weren't *doing* anything for them. But once we got involved with designing the albums, we also got a little more involved in their promotion and then a little more involved in their creative aspects. And so, being in advertising, we *marketed*, pushing those types of ideas that eventually helped make them what they were, what they should have been from the beginning."[6]

"Once Howard Marks was involved, things changed," remembers Larry Harris. "This was the advertising industry: they had a whole bunch of various artists and people who worked for him and created advertising stuff for his company, and I think a lot of that was Howard and us going, 'Yeah, let's go for the gold on it.' I mean, you know, we didn't really have a whole lot of choice."[7]

The absence of this vital element of sonic imagery is hard to fathom in the overall directive of KISS. Balancing on a thin tightrope between oblivion and stardom, the four members were running out of viable options. Another failure could have spelled the end for everyone: KISS (totally dedicated to the blood-and-sweat illusions of The Act), Rock Steady (its only client struggling to survive), and Neil Bogart's Casablanca Records (mired in the bombing of a two-record collection of highlights from Johnny Carson's *Tonight Show* that the company had dumped its remaining funds into). But *Alive!* did not fail. It sent a cracking shot across the bow of the rock industry and became the bridge to greater things to come.

There are far better live rock-and-roll records. One that quickly comes to mind is *Woodstock* (1970), of course. In the realm of pure soul and funk, the original *James Brown at the Apollo* (1963); the Rolling Stones' masterwork of stage boogie, *Get Yer Ya Ya's Out* (1970); the Who's *Live at Leeds* (1970) is a war machine personified; *At Fillmore East* (1971) is the Allman Brothers' most stirring contribution to the genre; *Sam Cooke Live at the Harlem Square Club* (1963) will make anyone with a pulse weep; Van Morrison's scorching live band of the early '70s, the Caledonia Soul Orchestra, captured on *It's Too Late to Stop Now* (1974), is unfair advantage; and any of those Johnny Cash prison recordings, from *At Folsom Prison* (1968) and *At San Quentin* (1969), induce chills. There are unquestionably more popular live records: *Frampton Comes Alive* (1976) advanced the standard. Talking Heads' *Stop Making Sense* (1984) made a theatrical impact, along with the Band's *The Last Waltz* (1978). The Grateful Dead's *Live in Europe '72* (1972), the Blues Brothers' showcase *Briefcase Full of Blues* (1978), and the one that made U2 important, *Under a Blood Red Sky*

(1983), make a forceful case. But none is more seminal to its creators, pertinent to its backers, or precious to its fans than *KISS Alive!*

Alive! climbed steadily up the charts during and beyond the 1975 Christmas season, nestling just inside the *Billboard* Top 10 at #9—making it by a long shot the highest-charting record for KISS. Boosting its unprecedented ascent was "Rock and Roll All Nite." A month into the double-album's precarious arrival on the scene, the now-celebrated live single, which topped-out at #57 on the *Billboard* pop singles charts in studio form, skyrocketed to #12 in America and #18 in Canada.

"The success of the live album shocked us as much as anybody else," admits Larry Harris. "We were like, 'Holy shit, look what's going on!' We didn't realize that it would explode the way it exploded. We were grasping for the ring and luckily we got the ring."[8]

Alive! indeed became a watershed moment for a band on the fringe, turning KISS from a cult oddity into a fully fledged national rock act. It saved Casablanca Records. It rescued Bill Aucoin from a mountain of debt and helped solidify his bargaining position with the label. A mere three days after Bogart countersued Aucoin, on October 6, KISS was offered, and signed, a lucrative new two-album deal. "Neil's biggest fear was losing a band that would later be successful," says Harris. "It happened to him with Melanie, and it drove him crazy because he was very close to her, and it was always a point of contention with him about losing a band. There was a point where the Village People had come back and asked us to redo their contract and they wanted a half a million dollars an album, and this was after 'YMCA' and 'In the Navy' and all their big hits. And I had to fight like a dog for him *not* to sign that contract, but he was afraid that they'd still have hits. I tried to explain to him that they were over. Neil just could not fathom losing a band that somebody could later come back to him and say was a hit."[9]

Ultimately, KISS remained loyal to those who had the prescience to initially throw in their lot with The Act. "We had a lot of offers," Peter Criss told *Goldmine* magazine in 1976. "In the beginning, nobody wanted us, and here's the same people calling back and saying 'We want you,' but we figured, fuck you, let's stick with Casablanca since they're new and we're their first babies and we know they're going to bust their balls for us."

Looking back years later, in *KISS Alive Forever*, Aucoin concurred. "Truth be known, I loved Neil and Casablanca, and Neil Bogart was the only person crazy enough to buy into all the nutty things we came up with; you really need that kind of flamboyant person who shared your enthusiasm."[10]

The money sure didn't hurt. More than anything, the success of *Alive!* meant

Casablanca could make KISS happy in more ways than one. "Bill got a check for heavy seven figures, which he was more than thrilled with, and everything was fine after that," recalled Harris.[11] Over twenty years later, Aucoin again concurred. "We got our first check for two million dollars, and I can remember just staring at it, counting the zeros. I had never seen so many zeros."[12]

As KISS continued to tour with no end in sight, the double live album everyone had wagered on climbed up the charts for 110 weeks and outsold anything that had come before it tenfold. Three months after its release, it went gold, a certified 500,000 copies moved worldwide. At a New Year's show at Nassau Coliseum in Long Island, New York, a few miles and two years removed from the night Gene Simmons first lit his hair on fire, KISS was presented with a gold record, signifying that the days of struggle for notoriety had suddenly become the struggle to prove the band was no fluke, that The Act truly belonged in the rock-and-roll firmament. A few months later, the newly formed KISS Army franchise, with its monthly newsletter to fans, announced *KISS Alive!* had gone platinum, meaning one million copies sold (and while some data refutes its reaching platinum status by that time, it would do so soon enough). The band that had been conceived, formed, and built on the single notion of stardom or bust, had hit the big time.

So, after what appeared to most to be an overnight success, the music industry and the growing fan base asked . . . what next?

KISS Alive! proved Casablanca, Aucoin, and KISS correct. This was a worthy cause, both creatively and professionally. It also proved antithetical to how a music career is forged. As a showpiece filled with pyrotechnics, costumes, and general revelry, KISS had few peers, but the live setting—while literally breathing life into the structure and presentation of its songs—had also revealed glaring weaknesses in what preceded it. *Alive!* made the previous three studio albums appear more trite than ever. What should have been fair sampling of artistic merit only served to weigh down The Act. Antiseptic studio environs, tension-filled sessions, vacillating producer theologies, and half-assed song construction proved a damaging cocktail. While *KISS* set the stage for the sledgehammer material needed to seduce the hard-rock connoisseur, its best work sounded hollow in the impressive wake of the *Alive!* treatment. The signature songs from *Hotter than Hell* sounded gauche and *Dressed to Kill* ham-fisted. The exploding popularity in both pure sales and genre-crossing recognition of "Rock and Roll All Nite" as a live track—complete with a rip-roaring guitar solo absent from the studio version—offered a glaring distinction in quality and success between KISS onstage and KISS on record. There was little denying that, despite the band's growing status among the rock elite, there was still a huge professional hurdle for it to overcome and a looming industry dragon left to slay.

To wit: despite rapid sales and a growing fan base, the reviews for *Alive!* once again centered on the negatives and further pushed KISS from a legitimate (whatever the hell that is) rock-and-roll band to something of a peculiar fad. Alan Niester of *Rolling Stone* was particularly harsh in his criticisms, hitting the band where it was most vulnerable: its songbook. "KISS onstage could possibly be mildly entertaining for about ten minutes," he wrote, "but on record, minus the impact of gaudy painted faces and stage theatrics, the band must be judged solely for its music. It's awful. Criminally repetitive, thuddingly monotonous. And like the legions of equally talentless bands across the country, KISS attempts to get by on volume and tired riffing. Unlike these other bands, however, they came up with the idea of dragging rock further into the pits of theatrical overkill."[13]

Although as a profession it was hardly yet legitimate, rock criticism was still an evolving form in the mid-'70s. Most of those forced to listen to newer rock records were jaded veterans of a bygone age not yet ready to throw off the ghosts of Woodstock or not quite done grieving the deaths of Jimi Hendrix and Janis Joplin. There were also voices that felt the need to protect the brand that paid their bills—in some cases, daring to eviscerate those who had taken the heretofore-limited scope of rock music to unimagined heights. During the 1970s especially, the ex-Beatles were put through the press ringer for failing to live up to the social and cultural utopian dream they had once foretold, as the Rolling Stones were harangued incessantly for becoming soft in their descent into faux-celebrity dope-fiend chic, and once-edgy street troubadours like Lou Reed were shoveled over with funereal dirt with every record release.

In an extensive overview on the origins of rock criticism, Devon Powers's 2013 *Writing the Record* reveals the not-so hidden agenda of the medium: to view theatricality and pomp as a personal affront to the process. When discussing the backlash some critics laid on the culture-shifting Beatles' opus *Sgt. Pepper's Lonely Hearts Club Band*, Powers minces no words. "Dismissing the Beatles was a metaphor for dismissing this process of hype more generally—necessary in order to protect critical practice."[14]

Popular acts with little or no '60s credibility, like the flamboyantly prolific hit-maker Elton John, were not merely dismissed but openly mocked. Even bands with underground traction in the growing heavy-metal community, like Black Sabbath and Judas Priest, were routinely held up as a brutal assault on the art form. Many in their highbrow periodical towers pointed to enormous records sales and packed stadium shows as some sort of affront on rock sanctity.

Under these constraints, KISS had no shot—and, to its members' credit, they were happy to be ostracized. "We had no problem with the public," Paul Stanley intones, during his commentary on the *KISSOLOGY Volume I* DVD set. "The public was there to see us and champion us and we lived up to their expectations. Our problem was always with the people who wished we would go away, the hierarchy, who thought they could decide and spoon-feed what kind of music they liked to an unwilling audience. I think we gave everybody a wake-up call by saying, 'We're here, we're not going away, and we're taking everyone with us.'"[15] To KISS—and certainly *Alive!* cemented it—the fan was king; or as Gene Simmons, most vocal in pissing up the criticism rope, called them, "our bosses."

Still, as much as the generation gap and intellectually nuanced lines were being drawn between rock critics and KISS—and despite many underground weeklies, and Detroit's stalwart anti–*Rolling Stone*, *Creem* magazine, championing the band—there was a good deal of truth in the telling. Although *Alive!* would soon save the day and subsequently transform KISS from a money pit into a measure of the colossal mega-group it was conceived to be, a cloud hovered over the band's prior studio work. Certainly, once *Alive!* began to sizzle, the follow-up had to be better than good—it had to seal the deal proffered by what ostensibly was a greatest-hits package with cheering.

"*Alive!* was kind of a bookend of what we had done up until that time," Gene Simmons declared, in *Behind the Mask*. "We thought it was time to take a step forward."[16]

Suddenly, the band would be forced to consider what reaching the summit's edge had wrought: a spotlight on the image, the concept, and The Act—the very mission statement of KISS. Songs about getting tail, cramped hotel living, sexist rants, and street miasma were no longer going to cut it. It was time for KISS to conquer not only the studio but also the song: to marry The Act with musical imagination and put it all together in an unforgettable package that could cash in on this new fame and solidify its standing in the pantheon of rock.

Simmons, Stanley, Frehley, and Criss were now changed men. They had tasted true success for the first time. Having been chopped down to size and run through Bob Ezrin's boot camp—and forced to reevaluate their songwriting skills and how they approached expressing their image, which was being driven out to the public with great precision in the packaging of *Alive!*—they would head back to New York in the first days of the nation's bicentennial year and make their ultimate musical statement.

SIDE TWO

"Flaming Youth"

Our flag is flying higher!

The band thrashes forth, unimpeded by shock, outrage, or puritanical restraint. Its trumpet call summons the brave and the bold into battle. Those unafraid to herald the joys of unbridled individualism may now wear their hedonistic liberty as a badge of honor. "Oh yeah!" the singer attests.

It is the voice from the first two songs: the young rider on the storm and the suburban dreamer of headlight queens resurrected! He is now our ringleader. The circus is in town, and we too can join it—or perhaps we already have. The circus, the music says, is us: the young and the strong, a stirring human spectacle come to life on the command of electric guitars. They speak of the promise of rock and roll, a radiant howl that sears the skin from our bones, brushes the locks of our freak flags, brands our tattered leather jackets, singes our concert tees, and bulges beneath our faded jeans.

My parents think I'm crazy and they hate the things I do
I'm stupid and I'm lazy, man if they only knew
How flaming youth can set the world on fire
Flaming youth, our flag is flying higher and higher and higher!

Oh, how those glorious guitars swirl in a tempest and then veer off into the ether once more, leaving the drums to lay the groundwork for the blissful march onward and upward.

My uniform is leather and my power is my age
I'm getting it together to break out of my cage

'Cause flaming youth can set the world on fire
Flaming youth will set the world on fire
Flaming youth, our flag is flying higher and higher and higher!

The tension shreds the carnival barker's vocal chords, serving due warning to an unsuspecting world that the ignored, the shoved aside, the kicked around, this ragged army of misfits has grown strong on the music. Exploding from the shadows of silent oppression, feral rhythms loudly testify to the ecstasy of apathetic rebellion. There is power in numbers, and perhaps an even greater power in the number *one*.

Straining our tattered throats, we bellow impatiently with playful arrogance, paving the way for a pulse-quickening guitar solo. It bounces along as if an electric current riding the crest of a summer storm. Bolts of furious lighting crack.

The band provides the thunder on which it must flash. The beat quickly turns 'round and back down again, skidding a hairpin turn into a vivacious calliope interlude. Our circus has come full circle now, welcoming one and all into the big top of thrills, where the band, the music, and its throaty youth have formed a holy trinity—an unstoppable force flying high on the trapeze, traversing the tightrope and taming the beasts. The clowns, emboldened by greasepaint and trickery, have emerged messiahs!

> *Flaming youth will set the world on fire*
> *Flaming youth will set the world on fire*
> *Flaming youth will set the world on fire*
> *Flaming youth will set the world on fire*
> *Flaming youth will set the world on fire*

The divine mantra is released unto the heavens. Out of the speakers and straight from our hearts it rises as the undying spirit of youth, leaving behind parents and school and braces and acne and bullies and boredom and confusion and the uncertainty of what comes next.

> *Flaming youth, our flag is flying higher and higher and higher!*
> *And higher, and higher, and higher, and higher, and higher!*

What comes next? Who cares!

9

The Songs, Part One: Origins

With Bob, a lot of his stuff—the creative ideas, the visual underpinning—a lot of it happened in preproduction, where he hadn't even come near a studio at that point. So the band and Bob were off wherever, putting the basic album together. A lot of his concepts happen there. So when he got to the studio and started laying the tracks down, that sort of filled in more of the blanks.
—Allan Macmillan[1]

There are nine tracks on *Destroyer*, the musical and lyrical scope of which completely obliterates the entire KISS canon that precedes it. The band—ably guided, prodded, and cajoled by Bob Ezrin—set a course to expand its musical limits and broaden its manner of subject. This took place gradually, over a three-month period when the band met with the young producer to set the thematic groundwork for the album's motif: a heavy onslaught of illusionary aural dreamscapes that would heavily build on The Act's theatricality while unveiling a vulnerable subtext to the KISS personalities.

Sometime in July of 1975, Paul Stanley and Gene Simmons recorded demos of material they hoped Ezrin would embrace; then, in August, throughout the long days of "boot camp," most of the chosen songs were fleshed out and put on the table to soon be manipulated into *Destroyer*-worthy material. The remainder were culled from outside sources or written and arranged during the rehearsal period, which may or may not have included recording that September in one or more of the several locations alluded to already by varied sources. All of this working and reworking of songs would outlast all of the previous KISS studio experiences by a long shot and put to the test the challenges the band, its producer, and now its audience had demanded.

If Ezrin was looking to add pathos to proceedings, Paul Stanley strategically accommodated him with "Detroit Rock City," a song its composer would later tell me "embodies my work within KISS. It still goes over like a storm, because it's a great song. And I still look forward even today to playing it."[2]

Even with the song in its gestating state, Stanley had clearly broken boundaries in his songwriting. It was less riff orientated and far more thematic. On its surface, "Detroit Rock City" is an indelibly Kiss-esque number punctuated by a driving *ostinato* dual guitar line. It deftly expounds the chanting flavor of his contribution to "Rock and Roll All Nite" with the "Get up, everybody's gonna move their feet / Get down, everybody's gonna leave their seat!" refrain that would become a KISS imprimatur, but its spatial structure left room for Ezrin to add deeper emotive flourishes. These were inspired by the song's subject matter, which was another major leap for Stanley. While the verses are filled with recklessly liberating nods to drugs, speed, and booze, beneath this overt ode to hedonism resides a poignant depth never before mined by the band.

Stanley brought the skeletal makings of the song to Ezrin as a living tribute to the town that backed The Act from its first visits to its triumphant *Alive!* shows. However, as Stanley recalled in *The Box Set*'s booklet, "Detroit Rock City" was also "very much a tribute to all the cities that live for rock and roll."[3] He simultaneously planted the seed of a melodramatic underscore in the face of the youthful exuberance that turns the song into a requiem for a KISS fan allegedly killed in a car accident on his or her way to a concert.

Stanley: "At the time I was writing the lyric, I remember we had played somewhere in the South—and I'm not sure if it was Charlotte, but someone had been killed outside the arena in a car accident and I thought, how strange to want to come out to an event that's such a celebration of life and you lose yours going to it."[4]

Interestingly, geography played a part in the construction and eventual recording of Stanley's baleful lyrics, with the band inadvertently referring to a New York State highway as being inside Michigan. "We made a terrible mistake, because we called out the wrong highway," Ezrin admits. "We're supposed to be in Detroit, and it's 'Movin' fast, down 95'—and it's actually 75. So we had to change the lyrics on the sleeve, 'Movin' fast, doin' 95.' But we didn't sing 'doin' 95.'"[5] (Ezrin sonically corrected this roadway *faux pas* in his 2012 *Resurrected* version by way of "digital manipulation.")

The other striking aspect of Stanley's thematic structure for "Detroit Rock City"—one that made it an obvious choice for Ezrin to eventually use to kick off *Destroyer*—is its lyrical presentation in the first person. The song is unmistakably sung as a characterization of a fan and not that of the author and singer, the rock star Paul Stanley. It immediately portends the playful masquerade of the album to come. This is the cinematic resonance of Ezrin's vision: presenting an atmospheric anomaly, inviting the audience to a known commodity, and immediately turning the tables to create an unease that eradicates expectation. "Detroit Rock City" is KISS literally wiping away any preconceptions instilled by the band's heretofore failed studio efforts and replacing them with distinctive intensity, while also accentuating what The Act's model promises: a thrill ride unveiling moments of apprehension that heighten exhilaration. The invincible power of rock and roll, preached from the stage nightly by Stanley, has a darker side.

"We had decided to get a little cinematic with 'Detroit Rock City,'" explains Ezrin. "They lived in that frame of mind when they got all dressed up and hit the stage, but they didn't have songs that allowed them to go to that place; musically and lyrically."[6]

The opening line of Stanley's demo of the song, "I feel uptight on a Saturday night," would remain in the final rendition, but the rest of the lyric and its ensuing melody belie its early promise. For instance, the second line of the first verse is delivered in a British blues style—"the music playing in my head!"—which Ezrin would replace with an answering bass run by Simmons. Stanley then repeats the second part of the stanza with, "Get up, get down, I'll tell what I'm gonna do!" which ushers in his infectious, "Get up, everybody's gonna move their feet / Get down, everybody's gonna leave their seat!" as the chanting chorus completes each verse: "You gotta lose your mind in Detroit Rock City!" This line, which is repeated once more in Stanley's demo, was later removed from the other sections of the song for the final version. However, it was later returned by Sean Delaney for the 1978 greatest hits package *Double Platinum* and eventually added to two sections of the riff by Ezrin for his 2012 remix/remaster, *Destroyer Resurrected*.

Gene Simmons is quick to point out, even today, that his contribution to "Detroit Rock City" is found in no small part within the basic structure of his own unfinished composition "Too Young," which evolved into a section within a longer instrumental built originally from an Ace Frehley guitar riff titled "Acrobat." Another segment of the instrumental appeared, excluding Simmons's part, as "Love Theme from KISS," thanks to a suggestion by co-producer Kenny Wise during the *KISS* sessions. *The Box Set* includes a recording of a 1973 performance at the Daisy Club in New York City in which, at the 3:20 mark of a more than six-minute jam, Peter Criss picks up the tempo with a drum beat strikingly reminiscent of the one he later performed on "Detroit Rock City," which is followed by a half-measure of that familiar opening *ostinato* before the song resolves into a James Gang–style riff. A little later in the song, after a series of rough-edged falsetto harmonies, Simmons sings, "You're much too young!"—a section of "Acrobat" that was never fully fleshed out by KISS, but that leaves little doubt that its driving (albeit truncated) *ostinato* inspired "Detroit Rock City."

Stanley's demo of the song bears this out. Its tempo is practically identical to the final version, with the *ostinato* acting as the primary driving force of the song, accompanied immediately by a wild Ace Frehley–type lead (possibly played by Frehley himself, although most of Stanley's demos were recorded for *Destroyer* at Magna Graphic Studio in Greenwich Village with only Simmons on bass and tour manger J. R. Smalling on drums). None of the funky bass runs Simmons would bring to the eventual track are yet present, and nor are the rhythmic dynamics, the guitar harmonies during the *ostinato*, or anything resembling the song's intricate interlude, which would soon turn "Detroit Rock City" into a classic. The dramatic pauses and drum fills that ignite the finished song would also seem alien in this almost punk-rock, Ramones-like take.

After its transformation during "boot camp" rehearsals, "Detroit Rock City" would combine Stanley's original vision with Ezrin's instinct for structure and nuance. Placed as *Destroyer*'s opener, it immediately assaults the listener with a rumble of lashing guitars bearing down into overdrive, but is equally haunted by a shade of melancholia clearly evident in the lyric and echoed by the wistful key of C minor. The rising dual guitar part—C-sharp to B repeated—ascends to a harmonious fifth above the main lick, the guitars roaring as if beneath the hood of a sports car unleashed. They then shift seamlessly into octaves above the chords which fuel the tempo at breakneck speed, providing the track a swath of resonance, presaging the open road and allowing the type of space needed to lay down an ephemeral landscape for the starkly pitched vocal.

It is here that Bob Ezrin stepped in to suggest a thunderous bass line repeat a pattern that peddles between the chords at the end of each progression. By far Gene Simmons's funkiest moment of Motown distinction, the bass riff exquisitely answers each anxious vocal line with a rumbling exclamation. These unique runs were given a substantial boost in the mix when Ezrin remastered the tracks in 2012 for *Destroyer Resurrected*. Simmons's picking (as opposed to fingering) is prevalent in the attack. Amid this furious guitar symphony, the rhythm section is well represented. "Bob sat with Gene and came up with a bass line that was influenced by a Curtis Mayfield song called 'Freddie's Dead,'" Stanley recalled, in the booklet accompanying *The Box Set*.[7]

"That was very non-typical of me," Simmons told *Goldmine* in 1998. "It's very R&B, almost like the song 'Freddie's Dead' by Curtis Mayfield. That's the bass line from 'Shaft.' The bass line from 'Detroit Rock City' is similar, but not the same thing note for note."[8]

"Some of the bass playing on that record is just remarkable," Ezrin exclaims.

"Gene was punching way above his weight class. And how it got there is the way he gets through anything; he's just the most determined person you've ever met in your life. He was determined to be able to do it. If I asked for it he'd be determined to do it. So, just by perseverance and repetition and determination he was able to learn some really complex parts and execute them really well. In fact, it wasn't that he was just learning parts, he was actually inventing very complex parts, much more complex than he had done in the past."[9]

The second melodic undertone to the song arrives with the counter-melody present below the memorable vocal line, "You gotta lose your mind in Detroit Rock City!" The second time it comes around, Ezrin introduces an interlude featuring a strangely seductive key change from C-sharp minor to D-sharp minor for two-and-a-half measures before returning to C-sharp minor.

The true complexity of "Detroit Rock City"—which coalesces Stanley's ballsy verses with the underlying notion that it may well be a final bellow against *the dying of the light*—resides in an inspired eight-measure motif wherein the guitars replace the vocal as a narrative element. Built upon a harmonic-minor scale most prevalent in classical composition, this musical bridge unfurls as if an empathetic interlude. It introduces quite literally another movement within the song rather than the traditional solo found in most rock numbers—much less one performed by KISS, a band that almost always used sections of choruses and extended verse parts to allow Ace Frehley room to roam expressively. This introspective turn is triumphantly ushered along upon a bevy of guitars playing within the same pitch class, but in varying octaves. As Ezrin originally worked it out with the band, however, it begins simply enough, with two guitars playing within an octave of each other, followed by two more guitars laying down harmonies of those octaves.

"I knew exactly what that section was going to do in my head in terms of melody," recalls Ezrin. "I wrote it on piano. It's a very simple melody. It was just knowing what to do at that moment in the song—coming up with something that would elevate the mood and create a little more tension—because here we were telling the story about a kid that was gonna die. So it had to have, on the one hand, a feeling of soaring, flying, because he's driving really fast, but on the other hand, it had to have an undertone of impending doom. Something was coming. What is the phrase, 'Something wicked this way comes?' You just have a sense that something was gonna happen."[10]

"Bob did a great job of coming up with the guitar solo," said Stanley. "He literally sang that guitar solo note-for-note and the harmonies as well."[11]

"It's very flamenco," recalled Simmons in 1998. "We thought he was on crack when he suggested it. We said, 'What are you, out of your mind? This sounds like we just came from Spain, like we were Los Bravos or something.' But as soon as we heard it put together with the drums, he knew more than we did. What can we say?"[12]

"It wasn't that hard," Ezrin replies. "I showed it to them on the piano: Stanley got it right away, and it was just a matter of showing it to Ace, and once he found the notes on the guitar, he could play it. It's not a very difficult part at all."[13]

Having been hampered throughout rehearsals and eventually the *Destroyer* sessions by his lack of enthusiasm to play within a rigid musical structure and kept from his signature freestyle lead work, Ace Frehley nevertheless made it a point in his memoir, *No Regrets*, to pay homage to Ezrin's efforts. "As a guitar player this is hard for me to admit, but the solo on 'Detroit Rock City' is one of the single best moments in any KISS song. And I had nothing to do with creating it. I always loved the song, and I would be the first to credit Bob Ezrin for writing the guitar solo. He came up with the melody, and I learned how to play it, and Paul figured out the harmony. It's a classic guitar solo, as good as anything you'll find on a KISS record. I wish I thought of it, but I didn't. It was all Bob's."[14]

As a feral counterpoint, Ezrin worked Peter Criss on "Detroit Rock City" as hard as on any song on the record, forcing the drums to maintain a strident gallop. "At one point, Bob dismissed us all from rehearsal while he worked with Peter on the drum part," Stanley remembered.[15] The end result is arguably Criss's finest recorded performance, denoting a sense of unimpeded momentum careening toward oblivion.

"It was really important for me that we set the guitar solo part up in the beginning without having the rhythm part," explains Ezrin. "Just having that drum section, and then introducing that melody with those pounding, incessant drums evoking a sense that something was gonna happen and that it wasn't gonna be pretty."[16]

It is a drum part that again may have originated from the "Too Young" section of "Acrobat," as is starkly illustrated during a lengthy drum break at the 5:06 mark of the aforementioned bootleg, which includes the same full-measure drum roll that introduces the coda of the song, although in the final arrangement of "Detroit Rock City" it would signal Ezrin's dramatic guitar interlude.

"Detroit Rock City" would become the perfect overture for *Destroyer*, announcing the presence of a big, brash ensemble taut with youthful defiance. It careens across a sheath of deafening volume while also remaining aware of the looming shadow of mortality. Its indelible clarion call became the band's opening number on the Spirit of '76 tour all the way through a litany of "final" world tours well into the next century.

Ezrin also loved a second song Stanley had demoed back in July, but for wholly different reasons than the composer had envisioned when he enthusiastically presented it. The atmospheric "God of Thunder" would become the quintessential Gene Simmons vehicle—in many ways the origin of his signature "demon" growl so prevalent in future KISS staples like "Almost Human," "Larger Than Life," "War Machine," and "I Love It Loud," to name just a few—and was to be his vocal debut on *Destroyer*, but it was actually written by Paul Stanley. Eventually placed as the third track of *Destroyer*'s side one, deftly following two rousing Stanley lead vocals, shifting the narrative from the Star Child's reckless exuberance of youth to a demonic manifesto, it was originally intended by the songwriter as another playground for his rote braggadocio. Once again instituting his well-worn mantra of following whatever fit the core element of a song—be it musician, arrangement, key, or singer—Bob Ezrin observed its potential as a way to brand Simmons in sonic form, once and for all, as the bestial Grendel persona he was emoting nightly onstage.

"It was completely obvious," Ezrin states emphatically, while recalling his initial conversation with Stanley on the direction of the song. "I was listening to this thing and going, 'Wait a minute: great song, Paul, but isn't Gene's character the God of Thunder? Isn't he that guy onstage? He's the monster, right? You're the lover. He's the bragger and you're the lover.' I mean, you can't really argue with that, can ya? So it was basically really obvious to me, and I thought that it was a much heavier song than the demo showed, so I just turned it into something that was suitable to the character of the monster."[17]

In interviews over the years, Simmons has had his fun with Stanley by pointing out that "God of Thunder" was always going to be his for the taking. "By the end of our third record, we had gotten very used to each other's songwriting styles; Paul's songs were always a little snappier and happier, and mine were always darker and gloomier. So we'd poke fun at each other sometimes, and Paul said to me, 'Anybody can write a Gene Simmons song.' To prove his point, he came back the next day with 'God of Thunder.' I changed some of the lyrics and sang it. When I first heard the song, I immediately had visions of the scene from *Fantasia* when the mountaintop opens and this big winged thing is standing there—something from the dark shadows. But Paul's 'God of Thunder' lyrics totally missed the point—they were almost all about Aphrodite and love."[18]

Simmons may be the one who missed the point, as according to both Stanley and Ezrin's recollections, the song was never meant for Simmons. In fact, when Ezrin approached Stanley about reworking the arrangement, slowing the high-energy tempo to nearly a crawl and handing the foot-stomping rocker over to Simmons, it was a bit of a shock. Stanley told KISS official biographers as much: "'God of Thunder' was originally written as my theme song. There's Apollo, there's Zeus, there's the God of the Sea, Neptune, there's all these icons. And then the God of Thunder is me, yours truly. I went in and did the demo and we started rehearsing it with Bob, and he wanted to slow it down and that was great, it sounded really heavy. And then Bob said, 'And Gene's gonna sing it.' I was devastated."[19]

Stanley's version of events runs parallel to how the original meetings with Ezrin had gone all the way through the "boot camp" rehearsals into the obligatory rewrites. Ezrin stressed that each member must have a song that provided more depth to their stage personas in order to gain a softer, more empathetic side for female fans. The Star Child's "love" demeanor that he affected for photographs, coupled with his effeminate prancing and sexual stage posturing, made him the obvious choice to set a course to that end. Moreover, Stanley possessed an emotionally sensitive background, later revealing in his 2012 memoir, *Face the Music*, that he was born without a right ear (a condition known as microtia), which forced him into a lonely, antisocial world of his own making. Well read, and with an imagination that worked overtime in the metaphors of "Detroit Rock City," Stanley effectively realized this agenda by attempting to fashion a "theme song" saturated with mythical references to the daughter of Aphrodite, the goddess of love, whose name in Greek mythology is Harmonia (the origin of the musical term, harmony). His chorus, kept intact for the final version, borrows the classic blues symbolism of heralding one's libido, as in "God of Thunder and rock and roll." (The term "rock and roll" was originally a euphemism for sex.)

Ezrin, however, heard the polar opposite. Where Stanley envisioned roses and seduction, the young producer imagined fire and brimstone: "It didn't fit with the more sensitive and vulnerable persona that we were developing for Paul, like 'Do You Love Me?' We arranged it to be as heavy as we could make it and Gene was in full monster mode when he sang the vocals."[20]

Stanley eventually echoed his producer's instincts and gradually came to grips with the decision to let Simmons have at it to accommodate the all-for-one mentality of the sessions. "Our rule was the producer had final say," he recalled, "because Gene and I could bat something back and forth so endlessly that we needed somebody else to come in and be able to put an end to that. If you're gonna play that game, it has to apply even when you don't want it. So I was floored and completely incredulous that Bob wanted Gene to sing the song. But you know what? It's a perfect Gene song and I never could have done what Gene did with the song because it's really the embodiment of who he is. It's always interesting that Gene's signature song is mine. So I get a certain amount of solace in that and clearly at this point it's impossible to separate him from that song."[21]

As if to demonstrate how seriously he took the idea of "God of Thunder" being his "theme song" for *Destroyer*, Stanley recorded a complete demo of it at Magna Graphic Studios, once again with Simmons on bass and road manager J. R. Smalling on drums. The raunchy Black Sabbath riff, played in E minor and tuned down to E-flat minor, that races alongside a driving hi-hat rhythm is antithetical to Stanley's seductive pleas, sung with the type of melodic precision later displayed in his contribution to the 1978 quartet of KISS solo albums. Yet the opening lines—"You've got something about you, you've got something I need / Daughter of Aphrodite, we'll make love till we bleed"—distinctly evokes a violent, Alice Cooper–tinged sexual deviance that would have definitely caught Bob Ezrin's ear and moved the song away from the Star Child and into the voice of the Demon. Stanley's original line, "I was raised by the women," would be dramatically changed by Simmons and Ezrin to "I was raised by the demons," while the apparent spell the subject is under was transformed from something to do with making love to the robbing of a virgin soul—both changes prime examples of the direction "God of Thunder" would take on its way to becoming track three on *Destroyer*.

Pressed in 2006 to name his favorite KISS composition, Stanley admitted that alongside his affection for "Detroit Rock City," "God of Thunder" may well be his proudest songwriting moment. "It's funny to have written the song that most embodies Gene, and the song most people associate with his character. So there's an irony and a pride in that."[22]

Out of all of Simmons's original compositions, some of which were demoed, some played live in studio for Ezrin, two survived the strict *Destroyer* litmus in rehearsals. The first of these is the predictably salacious "Sweet Pain," by way of the discarded "Night Fly" / "Rock and Rolls Royce," which would eventually settle in as the second song on side two.

"'Sweet Pain' started off as a lick that I had for a song called 'Rock and Rolls Royce,'" remembers Simmons, in *KISS: Behind the Mask*. "The song wasn't up to snuff. Bob Ezrin stuck in the riff at the end of 'Sweet Pain.' The riff that's on the bottom of the solo is that riff from 'Rock and Rolls Royce.'"[23]

Ezrin's liberal use of Simmons's segmented chord patterns and loose riffs in the key of A major is evident in the opening strains of the song, which he would later spice with Hammond organ and acoustic guitar. This slight progression also acts as a chorus beneath the "Sweet pain / My love with drive you insane" refrain, which quickly changes to D major as the vocals kick in and remains so for the verses. The verses are a V-I-IV-I progression, with the bridge ending in a big, fat A major—not unlike the popular head-bobbing rocker "Free Ride," a 1973 hit by the Edgar Winter Group. However, to simply have the band pedal on an A major chord would sound anything but sophisticated, so Ezrin rearranged the chords to shift tonal centers in and out of a D Mixolydian mode (tuned down a half step to D-flat). He would later incorporate several electric and acoustic guitars, along with a driving keyboard in the background to fuel the track's momentum.

"In those days songwriting came very fast," Simmons concluded, in *KISS: Behind the Mask*. "Bob rearranged the song."[24]

Simmons notes in the same account that he was originally attempting to pay homage to the Troggs' 1966 hit "Wild Thing," in which the vocals plod along with the power chords as if merely another guitar. "The thing about 'Wild Thing' that impressed me is the vocal didn't soar above it or didn't go underneath it. I tried to keep the vocals close to the chords."[25] A bootleg of rehearsals for the song gives credence to this point. As the band works through the backing for the verse parts, Simmons is singing along in a monotone, Lou Reed moan. Although he did not recall it specifically, Ezrin does not deny that his recent work with Reed, in which he counseled the eclectic rocker to recite more than sing for his work on *Berlin*, may have inspired him to support Simmons's baritone, which meanders flush against the chiming chord pattern. The subject, a playful introspection into sadomasochism, allows Simmons to reintroduce the sexual side to his demon character—a trait he had heretofore molded into an art form.

"'Sweet Pain' is a personal statement by me," Simmons told journalist Frank Rose, a few weeks after the band recorded it. "Let me give you more than pleasure, let me give you pain. When you get to the point where you're getting excited, love bites are exchanged—just a little bit of pain. It heightens the pleasure always. Now how far you want to take it depends on the extreme."[26]

With Simmons's cocksure sexual deviance well represented, Ezrin was able to cull the seductive if not restive side of the Demon in the second song he received from Simmons: a lush mid-tempo number that its composer described to KISS's biographers as an "ode to groupie-dom."[27]

Once again, Simmons reworked one of his "dark" earlier compositions, this time one called "You've Got Nothing to Live For," which was originally conceived to give voice to each member of KISS in communicating their otherworldly perception by female fans. The new title originated from the 1946 film adaptation of Charles Dickens's *Great Expectations*, starring British stage actor Alec Guinness and, ironically, Jean Simmons. Aside from the title, and maybe the black-and-white temper of the film, little of Simmons's "Great Expectations" is derived from Dickens's coming of age tale, which depicts the travails of an orphan named Pip.

On which instrument Simmons wrote the song is up for question, as he contradicts himself in two accounts. Perhaps cross-mixing the previous song with the refigured "Great Expectations" presented to Ezrin, in *KISS: Behind the Mask* he remembered writing it on bass, but in the liner notes to *The Box Set* he would recall strumming an acoustic guitar in what he calls a "Beatles-esque" style—something that was normally not accepted in KISS-land but was now fully embraced in the sudden priority of Ezrin-ville.

Simmons does not vacillate, however, in giving full credit to Ezrin for "changing and modulating the chords" in the former account[28] and "making a number of lyrical changes" as well as adding a "classical feel" in the latter.[29] "In particular, I took the verse and re-wrote it as a song about the band: 'You watch me playing guitar, you see what my fingers can do, and you wish you were the one I was doing it to,'" he explained. "The song kept referring to the singer and the drummer, and so on, and all about the expectations of some of our female fans. And the point of the song was what you can see onstage may not be something you can take home."[30]

Although he was enthusiastic about the idea of taking Simmons's "demon" character and splashing a bit of seductive melancholia on it, Ezrin's main lyrical suggestion was to replace the collective stance indicative of the verses—as in, "Paul is playing guitar" or "Peter plays his drums for you"—with the near-whispered intimacy of first-person: "You watch me playing guitar." At the same time, Ezrin surrounded this intimate "come hither" to the fans in a sweeping orchestral monolith, which he described in *Behind the Mask* as being the equivalent to "Dance of the Hippos" from the 1940 Disney animated classic *Fantasia*, wherein cartoon figures cavort to classical pieces by Bach, Beethoven, Tchaikovsky, and Stravinsky.[31] It stands to reason that the classically trained Ezrin, a student and ardent fan of sound innovations and cinematic designs, would evoke such a seminal film work, seeing how the advent of Disney's "Fanta-Sound" was an early breakthrough in surround-sound recording, elements of which are still in use today. He told KISS's biographers, "It presented a caricature of the already larger-than-life character that Gene already portrays wrapped in a musical brocade and chintz as outlandish as any romantic opera."[32]

Musically, Ezrin would not stray far from the *Fantasia* analogy by literally lifting Beethoven's Piano Sonata No. 8 in C Minor (or, as it is more widely known, "Sonata Pathetique") for the song's opening strains and interweaving its cantabile melody into the choruses. The Sonata was composed by Beethoven when he was twenty-seven, one year older than Ezrin was at the time of the *Destroyer* sessions; the exact part that's molded here to such shameless parody is its second movement, or the Adagio, immediately recognizable to any casual listener of Beethoven. This may explain why, in a subtly playful move, Ezrin, who radically reworked Simmons's basic chord structure to follow the Beethoven template step-for-step, opens the song in F major instead of the master's original A-flat. Otherwise, the progression remains in a classical construct throughout the first half of the verses, staying in the key of F major until Ezrin introduces the G minor chord, which leads the listener's ear to a new tonal center when it resolves to C major. The resolution only lasts for one measure, however, as the second part of the first verse changes the tonal center again; erasing any doubt on whom the song relies when it respectfully returns to Beethoven's A-flat and then to E-flat, basically the same run as the first part but a minor third up, before changing back to F major with a new chord thrown in; B-flat. Ezrin effectively lifts the first four measures of Beethoven's vision note for note and deftly arranges it for a rock band.

Ezrin: "I sat down at the piano and the chords screamed out: 'Okay, here we go, into 'Pathetique,' which I played as a kid, so that sort of just came on the moment. We played around a lot with that song. And it worked. Love it."[33]

Ezrin's playground in "Great Expectations" expands in the memorable chorus, "You've got great expectations," which is later accompanied in grand fashion by a full choir, once again unflinchingly arranged in Beethoven's A-flat. With the help of composer/arranger Allan Macmillan the vocals would eventually be laid on a lush orchestral bed of chimes descending into the dramatic fade.

"This was an era when we were experimenting," said Macmillan, who worked on the orchestral charts for the song with Ezrin soon after the young producer began putting his stamp on it. "We were sort of cross-pollinating, in a sense, not exactly classical music but well-written music to accompany rock and roll, and that expanded the opportunity to express ourselves. That's what Bob felt, and all this orchestral input was a means of broadening what he had conceived for this particular project."[34]

Having absorbed the best of what Simmons and Stanley could offer, *Destroyer* would fill out with songs from collaborations both inside (Ezrin as composer) and outside the inner sanctum (material from another source entirely) to further enhance the idea that this would be a KISS album like no other.

10

The Songs, Part Two: Collaborations

If it makes the hair on my arms stand up or makes my scrotum tighten, if I have a deep, visceral reaction to something, then I know something great is happening here. That's what you call a "Holy shit!" moment.
—Bob Ezrin[1]

Ezrin's songwriting contributions to *Destroyer* would be indelibly etched in the remainder of the tracks, not the least of which is the implausible puzzle that became side two's opener, "Flaming Youth," and a song on which he worked side by side with Stanley and Simmons to create the penultimate KISS anthem, "Shout It Out Loud."

A microcosm of the *Destroyer* sessions, the concept, writing, arrangement, rehearsals, and recording of "Flaming Youth" reflects the band's self-awareness of its audience and the way it underlay the creative efforts of three composers and the dedication of raw musicians striving to raise their talents to the challenge. It is also the mission statement of an all-encompassing producer's vision realized.

As with the remainder of the songs on the album, save one monumental ballad, there was no "Flaming Youth" prior to the late summer of 1975. Paul Stanley had part of a chorus; Ace Frehley had a loose riff; Gene Simmons, merely by mentioning to Ezrin the band having once played with a girl band named Flaming Youth in the early days (Coventry Club, December 21–22, 1973), prompted an enthusiastic, "Great title. We're going to write a song called 'Flaming Youth.' What have we got?"[2]

Simmons's offering was a fully developed song called "Mad Dog" that would soon be gutted and transplanted as if a vital organ to another living being. Frehley's part turned out to be the perfect guitar clarion call, neatly prefiguring the chorus Stanley had been carrying around in much the same way as he had astutely attached his fist-pumping youth anthem to Simmons's rumbling verses for "Rock and Roll All Nite" a year earlier. All of it somehow fit together, as Ezrin played his most convincing Dr. Frankenstein to the willing four-headed monster.

Despite its difficult shifts in time signatures, which spurred the infamous "boot camp," these disparate musical notions would converge to provide the perfect opening to side two of *Destroyer*.

Perhaps more than any other song on the album, "Flaming Youth" pushed the musical efforts of everyone involved to the limit. Although the final track appears to sound like a straight-ahead rock song, hardly approaching the intricacies of either "Detroit Rock City" or "Great Expectations," it manages to change time at three different intervals. Most rock songs are built in measures of four or 4/4 time: four beats per measure, including bridges or choruses, instituting the same grouping, which may also expand to larger groups of four (eight, twelve, or sixteen). The Beatles, for instance, referred to a bridge or musical change in a song as a "middle-eight." In "Flaming Youth," however, the chorus—"Flaming youth, you set the world on fire!"—is repeated twice over the course of an odd five measures before heading into Gene Simmons's "Mad Dog" riff, which rumbles under, "higher and higher and higher!"

"They called me the 'bridge-maker' then," recalls Ezrin. "Part of what I used to do and part of what I still do is come up with a great bridge—something that would really take a little musical diversion in the middle of the song and set up a big finish. People would come in with these great songs—verses and a chorus—but very few people could write a good bridge. So I was always the guy who could do it."[3]

For the solo, played over this riff, Ezrin shortened what would traditionally be a pair of two four-bar measures by one beat to a single measure of 7/4 time over six measures, switching the riff back to its full complement of beats for the final three measures of 4/4. The entire solo, wherein Peter Criss continues to play quarter notes on his snare drum, runs for nine measures before resolving on the descending guitar lick and Criss's *rat-tat-tat-tat* interval. It is here that the eventual accompanying calliope drives the chanting chorus back into the full band for the fade. None of this had ever been attempted by KISS before, and, as the well-documented "boot camp" attests, it took some time in rehearsals to get it all down.

"It's very much like you're the coach of a team," explains Ezrin. "You know your players strengths and weaknesses and you need to position them to succeed. So the idea here was I didn't want to throw anything at the band that they couldn't handle or if they couldn't handle what I was thinking of then I would modify it so it was handle-able without completely sacrificing the idea. Like that whole section in 'Flaming Youth,' the 7/4 time—in no way could Peter Criss count seven. It wasn't gonna happen. So I told him, 'Don't count seven; you just count 'one-one-one-one-one-one-one' and I'll tell you when it's over.'

And so that's what he did! It's right there on the drum part: *thump-thump-thump*. He's just playing steady in the background while everybody else is doing something in seven, but it worked! And it doesn't sound stupid and it doesn't sound unschooled or unprofessional. It sounds really good, like everyone knew exactly what was going on. That was my job: to take my players and position them for success, to give them assignments that they could actually execute. Or, if they couldn't quite execute it, then stay with them in rehearsal and practice, practice, practice until they got it, and then we'd be good."[4]

Principally, the song embodies the essence of The Act as it had been conjured by Simmons, Stanley, Criss, and Frehley from day one and spread as a cult of personality throughout a rabid fan base across America for three long years. Its theme evokes the plight of the KISS Army, many of whom were deemed "crazy" and "lazy" by parents and society at large, and who needed more than a voice of a generation—they needed the physical and psychic embodiment of it. To that end, Ezrin tinkered with the original lyrics, moving them once again from a group element, as with "Great Expectations," to a first-person harangue. The insulting "We're stupid and we're lazy" becomes the more defiant "I'm stupid and I'm lazy." What "Flaming Youth" presupposes, like all of *Destroyer*, is that KISS is not the *leader* of this crass, leather-clad youth but its brethren, laying down an alliance longed for in the disconnected. It replaces mere protest with proclamation; its flag flying higher, higher, and higher to claim a victory of imagination over the daily humdrum outside the headphones.

While "Flaming Youth" would open side two as a reminder of the chanting solidarity of the KISS brand, it would be overshadowed by the rousing "Shout It Out Loud," a song so perfectly structured to be an anthem of youthful exuberance, both musically and lyrically, it could well be Ezrin and the band's strongest collective proclamation. Stanley calls it "our mission statement" in his memoir.[5]

Unlike "Flaming Youth," which was a composite of disparate riffs carefully crafted together by Ezrin and the band, "Shout It Out Loud" was one of two of *Destroyer*'s original collaborative compositions (the other being "Do You Love Me?") that were conceived by Ezrin, executed by Stanley, and completed with later lyrical flourishes added by an outside source. It was quickly written by Simmons, Stanley, and Ezrin during the sessions without the aid of an existing demo or restructured segments of songs. It was inspired by the times, the band, the young producer, and the dynamics of the tireless creative pursuit to nail a theme song for The Act.

Ezrin: "In some cases we wrote in my apartment, across the street from where Stanley was living and not far away from Gene, and they'd come over. I had a grand piano in my living room, so we would sit there at the grand piano.

'Shout It Out Loud' was written there, hence, the very pianistic nature to that song. That whole bass line is really just my left hand on the piano."[6]

"We wrote 'Shout It Out Loud' one morning before we went into the studio," Stanley recalled, in *KISS: Behind the Mask*. "That was when Gene lived across the street from me [on East Fifty-Second—mere blocks from Ezrin]. So Gene came over and we went over to Bob's house and Bob had a piano. Before we went in to do one of the *Destroyer* sessions, we went to Bob's house and played piano, and we were writing the song."[7]

Simmons told *Circus* magazine, "We were sitting together in Bob Ezrin's room, Paul, myself, and Bob. Originally, we were going to come with something hard-edged—the wanting and never getting. How about—the moon is out and you're howling, and my love's what you're thinking of. Okay, that's really good. Well, but we're really looking for a kind of general statement for everybody, the way 'Rock and Roll All Nite' is. And one of the few things you can really do collectively is shout. It doesn't matter what you're shouting about—when you're young, you can really get off on the noise and shouting and just kind of letting it out."[8]

Although written in spontaneous fashion, the song was not entirely without ancestry. According to Gene Simmons, "Shout It Out Loud" had its origins in a Wicked Lester cover of the Hollies' "I Wanna Shout," which features the prominent chorus, "We wanna shout it out loud!" Both the Hollies vision and the Wicked Lester version that was to appear on its defunct Epic Records debut bears little resemblance to what Simmons, Stanley, and Ezrin had in mind, however. "I always thought the idea was bigger than they were trying to say with it, with the lyric implying, 'We have a secret, but don't tell people, we have a relationship.'" Simmons noted, in *Behind the Mask*. "I always thought just like that commercial on TV, that it was just, 'Shout it!' When you've got something you want to shout it out to the world, it doesn't matter what it is. Bob and Paul kept saying, 'Shout *what?*' I said, 'Who cares?' Whether it's national fervor or my team's better . . . it's a team rally. And then Paul came up with the verse."[9]

An "oldies" foundation was certainly present in the song's composition, with its rather shameless homage to the type of R&B call and response featured in such classics as the 1964 international Motown hit "Dancing in the Street" by Martha & the Vandellas or more blatantly in the Isley Brothers' 1959 rouser "Shout!," made famous to the KISS generation in *Animal House*, the 1979 National Lampoon comedy film about early-1960s college life. The incestuous nature of "Shout It Out Loud" goes back even further, as the Isley Brothers literally intended "Shout!" to be their answer to "Lonely Teardrops," a hit for the dynamic Jackie Wilson the year before.

By challenging Simmons and Stanley to conjure an anthem—just as did Neil Bogart in January of 1975, with "Rock and Roll All Nite" the result—Ezrin drew on his own encyclopedic pop sensibilities to add a little soul into the mix. Stanley would later admit to his biographers, "We were trying to cop some Motown kind of stuff, Four Tops kind of stuff with the answering background vocals."[10]

In the manner of a vocal group featuring various "lead singers," such as the Four Tops or the Temptations, Simmons and Stanley share verses, with each line followed by a group refrain to finish the thought, effectively driving home the rallying cry Simmons had suggested. The enthusiastic writing session came together quickly, as if the song was already in the ether to be plucked. "I knew exactly how I wanted to treat the song," Ezrin concluded, in *Behind the Mask*. "I loved writing with those guys. It wasn't often they would actually write together. Most often they would work at their individual apartments and record ideas to cassette that they would bring in and show me. But every once in awhile we'd get together and churn something out. It wasn't the music that made those times work for me. I felt like I was hanging out with my cousins. I was so comfortable with them both and so enjoyed their company."[11]

Moments like the composing of "Shout It Out Loud" had a lasting effect on what would soon build into a strong alliance between Simmons, Stanley, and the young producer, all three dedicated to making *Destroyer* the band's signature statement. During interviews for this book, Ezrin revealed why he was immediately keen to this bond being as much ancestral and behavioral as it was professional, expounding on his previous statement about feeling as if he were "hanging out with cousins."

"You cannot diminish the kind of kindred sense of connection some of us, and I mean Paul and Gene, had, growing up Jewish boys. The three of us growing up in Jewish households with that same sort of Eastern European ethic of trying to push the kid to be great and supporting the kid and putting an emphasis on education and putting an emphasis on the arts, you know; having to take piano lessons, having to learn to dance, doing all this stuff we had to do as kids, we had kind of a common ground. So when we all got together we felt like long-lost cousins in a way."[12]

Ezrin would leave the bubble of the close-knit trio to fill out the remainder of *Destroyer*'s tracks. Two of them came from an outside source, one collaboratively and the other completely. "King of the Night Time World" originated from beyond the creative enclave and came to KISS via Ezrin through the interwoven pipeline of the Record Plant. The original demo was recorded at the Los Angeles studio in 1974 by a fledgling band called the Hollywood Stars—

its most intriguing aspect being the involvement of songwriters Kim Fowley and Mark Anthony. Two years prior to cutting the demo, Fowley, an industry impresario whose career as a networking master stretched all the way back to 1957, had been introduced to Ezrin through Alice Cooper.

"In 1972, Alice Cooper, whom I'd known back in the Zappa and GTOs days, told me to go see Bob Ezrin for song ideas," Fowley later wrote, in a piece titled "Into the Sinister '70s" for Rock's Back Pages in 1999. "He was presented to me as the boy genius of the Guess Who organization. I went over to DCT Recorders at the corner of Sunset and Cahuenga, and there was Ezrin, who reminded me of Al Pacino. I told him I had a lyric called 'Alice Cooper for President' and said Alice should dress up like Uncle Sam. Well, of course, that became 'Elected.'"[13]

Considering his vast experience in the cutthroat world of the music business, Fowley never expected to see so much as a dime for an idea that eventually became a phenomenal single for Alice Cooper the very next year. He was stunned, however, to receive a strange offer of compensation when Ezrin contacted him as soon as the song became a hit. "Ezrin is a very honorable guy," Fowley affirmed, during an interview for this book. "He told me he played poker up at Capitol Records, and Herb Belkin [then head of A&R at the label] owed him ten grand for a poker game. He said, 'I'll call him and tell him to sign you with a $10,000 advance and a recording contract. Can you sing?' I told him, kind of, and so I went up to Capitol and Belkin met me there and handed me a check and asked me to sing like Jin Dandy from Black Oak Arkansas. I growled out some nonsense and he said, 'Welcome to Capitol Records!'"[14]

Fowley's brush with Ezrin is only one of an endless array of anecdotes from his incredible rock-and-roll life. By the autumn of 1975, when "King of the Night Time World" was being considered for the *Destroyer* sessions, his circuitous route through the music business already read like a who's who of rock royalty: Alan Freed, Phil Spector, Jimi Hendrix, Richie Blackmore, Gene Vincent, David Bowie, Gram Parsons, Leon Russell, Warren Zevon, Kris Kristofferson, and many more. His resume, which ironically included being the emcee at the infamous Toronto Rock Revival that launched the Alice Cooper rumor machine, had run the gamut of songwriting, performing, producing, promotion, publicity, and management. Soon after his brush with KISS, Fowley would go on to greater fame as the founder of the first ever all-girl rock group, the Runaways, who would enjoy a brief but electrifying underground success as well as yielding the hit-making '80s careers of Joan Jett and Lita Ford.

Conversely, Fowley's songwriting partner on "King of the Night Time World," Mark Anthony, would achieve only a modicum of success with the sudden arrival and quick exit of the Hollywood Stars debut album for Arista Records in 1977. Fowley "discovered" Anthony, as he recalled it, when the guitarist was twenty-one years old, wandering the streets of Hollywood, where would-be musicians and fast-talking manager types convened to be discovered. "You know how it is: you go to the same clubs and the parking lots and stand around and you eventually talk to someone who's standing there," Fowley remembered. "'Hey, you play an instrument? Okay, let's write a song or join a band or just ignore each other or insult each other, whatever.' Well, Mark had a gift for melody. He could play guitar. He was a good singer—not a great singer, but had a good image and could write really good melodies. I was a really great lyricist. He wasn't as good a lyricist as I was, so we decided to form the West Coast New York Dolls, where Mark would be the Keith Richards guy or the John Lennon guy, and we would try and find other guys in Mark's age group, and I would be the Brian Epstein, George Martin guy."[15]

Anthony, a runaway at age thirteen, had survived the seedy back alleys of Hollywood on his wits with literally nothing more than a cheap bag of magic tricks and a beat-up guitar he'd brought from his suburban purgatory. He jumped at the chance for stardom as prophesized by the well-connected and well-traveled Fowley. The Hollywood Stars—a band of spitfire club mercenaries whom Fowley threw together on looks and bravado—fashioned a sound from his and Anthony's compositions akin to what Fowley recalls was "not quite metal and not quite bubblegum, but something in between."[16] Most of what was "in between" in "King of the Night Time World" surrounded the salacious promise of the "headlight queen" to the narrator's "king," the lyrical origin of which Fowley said was inspired by his ogling a member of the Hollywood Stars getting a blowjob in an alley while bathed in the glow of headlights from an idling vehicle.

Having produced three songs that would appear on what would soon be a blockbuster soundtrack for George Lucas's hit film *American Graffiti*, Fowley now landed the Hollywood Stars a record deal with Columbia Records, but he could not convince the label's execs to let him produce it. Instead, his band of misfits—whom Fowley admitted "had issues with each other"[17]—imploded before the album was mixed.

Before the smoke cleared, the opportunistic industry veteran in Fowley leapt into action, recalling an opportunity proffered by his old friend Bob Ezrin. "Ezrin was considered to produce the Hollywood Stars early on, and right then he said to me, 'Don't like the band, but I like two songs. If the band ever breaks up, then I will do something with those songs. Okay?' So right before the band broke up, I called up Ezrin and he said, 'Great! Alice Cooper will rewrite "Escape" and the guys in KISS will rewrite "King of the Night Time

World" and you'll make more money with this band breaking up then if the band would have survived.'"[18]

"That's exactly how it happened," Ezrin agrees, upon hearing Fowley's recollections. "I used to talk to Kim a lot in those days. He was a very entertaining guy, totally encyclopedic about music. We'd have long conversations about what was going on—who was playing what and who was doing what—out in Hollywood particularly. He was my eyes and ears in Hollywood. So he knew I was doing KISS and it was his idea we do the song. Once I heard it again, I knew it was in perfect keeping with the project and it kind of defines who Stanley is."[19]

The demo of the Hollywood Stars' "King of the Night Time World" as Paul Stanley eventually heard it from Ezrin begins with a pounding drone on a single guitar note, which is joined after four bars by an accompanying guitar hammering away on a full chord. When a rolling drum line is introduced, the guitars coalesce into a funky rhythm that's soon accentuated by a sparsely rendered lead-guitar melody sloppily played in the upper register as if in shameless homage to Mott the Hoople. Singer Scott Phares, doubtless the "Mick" to Anthony's "Keith," comes slithering into a catcall, as he lasciviously recounts the nocturnal urban wet dream. The chorus cuts to half time with crashing symbols and groaning guitar lines powering the lyric, "I'm the king of the night time world / And you're my headlight queen!"

Aside from a serviceable guitar lead and gang vocals at the coda, the demo is represented well in the KISS version. After Stanley and Ezrin had at the lyrics and much of the arrangement, the tone of the song would evolve from a party-rock number about a back-alley hummer into a teenage ode to fantasy escape.

Ezrin and KISS ultimately decided to perform the song in D major, but the guitars, from the first squealing feedback note, are tuned a step down, to D-flat. Interestingly, the Hollywood Stars' version is tuned one step lower than the eventual *Destroyer* cut, which allowed KISS to make it brighter and more upbeat; the lyrics, when sung with the requisite Stanley bravado, appear—even allowing for Fowley's spicier lines—as a romantic salutation to a dreamscape seductress.

Peter Criss's thunderous pattern of sixteenth notes on the snare to eighth notes on hi-hat, while being true to the demo version, actually gives the midtempo number a quicker pace. "I think 'King of the Night Time World' was really great," Criss told *Goldmine* magazine in 1998. "I played the shit out of that. It was amazing if you listen to the drums, all the work in it is really brilliant. That was a lot of physical work and yet it was tasteful. The dynamics of that song were incredible. I felt like I was marching to a war and then all of a sudden I'm rockin' and rollin'."[20]

Ezrin arranged the verses of the song to accentuate Stanley's vocal by the conspicuous absence of bass. When coupled with the drums falling into a standard 4/4 time allowed ample room for Stanley's muscular vocal performance. Once again, as with "Detroit Rock City," a heavy emphasis on storyline plays out unimpeded, which wasn't entirely an Ezrin invention. As early as the first record, KISS perfected arrangements that although they thrashed along never impeded the vocals. This gave much of the band's most lasting material the kind of legs that would sell millions of records well into the next century.

Fowley's contribution to *Destroyer* doesn't end with "King of the Night Time World," as he was asked by Ezrin to add lyrics to a song he was sure was going to drive home his *The Wild One* theory of infusing a measure of vulnerability beneath the KISS machismo. Ezrin believed this was especially important for Stanley, who had fashioned his character as that of a master showman with puckered red lips to better connect with the glam side of The Act's barrage. This is the origin of "Do You Love Me?," which Ezrin had conceived and begun to work through the basic structure of before eventually co-writing it with Stanley and then shipping the concept off to Fowley to fill out the imagery.

Fowley: "Ezrin said, 'I have a title, "Do You Love Me?" It's about a groupie bothering a singer of a band and the singer questions her motives. I want you to write the lyric.' So I said, 'Well I have to work with Joan Jett. We're putting this girl band together and we're meeting a new bass player at the airport.' So he says to me, 'Co-publishing two songs on a KISS record will make you more money in your lifetime than anything the Runaways ever do.' Well, wasn't he correct. And so, we went down to the airport and I wrote the lyrics of 'Do You Love Me?' while we were waiting for the plane to land with Alison East, who later had a career in New York punk music and died of leukemia. Nice girl. She and Joan, Joan's mother, and I rode away and I had the lyric on a napkin. And I remember Joan's mom gave me the ballpoint pen. And she asked, 'What are you doing?' and I told her, 'I'm taking care of my pension.'"[21]

"We had finally hit upon something with vulnerability," Ezrin enthusiastically explains. "Paul Stanley going, 'Yeah, I'm beautiful and I'm a rock star and I got all this and I got all that'—kind of like the rappers of today. 'I drive this and I drive that and you ain't nothing, but . . . do you love me? I mean, do you *really* love me?'"[22]

"I love 'Do You Love Me?' because of what it says," Peter Criss told *Modern Drummer* magazine in 1999. "Do you love me, or all the cars, the money, and the rock and roll? That always got to me. I love the beginning, real Ringo Starr drumming."[23]

Sometime after his initial meeting with KISS and the first days of "boot camp," Ezrin escaped to Los Angeles to begin preliminary work on the songs that would wind up on Alice Cooper's second solo album, *Goes To Hell*, when he started fiddling around with an idea he'd discussed directly with Stanley. "I remember doing some writing on 'Do You Love Me?' when I was up in L.A. working with Alice Cooper," confirms Ezrin. "The guys weren't even around then. I don't know who started it, but we worked on it like that."[24]

"Ezrin had a rental up in Benedict Canyon in Beverly Hills," said Fowley. (According to Ezrin, it was around the corner from where the Tate murders occurred during the summer of sudden terror sparked by Charles Manson and his murderous "family" in 1969: "a Gothic living room with high windows and the piano right in the window."[25]) "I went up there the following Monday," Fowley continued, "and he said, 'Okay, I'm going to play the chords I've already come up with. I don't have the melody yet.'"[26]

"My recollection is that I came up with the chorus up in Los Angeles," says Ezrin. "I distinctly remember just playing those chords over and over and singing, 'Do you love me?' and just getting that feeling that I knew I was going to try and reach for in the song. I loved Kim's sensibilities, so I brought him in and the boys also contributed to the lyrics. I didn't word-count, but everybody played a role."[27]

"He put the words up on the piano and all of a sudden the lyrics sang themselves," Fowley concluded. "He played it, singing them, and when he was done, he turned to me and said, 'Congratulations, you've got a second song on a KISS album.' Wow. And then Paul got in there and messed around and added to that."[28]

"Quite a bit of 'Do You Love Me?' was written and brought in to us during *Destroyer*," said Stanley, in *Behind the Mask*. "I still think it's one of my favorite tracks. To me it's closer to some of the Mott the Hoople stuff in its glorification of rock 'n' roll, celebrating being a rock star and that kind of life."[29]

Straying from Ezrin's motivation to give him a more sensitive side, Stanley would expound on the bravado behind the verses that were inspired by Ian Hunter's work with Mott the Hoople in *The Box Set*. "They were storytellers, who sang these great rock 'n' roll songs, and seemed to really capture a moment of a life that I found myself wishing I could be a part of. A lot of the English bands had so much more flair and seemed to live such a more interesting rock and roll life than what American bands did."[30]

Ezrin: "I love how it goes, *but* then it sort of breaks down to 'Do you love me?' In my head, onstage, I could almost see Paul getting down on his knees and shouting, 'Do you love me?' I just visualized all the girls in the audience running to the front and throwing their bras at him, screaming, 'I love you,

Paul!' I just thought that was the thing that was going to open up the flood gates for us, that was going to really make them human enough to become romantic figures to the women in the audience."[31]

Even at its most sympathetic, "Do You Love Me?" still rocks: the thudding 4/4 backbeat, the crunching guitars, and bellowed vocals belie its true intention. Most of the song is filled with images of money, sex, and posing—even the woman in question whose love the narrator is beseeching seems to be obsessed with "the life," leaving narrator *and* listener in the dark as to who loves whom. For Ezrin, there was still one more step to go to uncover the hidden sensibility beneath *The Wild One* tough guy exterior he was aiming for. He knew how it scintillated for Alice Cooper months before on the tender ballad "Only Women Bleed," its themes of raw sympathy filled with weepy imagery. Ultimately, The Act's true vulnerability would reside in the most unlikely of places, written and sung by the most unlikely of people, all of which allowed the young producer free rein to provide *Destroyer* with one last unexpected turn.

11

And Suddenly... "Beth"

We were knocking the guy's wife: shut the fuck up, quit calling.
—PETER CRISS[1]

The two-minute-and-thirty-eight-second recording of what can best be described as a fragmented ditty begins hesitantly: the guitar player, nineteen-year-old Stan Penridge, lightly plucks out a two-chord progression, accompanied by the twenty-five-year-old Peter Criscuola tapping erratically on a conga; his voice, a three-in-the-morning after one-too-many cigarettes rasp, croaks, "Beck I hear ya callin', but I can't come home right now / Me and the boys been playin', but we just can't find that sound." The duet, although crude, is sweetly aching, a siren song to a lonely musician's lover. That is until a minor chord turns the sentiment to playful mockery. A second voice, that of Penridge, softer and barely on key, sings along, "Won't you wait an hour, and I'll run right home to you / I know you love complaining, but Beck what can I do?" A short break in momentum, whatever momentum there is, ushers in the same two haunting chords, made manifest by the warped muffle of the aged tape.

It is 1971, and Chelsea, whose mish-mosh sound is caught halfway between coffeehouse hootenanny and cool R&B, has bottomed out in a fruitless Decca Records deal and is breaking from a bevy of dreary bar gigs. The drummer and guitarist, close friends and budding composers, have taken a few minutes to finally lay down a goofy lyric hung on a rough melody Criscuola fashioned while enduring lengthy subway rides. The band had built upon it by sarcastically serenading guitarist Michael Brand in order to better bust his balls over what the members felt were pathetic excuses to keep his forever-complaining wife Becky at bay. "Beck I hear you callin', and you say you feel so bad / I know you need no doctor, but I know you need me bad," goes the second verse, with Criscuola now soulfully adding a tinge of regret to the voicing with a falsetto accent. The duo runs through the bridge/chorus structure twice more as the tape fades out with a refrain of the opening notes and Criscuola vamping background *ooohs*.

"'Beck' was written, almost word for word, from Mike Brand's responses to his wife's constant calls that interrupted our rehearsals," Penridge explained to Julian Gill in a 2000 interview, which appears in his www.KISSfaq.com compendium, *The Other Side of the Coin*. "It got to the point where I wrote down his remarks over a period of three or four days in what I called my 'wizard book.' It was merely a small notebook I carried to jot down silly sayings, sketch in, anything . . . to save ideas. If you look at the lyrics and view them as a henpecked hubby's remarks to his nagging wife, you'll see what I mean. Just pause after every sentence and pretend there's a bitch at the other end of the line."[2]

Penridge, something of a child prodigy, entered the New York School of Music at age seven and as a teenager was a fixture in the early-'60s Greenwich Village scene, honing a folk act opening for such New York staples as the Lovin' Spoonful and appearing on the same bill at the famed Café Wa? with Jimmy James & the Blue Flames, an early vehicle for the man the world would soon come to know as Jimi Hendrix. It was this Downtown scene that led Penridge to meet Peter Criscuola when auditioning for Chelsea, a band he knew from its repeated bookings at the East Village's Electric Circus. Criscuola, incensed over not being consulted on his eventual hiring, quit the band when Penridge came aboard. But in keeping with the drummer's celebrated mood swings, the angst faded, and the two became fast friends and songwriting partners.

Not long after Penridge joined the band, he and Criscuola bagged Chelsea for the short-lived trio Lips, which ironically received a tentative deal from Karma Sutra Records, headed then by one Neil Bogart. Myths abound of another rough band demo of the song being recorded at Bell Sound Studios—the very place KISS would enter nearly three years hence to record its debut album. But although Lips did indeed lay down demos in early 1972 at Bell Sound and RCA Studios, court records from a royalties case in 2002 between Penridge and KISS reveal that "Beck" was never officially recorded. Criss would later regale interviewers with what by all accounts was another of his famous tall tales of Bogart tossing Lips out of his office after hearing the crude 1971 recording of "Beck," a song that in five years would pull the very same Bogart and his struggling Casablanca Records from its financial morass and expand the KISS brand into realms of which even its fanatically confident members would never dare dream. As with most KISS tales, it's a good story without an ounce of truth. "'Beck' is one of the only songs we didn't perform for [Karma Sutra VP] Bob Reno or record during either session," remembered Penridge. "At that point it was still a 'joke song' or novelty tune."[3]

The "joke song" would register on the KISS radar in the late autumn of 1975 when, according to both Peter Criss and Gene Simmons's autobiographical accounts, Criss idly sang the long-lost melody while sharing a limo ride back to the hotel after a show in Flint, Michigan—which if true, would date it to November 17, a few weeks after part one of the *Destroyer* sessions commenced. Simmons immediately told Criss how much he liked it, but that he thought it would be more comprehensible or marketable if they changed it to "Beth," so as not to have anyone mistake it to be an ode to guitar hero Jeff Beck.

It is quite possible that—judging from the proximity of this key incident in the evolution of KISS within *Destroyer*'s expanding the brand beyond macho posing to more sensitive themes shrewdly developed by Bob Ezrin—Criss and certainly Simmons were inspired to never dismiss any musical idea, even something as seemingly corny as "Beck." Simmons enthusiastically suggested that Criss bring it to Ezrin, as the producer had recently helped him overcome similar reservations about his own folksy ballad. ("I didn't think it ['Great Expectations'] would be right for the group," Simmons admitted in 2001, in an interview for *The Box Set*. "A lot of the songs I had written stylistically veered more toward the Beatles and three-part harmonies, and only the tougher songs wound up on the record. But when Bob Ezrin was producing, it was clear this was going to be a record unlike any other KISS had recorded."[4])

As it was, until the autumn of 1975, no Peter Criss songs, Beatles-esque or otherwise, were ever considered for a KISS record. But with Ezrin's insistence on smoothing out the band's harder edges, and in searching for some heart behind the braggadocio, "Beck" was offered to the young producer, who describes its inclusion in terms akin to desperation. "There was a political thing where Peter had to have a song on the record, one song that he sang," Ezrin told Vancouver's Rock 101 *On the Record* radio show in 2010. "So we were going through material to come up with something that Peter could do that would suit the record [which possibly explains Ezrin's ill-suited pitch for the discarded 'Ain't None of Your Business']. I was just tearing my hair out, because just nothing was grabbing me. But there was this song, 'Beth,' that he had written with Stan Penridge, and it was different. It was more bouncy and kind of, I don't know, I can't even describe what it was. But anyway, I said, 'Do you mind if I take it home and play with it a little bit?' And they said fine. So I took it home and rewrote the lyric and the melody a little bit, slowed it down and turned it into this kind of love ballad and brought it back. Peter loved it. The other guys were kind of unsure about it, but I sort of said, 'Trust me, this is really going to be great and we're going to do it entirely differently.'"[5]

Criss expounds on Ezrin's enthusiasm in his memoir, recalling that when he first sang the song to Simmons in the limo, he was sure neither he nor Stanley would accept a ballad, but that the young producer "immediately understood it for what it was."⁶ Ezrin promptly told Criss he would get the New York Philharmonic to play on it, adding in no uncertain terms that it was going to be a hit. Criss figured it was a long shot and was not shy in telling Ezrin, whom he recalls merely smiling impishly. Later, according to Criss, Ezrin explained that even in its rawest form, he heard in the song a universal theme: "This little song says so much in so few words. 'I wish I was home, but I can't be.' Everyone will relate to that—businessmen, doctors."⁷

Ezrin was true to his word. The "Beth" he returned to the studio with resembled only the bare bones of the "Beck" of old, with just Criss's haunting melody fairly intact and some of Penridge's more sympathetic lyrics remaining. Otherwise, it was as much a Bob Ezrin piece as any he had worked on in all his years with Alice Cooper.

"I'm replaying it in my head, and I can see me at the piano and see what I was doing," Ezrin recalled, during interviews for this book. "It didn't take very long, because once I had that [opening piano] figure in my head, it sort of set the stage and the backing track began to write itself. My recollection is that it was done either over a weekend or over a couple of days. It didn't take very long at all. I think it was a weekend during the daytime in my apartment, so it must have been when we weren't rehearsing. And the chart itself is actually embedded in the piano part. Well, that musical bridge . . . if you think about it, I used it on fifty things! It was my signature approach. It was on 'Comfortably Numb'; Alice Cooper's 'Steven'; it's all over the place."⁸

The "Beck" Ezrin took to his Midtown apartment followed a rudimentary folk chord progression:—D major to G major to E minor, the chorus an A major to B minor bridge—played on acoustic guitar. Ezrin immediately shifted the song to piano and the more common key of C major and then completely altered the chord structure from a back-and-forth I–IV rock-and-roll-style progression to a classically influenced climb over the C major chord during the verses. This includes a C bass-note pedal, while the chords climb from C major to D minor to E minor. Immediately, even without the lush strings and brass accents that would be added later, this was a significant departure from anything a heavy-rock band would conjure. Although every measure shares the same melody, in the song's rawest, stripped-down form, Ezrin never repeats a chord in the verses.

"It really didn't match anything we were doing at all," Ezrin told KISS biographers David Leaf and Ken Sharp. "But I heard something in it and I took it home and translated it to the piano. I rewrote it a bit and thought about a kind of orchestral approach to it, in fact, I rewrote it substantially, and brought it back in and said, 'You mean something like this, Peter?' It was important that he felt that he was participating as much as possible. It was something I heard in another form, but it didn't become the 'Beth' you know and love until it went to my house for a while."[9]

For all intents and purposes, the "Beck" melody remains untouched, but with each pass the chords change beneath it: C major, D minor 7, C major 7, E minor, F major, G major over F, E minor, E sus, E major. Although the movement stays the same, two chords within it, the chord movements vary. The original composition has a I–IV–I–IV repetition, whereas Ezrin expanded "Beth" to ten different chord changes. The most interesting chord progression follows a scale down from A minor to G major after the verses into the song's first bridge, "Just a few more hours / And I'll be right home to you" (F major to E minor), followed by the next line, "Beth I hear you callin'," which changes to D major. This classical music technique—similar to the one used in "Great Expectations," the foundation of Ezrin's schooling and unflinching dedication to song structure—is anything but the rock norm. While what would usually follow would be a minor chord, here Ezrin chooses a major dominant-seventh chord, which briefly changes the tonal center to G major, before ending the phrase on an A-minor chord.

Within the essence of what has now gone from mocking folk ballad to gut-wrenching torch song, Ezrin's most stunning achievement is easy to overlook. It is subtle but not without purpose or musical note. The use of the shifting chord structure is a highly effective method to evoke powerful emotions in the listener—an undercurrent of sentiment that *Destroyer* assistant engineer Corky Stasiak calls "making music smile."[10] The understated addition of a piano line that follows the song's lasting hook, "Oh, Beth what can I do?," which wasn't musically available in the "Beck" demo, skillfully delivers its enduring tenderness: F major, G sus, C major; "Beth what can I do?"

Now a sweeping, epic ballad, opening solemnly with piano at the forefront of what begs to be a fully orchestrated arrangement, Criss and Penridge's novelty number had to sacrifice its references to an irritated girlfriend's complaints for a more tender ode to the pining of an impatient lover's lonely vigil. "Oh, Beth, what can I do?" the vocal now laments. The second, more wiseass verse, which impishly jabs at a nagging hypochondriac, is scratched in favor of a narrator's reflection on what the song's namesake—changed to "Beth," according to Ezrin, to remove any gender doubt—has told him. "You say you feel so empty, that a house just ain't a home / I'm always somewhere else, and you're always there alone" does more than merely erase immature ridicule: it pours gallons of syrupy pathos on what is unquestionably a full-scale sentimental opus. Ezrin's new lyrical epilogue, following an ornate musical interlude, is to be sung over a bed of strings and once again a single grand piano. Criss's soulful refrain, hardly reassuring, is almost wistful: "Beth, I know you're lonely, but I hope you'll be all right / 'Cause me and the boys will be playin'. . . ." A slight dramatic retard extends the pensive moment, until the vocal, drawn out in an anguished note, forlornly concludes with "all night."

Ezrin: "I started playing with the idea that's it's really his heart that was broken. He's not being the macho asshole; he's actually using that as a defense. But because their relationship is falling apart he regrets it desperately. He's hurt and he won't come home. So, anyway, we changed it into that. So I brought that in and everybody liked it. But I don't know if they believed it was going to be an important part of the record when I brought it back in. I think everybody kind of liked it and went, 'Okay, that's nice, there's Peter's thing, so now let's get back to the real record.' But I always felt there was something really magical about it. And I didn't care who wrote what. I never cared who wrote what. For me, what works is what counts. I didn't love a song simply because I had something to do with it. I had something to do with other songs. I had a lot to do with 'Detroit Rock City' and 'Shout It Out Loud' and 'Do You Love Me?,' but with 'Beth' there was just something about it that was just so perfect for the job at hand."[11]

To best drive the heartrending musical strains of such a composition, Ezrin turned to a man who first put his theatrical prowess to professional use by entrusting the musical balance of Toronto's Spring Thaw revue to his creative spirit. Years after Hugh Allan Macmillan plucked Robert Alan Ezrin from Toronto's folk underground to work as musical director for the burgeoning Nimbus 9 production company—which, after an unexpected encounter with the Alice Cooper group, catapulted his career—the young producer returned the favor, calling on Macmillan to arrange the pensive score for Lou Reed's dark heroine of *Berlin*. The roles now reversed, Macmillan flew to London at Ezrin's request to conduct the orchestra and sit in on piano. "This was Bob reaching back and grabbing someone who was at hand who had cabaret experience," says Macmillan. "It was an amazing exercise: pretty crazy, but it turned out to be an incredible album."[12]

Macmillan then joined the talented team of musicians that created the ambitious *Welcome to My Nightmare* the following year, once again scoring, arranging, and conducting the orchestral themes that brought Alice Cooper's nocturnal drama to life. Macmillan describes his and Ezrin's process: "Basically, I sat down with Bob after the basic tracks were done. In many of the situations Bob would be the primary arranger. He had some ideas where certain musical expressions would take place. He would actually even have the melodies worked out. It was up to me to orchestrate it, but all of those elements would have been discussed. So we would have a private session in which all this stuff got together, and then I would go away and score the stuff and the backing band would get hired and record it and hopefully it worked out as Bob had envisioned it. A lot of cases it did and a few cases it might not; some of that would end up on the cutting room floor. Generally you record more than you actually intend to survive the mix."[13]

For "Beth," Ezrin took the song's basic musical structure to Macmillan at Nimbus 9 in Toronto, so they could quickly begin their collaboration. By then, he had decided that the Beethoven-saturated elements of "Great Expectations" also needed orchestral accompaniment.

Macmillan: "The first thing that was done in preparation for getting together was I'd prepare lead sheets for the songs that Bob wanted to add orchestral input. In the case of the two songs on *Destroyer*, he sent me a tape containing the finished two tracks with a rough working vocal that I would transcribe into a rough score, so we'd have in front of us the natural structure of the song musically. Then he would often sit at the piano and play a line or a musical phrase and go right through the song, indicating where he thought the orchestral input ought to be, and he would frequently sing the actual notes he wanted. I would be suggesting orchestral colors that would help the thing to express what I thought he was trying to express and I'd notate them right into the sketch. At the end of the session, we'd have a filled in musical outline. Then, after Bob scuttled back to New York, I would go off and score the thing for orchestra."[14]

While Ezrin leaned on Macmillan's expertise and input, the veteran arranger insists that there was little doubt how much the young producer had already worked out in the original composition of the song. "Bob was really doing the arranging work at that time," says Macmillan. "In a lot of cases, Bob was really the silent co-arranger, and my role was co-arranging and orchestrating. There were numerous occasions where Bob was entitled to take the credit for arranger or co-arranger, but you generally try and keep the credits as simple as possible. I think Bob thought that ethically it was better to keep it simple and perhaps not have his name overexposed on the album credits."[15]

The formal but fluid Ezrin/Macmillan collaboration was just another example of *Destroyer*'s selfless, all-for-one ambiance. Ironically, as much of a departure as "Beth" is in the KISS pantheon, it is everything *Destroyer* was to be, and what it inevitably became: a full and complete creative alliance, which meant sacrifice and compromise, that all ideas were welcomed and traded openly, as in Stanley's disappointment over Simmons's taking the lead on his "God of Thunder" or Simmons feeling fleeced of the signature guitar opening for "Detroit Rock City," or the three segments of chord progressions absorbed into "Flaming Youth," the latter being as much an entire band composition as had existed before in KISS. This was The Act in full swing: commitment to the cause, a hazy mist hovering over proceedings about which song or lick or bass part or drum signature or lyric belonged to whom. To claim individual taste or personal gain over the group was never the KISS way, and *Destroyer*—and specifically the inclusion of "Beth"—was the culmination of this edict.

Absent of guitar or any instrumental solo, the middle-eight section, beautifully arranged by Ezrin and Macmillan, repeats the intro/outro along with the chorus/bridge part into an orchestrated interlude before the dramatic tag line returns, this time brush-stroked with single-note violin and viola lines classically balanced by counter-melody cellos changing key from C major to A minor into a crescendo. Enter the horns (trumpets, trombones, tubas, French horns), accentuating the hook line with a flourish.

Macmillan: "Bob wouldn't necessarily pinpoint the instrumentation of a musical line that he had hummed and wished to be written down. That would frequently be suggestions coming from me; that the strings could take that line, or there could be a secondary line in the brass, or whatever. This was all very collaborative, but then again this is generally the pattern that a lot of producers worked on. The concept is there with the producer or the musical director, and that concept could be developed as the tracks are being developed."[16]

The Act now had its sensitive side. "Beth" rounded out an eclectic lineup of songs to both separate the agonies and failures of past sessions and provide the soundtrack to superstardom. With the inclusion of this song's anguished plea for connection from the lofty heights of fantasy, *Destroyer* would now successfully elevate KISS from mere rock band, featuring as it did thematic tales of youthful exuberance and melodramatic consequence, signature theme songs for the Demon and the Star Child, expanding on the anthemic nature of "Rock and Roll All Nite," and laying the groundwork for imagination and camp.

It was now time to finally put it all down for posterity; leave the costumes, makeup, photo shoots, clamoring rock media, arenas, cheering crowds, exploding stages, and theatrics behind for the solitary environs of the dreaded studio—KISS's final conquest. Next stop for the new stars of rock would be the most state-of-the-art recording space in world.

12

The Palette

I lived in there.
—Jay Messina[1]

Upon receiving word that the KISS camp and Casablanca had settled and he would be retained as the producer on the suddenly crucial follow-up to *Alive!*, Bob Ezrin began assembling his team, specifically engineers for whom he felt a working comfort and who, in turn, were comfortable with his methods, which by the autumn of 1975 had become something of legend. "I was known as the assistant killer," Ezrin states emphatically. "They would send assistants on my stuff, 'cause I basically chewed them up and spit them out, worked them harder than anybody had worked them, was more demanding and kept them on their toes more than some of the other clients."[2]

"I remember distinctly the first time I met Bob," recalls heralded sound engineer Rod O'Brien, whose list of credits includes Aerosmith, Alice Cooper, Grand Funk Railroad, Patti Smith, Talking Heads, and Cyndi Lauper, among others. "I was assisting Shelly Yakus and he introduced me—it might have been on one of Alice's records, but Bob was like, 'Hi, I'm Bob Ezrin, you screw up my tapes and I'll kill ya.' I went, 'Okay.'"[3]

Most importantly, the young producer homed in on a studio that would provide him and his team an infinite palette of aural possibilities: a room in which the independent phase of his career had been launched. In New York, a mere eight blocks from what he describes as his "home ground," was the legendary Record Plant on West Forty-Fourth Street between Eighth and Ninth Avenues, in an area of Manhattan known as Hell's Kitchen. It was in the spacious Studio A where Ezrin worked his magic for the Alice Cooper group's most compelling and popular albums, *School's Out* and *Billion Dollar Babies*, and where he recorded overdubs and mixed Lou Reed's *Berlin*.

"The first thing I discovered while working at the Plant was that everybody there was feverishly experimental," Ezrin recalls. "Everybody was trying new stuff. Everybody was building or trying out every new piece of gear that was ever invented. In the RCA Studios, where we had worked before, everything was quite traditional, even down to the fact that the engineers belonged to a union, and we had to live by union rules. At the Record Plant, everybody was living out on the bleeding edge. All the studios were equipped with an eclectic collection of high-end classic gear along with new-fangled stuff, custom-made stuff, and things made by small but cutting-edge manufacturers at the time like Peter Flickinger and Roger Mayer, so every room had this jungle of cables and a landscape filled with exciting machinery and technology, and some machines that I had never seen before. It was just the most amazing playground for somebody who was just beginning to come into their own, and at that stage of my career, I didn't know anything, therefore I didn't know you *couldn't* do anything. I was just too stupid to know what you shouldn't do, so I just did it."[4]

Ezrin had first come to the Record Plant when the Alice Cooper group had moved its operations out of the Detroit/Chicago rock scene to be closer to New York City—in order, in Ezrin's words, to "bust out."[5]

"It was decided they would move the whole operation to an estate in Fairfield, Connecticut and, of course, we had to move our recording facilities from Chicago. Basically, I had set up the whole Alice Cooper thing for Jack Richardson. I had recorded these guys in the studio where he liked to record with the engineer he always used, Brian Christian, whom I loved, and so I did what Jack did. But when the decision was made for Alice Cooper to go to New York, we had to find a base for us to work. I had done some work before at A & R Studios, really, really early on—perhaps right after *Love It to Death*. I produced an album by a guy named David McCue and we did it at A&R Studios, Phil Ramone's place. I worked with an engineer called Dave Greene, and all of the Record Plant guys came out of A&R, so I knew about these ex-A&R guys. Not sure who was the person that suggested we go to the Record Plant when the whole Alice Cooper move went about, but that's where we went."[6]

Once there, in the early months of 1972, Ezrin began the *School's Out* sessions, which challenged and inspired him as never before. "For me, that was a physical, emotional and philosophical transition from being Jack Junior to actually becoming Bob," he recalls. "I was out of the environment that was Jack's and was in a place that they didn't do things the way he did things, working with people that he had not worked with before. So this was really my growth moment as a producer and my matriculation from being Jack's protégé to being myself."[7]

Beginning his work on *School's Out* with new Record Plant owner and top engineer Roy Cicala—who according to Ezrin had a penchant for routinely disappearing, which in turn forced him to push his abilities and fire his imagination by mere circumstance. "Roy was a real character and really eccentric," Ezrin continues. "If Roy suddenly got distracted or got an idea that he needed to pursue or he was hungry or he was just bored, he would go off to the bathroom and he wouldn't come back. Suddenly there you'd be in a session with a band sitting behind a console with faders and machines and no engineer! And every time that happened, it would force me to sit behind the console myself and push faders and turn knobs and try things and plug things in, because there was no Roy to do it for me.

"I learned a huge amount on the job during the making of that one album. I would say *School's Out* was probably, from a career point of view, the watershed moment for me. I was forced, in the making of that record, in that environment, to find my way around the technology and use it to do stuff that I was imagining, which sounds easy, but it's not so easy to be looking at a bunch of knobs and switches and nobody tells you what they do. But it was also great. I had to discover by using my intuition. I found out that if you push a button nobody dies, so I was just pushing buttons! I pushed whatever button I could to see what it did and every once in awhile I'd go, 'Whoa! Yeah, that's what I want!' And that's how I kind of found my way around the instrument that is the studio, and all of that was happening in Studio A. So that console, that array of outboard gear, those particular machines, that room—the way it was set up acoustically, that was the sort of birthing ground for me as an individual producer. From that point on I wanted to do everything in that room that I could. The Record Plant was the place where I felt the most comfortable and confident about what I was hearing and knew that what was coming out of those speakers is what I intended."[8]

By the autumn of 1975, when Ezrin was preparing for the *Destroyer* sessions, the Record Plant was *the* state-of-the-art recording studio, and also a template for what would soon be considered a standard recording experience among popular music's elite. Before the Record Plant opened in 1968 and began offering living room–type comforts—mood lighting, soft interior designs, and even a Jacuzzi—artists were expected to create in cold, starkly white environs surrounded by stringent baffles cutting across expansive open rotundas. Restrictive vocal and dubbing booths held limited communication through impersonal intercom systems also added to the drably oppressive factory vibe. The new age of rock, along with the burgeoning album-as-statement landscape, demanded a more intimate space: a home away from home to alleviate the pressures that come from the continuous daily grind of recording at all hours for weeks on end. This new age also expanded the range of sonic experimentation, therefore requiring a higher level of quality in the studio's equipment. Providing the best devices for these experiences was essential to the process. Co-founder Gary Kellgren and businessman Chris Stone understood these challenges. Kellgren used his years of experience behind dozens of studio consoles to design and build his Record Plant from the ground up.

Grammy Award–winning producer Bob Margouleff (Stevie Wonder, Billy Preston, Devo) described Kellgren's Record Plant origins in a 1977 *New Times* piece. "Gary opened up a regular studio, with like a two-track taping system, the early days of stereo. But he was never satisfied. All the studios were bare rooms with green paint and linoleum floors . . . it was like making music inside a hospital ward. So finally, in 1967, he got together with Chris Stone, who was working for Revlon, and this heiress to the Revlon fortune. Stone was the businessman, Gary was the engineer, and the lady was the bread. When they built the first Record Plant, it was like a spaceship."[9]

By the time he'd dreamed up his picture-perfect studio deluxe, Kellgren was already known as an instinctive technological innovator. Advancing on the original late-'60s eight-track methods to up to twelve individual tracks of recording, Kellgren also expanded upon the EMI Studios famous "flanging" or ATD (automatic double-tracking) technique while introducing into the mainstream the elements of "phasing"—the art of recording one instrument played slightly out-of-sync on top of another to create a new melodic effect.

Heavyweight acts such as the Velvet Underground, Jimi Hendrix, Sly & the Family Stone, Frank Zappa, Stevie Wonder, Barbara Streisand, Rod Stewart, and Neil Diamond, as well as several ex-Beatles, all spent time at the Record Plant. Major sound mixing for the film and album of *Woodstock* and later the *Concert for Bangladesh* was completed there. Certainly, some of the most important and successful albums of the era were realized at the Record Plant, including Jimi Hendrix's masterwork, *Electric Ladyland* (1968); the Don McLean epic *American Pie* (1971); the Allman Brothers' *Brothers and Sisters* (1973); the New York Dolls' debut (1973); Bruce Springsteen's breakthrough, *Born to Run* (1975); Aerosmith's tour de force *Toys in the Attic* (1975); as well the aforementioned signature Alice Cooper records. In the ensuing years, Patti Smith, Cheap Trick, Blondie, David Bowie, Iggy Pop, Queen, Cyndi Lauper, the Beastie Boys, and Guns N' Roses, among many other top acts, would record seminal works there. It was the place where John Lennon spent his last hours on earth, on December 8, 1980, mixing down a single for his wife, Yoko Ono, in the very same room where, nine years earlier, he'd recorded the brilliant *Imagine* (1971).

The Record Plant's sound and atmosphere became so popular that Kellgren sold his interest in the New York location to TeleVision Communications in 1969 and moved his operation to Los Angeles, before opening a third studio three years later in Sausalito. Among many other records laid down for profit and posterity were Stevie Wonder's *Songs in the Key of Life*, Billy Joel's signature *Piano Man*, the Eagles' haunting *Hotel California*, and arguably the '70s' biggest smash, Fleetwood Mac's *Rumors*. And as the studio attracted the most compelling talent of the day, so did it produce some of the finest engineers. Among the famous roll call was Shelly Yakus (the Band's *Music from Big Pink*; John Lennon's *Imagine, Walls and Bridges*, and *Rock and Roll*; Van Morrison's *Moondance*; Alice Cooper's *School's Out* and *Billion Dollar Babies*) and Roy Cicala, who worked with everyone from Frank Sinatra to Patti Smith, and in 1972 became the New York location's owner and proprietor. An impressive list of perennial studio wizards got their start in the Record Plant's heyday, including the incomparable musical entrepreneur Jimmy Iovine (Bruce Springsteen's *Born to Run*, Patti Smith's *Horses*, Tom Petty & the Heartbreakers' *Damn the Torpedoes*, Meatloaf's *Bat Out of Hell*, Dire Straits' *Making Movies*, Stevie Nicks *Belladonna*) and Jack Douglas (Alice Cooper's *Muscle of Love*; Aerosmith's *Get Your Wings, Toys in the Attic*, and *Rocks*; John Lennon's *Double Fantasy*) who rose from general custodial duties to one of the most influential producers of his time.

"What I loved about the Record Plant [was that] it was very much from the A&R tradition," Bob Ezrin explains. "It was a teaching studio. When you got a job at A&R, you went in to a kind of apprentice system and you worked in every single department within that building. You started off in the library, then you went to master, and then you went to assisting, and so on. You went all the way through the system before you were allowed to become an engineer. And the same was true at the Record Plant, so people who came to work there had gone through a very similar system. The assistants all had to go through every stage of the process and prove their mettle each step along the way if they were going to survive and actually get a chance to sit in the main chair behind the console. There were assistants, junior assistants, and then there were more senior assistants who'd be in the room with you and you could turn to them and say, 'Take over!' and they would sit in the main chair at the console and do some engineering for you."[10]

Not the least of these master musical craftsmen were Jay Messina and Corky Stasiak, both of whom were at the top of their field by the autumn of 1975, and would play major roles in the making of *Destroyer*.

Jay Messina, while being no stranger to the rock scene, having spent the previous two of his then ten years of professional session work at the board for Aerosmith's *Get Your Wings* (1974) and the band's breakout release, *Toys in the*

Attic (1975), worked in a wide array of musical genres. Pop/rockers Three Dog Night, folk icon Judy Collins, and the mixed rhythm-and-blues sound of Booker T. & the MGs are among the contrasting artists that fill his extensive resume.

It is a resume that began quite abruptly in 1966 when, at twenty-four, the day before he was due to start a quality-control job testing meters after an extensive education in technical engineering at the RCA Institutes, the Brooklyn native received a last-minute offer from a friend to become a music engineer for $25 a week and the promise of "a lot of fun."[11] Quitting a job he never actually held the very next day on a "gut feeling," Messina headed instead to Don Elliott Productions studio on Sixth and Fortieth in Manhattan.[12] There he was privileged to work on one of only five one-inch eight-track machines in the world at the time, purchased by the studio directly from Les Paul, the godfather of modern tracking, in addition to his renowned guitar ingenuities. "My entrance into engineering was odd for the time," Messina recalled, during interviews for this book. "The norm for 1966 was three to four multitrack recording, and I'm working on original, rare, and prestigious equipment, and my first session is Ravi Shankar playing Indian music for a 16-millimeter film that we had to set up in the control room. They're loading in the studio, hanging pictures and lighting incense; it's all very exotic, middle-'60s stuff. So the session's over, and Don tells me there is a doctor that's sponsoring the recording and he would be paying me, and when I looked at the check it was signed *Timothy Leary*. That was my introduction to studio work!"[13]

Messina's evolution was not only eclectic but vast, and involved working solo in every avenue of studio duties: taping ad jingles, mastering albums onto eight-track tape format, and splicing radio spots, as well as adding vocal overdubs to movie soundtracks for master producer Quincy Jones and recording basic tracks for an array of Motown artists. After a year, Messina moved on to cutting masters at A&R Studios, a state-of-the-art studio run by famed producer, Phil Ramone. "That was a key move for me," says Messina. "I learned all the problems with a mix, whether phasing issues or bass modulation, when it's set to be put on a disc."[14]

Between mastering, Messina expanded the art of recording jingles and editing radio spots, but at the encouragement of Ramone he also spent his weekends recording a variety of bands that came through the studios. Messina even offered free studio time to his friends' bands for the opportunity to cut his sonic teeth. This led to working with soon-to-be stalwart studio musicians like drummer Steve Gadd and bassist Tony Levin, among others. "Musicians are the best salesmen for engineers," says Messina. "They go from studio to studio passing on the word of your work, and if it's good, you're in demand."[15]

Demand and reputation, along with talented colleagues like Shelly Yakus and Roy Cicala having left the mostly sterile environs of A&R, allowed Messina to move onto the Record Plant, where he would eventually thrive.

A twenty-six-year-old Messina walked into Studio A for the first time in the autumn of 1971 and was immediately mesmerized by the Record Plant's exotic décor and ambiance. His first impression was formed the week the Who happened to be working out the basic tracks for what would soon be the remarkable *Who's Next*. "It was like walking into the coolest nightclub," Messina recounts. "The lights were all dim and it was a totally different vibe from anything I had worked in to that point. The monitors were turned all the way up, so much so I could hear breathing as vocals were being rehearsed. It was very impressive. It was the cool place to be. I knew instantly that was where *I* wanted to be."[16]

The ultimate craftsman, Messina quickly focused on the Record Plant's contrasting environment to that of the more stridently professional A&R Studios: "A&R was turning out big-name records in those days; the rooms had a very lively sound. The place was brightly lit, and the overall operation was *efficiency first*: the staff and the acts were expected to be on time. Therefore the atmosphere was geared toward service. We were mostly doing commercials for Madison Avenue, and also movie scores. The Record Plant was literally *a record plant*—it was about making records. So there was some adjusting to the whole laid-back atmosphere, but mostly I had the hardest time adjusting to the sound of the place. There were rugs everywhere, sort of where 'the sound' was going back then, very dead and dry, which is not what I was used to."[17]

Soon Messina attuned his ear to the Record Plant milieu and realized his days juggling a disparate series of aural tasks would inevitably lead to a steady career making records. His years of wearing many hats—sometimes all at once—proved invaluable to his ultimate destiny. "When I was at A&R the stigma for engineers was that the cool thing to be doing was to be making records," he recalls. "Most of the engineers were always bitching about one lousy job or another, but I didn't approach it that way. I was always into what I was doing. I was present for every moment I was in the studio. The exercise for me was, if I had two minutes to get a drum sound and I complained for thirty seconds I now only have a minute and a half. And there was also the editing that you learn working on radio jingles: if they tell you it's a second over, you have to lose that second without any apparent notice. The bonus of all this was when I started doing rock records, I appreciated knowing how to get a drum sound quickly. Sure, most times it was okay to take your time getting a drum sound, but sometimes, when the drummer is ready to perform or the singer is ready to sing and you're not ready to press record and it's going to take you twenty minutes, and say the singer suddenly doesn't feel like singing after those twenty minutes, you blew it."[18]

"That's how they did things," Bob Ezrin adds. "Jack Richardson, my boss, taught me in a very similar way. Also, he was very close to Phil Ramone, and both of them have passed sadly; they were both great men who have a great deal to do with my being here in the first place. Phil and Jack were very close and had similar ethics; basically, you had to know everything, you had to be on your toes; you don't get it right they send you back to do it again over and over and over until you do. It's really kind of a baptism by fire. So I got taught that way and I felt that it was really good. It was strong, and led to a respect for the system, it led to a depth of knowledge, a confidence you get from being put through boot camp that you didn't get if you were dropped in there from a school or something like that."[19]

Ezrin was first introduced to Messina during the Alice Cooper group's *School's Out* sessions, and explains how working with the engineer would become an organic tag-team experience. "The interesting thing about the Record Plant was there were these groups of engineers that were the superstars; there was Roy, Jay, Shelly Yakus, and a couple of others at the time that I didn't work with, so I didn't really know them very well. In hiring Roy to do *School's Out*, it came with the understanding that this is the guy who owns the studio—he's the chief engineer and there will be times when he's not available, so other people will be coming and going on the session, which was fine with me. By the time Roy had left me alone a few times in that room, I got to the point where that room and I were becoming really good friends, so whoever came in to do engineering, I felt comfortable with, simply because we were in *that room*."[20]

Soon after *School's Out*, Messina assisted the young producer during intense overdubbing sessions for Lou Reed's *Berlin*. Ezrin, whom Messina described as "being around the Record Plant a lot in those days,"[21] was acting in the capacity of executive producer for Aerosmith's second record, *Get Your Wings*, in 1974 when he tagged Jack Douglas as lead engineer, which essentially meant becoming Aerosmith's resident hands-on producer. "Jack Douglas came in as an assistant and was working on a bunch of stuff," says Ezrin. "I love Jack and had an instant sense of report with the guy, and I developed a real respect for him when I was unable to kill him."[22]

By the time Aerosmith came calling, Douglas and Messina were already fast friends, and according to Messina had coalesced into a solid studio team. Douglas was invited on several of Messina's projects and subsequently flipped roles to support the Aerosmith sessions. The duo became the architects for an impressive run of '70s hit albums for the Boston band, solidifying the engineer's rock pedigree and his inclusion in the *Destroyer* sessions.

"It was very much a family, and very much a group of people who were excited about working with each other and together were on this adventure as a team," says Ezrin. "I never got the sense that one of them was trying to push the other aside or there was anything in the way of jealousy or resentment from one of them toward the other. They all seemed to be good friends and all the junior people were incredibly respectful of senior guys, 'cause the senior guys were really amazing. I mean, the house engineers in that studio were as good as or better than anybody I've worked with my entire career. And they came with the studio!"[23]

Corky Stasiak was another young, up-and-coming engineer anxious to find a spot on the Record Plant roster. "I would walk over fire and hot coals just to run the tape machine for Jay Messina," he says, "because he was the greatest engineer of his day."[24]

In 1969, long before he knew of Messina's work, Stasiak had come across a photo of his musical hero Jimi Hendrix with Record Plant founder Garry Kellgren in *Time* magazine. He immediately applied for a job there, but was told there was no room at the inn. Having already carved out a productive career at National Recording Studios in Midtown Manhattan—where, fresh out of high school at the tender age of seventeen he first performed menial tasks such as running errands, fetching coffee, and sweeping up while hoping to network a record deal for his burgeoning rock band—he was thrown right into the professional deep end when, after just three months, the entire engineering staff was sacked. Soon, he was recording high-profile movie soundtracks, including *The Producers* with Mel Brooks, as well as the directorial debuts of Paul Newman (*Rachael Rachael*) and Woody Allen (*Take the Money and Run*). But like Messina at A&R Studios down the street, the bulk of Stasiak's time was spent recording advertising jingles for the studio's main clientele, Madison Avenue.

As the only young "longhair" at National Recording Studios, as he puts it, Stasiak gained the reputation as "the cool kid," energetic and willing to do most anything.[25] This led him to his first rock-and-roll assignment: working with singer/songwriter and future studio wizard Todd Rundgren's first band, the Nazz, as they demoed the song "Open Your Eyes." Ironically that song would figure into KISS lore, as the opening riff was lifted note-for-note on a track from *Dressed to Kill* called "Love Her All I Can."

Getting a taste for laying down the rock-and-roll sound and having been rebuffed by the Record Plant, Stasiak began the '70s as the main assistant engineer at the newly christened Hit Factory, which was being designed and built by Brill Building veteran Jerry Ragovoy with royalties earned from "Time Is on My Side" (written under the pseudonym Norman Meade), which became one of the first hits for the Rolling Stones, and a little later "Piece of My Heart," made famous by Janis Joplin. After hearing a demo recording Stasiak produced one weekend, Ragovoy beamed, "Hey man, you really got ears!"[26] It's no surprise then that, mirroring Messina's versatility, Stasiak worked as one of the main engineers for an incredible run of hits for folkie Jim Croce (his "woo!" heralds the boogie-woogie piano opening to Croce's smash 1973 hit, "Bad, Bad Leroy Brown").

Around this time, Messina crossed paths with Stasiak when he was invited in to work a weekend session at the Hit Factory. Although he was not present for the recording, Stasiak was instructed by Ragovoy to "check out Messina's handiwork."[27]

"When I put that tape on the two-track machine, I had never heard bottom like that before at *any* studio," Stasiak raves. "At that moment, I thought, 'This is what music should sound like' and I became his number one fan, looking up his records and each one was just amazing. This guy had such control on the bottom end. Once I heard that tape, man, I said, 'I've never heard a better engineer in my life, that's the guy I want to be like. I've got to find a way to meet this guy and work with this guy.'"[28]

He would soon get his wish, for in May of 1973 Ragovoy had to let Stasiak go, ostensibly for financial reasons, but while also whispering, "I'm holding you back as an engineer."[29] Keeping his Record Plant dreams alive, come autumn Stasiak heard that a night maintenance man at the Hit Factory was spending his days upgrading the studio for Westlake Audio. Inquiring about an opening—and, much to his surprise, quickly getting an interview with studio manager Ed Germano and new owner Roy Cicala—he was quickly asked when he could start, to which he enthusiastically replied, "I'll start right now!"[30]

Over the ensuing months, Stasiak found himself in awe of the allure of the Record Plant. "I had been to a few studios in my time, but when I walked into the Record Plant and saw the kind of operation they had, my tongue was on the floor. These weren't just speakers hanging on chains from the ceiling. These were molded into the walls with black walnut wood and big Ubangi lips as midranges, and a beautiful high-tech console, two or three headphone cues. I looked around and said, 'Holy shit, this is the big time. I made it!'"[31]

"Making it" meant engineering Bruce Springsteen's seminal album *Born to Run* (1975), which Stasiak vividly recalls as the Boss's "do or die album."[32] The sessions' lead engineer was the now-iconic musical entrepreneur and master producer Jimmy Iovine, who came by way of Alice Cooper (according to Bob Ezrin, one of Iovine's first chores was assisting him) and who would, like Roy Cicala with the young Ezrin, sometimes disappear for up to a week. "I jumped at the chance to assist, because I loved Springsteen and I loved Jimmy," recalls Stasiak. "Jimmy was cool and always fun to be around, but he was easily bored, and I always knew that he would give me a call one day and say, 'Corky, I can't make it today, you be the engineer.' And I don't know how he got away with it, but Jimmy, who wanted to be an engineer and got handed this big project, started taking days off here and there, and he assured those guys that I could handle it. Springsteen spent a year making that album, so we had to jump between four different studios!"[33]

The same year, Iovine tapped Stasiak to assist him on John Lennon's *Walls and Bridges* (1974) and promptly left for a three-week trip to California, once again placing the main engineering responsibilities firmly in Stasiak's lap. He responded by helping to create one of the most memorable studio moments in all of rock history: the famous duet between new megastar Elton John and the ex-Beatle on Lennon's funky "Whatever Gets You Through the Night." It would soon become the #1 hit Elton had predicted it would be, prompting a stunned Lennon to make a walk-on appearance at his Thanksgiving concert to grand applause, and, most importantly for Lennon, reuniting him with his beloved Yoko Ono, with whom he had been estranged for over a year.

Throughout it all, Stasiak bent an ear whenever he heard that his hero, Jay Messina, was in the building or might be working a session. He would sneak in to write down all of Messina's settings, trying to catch a glimpse of the techniques that had so enthralled him months before. But nothing could have prepared him for their first session together, which ironically came on the day the twenty-seven-year-old first encountered the looming presence of Bob Ezrin.

"I was scared shitless of Bob because of the stories I heard about him taking assistant engineers and chewing them up for breakfast and spitting them out," remembers Stasiak. "Getting them fired, embarrassing them in front of a room full of people. Bobby was really into coke and cognac and cigars, and he was *the boy wonder*. I thought he was like five years older than me, and it turns out he was two years younger! He was a concert pianist and had a super ego, and rightly so, 'cause he was a talented motherfucker."[34]

Deep in professional worship for Jay Messina and duly intimidated by Ezrin, Stasiak was called to participate in a weekend session for the '50s-style doo-wop band Sha Na Na (*Hot Sox*, 1974), a project Ezrin had handed to his protégé Jack Douglas prior to his stint on Aerosmith's *Get Your Wings*. This would mark the first time the team of Ezrin, Messina and Stasiak—the core of *Destroyer*'s aura and sound—were all present at a session. "Jack Douglas was producing and Jay Messina was the lead engineer and I was just helping out; running the tape, doing punch-ins, doing edits, setting up microphones, breaking down the studio, that kind of stuff," Stasiak recalls. "I was just in my glory, and I distinctly remember Jack Douglas coming over to me and saying, 'You better be on your toes, because this guy Bob Ezrin doesn't suffer fools lightly, and if you fuck up, he's gonna chew you up and spit you out. He doesn't take shit from anybody, and you better keep your eyes on him and when he tells you to stop the tape—if he just gives you the finger to hold the tape—you *fucking* hold it. And I don't want to hear a peep out of you, because if you say something while he's talkin', he's gonna cut you to ribbons.'"[35]

With Messina at the console, holding back laughter, Stasiak nervously assured Douglas that he'd worked enough big sessions to keep his head down and dutifully fulfill his chores. "Well, Bob walks in," Stasiak continues. "He looks at me and goes, 'Who's this guy?' And Jack says, 'Oh, that's Corky Stasiak.' And Bob goes, 'Stasiuk?' Jack corrects him, repeating my name. And Bob looks at me and says again, 'Stasiuk? Do you know Vic Stasiuk? Vic Stasiuk is my hero.' I didn't know at the time that Bob's Canadian and loves ice hockey, and Vic Stasiuk was his childhood idol. Thank God my name was Stasiak! From then on he would yell out, 'Vic! Stop the tape!' And he and I got along famously the whole weekend."[36]

Bob Ezrin agrees. "I connected with Jack better than anyone. I connected with Corky, too. Corky wasn't quite on the same level as Jack at the time. He was younger. But I loved Jack and Corky was right there."[37]

The duo would again collaborate with Jack Douglas in 1975 to complete Aerosmith's breakout album, *Toys in the Attic*, with which Stasiak felt like he had finally been "accepted into that group."[38] Ezrin then tabbed him to help guide Alice Cooper's solo project, *Welcome to My Nightmare*.

Ezrin would return once more to Messina and Stasiak, however, to help him supply KISS with the time, efforts, and talents Bill Aucoin and the band felt had been missing during its previous studio experiences. Stasiak recalls Ezrin giving him a pep talk while painting a desperate scenario. "Bobby told me, 'Listen, I've got something in the works here with this group, KISS. They're about to get dropped from their label. It's a disco label, Casablanca, and they don't know what they have. I've seen these guys: they put on a great show but they don't sell records. These guys are so theatrical, and they need a big sound and a big production to suit them, and we're gonna give it to 'em. They're on the balls of their ass. They're so depressed. When they come in, let's really make 'em feel good.' So Bobby was masterminding the whole thing. He said, 'We got to make them a great album. There's a great album in that band, I'm tellin' ya.'"[39]

"At that time, I would have said yes even before the end of the sentence," Messina recalls of being asked by Ezrin to be lead engineer on the KISS project. "If I thought it was going to be fun, I was there! Working with Bob made it appealing, and doing a KISS record was certainly exciting. I knew there would be a lot of glamour. I definitely jumped on it."[40]

"I was so happy to work with Bobby on that project," Stasiak concludes. "Being in the room with Ezrin and Messina—I would have paid *them* to be in that room!"[41]

With a hungry and talented recording team in place, Ezrin prepared to enter Studio A, his home away from home, to take the songs the band had rehearsed under his tutelage and unleash the aural elements of The Act to realize the ultimate KISS album.

"Sweet Pain"

My love will drive you insane

A chiming waltz of sinuous twelve-string electric and acoustic guitars dance above a staccato feast of Bach piano, teasing the ear before being abruptly interrupted by an ascending baritone, "Ahhhhhhh!" A salutation to unspeakable pleasure exhaled by a sinister rogue. The eager rhythm section joins the sonic orgy, accompanying Fellini hallucinations clad in chains and aroused by the lash.

> *My leathers fit tight around me*
> *My whip is always beside me*
> *You want the same thing every day*
> *I'll teach you love a different way*
> *You'll learn to love me and my sweet pain*

The dark dungeon master is joined by his concubines, whose soulful harmonies may soften his exterior, but whose sharp tongue is sweetened by the nectar of honey-dipped amore:

> *My love will drive you insane*
> *Sweet pain, my love will drive you insane*

This paradoxical proposition hints at forbidden temptations; an underlying lust cannot be quelled. Hesitancy is no longer an option. Discretion is abandoned. Secrets are revealed.

> *And pain has got its reason*
> *And if you don't stop your teasin', baby*
> *I'm gonna show you now*
> *You'll get your lovin' anyhow, anyhow*
> *And you'll get to love me and my sweet pain*

The accompaniment turns; the band rumbles forth as if no longer seducing but getting on with its business. The lead guitar screams its pleasure, shredding away inhibition as cymbal crashes hint—nay, exclaim—the searing taste of the lash. Suddenly a machine-gun snare arouses the dominant growl: "You'll get to love me . . . anyway I say!" The final word hangs on a line of pure desire. "Ahhh, you'll get to love me and my sweet . . . ," the girls return, pleased to fulfill their master's demands and sing the sleek harmony down the scale, down, down, down . . . as if tumbling further, deeper into the dungeon, unable to deny the glorious "*pai-ai-ai-ai-ai-ai-ai-ain.*"

The drums cut deep, as if a strike once again across the reddened skin and a wailing, high-pitched guitar howls, scaling the heights of sensuous rapture. It is the sonic orgasm of the initiated. It is the taste of forbidden fruit, its nectar streaming a crimson river, arched back, clenched fists.

Oh . . .
Pain has got its reason
You find it pleasin', yes you do, yes you do
And I'm gonna show you now
You'll get to love it anyhow, anyhow and
You'll get to love me and my sweet pain

The master has gotten his prey—as she intended, as she fantasized. He serenades her once more, assuring her that the conquest is her own. She is indeed the dominant one; he lives to serve her up a measure of sexual vengeance, which she sinks her teeth into, and so the girls take over now. Their voices mesh with the return of the double-time waltz. It is how the song began, but now its willing victim; the concubine, the heiress, is the sexual victor. The female voices, so sure, so forceful, belt out the refrain as if their own.

Sweet pain, my love will drive you insane
Sweet pain my love will drive you insane
Sweet pain my love will drive you insane

And the master returns to lead his minions into the ether with a gospel chorale of dark secrets. The lead guitar slithers in and out of the words, not yet sated by their promise of endless perversions played out in hidden quarters where no one else shall tread, fading . . . fading . . . fading . . .

Ahh, sweet pain (sweet pain) my love will drive you insane

Sweet pain (sweet pain) my love will drive you insane
Sweet pain (sweet pain) my love will drive you insane
Sweet pain (sweet pain) my love will drive you insane

Fading . . .

13

All Right, Campers!

When I went into that novelty shop and saw the whistle, it spoke to me.
—Bob Ezrin[1]

A bitterly cold late Sunday morning in New York City. The lack of bustle inside 321 West Forty-Fourth Street signaled it was not business as usual: no phones ringing, no typewriters clacking away. Preparing a session in the middle of the weekend meant the first few hours of *Destroyer* would begin in relative privacy. Lead engineer Jay Messina and his assistant, Corky Stasiak, flicked on the lights and readied Studio A for a new recording project, as they had done for countless sessions, testing mikes and positioning amplifiers. Inside the control room, they fired up the Spectra-sonic console, both men, grizzled pros in the growing industry of high-tech recording, reveling in thoughts of once again plying their trade in the most celebrated studio in America: the Record Plant.

Stasiak, ever the stickler for detail, dutifully recorded the date in his ever-present journal: *January 4, 1976—KISS session—Day One*.

"I kept diaries," he recalls. "You have to keep diaries if you don't want to get eaten by sharks. 'What d'ya mean the check is light?' 'Well, the check is light because we did three other weeks of sessions.' 'No we didn't!' 'Oh yes, on the ninth of April we did saxophones, and on the twelfth we did the background singers—and remember the one guy spilled something on the microphone?' 'Oh, yeah, I didn't pay you for that?' 'No!'"[2]

Looking out through the glass of the control room, Messina carefully noted the dimensions of their sonic canvas, which had stood host to so many great artists. "I lived there," he admits. "Jack [Douglas] and I did records one after the other. There was one occasion when we were putting the final touches on one record while another assistant was setting up for the next one out in the studio."[3]

The thirty-foot room spread out from where Messina sat behind the glass, beginning with a shiny wood floor, twelve feet deep and stretched across its entire width, which separated slightly by blocks of hard Westlake Audio wood, gave way to thick carpeting. The wood blocks prevented what audiophiles call a "standing wave" that, left unchecked, might erase the precious "bottom end" needed to fill out the room's balanced sound. To Messina's left was a glass vocal booth, eight by twelve feet, accessed through a pair of patio-style glass doors. Almost directly across from there, on the right hand side, was another enclosed glass booth with a built-in drum riser surrounded by a small partition covered in colored fabric. The veteran engineer would always chuckle when he saw it, for although it was uniquely designed to contain the sound needed for ad jingles, pop tunes, or canned music beds, it was mostly ignored by rock bands, who wanted the "big room sound."

Further back, on the left-hand side, the long end of an old black Steinway grand piano extended out from a padded, L-shaped booth. The keys and bench were in the main studio, allowing the body of the piano to be sheltered while not completely isolating the artist from his accompaniment. The partition acted like a minor portal in a wall that descended from the ceiling, softening the sound of the piano while buffering the inevitable leakage of screaming guitars and pounding drums.

Many veteran engineers and producers, more used to higher ceilings in more traditional studios, would make immediate note of the lower overheads in all of the Record Plant rooms. This was especially true of Studio A, which allowed for a more intimate setting for group recordings but was not conducive to orchestral setups, where miking the musicians required far more depth. Along the back wall were double doors that opened to a second hallway, accessed during weekdays for deliveries and custodial duties. The hallway led to a classic marble lobby with a terrazzo covered in little stones grouted with brass inlays. Along one side of the hall was a service elevator with a garage-style door across it, through which janitors transported the day's refuse. Messina knew from experience that on a Sunday not unlike today—a respite from the flurry of weekday activity—he could place a drummer out there and produce a monster sound.

For the next month, Bob Ezrin's "home base," Studio A, would now also be home to The Act. The fortunes of KISS, its record company, and its manager would rest in the modest confines of this most austere palette.

In the silence of these pre-session hours, Messina and Stasiak could only guess to what was in store for them and their studio. Bob Ezrin was running the show, which could mean most anything at any time. Although they were braced for what they knew was going to be a wild ride, the mercurial young producer had prepped both engineers for what lay ahead. Ezrin gave Stasiak his own private pep talk, imploring him to pump up the band, "make 'em feel good," and work to achieve "a big production to suit them."

Messina fondly recalls a preproduction dinner at Jim Downey's Steakhouse on Forty-Fifth Street and Eighth Avenue, located just around the corner from the Record Plant in the heart of the theater district. The small but bustling bistro attracted stage actors, directors, and other showbiz impresarios to its private quarters, dramatically named the "Theatrical Lounge"; the "Backstage Room" would play host to the first of many meetings between the producer and his lead engineer. It was a ritual Ezrin had always followed to great effect, to keep the lines of communication open and maintain a likeness of vision throughout the entirety of the sessions.

"Bob and I would go around the corner to Downey's, maybe have dinner and a few drinks, and just talk about the record," recalls Messina. "We would take our time in the studio experimenting with sounds, so it unfolded right in the studio, but we needed to know what the overall goal was for each session."[4]

Ezrin: "We'd probably start around noon or one o'clock in the afternoon. We were very much night owls, and so the first break we would take was sort of a dinner break and we'd go around the corner to Downey's—it was a very convenient, good steakhouse—and talk about what we had done and what was coming up. For me, every minute we were there was part of the process, and we were *always* making the music in one way or the other. Even when we just sat out in the hallway, I was thinking about what we were doing and trying to keep everybody focused on the job at hand. So anytime I could, if I could sit with Jay and talk during the making of the album about where we were going, just bounce ideas off of him and explain what I was thinking of, that was useful to me."[5]

"We always had a good relationship," says Messina. "In fact, whenever we'd go home after a day's session—he was located on the East Side someplace and I'm on the West Side—we'd talk to each other over the CB" ("citizens band" radio, a mode of communication between truckers that became a domestic fad in the mid '70s)."[6]

According to both Messina and Stasiak, despite these pep talks and offsite meetings, Ezrin strongly believed in the organic development of creation: of letting the sounds in his head mingle with those being translated by live musicians on acoustic and electric instruments meshing with the room, passing through wires and out of speakers that poured into a control board with a myriad of dials and faders, all capable of changing the slightest tone into vinyl magic.

"Bob is one of those guys who has an idea in his mind and knows how to achieve it," Stasiak explains. "After each session we'd plot out what we would do the next day, but sometimes, and I love this, he would have an idea and we'd take it one way and he'd go, 'Oh, man, wait a minute, I've got a better idea, let's do this!' When you're producing an album, you have an overall plan, but it really depends on how the songs are played and how it sounds. Sometimes the idea you had is right on the money and sometimes the idea you had is almost there, but when you put it down on tape and listen to it, you might say to yourself, 'Gee, you know, I've got a better idea for this.'

"It's no different than building a house or making shoes or cutting cloth for fashion, as you go along you're calling audibles, and Bob, the genius that he is, really had his homework done and knew how he wanted it to sound. Shit, he wrote half the songs. And when it all comes through the speakers, he hears how it's performed and may have been hoping for one thing, but maybe it should be something entirely different and then he'd call his audibles. It was great working with Bob simply because he had so many great ideas and he knew how to get 'em."[7]

"I seem to remember Bob saying that what he liked about me was that I would come up with a lot of different choices," Messina notes. "So that if I gave him, for instance, a certain snare sound, he might say, 'No, that's not it, it should sound more like this or that.' I could quickly and easily come up with another choice for him to listen to. I remember working on a drum sound for a whole day, and at the end of the day Bob wanted to tear them down and set them up in another part of the room starting the next day. It was almost like a work in progress. Things would develop and would inform your decisions going forward."[8]

Ezrin: "Once you've got the band on the floor, particularly that group at that time, there were such disparate personalities and they were so much larger than life and any one of them could have taken up all of my attention and all of my time, and having all four of them there sometimes required that I be so attuned to what was going on with these four disparate personalities plus being completely aware of what's happening with our music and all that stuff, it didn't leave me a whole lot of time to turn to Jay and say, 'Okay, here's what I have in mind *for this*.' So it was better to have had that conversation before we got in the room with everybody. I still do that to this day. I'll sit down with the team and explain what the concept is and how things are going to run and what I'm looking to achieve that day and make sure that everybody's aware of their roles and responsibilities. That just helps make things run very smoothly."[9]

According to Stasiak's journal, KISS arrived at the Record Plant the following afternoon, January 5, with a renewed vigor. With instruments at the ready, they prepared to chase the elusive "live" sound: the larger-than-life, blasting-to-the-rafters barrage that had haunted them for over two years across three studio albums. Everyone involved with the project knew from the very beginning that whatever transpired, it could not be another fabricated overdub of a live show. This time the music, performance, production, and final product had to express the raw dimensions of a worthy rock band: mythologizing, one groove at a time.

Having endured Ezrin's' "boot camp," survived a contentious law suit, and seen its fortunes suddenly thrust up the charts with *Alive!*, there was nothing left for KISS but to gorge on the fruits of its labor. By now, Simmons, Stanley, Frehley, and Criss were fully aware of what was expected of them: a follow-up to the astonishing explosion of *Alive!*, which by the opening days of 1976 had become a monster.

When the sessions began—the demos, rehearsals, and the Bob Ezrin Music School 101—KISS was a desperate bunch. Bill Aucoin had to find a producer capable of wringing quality performances from his boys, and he was fully willing to pay for it out of his own pocket, just as he had dutifully bankrolled the tour that produced the tapes that eventually saved their hides. As the band entered the studio to begin recording the follow-up, there was suddenly a heightened pressure, bringing with it a whole different agenda: to produce a studio recording worthy of superstars. Big, loud, brash, and uncompromising—this was now the goal for the band, guided by Bob Ezrin and assisted ably by Jay Messina and Corky Stasiak, all of whom would effectively become honorary members of The Act for one month. Thirty days in Studio A carrying the fate of KISS.

"I always thought that sonically what we were about always eluded us," Paul Stanley bemoans, of KISS's prior studio woes, in 2013's *Nothin' to Lose*. "I was always desperately trying to get the sound that I heard in my head onto a record and I didn't know how to do it. We didn't have the ability in technique and the technology and the people we were working with were not up to the task."[10]

Bob Ezrin fully understood the band's frustrations and also believed that the success of *Alive!* proved that the previous studio albums failed to achieve the "live sound" KISS had rested its reputation on, but he did not get caught up in looking backward. "I intentionally did not go back and listen to the old KISS stuff, because I just didn't want to be prejudiced by it," he admits. "Once I saw the band play live, to understand who they were and get a sense of what I could and should do with them, the best thing was to see them play. I was worried [that] if I listened to their records I'd be prejudiced toward or against certain sounds, and I wanted to have an open palette. It's human nature. You're taking on a project someone else did before you, so you go and check out what they did and you make a resolution that you're going to make something different. Well, I didn't want to be forced into *differently* if that wasn't the right thing to do. And I'm competitive by nature, so the best thing was just to go in with an agile mindset, see the band live, and use that as my baseline. My comparative baseline was the live performance."[11]

Ezrin—whose vision for The Act would now be realized—hit the ground running. He was a whirlwind presence in the studio from day one, equipped with an ample supply of cigars, cognac, and cocaine—the use of the latter eventually becoming the stuff of *Destroyer* legend. Cocaine was so ubiquitous and its use so effusive there are stories to this day of mirrors being built into the console and mounds of it piled everywhere. In their memoirs, released within a year of each other in 2011 and 2012, respectively, Ace Frehley and Peter Criss agree that the amount of available coke almost immediately had an equally dynamic and harrowing effect on the sessions.

"I had never seen that much coke in one place," writes Criss, who admits having been introduced to the drug while recording *Hotter Than Hell* in Los Angeles over a year earlier. "I'm not talking grams—it was more like bags full of blow that would be laid out in pyramids on the mixing board."[12] For Frehley, a boozer of renown, this would be an auspicious introduction. "Once I started doing cocaine, there was no stopping me," he confesses, in *No Regrets*. "It really was that clear a line of demarcation, and it began with *Destroyer*. For a while it didn't have an adverse impact on my playing. Cocaine can actually make you sharper. For me, in smaller doses, it was like guzzling coffee. I had tried speed a few times and didn't like it—made me too jumpy. But coke worked beautifully, especially in combination with alcohol. I'd get comfortably numb, as they say."[13]

"We were all doing coke," says Ezrin. "Well, not all of us—Gene and Paul never touched anything—but I mean everyone *around* at the time was playing with drugs of all sorts. Everybody was doing drugs."[14]

"It was always there," Stasiak concurs. "Jay and I liked to smoke weed. The sessions can become pretty strenuous and fast paced, and also pretty boring, so we'd liked our weed. Bob liked his coke. In almost every session I worked with Bob, it was there. He had this little bowl always available of some great, clean stuff. There was an engineer at the Record Plant who could pick up the phone at two in the morning and there would be half an ounce of blow on the board."[15]

"Everybody pretty much did it, except Gene and Paul," Messina adds. "I don't remember it being very obvious or visible during the making of the record, mainly because of them. They wouldn't have approved. They probably knew that everybody was doing it, I suppose. Other records that I've done I could remember clearly incidents of drugs, but on that record it was discreet, because of Gene and Paul."[16]

"Don't get me wrong, the *Destroyer* sessions were not a drug fest," argues Stasiak. "It was more like someone saying, 'Let's take five and have a cigarette!'

We were all partaking here or there. Jay and I were never addicted to it. It was something that was always around and we'd partake, but we could take it or leave it. We weren't going crazy like a lot of acts I worked with—'Gimme another toot! Gimme another toot!' It was much more like that when we worked with Aerosmith, where they wouldn't do a take if they didn't have a toot. But I never saw Gene and Paul so much as sip a drop of alcohol during the sessions, never mind cocaine."[17]

"Sometimes the drugs would render people incapacitated or would make the performance just horrible," Ezrin emphatically concludes. "But for the most part it didn't have a negative effect on the making of *Destroyer*."[18]

In his memoir, Simmons describes an incident where he was so oblivious of the drug use that he'd mistaken cocaine for the popular sugar-free coffee sweetener, Sweet'n Low. When stopped from pouring a spoonful of cocaine into his tea, he claims to have sought revenge by occasionally sneaking some of the sweetener onto the community coke glass to see if anyone would notice. No one did.

This naiveté about drug use in the studio struck Peter Criss in particular as dubious for someone as tuned in to his environment as Simmons, and he took his and Stanley's lack of outrage during the sessions as a form of hypocrisy. "It was interesting that Gene and Paul didn't say a word about Bob's drug problem," writes Criss, in *Makeup to Breakup*. "They were both majorly anti-drug, and if Ace or I would get fucked up on drugs, all hell would break loose."[19]

"Both Ace and Peter were fucked up all the time," Paul Stanley replies in his memoir, *Face the Music—A Life Exposed*. "I'd seen plenty of functional addicts. Bob Ezrin had been doing a lot of coke and chugging Remy Martin while we recorded *Destroyer*, but the quality of his work never flagged. Bill Aucoin, Neil Bogart, and much of the Casablanca staff were on a slippery slope, doing lots of drugs, too. Drugs and alcohol were like a Ferrari—there's a split second difference between being in control and being wrapped around a telephone pole. You're in control, and then you pass that line and don't realize it—until it's too late."[20]

"Ace and Peter were the ones who told me when they were first on the road and roomed together they started doing that stuff together," remembers Stasiak. "They were the partiers of the group before they were even in KISS, so they had no problems diving right in."[21]

"At that point in time I was a party animal," Frehley later told the band's biographers. "I was hitting Studio 54 a lot. A lot of times I'd show up late or with a hangover. There was no secret about that."[22]

Substance abuse was just one of the issues that surfaced during the *Destroyer* sessions that added to the inner turmoil within the band and would one day breed deeper resentments. But it was nothing that a veteran of studio chaos couldn't handle, and Bob Ezrin held fast to the role of taskmaster, showing up with "Time Is Money" printed boldly on his T-shirt and a whistle slung around his neck, which he didn't hesitate to blow at a moment's notice, abruptly halting any discord or goofing about with a hearty "All right, campers!"[23]

"I've worked with Bob on other projects before and after *Destroyer*, but that was the only time he ever used a whistle," says Stasiak. "Now Bob was an excitable guy anyway. I was scared shitless of Bob before I'd ever met him. Everyone knew that Bob could send you home crying if you didn't please him, but I think he believed that was the way to get through to these guys. If you let a rock group take advantage of you, they will."[24]

"The point of the whistle and the joking and the fun and the craziness was to *not* be intimidating," says Ezrin. "But I realize the effect that cocaine had on me was it made me more arrogant and a little bit less sensitive to what was going on around me. I got sober decades ago, but since having gotten sober I find that I can't muster the same level of arrogance. It just doesn't come. It's not natural. And I don't think I had it in the beginning, either. I think during the coke years it was more pronounced and I think it intimidated some people. For some people, my arrogance mixed with my sense of humor was actually exciting and fun and inspiring. I think it was a great catalyst for Gene. He had somebody to spar with that he felt he was challenged by, because he's so smart and so quick-witted and arrogant in his own way, and he could walk over just about anybody. He responded positively to having somebody who came into the studio who was as arrogant as he was, and also had a good sense of humor and was as quick-witted."[25]

Stasiak and Messina were immediately confronted by the brass, impenetrable personalities in KISS. "Let's face it," says Stasiak, "even though these were guys were in jeopardy of being dropped from their label and hadn't sold many records, you could tell right away they were used to always getting their way. As most rock people are, they were full of themselves. They were wild and crazy guys who got all the girls and got standing ovations and everyone close to them telling them they loved them. They were used to 'turn it up and play!'"[26]

"What Bob taught us was discipline in the studio," Paul Stanley recalled, in *Behind the Mask*. "He wore a whistle around his neck and would blow it and call us 'campers.' He was not above pointing a finger in your face and yelling at you. That's pretty funny stuff when you're selling out arenas all over and you have somebody in the studio that's treating you like an imbecile."[27]

Ezrin: "I don't know why I thought of it, but I went to a novelty shop one day and I bought a whistle. Why a whistle? It was there, that's why. And it was in the middle of, you know, 'The games are on!' Right? We were practical-joking all up and down the building. I can't remember what made me do it the first time, but I walked into the studio with the whistle and blew it, which got everybody's attention. Then I went, 'Campers!' I did this head counselor routine: 'Everybody up! Here's what we're gonna do!' And then we rolled into a take. Everybody was in a really good mood from that. They liked the joke. It was fun. Then I realized this whistle is a pretty effective way to get these people's attention, so I kept using it, and they began to respond to it. It was very Pavlovian: the more I used the whistle, the more they'd snap to and play, and it ended up becoming a really effective device for keeping them in the boat."[28]

Stasiak: "Bob challenged the band to reach for an emotional level. He was testing these guys. He'd come roaring out there and announce, 'I've got an idea, here's what we're doin'!' Bob was a 'lead, follow, or get the hell out of the way' guy. He wasn't one of those producers who coddled or pat you on the back. Bob had that great ability to get the listener involved, like when he wanted to punch someone in the face with a song, he'd have those guys play certain chords or he would play them himself. You tell me you can listen to *Destroyer* and not get emotionally involved in that album."[29]

Peter Criss would later recount one incident in which the band was bitching about something, causing Ezrin, menacingly brandishing a fire extinguisher, to throw a fit. "He had this crazed look in his eye. 'You cocksuckers are going to learn what this means,' referring to the slogan on his shirt (*Time Is Money*). 'You are not going to waste the time that we're paying for arguing over what you're going to eat or when you're going to get some pussy or whatever the fuck your problems are, because you can't even tune your instruments. I'm going to show you the value of time.' Then, according to Criss, Ezrin unleashed the entire contents of the extinguisher all over the studio, the band's instruments and amps, sending everyone scrambling into the relative safety of the control room. He then angrily marched back up into the booth and asked, 'Now who's wasting money and time?'"[30]

Having already established his authority during the weeks of "boot camp," Ezrin was formulating a wholly creative environment that succeeded within the constraints of hard work and discipline, taking the band out of the cushy world of the rock star to concentrate specifically on musicianship. He had seen what petty infighting and a defiant attitude did to the Alice Cooper group. He was forced to walk away from a goldmine, and, given a second chance with the solo Alice Cooper project, he was subsequently spoiled by hand-picking Cooper's studio musicians, all of whom gave themselves selflessly over to the greater good when it came to constructing the songs for *Welcome to My Nightmare*. Now, he'd been asked by KISS and its management to bring it home for them, and he was damned if he was to let them down by kowtowing to their impish whims.

"It's tough to suddenly be told what to do, but you have to consider the source," says Stasiak. "If a guy who doesn't know anything about music is telling you what to do, you may take the occasional good idea to heart, but Bob Ezrin was and still is a musical genius. He wanted to make a musically interesting, musically correct, musically magnificent record, and he had to corral them. I have to tip my hat to Eddie Kramer, who was also a fine piano player. I worked with Eddie on the follow-up to *Destroyer*, *Rock and Roll Over*, but he never challenged KISS musically the way Bob did. Bob was coming from a *completely* different place musically. He wanted to make colors in the music."[31]

Still, the magnitude of the sessions, the pressure of financial constraints and legal wrangling between management and label, and the reminder of what each of them had endured in constructing and rehearsing the songs for their make-or-break career record, focused the band as never before.

"In some ways, he was quite the disciplinarian," Simmons writes of Ezrin in his memoir. "When he didn't think we were getting a handle on something, he would send us outside the studio. Paul and I were excited, because we knew the experience was making the band better. We were rubbing our hands together thinking, *Oh, boy, this is going to a place we haven't been*. It was a really good adventure because we recognized that whatever we were doing, even though it was a step forward, it still sounded like KISS, but better than before. We literally heard the record coming together there in the studio, and it was the best version of the band to that point."[32]

Corky Stasiak: "Gene was a workhorse. If he had his way, he would sleep at the studio, get four or five hours' [sleep], and get up and record. Do a chick, have something to eat, and then record again; take a nap, get up, do another chick, and record again. Because Gene and Paul were the primary songwriters, they wanted to hang in there and be a part of everything. They were always great during the making of the record. And I saw a true chemistry there. When *Destroyer* was done, I went back and listened to the previous three studio albums, and they sounded as if they had five hours of studio time a day; do something and go home. I don't know how those records were made, and I never spoke to them about it, but you could see that they really put their heads to the grindstone with Bob."[33]

Paul Stanley and Gene Simmons both concur, as revealed by their statements in *Nothin' to Lose* about the band's experience during the hurried environs of the *Dressed to Kill* sessions with label president Neil Bogart. Stanley:

"Neil's function was to try and stop us from doing too many takes. He really wanted to move things along. I remember being in the studio with him and literally we'd do a take and he'd go, 'That's fine, that's good enough.' And I'd be like, 'I'm not so sure, I think we should do it again.'" Simmons: "In terms of producing, Neil was more of a cheerleader. We didn't take a lot of time with sounds. Everything went down fast."[34]

Bob Ezrin: "I have to say that, when people think of Gene Simmons as demanding and difficult to work with, Paul is actually more demanding than Gene. Paul is more precision-oriented than Gene, who is more gut-and-feel about things. Paul goes by feel too, but he's more meticulous than Gene is about the recording process. Together, both of them were a joy to work with, just fun and smart. It was so wonderful to work with intelligent people."[35]

"Paul was very excited," Corky Stasiak recalls. "He was like a kid in an amusement park."[36]

"I don't remember the guys in KISS having any particular ideas on where they wanted to go technically with their instruments," Jay Messina recalls, when asked about the initial days of recording. "They pretty much allowed us to take care of that end. They were pretty ready to take direction."[37]

The direction Ezrin had in mind—and in which he would guide the band, through an execution forged in blood, sweat, and tears—was a balance between the raw KISS live assault, its volume and extravagance, and the depth of Studio A's environs and its vast array of effects. These would be adroitly manipulated by the talents and experimentation of Messina and Stasiak, giving the tracks on *Destroyer* both a thrust and a sheen glaringly absent on the band's previous albums. The template was *Billion Dollar Babies*, on which the Alice Cooper group reversed the process of providing a sonic libretto for its outrageous concerts and succeeded in unleashing it full-tilt into the listener's living room.

"Those guys never stopped bitching and moaning about how no album— even when I did *Rock and Roll Over*, where we recorded the sessions in the Nanuet Star Theater—had captured KISS the way it sounded onstage," says Stasiak. "I have many times stood on the side of the stage during a KISS show, and the volume and the crushing sound that comes out cannot be recorded. It's like the explosions that go off during the show: you could be fifty rows back and you'll feel the heat. You can't feel that on a record, but I truly think *Destroyer* came as close as anyone has ever come."[38]

Destroyer would be the sound of The Act—a living illusion of invincibility and relentless power—while simultaneously pushing the boundary of expectation and allowing KISS, perhaps for the first time, to strip bare the personalities behind the supermen.

14

Sessions

When you learn to become an engineer, distortion is a bad thing, because you want to get good, clean sound, but there is a life on the other side of distortion called compression. That's why people love tube amplifiers and tube radios, 'cause it has that great ballsy sound.
—Corky Stasiak[1]

For the foundation of the *Destroyer* backing tracks, engineers Messina and Stasiak set the band up in a circular manner, allowing them to maintain eye contact and visually connect with each other while playing. Peter Criss's white, fiberglass twelve-piece Pearl drum set sat in the center of the room facing the control booth, and thus the rest of the band. The back half of the kit was positioned on the cement floor, with the front—specifically the bass drum—on the carpeted area. Behind him, the back doors leading to the freight hallway were left open, to allow for a booming effect and natural reverb.

Bob Ezrin: "My recollection is, the drums were in the middle of the room surrounded by a semicircular drum booth. It didn't have glass or anything over it. It was a semicircular platform, and it had a shoulder-height wall around it and then a big space where you could see over it into the booth, and then there was a roof over it that matched the shape. Above the head of the drummer there was a lot of open space, so it was sort of an infinite baffle. Peter was in the booth and the other guys were on the floor around him. But it was not like the drums were behind closed doors. When I say booth, it was more of a structure. He was within the drum structure that was on the main floor."[2]

Simmons, holding fast to his black Gibson Ripper LS-9 or switching to his newly acquired refinished Les Paul Triumph (he commissioned a custom Spector bass during the *Destroyer* sessions, but it is unlikely he used it while recording the album), stood in the back of the studio, off to the right, by his amp. "For bass, we used both a direct box and an amp," explains Messina. "It was an Ampeg B-15 we had modified, which was miked, but it also came directly out from the head of the amp just before the speakers, and we combined the sounds for one track. It's always easier to get definition with the pick, which Gene used, but you do lose the sense of the real bottom you get from the fingers."[3]

"We put Gene's amplifier in the little alcove—or I like to call it a 'sound lock'—at the back of the studio," adds Stasiak. "Just behind it was another door, and that opened to the back hallway. We always used a bass compressor called a Flickinger. This thing was a monster. It was like two-and-a-half feet wide by two-and-a-half feet deep, and it was all tube with one input and two knobs, and that was it. But man, it gave you that jukebox bottom. You know, when you go into a bar and put a couple of quarters into a jukebox and those records sounded better than they ever sounded."[4]

"The Flickinger was such a great old, tube compressor," Messina concurs. "It was a favorite of a lot of the engineers at the Record Plant. We may well have used it on both the recording and the mixing side of *Destroyer*. It just added a nice snap and really retained all the low-end on the bass, which added a feeling of power."[5]

Stanley switched between his Gibson Explorer and a '57 Firebird (he would use a 1967 double-neck on "King of the Night Time World") and set up to Criss's right, facing the drums; Frehley, his trusty Gibson sunburst Les Paul slung across his shoulder, stood across the room, parallel with him.

"We would have the amps cranked," explains Messina. "You want to have an amp sounding good in the room, if you want it to sound good inside the board. We used to have some great vintage Fender amps at the Record Plant that we used on a lot of recordings. We may have used those on *Destroyer*. We had a pretty good collection at the studio. I could see maybe Ace would have brought in a favorite amp that he liked, but with most records, like on the Aerosmith sessions, we used old Fenders: a real cool, old Gibson stereo amp that Joe Perry used a lot, although I don't think we used it on *Destroyer*."[6]

Stasiak: "The Record Plant had a special Fender Tweed twin-reverb amp from the early '60s that we kept covered in a special place. It was one of those rare amplifiers that just roared. People could rent it but they couldn't take it home. So many groups wanted to take that thing home. People who knew about it would book the studio predicated on whether they could use the Fender Tweed exclusively for their sessions. Very rarely was it just sitting in a back room for somebody to say, 'Hey, let's try this!' It had such a great sound, especially with a Gibson guitar. Head engineer Shelly Yakus had a side business called Moon Rentals that rented the Tweed out. Ace brought his own amp to the sessions, but once he heard the Tweed he just freaked out. In fact, that amplifier and Marshalls are what they primarily used on *Destroyer*. Nowadays you could use a Line 6 Pocket POD and plug it into the board and provide someone with the sound of a Fender Tweed. We didn't have that technology in '76, so it was all about finding the right guitar/amp combinations; switching up amps with different amp heads and then changing guitars to see how they worked. This was what our lives were back then, making records like *Destroyer*: finding that perfect match of amp with guitar to achieve the desired sound for the band and the songs."[7]

"On *Destroyer* we took our time getting the sounds out of the amp right," says Messina. "Bob gave me a fair amount of rope to play with in the studio, the creativity of coming up with different choices of sounds for him. His persistence was impressive, and how much time he would take for a particular sound, but it all came, as it always does, from the guitar, the player, the pick, and the amp. Then it's how you miked them."[8]

Stasiak: "Once we got the right sound, then it became what microphones to use and in what combination. Sometimes we would have three mics on an amp. We would always mic it off the center of the speaker, which in the case of Marshall amps would have four ten-inch speakers or four twelve-inch speakers, and you don't want to put the microphone in the middle of one of those speakers. We'd put it to the side of the cone, so we wouldn't get the direct pressure and crush the mic. We'd pad the mic down, but we would avoid that direct crushing sound. That was a common mistake engineers would make then, putting the mics straight into the center of one of the speakers.

"Our process was to place a Shure 57 off center of one of the speakers and combine that with a Sony mic that Roy [Cicala] had that was discontinued. We only had three of them. It was a cardioid-shape condenser microphone [a blue/gray/silver C-74 condenser mic], which was a *great* guitar mic. Sometimes we'd use the Sennheiser 421 shaver as a second mic with the 57. The third mic was a Neumann 87, set right in the middle but back three feet from the amp, and right on the wood floor to pick up the ambiance when doing guitar overdubs."[9]

Messina: "The Sony we used to use was either a C-37 or a C-38. We'd use a mix of microphones, including an SM57, which gave us a nice edge to the sound; a Sennheiser 421; and that Sony. We would get a lot of the meat from that Sony. It gave you a darker sound than the 421, a good mix against the 57 (which was brighter), and provided the bottom.

"Then, once the amps are miked correctly, it's time to decide whether to apply the process of parallel compression as you record it or when you mix it. In other words, you don't just put a compressor on a microphone. You have the microphone, and then you also send that microphone to a compressor, and then you add that compressor to it, so basically it's in parallel or 'parallel compression.' What I used to like to do, and still do, is compress something I know will sound better compressed when I record it. I don't want to think how it might sound good later. I prefer it sound good every step of the way."[10]

Stasiak: "Jay taught me a compressing thing which was just amazing. He would take a feed off of one of the microphones and feed it into a compressor, then take the output of the compressor and bring it up on a fader. He would then find a nice combination of say, the SM57 and the Sony, and then he would bring in the ambiance mic and mix in a real nice sound with that. Then he would take a feed off the 57 and send just one of the feeds, like a second leg, off of that feed to a compressor and compress the shit out of it, and bring the output of that compression on another fader, so you would have four faders on that guitar. And what the compressor does is bring up all the low passages and suppresses all the loud passages, so you don't have a great dynamic range, but what you *do* have is this great *sustain*. As the note is fading out it would give it this crunchy attack. In some cases, he would use the compression mic and the ambiance mic and do the same thing—close mic, ambiance, and a compressor thing—and mix them all together and it would make a great stretched-out, ballsy, bottom-end sound."[11]

"Say you've got the sound," Messina adds. "It sounds great already, but now you want to try to bring it up a notch, so you'll send some element of that combination of microphones to a compressor and then add that. The good thing about that is you can really do drastic compression with that compressor, and that, by itself, might not sound good, but when you add it to the non-compressed mics, it does something a little special. You could get a *grrrr* kind of sound from the compressor and another more crispy sound just from the mic, but the only way you could marry those two is to have it in parallel, so then you could add that *grrrr* sound to the more crispy sound, and you'd just add as much of that as you want.

"It might've been something I discovered, but I certainly wouldn't take credit for inventing it. It's just something that I used to do and still do. I do it in a lot in mixing. I'll do that same kind of parallel compression on drums. You know, you can pretty much do it on just about anything, and it's different than just putting a compressor right on the instrument."[12]

"When you're adjusting compression, you have an attack and release time you can manipulate," Stasiak concludes. "On a compressor, it's really pretty easy to do. On most compressors there are two knobs, and on the more elaborate ones they have other knobs for other things, but basically it's how hard you attack the sound that comes in and how you're going to release it. Are you going to give it a slow release, where it fades out but is just as loud as the guitar outputs until it starts to disappear when it's lost all of its dynamic range? It just kills all of the dynamic range, but that's good. That's why people love Marshall amplifiers. When you plug a guitar into a Marshall amp, those tubes compress the sound, like what our old Fender Tweed amp did. It had a regular input and a master input, so you floor the regular input and bring the master input down, compressing the shit out it. Queen and Roy Thomas Baker made their living compressing the shit out of everything they did."[13]

Messina: "My only rule is, if it sounds good, then it's good. I never had a formula for getting certain sounds, otherwise I'd have been bored a long time ago with what I do. Lots of times I don't remember how I got a particular sound. I may remember how I approached it, but I don't remember exactly what I did. It's the way I cook. I don't go by recipe, so a lot of times I don't remember how I made a particular thing. It's the same thing in the studio. It might be a spontaneous thing I might just go after, something that just feels right at the time. I might go to a particular compressor that I know how it works and I know I want to use it, but as far as the sound goes, lots of sounds I've come up with by mistake, like an accident that happens.

"What I would do lots of times, if the previous engineer didn't normal-out all of the controls on a particular piece of outboard, which was the courteous thing to do; if there was a particular setting on a compressor or an equalizer that was just there and my initial thought might be, 'Gee that's not gonna sound good on this vocal or this guitar,' that would be more of a reason for me to just plug it in and see what it would sound like, 'cause that wouldn't have been my initial thing to try. We know what we know and we know what we don't know, but that leaves out all the possibilities of what else there is, so when you try something that you don't think isn't going to sound good, you'll learn something from it, even if nine times out of ten your first thought might have been correct, that one time out of ten you'll learn from it something that's useful. I wasn't afraid to do those things."[14]

Both Messina and Stasiak agree that setting up the band for sound and performance was never rushed during any day or night of recording *Destroyer*. Ezrin could change his mind on how amplifiers were miked or where the drums would reside on a song-by-song basis—sometimes on a take-by-take basis. According to the engineers and the producer, the band members were also insistent on not rushing anything or ignoring the slightest mistakes, memories of "boot camp" still reverberating in their heads. And once the sounds of the amps and drums were readied, the band began to rip through live takes of each song: all four members playing off one another in a controlled version of their stage rapport.

"They played all the songs together, looking at each other in the studio, with all the tracks isolated," recalls Messina. "They'd wear headphones and react to each other for energy or to follow the changes, so if anyone made a mistake, it could be fixed later, in an edit. Maybe Paul would redo his part or overdub a lick or double a guitar or vocal, and it could be done cleanly without any problem, because in most cases we positioned the amps in glass booths, and occasionally in vocal booths, so there could be a completed drum track, and getting a solid guitar track could be accomplished later."[15]

This is why Bob Ezrin was adamant to the point of hysteria that no one under any circumstances quit playing the song all the way through, regardless of mistakes—something Simmons forgot on the very first day.

"Early on in the recording process, somebody made a mistake, Gene or Paul—I don't know who it was—but the band stopped playing," says Messina. "And Bob gets on the talkback and was kind of scolding them. And he says, wagging his index finger, 'Don't you ever, EVER stop a take unless I tell you!' And I remember the way Gene and Paul were looking at each other, like, 'We're getting yelled at!' The minute Bob got off the talkback we began cracking up, because it came out so forceful, it struck us funny. So, for the rest of the sessions, that became the joke. No matter what happened, it was, 'Don't you EVER...!'"[16]

"We would try to do matchups with guitar and amplifiers, but I don't specifically remember—and it must've happened—but I don't ever remember on *Destroyer* that we got a 'keeper' guitar take while recording the drums and bass," says Stasiak. "It was always, 'Let's concentrate on the drums and bass, get those guys locked in, and once we have them, we'll just build the whole pyramid.'"[17]

Playing the songs live was an effective way not only to lay down a solid drum take but also for the band to gather the structure of the number. If the guitars tended to bleed over into the mics set about the drums, all the better to create the kind of ambient sound that so well served many of the rock bands Messina worked with, including Aerosmith, with whom he had just finished working prior to KISS's arrival.

"Generally I would have some collaboration with Bob on what he was looking for," says Messina. "I preferred sometimes putting the amps in with the drums, because the leakage from the drum mics makes for a special kind of sound. Evidence of how leakage works best is how I specifically set up the orchestra on Aerosmith's 'You See Me Crying' for *Toys in the Attic*. I put all the violins in rows of twos and just set them up with three mics up kind of high, for the purpose of, when the brass played, it would leak into the violin mics."[18]

"Jay Messina recorded with a single, highly compressed microphone that was in the center of the room while we were tracking the songs and left it on its own track," recalls Ezrin. "That one track helped to provide the glue that tied everything nicely together, and gave each song the feeling that it was being done live."[19]

"When you have a mic in front of each instrument, you have more control on individual volumes, but the end result doesn't sound the way it would if you were in the room, ambiance bouncing off the walls, and so on," concludes Messina. "It is much more a realistic sound, as if you were in the room. Now, say Bob wanted to isolate the guitars—because he might be thinking of just getting a good bass and drum track—then you'd want to put the amps in a separate booth so there's no leakage, and then he can work with the guitar players individually and get what he wants out of that. Finally, I would ask the musician how they were comfortable, because if they're not comfortable, you're not going to get a great take to begin with. Of course, the drawback to all this is you have to get the complete take right with all parties, otherwise you have to go for another take on the drums."[20]

Capturing this thunderous backdrop to the foundation of *Destroyer* began with the natural cavernous reverberation achieved from leaving open the doors to the back hallway of Studio A, which provided the live room sound. The mics surrounding Peter Criss's Pearl set consisted of a standard SM57 coupled with what Corky Stasiak describes as a Sennheiser "lipstick" microphone. Both mics, when properly compressed, provided a solid punch to the snare, allowing it to slice through the heavy bass sounds Jay Messina famously leant to his "bottom-end" that sent Stasiak into orgiastic paroxysms of delight.

"One thing I wasn't afraid to do is turn knobs all the way up," says Messina. "One possible answer to that was going to an extreme, especially on the bottom end. So I might have done that on some EQ or compression or whatever the signal processing was. I was never afraid of turning everything up. That was something that I just did as I was recording. It kind of came naturally to me, 'cause I went with what it sounded like, not what it looked like. And the other thing is, since low end is really long waves, you can't mike it too close, and I was always in favor of having leakage, so that everything wasn't so sterile."[21]

The toms were also miked in different variations, depending on a particular song's mood. Both engineers recall the placement of additional SM57s and Sennheiser 421s, referred to by the pros as "shavers" for their resemblance to an electric shaver, an Electro-voice mic for the bass drum, and another 57 on the hi-hat. Each mic was filtered through a compressor and fed into a single track for later manipulation during the mixing of the album. For the ambient sound of the entire kit and the natural reverb and bleed-through of the guitar amps, a set of Neumann U87 overhead mics were placed around the circumference of the kit.

"We set the drums in the back of the room on a rug but left the door open to a hallway in the back, which was cement," explains Messina. "We placed microphones out there in addition to those on the kit to get the ambiance of the hallway added to the main room. But that wasn't the only setup. There were several different places we put the drums, depending on what song. There were some drum overdubs done with the kit completely set up outside, but most of the tracks were recorded in the original setup at the back of the room with the doors opened."[22]

"We recorded the drums the same way for *Billion Dollar Babies*," recalls Ezrin. "It was the only way to get that *booming* drum sound. Now, we may have gone back and forth from inside to outside the booth, as we did with the Alice Cooper stuff. The engineers would probably remember better than I do on that one."[23]

Corky Stasiak: "Normally, a lot of groups would come in, set up the drums and get a drum sound, set up the bass and get a bass sound, then the two guitars, and they'd try to plow through the songs. Once they got all the songs down, the drummer goes home, and then we'd work punching in the bass, et cetera. But Bob liked to mix it up a little bit. In fact, there was one song—I believe it was 'Sweet Pain'—that we put Peter in the drum booth, which I found very unusual. I hated that dead, padded thing. It was like a half moon–shaped little room that made you feel when you were in there like they had closed the door on an airplane and you had to struggle to pop your ears open. There's nothing live sounding about it. I would be surprised if we used that booth ten times in any session for all the years I was there. Peter didn't like it at all, but it didn't matter. When Bob gets an idea, he's pretty headstrong. If you whine about it, he has no patience. He did not suffer fools easily. If someone started bitching and moaning, he would turn into a tough baseball manager—you know, 'When I come out to the mound to take the ball from you, don't cry about it, take your medicine, and get back in the dugout!' Whatever was best for the team or the project, Bob was going to get."[24]

"Ezrin says to me, 'I'm going to put you in an elevator,'" Peter Criss told *Modern Drummer* magazine in 1999. "At that point it was three or four in the morning, and we were in the back of the building. He miked the drums from the fourteenth floor. There were mics in the elevator shaft, and I was in there with a bass drum and two floor toms going, 'Boom, boom, boom, bap, boom, boom, bap.' I was there all alone—they couldn't see me because they didn't have video setups in those days. In the middle of laying down the track, the elevator door opens and two garbage men came walking in to collect the garbage in the hallway!"[25]

Peter Criss's drum odyssey was one of the signature hurdles of *Destroyer*, but the results were stunning. "Ezrin got me to play things I had never played in my whole life," Criss recalled, in the same interview. "Or even *though*t I could play."[26]

"The funny thing is, when *Destroyer* came out there were people who said, 'Well, that's not Peter' [on drums]," Paul Stanley told *Goldmine* magazine in 1998. "I said, 'I have to say that there is stuff on *Destroyer* that Peter could never have played before, but he worked hard to be able to play it.'"[27]

The band, set up and ready for a run-through, hit a roadblock before ever getting off the on ramp—something Ezrin had already game-planned during rehearsals, when he noticing Criss's limitations. "Bob Ezrin told me that with Peter, he would say, 'Peter, watch my hand,' and he would move it up and down," remembers Jay Messina. "Then he would say, 'Peter, when my hand comes down, that's when you hit.' He couldn't get him to do it, and he couldn't get him to play with a click track. It was a problem in those days for drummers to play evenly. The shit would sound great and rocking onstage, but when you're making an album, if it's not even, it just doesn't make it. You can't have the time of the song be uneven. It just doesn't work. It's sloppy. Your foot stops tapping and the listener stops listening."[28]

"Bob insisted on the songs being in perfect time," says Corky Stasiak. "To achieve that, we first used a regular electronic metronome click track that we had for commercials; every studio would provide jingle players this device to play at a certain number of beats per thirty-second spot to hit the timing. It was standard procedure for that kind of session drumming, but Peter could not do it. He just did not respond to drumming to a clicking machine sound. And, to be fair, it wasn't standard procedure for a rock-and-roll record. By Peter's reaction, I could tell he hadn't done it on the first three records, and when I worked on the next two KISS records with Eddie Kramer, he didn't use a metronome or any timing device, either. In fact, I had and never have since worked on an album where the drummer had to be coached that way all the way through."[29]

"Working with Ezrin was the hardest experience of my life," Criss writes, in *Makeup to Breakup*. "For me, music is all about emotion and attitude. When you pick up those sticks, you have to feel it or else you're just tick and tocking—you're a mechanical clock. Most of the greats didn't play by the book—they played from the heart. But this was different. Ezrin actually wrote out every drum part for me and came up with some very intricate drumming that wasn't even in my musical style. I was a meat-and-potatoes Charlie Watts, Motown type of guy. Ezrin demanded complexity, so I got frustrated very fast that I wasn't giving Bob what he wanted."[30]

"Peter Criss will say that all I did was criticize him, but I *didn't*," argues Ezrin. "I didn't *criticize* him, I just made him play it over and over and over again, and he kept saying, 'You're killing me!' And I'd go, 'You can do it! Come on!'"[31]

Both Criss and Ezrin became so exasperated that the young producer reached for a completely unorthodox method and decided to simultaneously play along with the track and the drummer. Stasiak: "Eventually what Bob did was wrap a Shure 57 microphone up in a piece of foam into a four-inch square 3M leader tape box—leader tape being the white stuff you put on master tapes between the songs to separate them in silence—and just took a drum stick and beat out the beat. People always say that it was Bob banging on an ashtray, but that would have been too sharp a sound. You see, we had three headphone systems—maybe two, with Gene and Paul sharing one cue—which was perfect for KISS, because for most of the basic tracks we were working with three guys: drums, bass, and guitar. The drummer usually got the click track the loudest. He had his own mix. Peter could hear more bass drum or snare if he wished, and then heavy with Bob banging on the box. He could also hear more bass, too. Everyone had their own separate mixes. To my recollection, we never recorded the 57 with Bob banging away, but we would have erased it anyway, as soon as we got the drums down."[32]

In his memoir, Peter Criss writes that Ezrin drew his cat-man face on the box, playfully calling it the Cat Box. It added an occasional wrinkle to the proceedings: "I'd be playing along with it, but all of a sudden I'd hear an extra beat and I'd get thrown off and I'd stop the recording. 'Wait a minute. You just switched the beat,' I'd say. 'There's something wrong with that box.' 'Nah, there's nothing wrong with the box,' I'd hear him [Ezrin] say from the console room. There wasn't. He was just fucking with me, playing mind games."[33]

Criss's spectacular lack of patience and penchant to explode at any point over the most miniscule annoyance was being duly tested by Ezrin. While the other three members of KISS, having endured Criss's erratic mood swings on tour and occasionally during previous sessions, braced themselves for the explosion, the young producer showed no signs of letting up. He pushed the exasperated drummer to his inevitable brink, which by the winter of 1976 had become something of KISS legend.

"Peter liked to show off," C. K. Lendt, KISS's business liaison, explained to KISS Hell Online in 1998. "There are two things going on here: Peter had a substance abuse problem, and that's clear and that certainly affected his personality, but having said that it was also part of his natural personality that he had to impress people, that he had to show that he was the man in charge and he kind of liked the idea of unsettling people and making them crazy because he felt that gave him power, it was kind of a mind game in a way. The reality was that if you didn't pay attention to a lot of Peter's histrionics and craziness and you treated him as a regular person and said, 'Look I'm gonna deal with you as one guy to another and forget about all of your craziness,' Peter respected you more, and he calmed down and he settled into a more mature adult role and you could become very friendly with him. But some people have to put on this big act to impress people and get a reaction because they feel it makes them powerful, but they're just testing you, and with Peter he was really testing you because he felt that if you were really a down to earth guy that you would see through some of his silliness and when that facade came down he was much more enjoyable to be around."[34]

"Peter would get exhausted or get lazy, or sometimes he was just not into it on certain days," remembers Stasiak. "He was more, 'When can I go home? Do you really need me today?' or 'I'm not really into it today'—that kind of thing. Bob really kicked their butts to get those takes down. This is why our bass setup, when the guys played live was as simple as we could get it, because we had to get Peter right. Once we got the drums down, Peter could go home, and we could overdub the bass and try all different things."[35]

"If Peter had a problem with the click track, that was never a problem for me," says Jay Messina. "It might have been a problem for Bob or a problem for Peter, but not for me. I was there to make the drum sound as good as it could be."[36]

Before long, Ezrin had sent the rest of the band out of the studio or ordered them to leave the building entirely. It was then that he and his team began coercing Criss through each excruciatingly detailed take with astute precision. And for all of his alleged whining and complaining, the Cat Man persevered over several days—take after take after bone-rattling take—as Messina and Stasiak rushed around, moving his kit from one end of Studio A to the other: starting in the middle of the room, the back door flung open, pushing the sound into a cavernous explosion to achieve the four-on-the-floor attack of "Detroit Rock City"; into the deadened drum booth for the snapping pornography of "Sweet Pain"; closer into the carpeted area for the Stax-laden shimmy of "Shout It Out Loud"; and finally moving the bass drum and floor toms to the freight elevator for the monstrous backdrop to the cinematic themes of "God of Thunder."

When Criss would begin to wane beneath the physical toll that repeated takes of the violently concussive process of rock drumming can render, Ezrin began psychologically manipulating him, according to Criss's account in his memoir. "I started to really hate Bob at that point," he writes. "But, as with most of the stuff that Bob did, he had a hidden agenda. After a while, Ezrin realized that I had a trigger temper, and began to push me just far enough so I would begin to take out my anger on the drums."[37]

Ezrin's considerable ego and Criss's fury—both fueled by cocaine and the stress of the task at hand—combined to imbue *Destroyer*'s drum tracks with an aggressive passion never duplicated on a KISS record. Tales of the drummer's angered explosions—be it in the studio, during the *Hotter Than Hell* sessions, or onstage, as he repeatedly carped about having to risk his neck nightly on dangerously rigged drum risers that lifted him closer and closer to dubiously assembled shooting flames—coursed through the veins of KISS's inner sanctum.

C. K. Lendt expounds on the type of terror Criss wreaked daily on KISS office staffers: "The people who worked in the office—whether it was our office or Bill Aucoin's office—a lot of the girls that were assistants and secretaries at the time, they would be terrified to get a phone call from him, because sometimes he would call and be very abusive and start yelling and screaming and just really carrying on and making himself really objectionable and they would be afraid to take calls from him anymore because they were always afraid he was gonna go off the deep end. On the road crew it was the same: sometimes he would come into a sound check and start storming around the arena at some piece of equipment that wasn't set up right or he wasn't in the right mood to play and he started cursing everybody out. Because of his substance abuse he didn't sleep properly, he was up for days, and it's very difficult to deal with a person—particularly if you're a bodyguard or a road manager and you're responsible for getting the band to and from the next gig and on the plane—to deal with a person that hasn't slept in days and goes to the airport wrapped in blankets, and it's almost impossible to keep under control."[38]

Ezrin fused the notorious Peter Criss anger into the bedrock of *Destroyer*. "I would see him laughing hysterically, and I would hit those drums harder than I ever hit them in my life," Criss writes, in his memoir. "I just envisioned Ezrin's face on those drums and I hit them so hard it sounded nasty and evil, which was what he was going for all the time."[39]

The young producer's method for pushing Criss and the rest of the band fits in with Criss's theory about underlying agendas. For Ezrin, there was a sense that when the band was onstage—its most comfortable palette—Simmons, Stanley, Frehley, and Criss would live in the moment, reacting to the spectacle of performance while paying little to no attention to musicianship or approach. They thrived, Ezrin surmised, when each of them was unable to overanalyze. This was part of his method of guiding the band through each song in rehearsals, laying the groundwork for them to merely play each number as if by rote, so that they could then expend studio energies on attitude rather than style.

As with his exploitation of Criss's hair-trigger temper, Ezrin strategically used humor as a distraction. "One of the things that characterized all the KISS sessions was there was a large amount of humor," he recalls, "a lot of kidding around, practical jokes, a lot of fast repartee between us. My shtick was, every time the tape stopped rolling, I would fill the silence with something that would make the guys laugh. I felt like if you leave time for the performer to think of their performance between takes, all that happens—and this is my theory, and I could be wrong about that—but all that happens from having that time is they would start to get self-conscious. And once they start to get self-conscious, they lose that kind of automatic, unconscious, intuitive, inspired edge they had when they're performing. So I would try never to leave them out there *thinking*. To me, that was a dangerous thing.

"I still teach that, especially with singers, but really with anybody who performs. When somebody's just done a performance and the tape stops—or nowadays when you hit stop on Pro Tools—the minute that's over, the first thing that happens is they have a little bit of release of tension and they feel good or bad about what they just did, and then they start to think and they start to review their performance. They begin to self-criticize. The minute they get to self-criticism, you're in deep doo-doo. You're starting to get into the swamp, and you can lose them in there if you're not really careful. Remember, this is my theory—not everybody should strive for this—but for me, when that tape stopped, I let them have a breath, so they could go, 'Wow that felt pretty good,' and then I'd make a joke. I'd start something; I'd do something that would take their mind off what they just did and what we're about to do next. I wanted them to go into every take with a fresh, blank emotional slate."[40]

"It was excruciatingly painful," Criss concludes in his memoir. "But the outcome was genius. You listen to those songs on *Destroyer* and you go, 'Holy fuck, those drums are amazing.'"[41]

It wasn't too long into the *Destroyer* sessions, however, that Ezrin's Machiavellian distractions began to take on the anarchic overtones of complete madness.

15

Games

*As near as I can remember, you have a job to do,
and the first one that drops gets to go home.*
—Corky Stasiak[1]

"Generally, the Record Plant was kind of a boy's town," enthuses Bob Ezrin. "It was basically a locker room. You had a bunch of men, one or two poor abused women at the reception desk—some of them actually didn't mind it—and all of these guys with all of this testosterone rolling around and hanging out kibitzing, playing with each other, having fun, doing what they do. So even that, even our games, even the things that we did for diversion, in some way centered around the project in the studio."[2]

A few days into the *Destroyer* sessions, KISS had become absorbed into the sporadically festive world of the Record Plant and its master of ceremonies, Ezrin. Enduring the long days of being pushed to their creative limits, Simmons, Stanley, Frehley, and Criss began to wither. So too did Jay Messina and Corky Stasiak, especially since neither was given the obligatory "take five" afforded to band members, who could at least enjoy intermittent respites.

"There was so much to do and there were ideas going back and forth constantly," recalls Stasiak. "'Let's try this, let's try that, let's do this, let's do that.' And when we'd start to get tired, that's when we went home. And because they had the studio booked solid, we didn't have to break anything down because somebody was coming in the morning to record."[3]

Ezrin had cleared the entire month of January in Studio A for the sessions, which meant the studio team not only avoided the break down/reassemble process but also that of having to shift delicate mike positions or worry about anyone meddling with the precise settings on the master board in the control room. However, it also meant that the time spent working without specified breaks turned one day into the other, which became something of a blur. Once the summer's legal wrangling subsided, the recording of *Destroyer* would continue unabated, separated only by the necessities of sustenance, sleep, or simply the need to get fresh air.

Stasiak: "We'd come in at, say, eleven o'clock in the morning, and we might go home at six o'clock or nine o'clock the next morning. Maybe we'd push it until 2 a.m., and out of nowhere Bob would say, 'You know what? Let's get some sleep. Let's show up here tomorrow at three.' He could sense things had run their course for a particular session, but if you're in the booth, like me and Jay, you had to persevere."[4]

"It was tougher for an assistant like Corky," says Messina. "The session would get finished at, you know, five in the morning, and they had to be back in a few hours. So rather than take an hour and a half to go home and then another hour and a half to come back, they would just find a vocal booth or sleep under the piano someplace. It wasn't really the bands that practically lived there. They would come in and spend months—I've done Aerosmith records that would take months—but they wouldn't be sleeping in the studio. We would."[5]

"Working with Bob meant typically twelve-hour days, go home, and come back and do it again," recalled assistant engineer Rod O'Brien, during an interview for this book. "In fact I remember, for whatever reason, while KISS was recording *Destroyer*, my two twin daughters—and they were probably two or two-and-a-half at the time—were with me, and they were in the lounge, and Gene, exhausted from a session, came out to take a break and tried, in Gene's way, to be nice to them, leaning down and saying, 'Hi, how are you guys doing?' One of my daughters was a little nervous and my other daughter, Jessica, decided that she was going to protect her sister, and she looked at him and said, 'We don't like you, go away,' at which point Gene began to get upset. 'What the hell!'"[6]

The making of *Destroyer* quickly turned into something between a fluid exercise and a test of wills, as one or more band members enduring tired fingers (Peter Criss had his hands buried in a bucket of ice), a hoarse voice, or just a frustrating mental block and would be forced to temporarily bow out. Without missing a beat, as if a troop commander aiming to take a hill, Ezrin would turn to Messina or Stasiak and instruct the setup of a vocal mic or the moving of drums out to the back corridor for an overdub, or perhaps whip together rough mixes of the day's work for review. It was as if the young producer, fueled by drugs, tunnel-vision creativity, and a fast-approaching deadline to produce *the* KISS album, would instinctively play off the collective energies of whoever had not yet succumb to exhaustion and keep moving.

It was during these breaks that Ezrin began adding piano to certain tracks, specifically and crucially "Detroit Rock City," which was realizing its operatic framework. While it is usually used as either a song's main accompaniment or to add a subtle descant, the piano on *Destroyer* was employed for power.

"You want to make stuff big, because you've got all of those sonic oscillations going up and down, and some are phasing each other," explains Stasiak. "When that happens, it gives it a shimmer, almost like a 3D sheen that pops out a little bit. That's not an Ezrin trick or a new trick. That's been done since pop music began. Look to Les Paul, who invented the multitrack recording. He would play a guitar part and then an octave above and the third or the fifth of the chord and build a sound. It was nothing new, really, but it was effective."[7]

Additional hours of overdubbing bass, piano, and guitars further enhanced the depth of each song, cementing the uniformed enormity of *Destroyer* painfully absent from previous KISS studio efforts. This began with Ezrin's signature recording of acoustic guitars. From the very first Alice Cooper project to his magnificent work with Pink Floyd on *The Wall*, his use of the warmth and depth of acoustic instruments became a strategic element to his layering of sounds that vividly separates the sonic landscape of *his* artists from the pack. *Destroyer* is no exception. KISS had previously used acoustic instruments sparingly (piano on "Nothin' to Lose," from *KISS*, and acoustic guitars on *Dressed to Kill*'s "Rock Bottom"), but now Ezrin worked out the songs on piano, from the chord progressions of "Flaming Youth" and "Great Expectations" to the guitar solo interlude in "Detroit Rock City," later layering parts into the backing tracks to boost the guitars and add a foundation to accompany the bass. Then, of course, as with "Great Expectations," the piano and acoustic guitars were pushed to the fore to further enhance the romantic flavor of the song.

Ezrin: "What the Dolby machines used to do, in order to reduce noise, was they'd take the signal coming in and hyper-amplify the top end. On the back end of it, they'd bring the top end down, bringing down the noise level with it. So when it came out the other side, it would be attenuating noise. That was the design of the machine. What we did was to take the amplification of the top end and didn't process it out on the backend. When you left it amplified like that, you'd get this brilliant sheen to the guitar sound."[8]

Stanley concurs. "Sonically, Bob Ezrin didn't try to recreate the bombast of *Alive!* with its huge broken-up guitars and screaming vocals. He found power in other ways. He created an atmosphere of grandeur. He brought elements of things I loved—like the orchestral bells on 'Do You Love Me?' He gave the guitar chords heft by layering them with grand piano playing the same parts. In some ways it reminded me of what I liked about Roy Wood and Wizzard—that big, chaotic version of Phil Spector's Wall of Sound. Bob added things that really struck emotional chords in me."[9]

Ezrin was pushing to infuse *Destroyer* with an arena sound—a device he used spectacularly on Alice Cooper's *Billion Dollar Babies*, which brilliantly absorbed the mythology of The Show into the tracks—to create a booming, cavernous bludgeoning of the senses, as if the listener were at a concert. Having ignored what KISS had produced on its previous three studio records but now well aware of the impact *Alive!*, he was assured this tactic was the studio elixir for The Act.

"I took what you see with KISS live," he says, "the power, the drama, the joy, the horror—all those emotions that you see within those people performing and translate them into a soundscape. I was also trying to expand on all that. I sometimes found what they were putting forward to be less than three-dimensional. So I would help them to think about that. This was true of Alice Cooper, but particularly in the case of KISS."[10]

Stasiak: "Bob loved compression; he loved delay, all the little tricks. He used the control room as an instrument."[11]

"We used to call Bob Dr. Delay," adds Rod O'Brien. "He would turn to you and say, 'All right, take the guitar feed it into that fifteen ips tape delay, come out of that and put it into that seven-and-a-half ips tape delay, and then send the whole thing to the reverb.' You'd look at him like, 'Okay,' and all of a sudden we'd have this sound that was like, 'Oh my God this is great!'"[12]

"We loved the Eventide digital tape delay at that time," Stasiak explains. "We used it on just about every song for *Destroyer*. We'd have two digital delays going and a couple of tape machines doing delay on different things, especially when we mixed. It would just pop out of the speakers, melding everything together. And we used echo in different chambers. We had, I think, four or five different echo chambers—EMT echo chambers—that we patched into, and sometimes we had three studios, Studio A, B, and C that recorded, and then we had a mix room later, so that was four studios. And sometimes you wanted to use the good echo chamber, number one, which was on the roof of the building. It was in its own separate room. Roy Cicala built a separate room up there with the tape library on the top of the building, and he had a couple of EMT chambers in there, and they were these big wooden rectangle chambers that inside, if you cut it in half, one side had a microphone and the other side there was a speaker, and then there were plates in between, and you could control them remotely from outside the studio. You can say, 'Okay, patch me into chamber one,' and it would go into chamber one, which would go up to the roof, and whatever we fed into that chamber would come back down into chamber one, and then out and we'd bring it up to the board, and that would be chamber one. And then Bob might say, 'Make the chamber longer,' so there was a remote control button over in the hallway—just press it, and it would move the plate back so that you would get a longer echo delay."[13]

"Bob had great skill and vision to commit to sounds for a record while the performance was being recorded," concludes O'Brien. "For instance, you send a lead vocalist out to a microphone and you give them a certain type of reverb in their headphones, they are going to sing differently than they would if it was dry, or if there's a tape delay as opposed to an echo chamber. When you take all of that away, if you don't put that on tape, you're going to listen back to a dry vocal that's not going to have that same kind of feel or what they've done with their feel, because what they're hearing may not be the same. So we always committed these things. We would commit stuff in somebody's headphones—the guitar player, the vocalist, or even the drums—where we put him on the live side of the room, then on the next song he would be in the little drum booth because it needs to sound this way. Bob was never afraid to do it, and he taught us to never be afraid to do it. Every part of every song needed to be tailored and adjusted and found for each individual instrument or vocal."[14]

Technological "tricks" weren't the only effective way to add density to the tracks. Continuing in the tradition of every song KISS recorded up to and including *Destroyer*, the guitars and bass were tuned down a half step (a practice also known as tuning down one fret). While it is usually done to accommodate a singer's range, tuning down electric guitars also provides a fuller, deeper sound. The fatter punch is manifested in the use of "power chords"—the very staple of the heavy sound made famous by Jimi Hendrix and continued in the genre throughout the 1970s and beyond. For example, the band may be performing the song in C-sharp minor, but to the musically trained ear it is actually C minor. The result creates an impressive backdrop. Unconsciously, the listener is hearing a chord in a certain pitch: for instance, a standard A will appear as an A-flat, but has the same resonance as the A major.

Stasiak: "Bob wanted the guitars to sound like an orchestra. He told them to play an octave or maybe a third, and once they did it, they'd go, 'Oh, yeah. I've done this before on a Beatles song, or when I was learning it years ago.' A lot of times we'd find a little bit of buried treasure when you would have a guitar track that was great and you'd go, 'Fuck, that's great—let's double it!' Then you would double it and make it bigger or double it with a different guitar and give it a big layered sound, but most of that was calculated through overdubs."[15]

Stanley: "He [Ezrin] was the first producer we worked with who—finally—understood the subtleties we didn't understand about using different guitars for different parts, or doubling guitars with a different guitar, or slowing down the tape slightly and doubling the guitar over it to make the sound bigger because of the slight discrepancy in the tuning. Bob knew the essence of great production and great arrangements, and he brought it to bear on *Destroyer* in a way I thought was groundbreaking for the type of music we made."[16]

"I learned a great deal from Bob—how to record things and how to layer things—and there were a lot of overdubs on *Destroyer* to get that symphonic glow," says Stasiak. "It would do funny things; pop it out just a little bit. For instance, in 'Detroit Rock City,' on the *ba-daaa* [ascending phrase] there is a lot of that kind of layering going on. I would not be surprised if we ended up with eight parts."[17] As Stanley recalled for the liner notes to *The Box Set*, "I remember recording 'King of the Night Time World' in the studio with my sunburst Gibson double-neck with the toggle switch set to the middle position, so that as I was playing on the six-string neck, the twelve-string neck was resonating harmonically."[18]

And so it went through the first week of recording—specifically January 5 through 10, according to Corky Stasiak's trusty log, with a one-day reprieve (January 11) and back again on the 12th. The band and team soldiered on, trudging through takes, overdubbing guitars and piano, and experimenting with sounds and effects. The first casualties of this furious pace were Peter Criss, after his initial spate of drumming, and Ace Frehley, described by all involved as having little interest in laying the groundwork for the basic tracks and expecting instead to be called to perform once the sections for his signature solos were presented. Following a private discussion with Ace, Stasiak came to the conclusion early on in the sessions that the lead guitarist was burnt out from touring, and for him, being back in New York meant getting to hang out with friends and his fiancée, Jeanette, not wading through endless takes. "Paul and I used to talk about who was taking the experience harder," Simmons writes, in *KISS and Make-Up*. "In retrospect, I think both of them were feeling quite defeated, although their feelings manifested in different ways. Peter would come out furious that somebody was telling him what to play or how to sing. Ace would simply leave."[19]

"We began to have to work around Ace, who spent much of the recording process with his priorities far from where they belonged," Stanley writes. "He sometimes played his part with his rings and chains scraping against the fret board and pickups, and then wanted to quit for the day and take off. When I would ask him to remove the jewelry and do another take because of all the noise, he would say, 'Hey, that's rock and roll.'"[20]

"I play my best when I don't think," Frehley explained to *Vintage Guitar* in 1997. "I have an idea of what key I'm in, but basically, I go 'Hit the tape' and I close my eyes and let my fingers do the talkin'. 'Firehouse' was a one-take solo. In the early days, I used to sit home and try to plan solos, but what would happen is I'd get into the studio after working maybe two or three hours on the solo that I thought everybody would fall in love with and they'd say, 'You can do better than that!' Nine tunes out of ten, I'd just end up throwing out the solo I wrote, and come up with a variation of it, or just go in a completely different direction. Planning solos doesn't work for me. I'd rather just come in with a couple of licks to throw in and work around them. I have no idea why I do what I do!"[21]

True to form, while Criss had been driven into a rage and Frehley was clearly struggling with Bob Ezrin's strive for perfection, Stanley and Simmons fed off the pressure. They used Ezrin's creative cauldron to relentlessly challenge each other over the long hours, with both welcoming the mounting workload as proof that the magnitude of The Act was being realized. "Gene and Paul related to each other," says Stasiak. "You could tell that they were friends and that they trusted each other's opinion. They would call out, 'Gene, what do you think?' 'Hey, Paul, what do you think?' It was really a democratic society between those two guys, and they saw the end result. I mean, Ezrin was pulling great stuff from them, and I think they were real happy about that."[22]

On several occasions during intense periods of overdubbing, Simmons would call for professional women to ply their trade. Stasiak: "I can't remember what song it was, but Gene says, 'Listen, I can't do this. I need a hooker first.' And Bob said, 'What do you mean you need a hooker?' He says, 'I just, you know, I gotta get a blow job.' And everyone looks at me, and I said, 'I'm not going out. I'm sorry, man, that's not in my job description.' And then they looked at Bob, and Bob says to Gene, 'If you need this, make it happen, but I'm not going to help you out. I'll give you the money, but I'm not gonna help you out.' So Gene got up and went down the street. It's Hell's Kitchen, for Christ's sake, so in twenty minutes we're looking at the little camera at the front door and there's Gene with three hookers, and he brought them into the studio and, well, Gene did his thing and, you know, he did the take. But I don't know if that was a keeper or not."[23]

Simmons's legendarily insatiable appetite for women of all sizes, shapes, creed, color, and comportment became a thread throughout the sessions, and one that was established right away. "I can remember that we had been in the building for twelve minutes before Gene Simmons had the receptionist in the bathroom," says Ezrin.[24] Stasiak recalls Simmons bringing in two women and asking everyone politely to exit the studio until he was finished—and, to his amazement, everyone did.

Soon Frehley—whom Ezrin described in more than one interesting interlude tripping over himself without spilling a drop of his drink and exclaiming,

"Must have been an earth tremor!"²⁵—felt left out and began demanding sexual assistance before a take. Simmons once again volunteered for a recognizance mission, but according to most witnesses present returned with a prostitute so repellent that not even a blitzed Ace would touch her. "I remember the hooker and I remember Gene going in with her when nobody else would touch her," says Ezrin. "I'm not sure that it was because Ace refused to play until he got a blow job, but I like that twist on it. If that's the way Gene wants to tell it, I think that's a good way to print it."²⁶

"During the entire recording of *Destroyer*, Bob was the buffer," says Messina. "There were never any problems with me and the band. I got along with everybody. Paul used to get me hysterical with his impressions of Desi Arnaz. He'd get me every time, running around shouting, 'Lucy! Lucy!' Ace and I hit it off, and it's been a lasting friendship. I still keep in touch with Ace to this day. A good part of it was music-related, but also whenever I would see him out or when we'd go to parties together. Our friendship went beyond music. Sometimes we'd go to Studio 54 or to the Copa. We had a blast. But in the studio, I had fun with all of the guys. Lots of laughs."²⁷

Ezrin ran a tight if not chemically enhanced and sexually promiscuous ship, but he also knew when to blow off steam, and that usually came in the guise of a running joke or prank. His brandishing of the odd fire extinguisher had already given the proceedings a weird turn, as recounted by Criss in his memoir, but it wasn't always about rallying the charges, as had quickly become the custom with his trusty whistle. Soon he began enlisting the entire staff and the band in raiding nearby sessions with four or five fire extinguishers, blasting the offending foam all over the place before retreating to brace for the obligatory retaliation.

Apparently, the fire extinguisher battles had been raging for sometime around the Record Plant, as Corky Stasiak remembers during what he could only guess was an initiation into his early days while he was working with Shelly Yakus and decided to pay a visit to Jack Douglas and Jay Messina down the hall, where they were recording the New York Dolls' debut album. After being lured into a darkened studio by his hero, Jay Messina, and his partner in music and crime, Jack Douglas, with the promise of a couple of lines of premier cocaine, Stasiak instead found streaks of white grease pencil on a grand piano. Just as he realized he'd been had, the lights flicked off, forcing him to crawl back through the pitch-black studio groping for the door. Once he entered the main hallway, he was suddenly bombarded by several blasts of sticky foam. "When this stuff hits your clothes and then your skin touches your clothes, it burns like crazy! So I'm screaming, '*Ahhhhh!*' and running back into the dark studio," he recalls.²⁸ After enduring the hoots and hollers of his assailants outside for forty-five minutes, Stasiak slowly emerged, reaching the adjoining studio soaked and ill-humored only to find Messina and Douglas looking back nonchalantly and greeting him with nary a word of the ambush.

"Oh, there were friendly rivalries between studios, like between Studio A and whoever had the great misfortune to occupy Studio B," says Ezrin, who recalls declaring war on Grand Funk Railroad next door. "At one point there was a group in New York called J. F. Murphy & Free Flowing Salt. Jack [the band's lead singer and songwriter] was a real prankster. So, Big John—one of KISS's security guys, who was a wonderful character—and I walked into Studio B in the middle of Jack Murphy's session, and without saying anything we took three rolls of gaffer's tape and made a human dart out of him! We taped him from his neck to his ankles, and I said, 'John, let's load him up.' John put him up over his shoulder and went outside and threw him into the garbage dumpster just as the truck came along. The Greeks in the truck thought that this was the funniest thing that they'd ever seen. They looked at us like, 'What should we do?' We just said, 'Take him away!' So they dumped the dumpster, including Jack Murphy, into the truck and he was yelling as they drove away down Forty-Fourth Street, 'I'll get you for this!'"[29]

"We were all crazy guys and the sessions were always long, so it was very common to create havoc," says David Thoener, a Grammy-winning sound engineer and a victim of Ezrin's raids. "One of our interns got gaffer-taped to a studio chair and rolled out to Forty-Fourth Street. Being New York, he was out there for half an hour and people walked by and said nothing!"[30]

"One time we put somebody into an anvil case and rolled him into the lobby of the building," recalls Rod O'Brien. "We made sure we let him out before the air went away, but the thing is, Bob was one of those people where if you crossed that line with him it could be six minutes or six months, but he was going to get you back."[31]

"Rod O'Brien was a punky kid who was working in another studio when we were recording *Destroyer*," remembers Ezrin. "He loved to pull these little tricks or yell out something during a take or something mischievous. I'm pretty sure Rod did something like that, which we took as a challenge."[32]

"Bob came in one night and decided that we had declared war on him," remembers O'Brien. "We were celebrating an engineer's birthday and set up a little cake for him in Studio A. Long story short, a cake fight ensued; some icing got on the wall, and so I decided to write with the icing on the Studio A control room window, 'Hi Bob.'"[33]

According to O'Brien, Ezrin waited outside the Studio B door listening for the tape machine to stop, so as to not compromise a take, and then proceeded to cut all the circuit breakers. Just as when Stasiak was ambushed by Messina and Douglas, the windowless room was pitched in black.

"You could not see your hand in front of your face," continues O'Brien. "So I stepped outside of Studio B and was immediately grabbed by Bob and another engineer, Brian Christianson, who was this really big man, and they gaffer-taped me from head to foot and took me upstairs to the tenth floor to Studio C. Bob was like, 'How many fire extinguishers do they have?' because fire extinguishers were always the weapons of choice. They shut the lights off and left me gaffer-taped on the couch. I'm literally taped from my chest all the way down. But somehow I manage to get out of that and went down the back elevator to where our maintenance department tech guy was, grabbed the fire extinguisher, and ambushed Bob! But for some odd reason, the KISS guys had all these pies, and then a pie fight breaks out.

"This went on for a while, and by now it's sometime on Sunday, and there is cake and pie on the walls and every fire extinguisher in the building was empty. The lobby, the lounge, everything was caked, so we tried to clean up as best we could. Then the maintenance man shows up at six in the morning and he's like, 'Uh-uh, I'm not dealing with this,' so he calls Roy [Cicala]. By this time I'm home and I'm sleeping and Roy calls me. Very calmly, he says, 'Rod, I have a question for you.' And then he just went nuts. 'WHY IS THERE CAKE ON THE WALL AND THIS AND THIS AND FIRE EXTINGUISHERS!' And I'm still half asleep, so I said, 'Call Ezrin and he'll explain it all,' and I hung up. I believe Jimmy Ienner—whose idea it was to get the cake in the first place—and Bob each kicked in about two-to-three-hundred dollars apiece to get professional cleaners to come in and do a really good job. We used to have these felt and decorative things on the walls, and there was a cork wall with all these gold records on it in the lobby area, so they had to come in and pretty much steam-clean everything. But Bob said, 'It was well worth it. We'll pay.'"[34]

The next Studio B victim, twenty-one-year-old David Thoener, was assisting engineer/producer Shelly Yakus's work with legendary blues guitarist Johnny Winter when at 2 a.m., while transferring tapes to the tenth floor, he made the mistake of informing the very same Rod O'Brien that he would be "alarming" the first floor, so that no one would accidently set it off. O'Brien needed no further prodding to gather the KISS team together to pounce. "If Bob decided we were going to tape somebody up or handcuff them or whatever we were going to do, you were either with him or against him. Obviously, I never liked to be against him if I didn't have to be."[35]

"I was extremely tired," remembers Thoener, nearly four decades later. "And as I turned my back to walk out of Studio C, Rod tackled me and put a handcuff on one wrist and pulled me over to the studio door and clipped the other end around the handle on the outside of the door. I naturally started pounding on the door, and Bob came out and said, 'The longer you pound, the longer you stay handcuffed.' So I stop, sit down on the floor, and wait with my hand suspended in the air latched to the door."[36]

"I told him, 'Now, you can sit here, or you can say, 'I'm really sorry, Mister Ezrin for the nasty things I said and did earlier today,'" remembers Ezrin. "He looked at me defiantly—to him this was just a joke—and he said, 'Fuck you.' And I go, 'Really? Wrong answer.' So I opened the exit door, which led to the roof of the building, and took the key and threw it off the roof. That's when he sloped down to the floor and realized, 'Holy shit, I'm stuck here for life!' So we went back downstairs and did a few other takes of a song."[37]

"I watched as the key went over the ledge into oblivion," says Thoener. "They all walked to the elevator and Bob said, 'We'll see you tomorrow!'"[38]

Unbeknownst to Thoener, when Ezrin purchased the already legendary whistle, he was also moved to grab four pairs of handcuffs and the requisite number of keys. "By that point," Ezrin recalls, "he knew that we didn't really intend to keep him there forever, so he said something else wise. I don't remember what it was but, long story short, we ended up throwing three keys off the building and left the fourth key with the cleaner who came in the mornings and said, 'Could you please let Dave out?' So he was there all night until the cleaner came at 7 or 8 a.m. and let him out!"[39]

"I was not there all night!" Thoener argues today. "First of all, that wouldn't make sense. The maintenance guy would not have had the key. Sure, at first I figured I'd be there until the maintenance guys came in and they would saw me loose, but Rod came back about ten minutes after they all walked out and let me go. I was really pissed, but Bob was a very important client and I let the incident go. I never forgot, and he didn't either, but we later became friends."[40]

"I think Bob is correct, because I don't believe that I set David free," O'Brien retorts. "I honestly don't know who set him free, because we all left, and that was the thing: we left David up there. I know Bob gave someone the keys and it might have been this guy Willie. Willie was the gentleman who would come in the morning to clean up. Willie would show up around six in the morning, so he might have done it or it may have been one of the tech guys. They would come in to align tape machines anywhere between six and eight in the morning, depending upon schedules. So it could have been him, but I don't remember. I gave the keys to somebody, but I *did not* free David as far as I remember."[41]

Thoener rebukes this emphatically. "About an hour later, their session ended, they all came out, and then Rod came back and let me out, whether he remembers or not. That is a very distinct memory of mine. I am younger than these guys—they are all senile!"[42]

"I let David out," says Corky Stasiak. "I know the whole story. First off, Rod and I tackled David. Bob said to me, 'We have to get that David Thoener, he's obnoxious.' And I argued, 'David? He's such a nice guy!' But he insisted, 'He's a pain in the ass, we have to get him!' Then he says, 'Get Rod up here.' He knew Rod would be up for this, because he was always right in your face. Rod was not afraid to mix it up with anyone. So, when David poked his head in to tell us he was locking up, Bob yells, 'Get him!' And then everything went how the guys remember it, with Bob baiting him and then throwing the key ten stories down to Forty-Fifth Street. The whole time I'm pleading with Bob to let David go, but he just would not do it. I convinced him to at least give me the key when he left for the morning at around four—probably two hours after we first handcuffed him. I found him asleep with his hand dangling from the Studio C door and I set him free. Man, when he woke up, was he pissed off.[43]

Perhaps it was the day poor David Thoener was rescued by Stasiak, or embattled Rod O'Brien was gaffer-taped, or the time someone got around to rescuing the intern from the anvil case, or the day after the day after that—as each session overlapped into the other—when Stasiak received a notice that there was a special delivery for a Mr. Bob Ezrin at the front door of the Record Plant.

"I was blown away," remembers Stasiak. "I said, 'This can't be for our session. You guys probably delivered this to the wrong place.' And the delivery guy says, 'Nope. *Ezrin, KISS, Studio A*.' So I signed for it, but I couldn't believe that we were going to use a calliope!"[44]

Standing out on Eighth Avenue like the sorest of thumbs was an antique, circus-style calliope: thirty-two keys surrounded by a six-foot-tall, elaborately painted casing with gaudy pastels, flanked by four giant wooden wheels with yellow spokes. "We had rented this stupid-fucking-looking thing from SIR," chuckles Stasiak, even today mesmerized by the sight of it. "I mean, it was ridiculous. It was all painted up like it came out of a circus: white with Wonder Bread–type multicolored balloon colors on it. It looked like a street vendor's hot dog stand, and I said to Bob, 'You're kidding me, man.' And Ezrin goes, 'No, no. It's great. Listen, listen.' And I'm thinking to myself, 'Where the hell are we going to use this on a KISS record?' But Bob was great that way. He always had a little something in the back of his mind that he was going to spring on us at some point, which makes it fun to work with the guy. And it worked. I mean, what Bob did with it on 'Flaming Youth' worked!"[45]

"There is this bouncing eighth-note feel to the song when I played the piano part that just implied to me that circus vibe, and I thought if you're going to have that then why not go all the way?" says Ezrin. "I mean, the Beatles used to do that stuff all the time, where a strange instrument could be introduced into the song because it invoked a certain vibe for one moment. Almost like a cameo in a film: you would take a side trip into some other place in your memory or your consciousness. So, for me, that reminded me of a circus feel, and I thought, 'You know what would be cool, let's get a calliope!'"[46]

"Bob asked me to look into a calliope," recalls Jay Messina. "And I remembered we had once gone to Coney Island for a Ronnie Montrose record to record amusement sounds, and there was a calliope at a merry-go-round, and as we approached, the guy saw we had recording equipment and shut it off. He wanted $500 to record his calliope, so I knew it wasn't going to be that simple."[47]

"So we called around and, in fact, you can rent a calliope in New York City, which was a pleasant surprise to me," says Ezrin. "It was a mini steam calliope. It was electric, so it was blowing air through its pipes. You plug it in and you're playing circus music automatically."[48]

Rolling it in, Stasiak watched in amazement as Ezrin, smiling like the Cheshire Cat, sat down and began playing. The enormous rollicking sound of it bounced all around Studio A. Although the assistant engineer knew that the surreal was business as usual at the Record Plant, all he kept thinking was how in the world would they mike such a thing? "It had speakers on the side—or, you know, ports or something like that—and it wasn't stereo or anything," says Stasiak. "It was just like one port or one speaker, and I don't know what mic we used for it. I'm thinking that we used the Sony cardioid microphone, ones that Roy had gotten from Japan or something like that."[49]

"It was either a C-37 or a C-38," concludes Messina, who, in his inimitably stoic way, went about setting up this most usual rock-and-roll accompaniment, batting nary an eye and asking no questions.[50]

16

Exit Ace—Enter Maestro and the Kids

For me it was the ability to say something with the guitar.
—Dick Wagner[1]

Somewhere between the wild abandon and long hours of recording, Ace Frehley went missing. With no explanation other than his being Ace, the band and its producer began to lose patience. "Ace was always just Ace," recalls Ezrin. "He didn't become affected by success, he just was that guy—this party guy. He was the Ace in Space, a little spaced out and kind of stoned a lot, and even when he wasn't, he was always in his own private Idaho."[2]

"Ace's habits were heavily into alcohol, he did other things, but I certainly remember the alcohol because the alcohol was so flagrant," KISS business liaison C. K. Lendt told the KISS Hell website in 1998. "I mean, the guy would walk around with a champagne bottle all the time—not just once or twice, he was constantly drinking champagne and he would even go into a business meeting carrying a beer bottle."[3]

"There were a few times where Ace was maybe unable to play something because he may have been high or something," says Ezrin. "And it's partially true that Ace may have been intimidated and nervous by being introduced to coke on this project, but most of it had to do with Ace not making it to the session."[4]

A little more than a few days into recording, a growing rift had begun to develop between Ezrin's methods and what Frehley was willing to endure. Long before he put on makeup or made his bones as a rock star, Ace found it difficult to adhere to any set of rules. Taking into account Ezrin's frenetically uncompromising style balanced against Frehley's anti-authority stance—exacerbated by alcohol and cocaine—it was almost inevitable that things would begin to unravel.

"A lot of times for me to get a guitar solo right I have to get the right mood and I don't like pressure, " Frehley explained to KISS biographers Sharp and

Leaf. "Bob didn't have the patience the other producers that I'd worked with in the past have had. I'm not a schooled musician, if I didn't have something pat, a lot of times Bob would fuckin' make me feel inadequate, which I didn't find too thrilling."[5]

Despite allegedly being driven to primal scream therapy (a radical psychological treatment method that is pretty much as its name suggests) by the *Destroyer* sessions thus far, Peter Criss felt his experience was a walk in the park compared to Frehley's. "As painful as these sessions were for me, they were doubly hard on Ace. Ace didn't respond well to Bob's tough love. Once you get the drums and add the bass and the rhythm guitar, it's up to the lead guitarist to complete the picture. And then you're up there naked—you're on your own. Ace, like me, loved to play by feel. Ace's brother was a classically trained guitarist, but Ace hated his studied playing. Ace loved spontaneity, but Ezrin had other plans for him."[6]

"Ace felt overwhelmed," observes Corky Stasiak. "All the previous records, they would say, 'Okay, we need guitar here,' and he would put it in. He would do his part like a regular player in a band would do: two guys would jam and somebody would come in and the two guitar players would talk over the part: 'You do this and do that,' or 'Hey, I got an idea.' 'Okay, you do that.' 'Hey, I got an idea now that you're playing that.' That's the way it usually is, but when he saw how Bob was taking over the production, I got a feeling he didn't want any part of it."[7]

Ezrin: "I think that all of that stuff, for Ace, without trying to be too much of a shrink here, all that came from kind of an innate lack of confidence. I feel like insecurity was Ace's biggest problem, not the drugs or his disconnection from the other guys or even anything esthetically. It was that he didn't have enough faith in himself. And I don't even know how much he was aware of that. But I know often times when someone is afraid of a performance and they perform, they do a shitty job. For some people, that fear is their fuel. That's what makes them do better, like Olympic athletes or people like that, but musicians, for the most part, I think you have to roll into playing or singing or performing music with a clear head and an emotional impetus that's all about inspiration, passion, and desire, so there's not much room in there for fear."[8]

"I was intimidated by Bob," Frehley admits, in *No Regrets*. "You have to understand where Bob was coming from. I had heard that when he worked with Alice Cooper's band he had brought in a session guitar player to do a lot of the solos, and I got the feeling that there was a chance he was going to follow the same plan with KISS if I didn't produce quickly enough. The pressure was on—and with a hangover as a frequent distraction, I hit a brick wall occasionally."[9]

The constant partying and the excessive use of cocaine, the insecurities that stemmed from not being as musically expert as his brother, feeling intimidated by a classically-trained musician who demanded perfection—it all began to feed on Frehley's fears, which were not completely unfounded. Ezrin had indeed often used outside musicians during his maturation as a producer with the Alice Cooper group—especially guitarists. As early as the band's second album, *Killer*, he had asked celebrated guitarist Rick Derringer to step in to add a solo to the hit "Under My Wheels," and called in Dick Wagner, a Detroit axe-man of incredible pedigree, to play on several subsequent albums. Like Derringer, Wagner was not given credit, but he did receive (along with a generous paycheck) a congratulatory note of "Thanks Dick Wagner" somewhere on the busy sleeve of *School's Out*. Later, Wagner joined his Motor City brother in guitar-slinging, Steve Hunter, to become a staple member of Ezrin's cadre of talent that would tour Lou Reed's *Berlin* to great acclaim—so much so that it upstaged the brooding Reed, who summarily booted them from the show that produced one of the great live albums of the 1970's, *Rock 'n' Roll Animal*.

"Wagner and Hunter? Oh my God, when those two guys played you would get a woody," gushes Stasiak today. "I mean, if you loved guitar like I did, to listen to either one of those or both of those guys playing, it was just amazing. I'd never heard of Dick Wagner before I worked with him, and I remember Ezrin said, 'We're going to get Dick Wagner in here to do this,' and I said, 'Is he good?' And he looked at me and he gave me one of these eyes like, 'Are you kidding me?' Then he said, 'He'll come, you'll see, you'll learn.'"[10]

Ezrin: "I met Dick when he was in a band called Ursa Major. I produced their only album, fairly early on in my career [in 1972]. We shared a connection to Detroit and a love for heavy music and I found in him a guy who could play anything you could think of. So after we did the album, and situations would arise when I needed somebody to play anything we could think of, Dick Wagner was the first person I would call. I had already developed a relationship with Steve Hunter, who I got to know while producing the band, Detroit with Mitch Ryder [on 1971's *Detroit with Mitch Ryder*]. And Steve was another guy who had an otherworldly sense of melody and a kind of swampy feel that was steeped in blues, so whenever I needed that kind of thing, I'd call Hunter. On something like a KISS session for *Destroyer*, Dick was my guy."[11]

While executive-producing Aerosmith's second album, *Get Your Wings*, with Jack Douglas and Jay Messina at the controls, Ezrin brought in Wagner to spice up rhythm parts and take crucial leads. Wagner once again had to appear without public notice, much like his surreptitious turn on "I Love the Dead" from Alice Cooper's *Billion Dollar Babies*, an epic number that he not only played on but also co-wrote without an album credit.

"I received a lot of 'non-credit' credits and some attention, but my favorite may be one time a few years back when I took my sons to see Aerosmith at the San Antonio Convention Center," Wagner fondly recalled, during interviews for this book. "Steven Tyler put his arm around me in front of all those people backstage and said, 'This is the guy who helped us sell three million records.' I really appreciate that more than anything."[12]

Wagner's secret life as an invisible virtuoso allowed the thirty-three-year-old veteran of the Detroit heavy sound to take a front-and-center role in the Alice Cooper solo project *Welcome to My Nightmare*, composing, performing, and later shredding on the monumental live show.

Born and raised in Saginaw, Michigan, not far from the venue where Bob Ezrin first saw KISS perform, Dick Wagner was a rising star in the late-'60s Detroit rock revolution and a sought-after commodity. During an intense period of high competition, he was the guitar player's guitar player, making a name by forming bands like the Bossmen, the Frost, and Ursa Major, while becoming Middle America's answer to England's fascination with Eric Clapton. In a town bulging with fantastic acts playing jammed theaters that presaged the '70s heavy-rock arena experience, Wagner was well respected and imitated. In the forward to Wagner's moving 2012 memoir, *Not Only Women Bleed*, Alice Cooper writes, "I first saw Dick Wagner when he was playing with the Frost and I filed him under 'guitar players I'd like to steal.'"[13]

"The guitar for me is really like a lifelong marriage with a woman you meet who is your soul mate, who is always there for you and you always carry her with you in your soul and in your heart," exclaimed Wagner. "I used to sleep with my guitar, so that if I woke up in the middle of the night I could play it. I had a boom box I kept beside the bed and I had these tapes with backing tracks for the blues and I'd lie there in bed for hours and play guitar to it. That's how I learned how to play, to completely involve myself in it. It's like a marriage. It's the two of you: a way to hide, express yourself, and go outward. It can become all things. The guitar has been that important to me."[14]

Having reached the pinnacle of rock success, Wagner—who because of his incredible virtuosity and also an uncanny resemblance was rumored to be a direct descendent of the renowned nineteenth-century German composer Wilhelm Richard Wagner—continued to be at the beck and call of his benefactor, Bob Ezrin. The young producer would lean on him time and again to expand his sonic visions at a moment's notice. "Bob and I hit it off immediately musically," he said. "We think on the same level as far as structure and sound and all of it. It was compatible, but it was also kind of battle in those days, a back and forth of 'I love that!' or 'I don't like that!' Something he didn't like initially, and later he'd say, 'Oh, that's great!' And I'd say, 'I just played it for you a month ago!' and he'd just say, 'Well, okay, now I like it.' He was younger than me, but that was all right. He was a genius. I always enjoyed working with him, and we made a lot of great music together."[15]

By the winter of 1976, Wagner was living the solitary existence of rock-and-roll cliché, holed up in luxury suite 303 at the famously ostentatious Plaza Hotel at Central Park and Fifth Avenue. With Wagner looming only three avenues and ten blocks from the Record Plant, the specter of Ace Frehley's creeping paranoia was a simple phone call away—a phone call Bob Ezrin was fast being forced to make.

Ezrin: "Ace may have not even realized that he would miss a session, not because he was just flaky and stupid or he had just accidently fallen into a card game or a drinking bout or something like that, but I think it had a lot to do with him being sacred of the day. He was scared that we were going to do this following part, and he didn't know if he had it down or he didn't have it down and I don't think he was aware of it. But most of the problems Ace had had to do with him either getting there really late—where everybody had already been doing it for a while, and they were in the groove and he had to run to catch up—or sometimes he wouldn't show at all. So on a couple of those songs where he didn't show at all, I was encouraged by the other guys, specifically Gene and Paul, to call someone to play the part."[16]

According to his memoir, Frehley had some inkling as to what may have been transpiring behind his back, which added to his unease. "I get the feeling Paul and Gene might have told Bob about my drinking problem, and he may have put me in the same category as the guy's in Alice's band. The difference is that I had the chops; those just needed to be finessed."[17]

"At one point Ace wanted to leave early because he had a card game at seven that evening," writes Gene Simmons in his memoir. "At some point Bob didn't worry about Ace's excuses—he simply got another guitar player to come in and play Ace's parts."[18]

"The decision was made that we should just keep going," concludes Ezrin. "If Ace wasn't showing up, we should find someone to do his part. It was easy to call Dick, and he would show up in an hour and we'd get it done—as opposed to waiting the whole day or not getting it done or waiting and doing it at a later point. That was a problem."[19]

With the sessions temporarily ground to a halt on the whims of the Space Ace, whether by fear, foreign substances, or apathy, one frozen January evening, Ezrin summoned Wagner from his luxury Midtown lair. Stanley and Simmons were politely instructed to take the rest of the evening off; Criss had already blissfully escaped after surviving the drum tracks. It was the usual routine: like a hired gun in a classic Western, the expert session man grabbed his Gibson SG and his favorite Les Paul and hailed a cab to the Record Plant, where he was given his pay through the band on top of union wages.

"Sometimes I would know a couple of days ahead about a session and sometimes—like for instance with Aerosmith, when I did *Get Your Wings*—I got the call when I was sitting in my apartment at the Plaza, grabbed my guitar, and went down to the studio. So it comes at a moment's notice," Wagner recalled. "I was up for whatever—the next day or the next hour. I just wanted to play. I loved playing and the opportunities were a break and they loved my sound or they wouldn't have me doin' it."[20]

"This was just Wagner on the Q.T.," recalls Stasiak. "I can't remember now if Ezrin did it first and then told Ace or [if he] told Ace he was going to do it. All I know is Bob gave the guys the day off: 'Wagner's coming in, we're going to do some leads on this record.'"[21]

"I had done a solo on 'Sweet Pain' and it was okay," Frehley recalled, in *Behind the Mask*. "I said, 'Maybe I'll come in tomorrow and take another shot at it.' They didn't check with me or ask me if it was okay."[22]

Never phased by the who, the why, or how he was needed, just *what* was needed, Wagner, the ultimate professional, arrived, heeded instructions from Ezrin, and went straight to work. "I don't really read charts," he recalled, "except maybe chord charts. The most I would get was a chord chart to follow certain chord changes and then they'd play me the tape of what they had already laid down, then say, 'This is the section we need you to play in, these are the chords,' and then I'd try to learn the song as quickly as possible. To play the right part or to sing the right part, all of it, you have to get inside the song, learn it—you can't just guess at it. My philosophy in playing on somebody else's record was get inside and learn the song and treat your guitar playing as an extension of what the melody of the song is and the mood, the attitude of the song, staying of course within the confines of what the chord changes are. There are limitations, but you also have complete freedom when they just give you a spot and say, 'Go for it.' You got a chance then to come up with something that will be lasting."[23]

Imbued with considerable songwriting acumen, Wagner would approach the task at hand less as a soloist and more as an extension of Bob Ezrin's aim at creating moods, as if he were adding an arrangement to best serve the temperament of the track—in other words, a physical embodiment of the young producer's *raison d'être*. "I have a pretty natural feel for where songs are intended to go and where they can diverge off but still make sense, and you try to figure a way in that so you fit," he explains. "You don't want to do something just to do it and in the end you have to get rid of it, because it doesn't really fit. So you try and conquer all of that mentally first before you actually put something down."[24]

"Dick could just walk in, hear a song, and find the right part for it, no matter how sophisticated," recalls Ezrin.[25]

"Wagner was awesome to work with," says Stasiak. "He was one of these guys who you could describe a color, and he'll give it to you."[26]

Wagner: "I'm an artist and have been since I started doing this. For me, it's about playing well and doing different projects and being able to handle all these different kinds of music and being able to play something great every time. That was my goal always. It was never about the money, because when you're hired to come in and just play guitar on something, there's not that much money. I mean, it's okay, you can live on it, but it's not like being a star. I was a star when I was young in my local region. I knew what it felt like to be up front and be the focus of everything and then when I started working with Lou Reed, I had an opportunity to just sit back and play guitar. That was thrilling for me. I was playing with Steve Hunter and the two of us were the intertwining of silver and gold. The solo intro to 'Sweet Jane,' which Steve wrote and we worked out, was what I call 'restrained magic': we're working off as counterpoint to each other. I tried to weave in and out and not try and dominate. It was just a beautiful combination of guitars and I got off on that. Unless you become a solo artist or make it in a big selling band, you rely on what propelled you in the first place, and for me it was the ability to say something with the guitar."[27]

Messina and Stasiak set Wagner up in the center of the now empty Studio A, miked his amp, and then left him alone. "I'd sit for a minute or two by myself and kind of work out at least the basic core of what I'm gonna do," said Wagner. "But all those solos are improvised from an idea you have to develop quickly. It's a challenge. On the *Destroyer* album, for instance on 'Sweet Pain' they had already laid down a track, so I had to listen to it and feel as though somehow I had played on that track from the very beginning, really learn the song in my mind so I feel like I'm part of it. I don't want to feel like I'm an outsider just interjecting some music. Like with Joe Perry and Brad Whitford of Aerosmith, I listened to what they played on 'Train Kept a-Rollin',' and I would fit in that, make myself be an extension of it. That was always the best way to approach it for me."[28]

What Ezrin learned years before about Dick Wagner and his studio-experienced brethren was that there would never have to be compromises or ego-soothing or psychoanalytical measures applied to translating his musical vision, and whatever inequities that needed to be addressed in his work within an existing group dynamic like the original Alice Cooper group, Aerosmith, and now KISS could be rectified with little resistance. The fact that he had worked recently with Wagner on the *Welcome to My Nightmare* sessions, on which the guitarist acted as the musical director, meant there was an unspoken bond that must have seemed like a foreign concept to Frehley.

"For me, it was fundamental to apply basic music theory and classical orchestration techniques to rock and roll," Ezrin told *Electronic Musician* in 1996. "That didn't necessarily mean putting strings on a track; I could also orchestrate for the basic rock-band instrumentation. I would say things like, 'This sounds like a cello part to me.' Of course, it's a guitar, but we're going to treat it like a cello and play a cello line.'"[29] Dick Wagner, Steve Hunter, or Rick Derringer would take that as constructive information and not a threat.

Now, Frehley's aborted solo on "Sweet Pain" was at issue, and with Ezrin silently waiting for the magic, Wagner plugged in to a waiting Marshall amplifier and signaled to the booth that he was ready. Jay Messina began the tape that was queued a measure before the middle section of the song. Ezrin nodded in his direction, and Wagner was off.

Wagner: "I'm pretty sure I played a Gibson SG on 'Sweet Pain.' It has that good rock-and-roll sound. You're always trying to go for whatever is called for, and you've got to find a guitar that sounds that way. I used a variety of guitars for these fill-in sessions, but my '68 Les Paul was my favorite guitar, especially if you're looking for a real ethereal, singing lead line, because that Les Paul just *sings*. It was beautiful. But the sounds coming from whatever guitar you use is really a combination of the amps you use and also the primary element to any of it is the guitarist's touch. It makes all the difference in the world. You take the same guitar and the same amp, put it in two different guitar players' hands and it's gonna sound different, by the nature of the guy's touch. You bring your whole body and your whole psyche into the whole thing to make it an extension of what you do."[30]

In a couple of takes, Ezrin had his solo, spearing in at 1:22 on the track above a middle-eight bridge that rumbles along under a classic Gene Simmons bass riff interrupted briefly by the pre-chorus—"You'll get to love me, and what I say!"—which is extended out a full measure before the refrain until eventually revisiting the opening stanza. Through it all, Wagner weaves his solo somewhere between Ace-like trills and skull-thwacking Detroit scowls. Later in the song, as it begins its descent home, he bends up to a beatific high E before once again channeling his inner Ace toward the fade.

Deciding to take advantage of Wagner's presence, Ezrin instructed him to add a little more spice to the proceedings. By the gunslinger's estimation, there were four songs on *Destroyer* on which he took a pass. Later, Ezrin would ask him to accompany the team to A&R Studios for a separate session to record two songs ("Great Expectations" and "Beth"), but aside from applying his talents to "Sweet Pain," what was the fourth track? Interviewed for the 1996 authorized KISS biography *Behind the Mask*, Wagner was sure he also played on "Flaming Youth," but when pressed on the matter for this book, he mentioned another track that would take his ethereal slant on the guitar to the limit.

"I remember, but not specifically—which has always been a problem for me with this record—but I remember at the time noting that I played on four tracks. To tell you which ones, I don't remember. I haven't listened to that record for so many years. I've had people bring up 'Flaming Youth' and 'God of Thunder,' but I would guess that 'God of Thunder' is probably me. I'm one of the only guys that I've heard playing guitar on record that thinks that way, that dissonant. That happens to fit KISS and happens to fit Aerosmith. It's a theatrical way of playing the guitar. So that's probably me, because I do remember over the years that I had played on four tracks. I could never remember which ones, except 'Sweet Pain'—that for some reason stuck with me."[31]

During interviews for this book, I listened to the "God of Thunder" solo with Bob Ezrin, whose first reaction was mixed. "That doesn't sound unlike Ace to me. I would have come up with a sound like that for his playing, as well as Dick's. I can identify with how that sound was gotten, just by listening to it now. It could be Ace, but if Dick said he did it, then he did it."[32]

A careful examination of "God of Thunder" reveals several atonal guitar flourishes that merely act atmospherically—something Ace Frehley had not yet (if ever) attempted on a KISS record. Frehley's frenetic style preceded him, and while the substitute "Ace" made a valiant attempt to slip inside the head of KISS's lead guitarist for the out-front lead part of "Sweet Pain," on "God of Thunder," Wagner is literally meandering in the background, adding the type of "color" Corky Stasiak so aptly described. One can almost see the minds of Ezrin and his musical translator melding as the penetrating sounds of echoed menace slither from Wagner's fingers, roaring forth from the cranked Marshall inside Studio A.

"God of Thunder"—its overall feel akin to the sound of Godzilla's march over Tokyo—is played in Paul Stanley's demo's original key of E minor (once again tuned down to E-flat), but beyond the distinctive, almost monotone, repetitiveness of the original guitar progression, it is the revelry of discordant sounds that gives the track its spatial quality, while with his relentless kick drum pounding away, Peter Criss's gargantuan drum fills become more of a necessity to the arrangement than mere added flavor. Here is where the seismic shift in space and sonic turns from the first two songs to eventually appear on the final tracking of *Destroyer* ("Detroit Rock City" and "King of the Night Time World") becomes most striking—more so even than the choice of vocalist (Paul to Gene) or theme (sexual to demonic imagery). Where the first two songs are packed in tightly with a symphony of guitars, piano accents, and an array of background vocals, "God of Thunder" thrusts the listener into a chasm, echoing each instrument as if plunging the music into a subterranean mindscape. Eventually, Simmons's vocals will become more like spoken commands—sparse and drenched with reverb—adding to the atmospheric interplay. Unlike the carefully arranged, melodic playing on the previous two songs, the dissonant notes in the groaning agony of Wagner's Les Paul guitar descant fail to form a musical center until the searing last four measures of the solo. He forges into a classic blues lick and then descends into a minor scale that lands on the ninth, then breaks totally away from the backdrop to begin dancing about the carnage erratically, the guitar virtuoso at his most expressionistic.

The final evidence that Wagner and not Frehley played the dissonant guitar embellishments on "God of Thunder" is a black-and-white video of the band performing the number a few months later on the Spirit of '76 tour. Frehley is clearly putting his mark on the instrumental section with a "lead" in the Ace style that has endeared him to millions in the KISS Army, but it reflects none of the strange, atmospheric runs that give the recorded version its supernatural edge.

As for Frehley, the Spaceman told his biographers that he didn't learn of his "Sweet Pain" solo being replaced until hearing the final mix of *Destroyer*. "When I first played the record back, I go, 'That's not my fucking solo! What the fuck is this shit?' I called Gene and tore him a new asshole. He told me some bullshit saying, 'We tried to call you, but we couldn't find you.' One of many bullshit stories, lies lies lies."[33]

While this is an engaging story, the idea of Frehley being unaware of his replacement until after the sessions wrapped is yet another of the many myths that surround *Destroyer*. According to several sources, the band attended a listening party for the record company, where the entire album was played in its entirety. If Frehley had protested to what was and wasn't on the final mix, he could have—and may have—approached Simmons then. Additionally, assistant engineer Corky Stasiak distinctly recalls Ace having a fit in the control room soon after Wagner's session. "I remember sitting in the control room and Ace going, 'Look, man, we've got a lot of fans and I don't want his fucking name on my album!' I remember him being adamant about that, and rightly so. I mean, how would you feel if you were the guitar player of a band and you just couldn't cut it, and they got somebody else to play it? Of course, you might say, 'Let me learn the lead, and let me do it!' But it didn't work out that way."[34]

It is not known if Wagner, having added his expertise to "God of Thunder," was on Frehley's radar, but the song certainly was on Ezrin's, as the young producer looked outside the inner sanctum once more to infuse additional cinematic effects to the track, this time from an unusual source. "Bob's kids came in one day and had some toys that they brought in and were blowing, like whistles or something like that," recalls Jay Messina.[35]

Ezrin: "I had just come back from France, where I went to a very space-age, modern, fringe department store, and they had a space helmet and walkie-talkie set for kids. One kid would wear the helmet and the other kid would have the walkie-talkie, and they could talk back and forth. It was a glorified walkie-talkie set. So I bought them for my boys [David, ten, and Josh, eight] and they were in New York visiting at the studio, and we were playing around with the helmet and walkie-talkie. Listening to the sound of it, I said, 'Whoa, wait a minute: this is amazing! Okay, let's figure out a way to mike it.' So we actually broke into the circuitry to be able to mike the inside of the helmet—that sound—and all those *whooo-whooo-whooo*—I think there were little buttons that gave you effects on the voices. As soon as I heard that I said, 'Whoa, "God of Thunder," how cool would little monsters sound?'"[36]

"I remember turning the lights down in the studio and playing the backing track for 'God of Thunder,'" adds Messina.[37]

Rolling tape, ten-year-old David Ezrin shouted, "Okay? Now start singin!'" right before the track fired, which immediately prompted his dad to shout, "What a great way to start!"[38] In the final running order for *Destroyer*, the echo of a child's voice introducing the song is chilling in its unexpected leap from the silence as the album segues from the rollicking thunder of "Detroit Rock City" directly into the sprint of "King of the Night Time World." Added to the caterwauled gibberish coming from the roguish boys peeking through the deep is the pounding of Peter Criss's drums and Dick Wagner's dissonant wails, literally transforming 'God of Thunder' from Paul Stanley's ode to Greek goddesses of love into the groaning beast Ezrin envisioned.

"I love the sound of children," says Ezrin. "I think they're a phenomenal dramatic device in the same way that adult voices can be. You know, what are trying to do, what are you trying to say? What do you want people to feel? You use the stuff you got that will accomplish that goal."[39]

At closer inspection, the use of children as a "phenomenal dramatic device" is something of a signature Bob Ezrin approach. From the three-act homage to the silent-film era, "The Ballad of Dwight Frye," on his very first Alice Cooper production, *Love It to Death*, to the snot-nosed imps chanting "We don't need no education!" on Pink Floyd's "Another Brick in the Wall (Part 2)," Ezrin returns again and again to juxtaposing a child's innocence with darker themes.

When I confront him about this, his laughter says it all. At the beginning of "The Ballad of Dwight Frye," much like "God of Thunder," a child's lone voice calls out—"Mommy, where's daddy; he's been gone for so long?"—acting as an aural signpost to the sudden thematic segue from the previous track, "Second Coming," a mid-tempo rocker not unlike "King of the Night Time World" that fades into a distant music-box melody, played by Ezrin. The high-pitched treacle resets the mood, as if an establishing scene in a film. The chirping yelps bouncing around "God of Thunder" also revisit Ezrin's turns on "Dead Babies," from the second Cooper album he produced, *Killer*, where as the band halts prior to the shouted chorus, the time signature shift is broken by a tormented baby's cry. Cooper's subsequent album contains arguably Ezrin's most famous use of children: the puckish chant of "School's Out," which features an enthusiastic jailbreak flavor from a gaggle of well-trained brats (a trick repeated to lesser effect with the joyful mischievousness of "The Department of Youth" on the recently completed *Welcome to My Nightmare*). A hilarious insight into how the kids were motivated for such a rousing refrain can be found within the Alice Cooper *Old School* boxed set, released in 2012.

Ezrin's use of children also serves as an effective device for character development or to alter the mood, such as the aforementioned baby's cry before the chilling chorus of "Dead Babies" or the addition of folk singer Donovan, lilting in a prepubescent falsetto, as a counter-point to the perversions of "Billion Dollar Babies." It is used to its greatest effect on *Welcome to My Nightmare* (Ezrin's last studio work prior to *Destroyer*), adding an extra dimension to Cooper's story of frantically trying to return to the innocence of lost childhood. The record's—and probably Ezrin's—finest moment of aural terror comes during the "Years Ago" / "Steven" suite, a macabre musical masterpiece that combs through the rabid imagination of our deepest fears: loneliness, alienation, and death. Cooper sings in a flittering timbre, seemingly on the verge of tears, as he wanders through an abandoned playground calling out to childhood friends long gone.

Three years after *Destroyer*, Ezrin would turn Roger Waters's dismal diatribe against the brain-numbing affects of the iron-fisted British education system into a disco-fueled chart-topping hit for Pink Floyd. The mischievous sing-along that brings home "Another Brick in the Wall (Part 2)" from the otherwise dreary but brilliant 1979 classic *The Wall* was an act of desperation for the producer, who could not get Waters—who was already embroiled in the disintegration of his band due to his myopic recalcitrance—to finish the song. After the band left the studio for the day, Ezrin hired the school children to sing the first verse again. The moody Waters loved it, and the rest was history.

Undeniably the most controversial use of children as a "phenomenal dramatic device" resides in a haunting song from Lou Reed's *Berlin*, for which Ezrin used the heart-wrenching sounds of children desperately bellowing for their mother, whom the authorities are taking away, in the dénouement of "The Kids." The wails rise to an excruciating level at the song's climax, leaving the listener to ask the obvious question to just what method has been used to cull such a torrid performance from a minor. "It was so evocative there were people who couldn't put the record on again, because it was so disturbing to them," recalls Ezrin. "Well, you're not going to get that kind of reaction if you don't use that device."[40]

Indeed, what would be David and Josh's inaugural appearance on a seminal rock recording occurred only three years earlier, in an evocative pastiche of jealousy, paranoia, and the price a promiscuous, drug-addled German beauty had to pay for a damning lifestyle. Their performance as the crying, begging children was so believable it caused a stir with RCA, Reed's record company, and then the press and fans, who bought into Alice-Cooper–esque stories of the young producer actually harming his own children in order to get the take. Ezrin recalls Reed's assistant running from the room weeping upon hearing it. Of course, while this proved to Ezrin he had pushed the correct emotional buttons, the reality was less dramatic.

Ezrin: "Contrary to the story that I beat my children, the reality is that, by that time, David was old enough to understand theater, so I was saying to him, 'Look, we're doing this for TV.' I didn't tell him we were doing it for a rock record, which wouldn't have meant anything to him at the time. I had this portable recorder. So I said, 'Here's the story: the kids are outside and the doors locked and they can't get in and their mother's inside and they're getting scared and they start beating on the door, and they start yelling, "Mommy! Mommy!" and she doesn't answer and they get more and more scared. So that's what I want you to do, beat on the door, and start yelling.' And his brother Josh, who was tiny then—he was maybe a year and a half old or two—was standing beside David and emulating what David was doing. And actually if you have the solo tracks you can hear Josh at one point go to David in little-kid gibberish, 'What's going on, why are we calling for Mommy, she's right over there!'

"So they're pounding on the door and pounding on the door and screaming, 'Mommy! Mommy!' And the crying, which people said I beat my children to get? Well, for the first few years of his life, every day Josh was the happiest child you ever saw in your life, but every night around eight o'clock when you would say the two most dreaded words in human language he would start to cry; and those words were 'bed time!' So Josh would go, '*Ahhhh!*' and I'd go, 'I'm sorry you gotta go to bed'—and more, '*Ahhhh!*' He hated to miss anything. He never wanted to sleep. So that's what we did. I said, 'Bed time!' and then I recorded that cry and I amplified it and distorted it and messed with it; I changed the speed of it. I just, you know, screwed with it with sound design to make it as scary as possible and put it on the record. How else could you possibly get that effect if it wasn't with kids?"[41]

"Bob always liked a big product, big anthem, kind of sound," Jay Messina surmises. "The idea of having kids there is just part of it. Maybe that's why he had kids."[42]

And so, with "God of Thunder," Ezrin continued his cinematic expression, manipulating tiny voices to create an eerie backdrop. But perhaps more so than even Ezrin's use of children to spark emotions, the classically trained pianist had made his bones by being more than partial to grander accompaniment. Very soon, he would splash another signature "effect" into the making of *Destroyer* that would take the band and its team outside the creative madness of the Record Plant and into the lush environs of the legendary A&R Studios.

"Shout It Out Loud"

Shout it out louder!

The chorus melody bounds from the silence like a clarion. Drums pound a four-on-the-floor R&B beat tickled by a high-end bass line that lays the groundwork for the guitar harmonies to sing along. It repeats, dragging us behind it. We follow the music down, lower, lower, and lower still. The voice—our speeding concert fiend whose song blared on the car radio, the dreamy teenager yearning to burst free of the suburban mundane, the ringleader of our flaming youth—now bounces on a raucous trampoline crunch of chords. It rings true, asking one poignant question . . .

Well, the night's begun and you need some fun
Do you think you're gonna find it?

Choral voices echo this most pointed query. It is a call to action this time; all the craving and speeding and beseeching and terror and seduction and strange sexual delights have led to this. It is time. We can no longer be the passive listener; now we get down into it, break the fourth wall, and absorb the aura of The Act. It challenges your insides. It fuels your desires. It has a bold piece of advice:

You got to treat yourself like number one
Do you need to be reminded?

Once again the choir sings, "Do you need to be reminded?"
Well, do you?
The band hits its stride, rollicking forth beneath the growling timbre of our second more bestial voice, the troll of the underworld, and our pied piper into the spotlight world. The moaning libido at the lash announces without restraint:

> *It doesn't matter what you do or say*
> *Just forget the things that you've been told*
> *We can't do it any other way*
> *Everybody's got to rock and roll*

He cannot contain himself; the music assaults him, the message leaps from his upper register, as if reaching for something just beyond his grasp . . . "Oh, Oh!"

> *Shout it!*
> *Shout it!*
> *Shout it out loud!*

The choir takes over now and they sing it again—"Shout it!"—even louder and with more purpose. "Shout it!" There is desperation in it. There is more than a sense that time and youth are fleeting. This is the moment—*your* moment. "Shout it out loud!" Those figures, the four heroes from on high, leaping from the mountaintop with the smoldering ruins of the past behind them, are blazing a new road to glory. It is not from a book. It is not from a dream. It is not in the song but inside you, and it needs, it begs, it demands to be let out.

Let me out!

As a raging stream alongside the shouts, the band pops and claps; a descending piano revelry rolls on, the music an uproarious counterpoint, if not a supernova, on which this impossible connection between the gods and their brethren must meet. The drums take charge, bridging the wild abandon of the reluctant souls to burst out of their cage and get on board . . .

> *If you don't feel good, there's a way you could*
> *Don't sit there broken hearted*

The choir is back, and it commands you: "Don't sit there brokenhearted!"

> *Call all your friends in the neighborhood*
> *And get the party started*

"Get the party started!"

That's right! Call the kid with the lisp and the kid with the zits and the kid with the ripped T-shirt and the kid with the matted hair and the kid with the skinned knee and the kid with the tattoo and the kid from the broken home and the kid from the swimming pool and the kid with the comic collection and the kid with the bully on his heels and the kid with the crappy car and the kid with the KISS albums—get them out of the house and into the street or the backyard or the edge of the planet and raise your voices in unison with one single unwavering purpose . . . to live, to breathe, to celebrate eternal youth!

> *Don't let them tell you that there's too much noise*
> *They're too old to really understand*
> *You'll still get rowdy with the girls and boys*
> *It's time for you to take a stand*

"Yeah! Yeah!"

In case there was any chance that you might not heed this battle cry: "Shout it!" Don't let anyone mock it. "Shout it!" Don't let anything stop it. "Shout it!" Make sure everyone and everything in its path knows it is coming—knows you are coming—knows that you are here and here to stay. "Shout it out loud!"

The voices jump another octave as if taking off on the wings of a shredding guitar lead, the sound of which breaks out to dance upon the roof of the rumbling riff below. The house is crowded; there's dancing in the streets and rocking and rolling all night and day. The entire lineage of rock and roll is here: the wang dang doodle, ripping it up and boogying down. The Act has exploded in all directions. Mayhem. Joy. Fist-pumping ecstasy.

Once again the drums beat out the march, and the voices sing in unison, "Shout it! Shout it! Shout it out loud!"

The bass picks up the groove.

You've got to have a party!

It is a soul revival, a rally for solidarity.

Shout it out louder!

Clap-clap. Clap-clap.

The piano tumbles down and around your ears.

Hear it getting louder!

Shout it!

Shout it!

Shout it out loud!

Yes, everybody shout it out!

Oooohhheewwwww!!!!!

17

Black Ties and Tales

"Kiss, I'd like you to meet the Brooklyn Boys Choir." With those words, producer Bob Ezrin launched a pairing so unlikely it could only happen in rock and roll.
—Frank Rose[1]

The moment Bob Ezrin listened to the four-year-old wobbly tape of Peter Criss and his former Chelsea bandmate Stan Penridge casually laying down the mock ballad "Beck," he could hear it all: the soft piano prelude, the mist of violins wafting above the delicate melody, the slight *restez*, and then the voice, raspy and choked with emotion, vulnerable and bereft of artifice. He could hear French horns and trumpets and the three vital chords that would wind up each verse as if a weepy Greek chorus answering the beseechingly serenaded lyric. In each aching barre is the kept woman's lament as a beacon as she tries and fails to reach her man, who is so far from home.

When the young producer retired to his Midtown apartment, he played the song over and over for two, maybe three days, as if he were in front of an invisible orchestra, each classical instrument lifting the notes high above the Manhattan skyline. It was then that Ezrin knew he had his *The Wild One* moment. Here, behind the mask of this goofy limerick about a bitchy wife, was the human face of The Act. He thought to call it "Beth," leaving no doubt as to the identity of the lonely woman whose name the singer recites as in prayer.

And so, having run it past the composer, who had been smarting over having his drumming stripped down and built back up again while shouting obscenities at the diminutive coked-up lunatic that pushed him to the brink, Peter Criss was now fully integrated into the story of *Destroyer*.

To hear Criss tell it through the years over many interviews, and again in his memoir, Simmons and Stanley were at first dubious about and then outright defiant against the idea of including a ballad on *Destroyer*. Despite Simmons's having prompted Criss to bring the song into the sessions, he and Stanley thought it would eventually have to become a mid-tempo rocker. Never would they dream that a sentimental love song would appear on a KISS album—much less one awash in orchestral tapestry.

Simmons, who would later claim that he, and not Ezrin, suggested changing the title to "Beth," does admit in his memoir that a lush ballad was a stretch for KISS but, in his inimitable style, he retreats to a more pragmatic stance. "We didn't really know what to do with it. Rock bands didn't do ballads, least of all in the midst of a concerted push for rock and roll credibility. The only way we validated the idea that there were strings on it was because of 'Yesterday' by the Beatles. If it was cool for the Beatles, then we could do it."[2]

The song's co-author, Stan Penridge, would concur in Dale Sherman's unauthorized biography of KISS, *Black Diamond*. "Paul always considered it a throwaway tune. Gene, on the other hand, seemed to be always open for trying something new. He had experience enough to take the chance to see what would happen."[3]

Regardless of whether Simmons or Stanley put up a stink—or even if Criss had second thoughts—it had become obvious to everyone from day one of this project that Bob Ezrin was the man in charge. The idea of fighting him had already proved futile. The young producer also had his original support group behind him. Bill Aucoin, for one, loved the idea. "Paul and Gene wanted to take 'Beth' off the album," he recalled. "I said, 'Look, I think it's a hit. I know it's not necessarily a KISS song, but it does have a rock and roll lyric to it. It's gonna stay on the album.' And they didn't fight me after that."[4]

"Beth" resounded with Aucoin, who admitted, in the same account, "I always thought 'Beth' could be a bellwether track for KISS, because no one else did." As far back as the week he secured Ezrin for the *Destroyer* sessions, Aucoin had sat in his Midtown office and crowed to *Circus* magazine, "I feel that KISS will have a major hit. Obviously the live album is a major hit, but I'm talking about more of a commercial hit. I think that will happen and all of a sudden everyone will say, 'Look at this overnight success!'"[5]

According to Criss, it was Aucoin who suggested the one-day orchestral session at which the song, along with the majestic accompaniment to "Great Expectations," would be realized. However, during interviews for this book, Bob Ezrin left no doubt that it was his idea to unfurl the haughty concept of what he audaciously dubbed the First KISS Grand Orchestral and Choral Recording Session.

"I didn't know when I started the project that we were going to do stuff that would require an orchestra," says Ezrin. "I didn't know that was the direction we would end up going until we started to compile material, but when we were getting into stuff like 'Great Expectations' and 'Beth' it became obvious what we were building, like 'Hello Hooray' in a way that was going to require more than your average rock recording, and I thought, 'Hey, look, if we're really going for it this time; taking these guys up to a new level and making them more legitimate—and I would put that in quotations marks—making them more "legitimate" by virtue of the fact of the record itself, then why don't we make an event out of the recording?'"[6]

Ezrin had already returned to Toronto for a couple of one-on-one arranging sessions with his scoring partner Allan Macmillan during the autumn hiatus caused by the Rock Steady/Casablanca lawsuits. After receiving the charts that resulted from their collaboration he booked the venerable A&R Studios at 799 Seventh Avenue for January 13.

Ezrin was well acquainted with A&R Studios and its co-founder, perennial Grammy award-winner Phil Ramone (the *R* to business partner Jack Arnold's *A*), who, since 1959, had in one way or another influenced a generation of producers and engineers while helping to realize the most successful music of the period. Having guided a wide variety of talent across every genre, from folk and jazz to pop and rock, Ramone's resume—which was for the most part A&R's legacy—is astonishing: Stan Getz, Lesley Gore, Frank Sinatra, Barbara Streisand, Paul Simon, Procol Harum, Harry Nilsson, Billy Joel, Chicago, Carly Simon, Madonna, Paul McCartney, Dave Grusin, George Benson, Barry Manilow, Joss Stone, Tony Bennett, and on and on. His work ethic, coupled with his determination to corral the right sounds and pull the best performances from artists, was passed on to Ezrin, who absorbed it under the guidance of Jack Richardson, whose own reverence for Ramone was duly imbued in his protégé and reflected in *Destroyer*.

The spacious main Studio A1—which lead engineer and former A&R employee Jay Messina calls "the only space big enough for that size orchestra"[7]—was saturated with New York City recording history, from radio (the inaugural broadcasts by the studio's original owners, the Columbia Broadcast System, in the 1930s) to music (CBS's formation of Columbia Records by the decade's end). Uniquely, it was one of the few recording structures in Manhattan to boast a cathedral-style A-frame ceiling beneath a forty-foot domed roof, which was made of metal to cut out the glut of Midtown radio signals swirling around the area. Located on the seventh floor, Studio A1 stretched sixty-five by fifty-five feet and was encased in high-diffusion plaster tiles, which helped minimize the natural reverb of the enormous space. This was later enhanced by the surrounding acoustic panels, which could be lowered or raised to diffuse reverberation off the shiny oak floors.

In his engaging 2007 memoir, *Making Records*, Ramone describes the structural nuances he and fellow producer Don Frey made to Studio A1 to achieve what he called "warm ambiance": "A well-designed room produces a balanced blend of high (treble), middle (midrange), and low (bass) frequencies. Too much of any one frequency range can mar an otherwise terrific record. To control the midrange and high frequencies and create spacious sound, Don Frey and I covered the walls with soft fiberglass and fabric. These 'drapes' had two layers, but there was some space between them so the fabric side didn't touch the fiberglass side. Because of this, the midrange would pass through the fabric and be absorbed by the fiberglass, while the high frequencies would bounce off and back into the room. We also redesigned the bass response in the room by creating 'bass traps' (fiberglass-covered battens that protruded eighteen inches from the wall) that would prevent unwanted bass frequencies from running along the wooden floor. Doing this reduced low-frequency muddiness, and gave our bottom end a clean, well-defined edge."[8]

Beyond its meticulous design, the space's history was daunting. Nestled at the corner of Manhattan's musically transcendent Fifty-Second Street, it was the site of some of the most dramatic moments in modern pop history, from Frank Sinatra's signature tracks to Barbara Streisand's translucent ascent; Bob Dylan's explosive "Like a Rolling Stone" to Simon & Garfunkel's indelible works; Elton John's first ever live concert recording event to a spate of mega-hits from legendary songsmiths Burt Bacharach and Hal David. The aura of Studio A1 was awe inspiring.

It was only fitting that Jay Messina would also return to the place where he, too, had developed his multi-tiered work ethic, conquering the mysteries of the studio, experimenting, and re-examining the tenets of sounds tamed from the unbridled attack of the artist, which was crucial in these first weeks of creating the epic KISS album. As he re-entered the grand room, the lead engineer recalled many days and nights working with similar orchestras and ensembles, but perhaps none of them could have prepared him for what would transpire on this day.

Part of Ezrin and Aucoin's grand plan was to once again make this a propitious occasion, adorning a KISS record with a full orchestra and the forty-strong Brooklyn Boys Choir. To achieve maximum effect, Ezrin fit his charges, Messina and Stasiak, with black tuxedoes and bowties, and so too Allan Macmillan (with added tails), who flew in to New York a few days prior to review the final charts.

"It seemed a little overwhelming, like things were really whizzing along," recalls Macmillan. "I had business to discuss with the contractor, and I'm not sure where all of the orchestra parts were. They may have been copied in New

York or maybe in Toronto. I just don't remember. But if they had been copied in New York, I would definitely have had to be there early with the scores so that I could give those to the copyist to get the orchestral parts prepared."[9]

Once again playing the part of ringmaster extraordinaire, Ezrin also showed up dressed to the nines, but with the added accouterment of a black top hat, tails, and a dramatic black cape with crimson inlay. An enthused Aucoin invited along select members of the press, including *Circus*'s Frank Rose, who would dutifully provide a blow-by-blow account in the magazine's upcoming issue. Also in attendance was KISS favorite Fin Costello, who had made an impact with his *Alive!* photos several months before, and perhaps the quintessential KISS photographer, Bob Gruen, whose exclusive access to the band had accelerated its ascent through such rock publications as *Creem* and *Rock Scene*, among many others.

"I did a lot of work with KISS, and generally Bill Aucoin or his assistant would call me, give me the address and the time and tell me to be there," Gruen recalled, during an interview for this book. "Bill was a prince, very creative and easygoing. I generally did these things for publicity for KISS on whatever occasion they called me up. I didn't work for them directly, so they didn't pay me, but [they] engaged me and gave me the access to record the event with the understanding that they would have some control over the images, go over them, edit them, and the ones they liked I would sell to magazines. Usually the decisions were made by management or publicists, not the band. That was never a problem for me. Some photographers are very adamant about not being edited. I'm very adamant about getting hired again. I was very comfortable working with a band and helping them create the image they want to create. I don't think I was on assignment for a magazine on that particular day."[10]

By 1976, Gruen was considered one of the best rock photographers in the business, having befriended John Lennon during his initial downtown residence in New York and recorded much of his exploits to grand acclaim (his famous shot of Lennon in the photographer's own sleeveless "New York" T-shirt has become one of the most iconic images in rock). His work adorned nearly every major music publication, which inevitably led to him shooting KISS for a *Creem* spread in 1975. It was during those sessions that the band ended up raiding his closet for the mugging, black-and-white cover of *Dressed to Kill*. Gruen's mere presence added further gravitas to the proceedings. "The orchestral session was a big musical step for a rock band from Queens," he states. "Only a couple of years before, they were playing bars."[11]

"We were turning the whole album into an event," says Ezrin. "KISS came in full makeup. I had my whole team dressed in white tie and tails. I came up with the idea of putting props in the studio, and we had the Brooklyn Boys Choir in African dashikis. The room looked amazing. The grand piano that I played for both 'Beth' and 'Great Expectations' was set up in the middle of the room, and we recorded those tracks virtually live. The whole thing was a little bit of the P. T. Barnum in me expressing itself."[12]

Aucoin made sure that each member of orchestra donned tuxedo T-shirts, partly as a tongue-in-cheek nod to the extravagance displayed by the recording team but also as a playful aside to saving a few bucks by not ponying up the outrageous funds it would take to nattily attire nearly fifty musicians. KISS soon ambled in, resplendent in new regalia designed specifically for the *Destroyer* rollout, which was simultaneously being incorporated into the album's cover painting. In fact it was on this day, thirteen days into the bicentennial year, that arguably KISS's most iconic costumes made their first public appearance of: Simmons in his battle armor and studded cod piece, his thigh-length lizard boots featuring crimson eyes atop fanged souls; Stanley bare-chested in a sparkled body suit and six-inch spiked heels; Frehley decked out in a black-and-silver space suit with knee-length space boots; and Criss in a shiny black-and-silver jumpsuit with jungle-cat collar.

The wide-eyed and rambunctious Brooklyn Boys Choir, mostly comprised of African American inner-city kids of preteen age, whom Corky Stasiak recalls were "kind of in awe of the place,"[13] filed in nosily, excited to pose for photographs with the seven-foot creatures surrounding them. The giggles and chirps of anticipation, set against the popping of flashbulbs and murmurs of incredulity among seasoned New York musicians, had Ezrin and Aucoin beaming. It was a spectacle anywhere one turned; a backdrop perfectly suited to what KISS had been striving for for years. The grinding hours of musical "boot camp" and the isolation of day-into-night-into-day recording marathons faded beneath its magical façade. They were stars once again—masks, costumes, cameras, and revelry!

Stasiak, whose strategic proclivity for keeping a daily journal of his studio work also extended to a photographic record, wandered through the bustle snapping his own shots. The orange-hued prints reveal the playful nature of KISS in its element, the thrilled and smiling faces of the children, and even an occasional bemused chuckle from the type of session musicians more used to stuffy high-pressured gigs traversing difficult passages by master composers. "I was stoked to be at A&R, the studio that'd I'd heard about since 1967," says Stasiak. "This was during its heyday. It was the earmark of great studios. It was *the* great studio in New York until the Record Plant came, and then the Power Station and the Hit Factory."[14]

Despite this being first public display of The Act and *Destroyer* in all its Technicolor glory, the flurry of activity—hardly a sidebar—could not be a distraction. This was an expensive day for Casablanca, and two full backing tracks had to be recorded in three-hour blocks, otherwise a large penalty would be accrued due to strict musician's union rules. As Stasiak recalls, "Those guys were pros. They were all union, so we had to remember that if they played one second over the allotted three-hour time per session, we had to pay overtime, or pay them a full three more hours. So despite the press and our being dressed up and festive and the band walking around interacting with everyone, we had a tight schedule and stuck to it."[15]

Allan Macmillan arrived to meet his players early and was stunned by the level of virtuosity assembled before him. "First of all, it was a great band," he enthuses. "I've forgotten the name of the contractor who contracted for all the players, and, of course, I'm from out of town, so I don't know all these people, but I did recognize the concertmaster was David Nadien. He was the concertmaster of the New York Philharmonic Orchestra, so this was something a little extra special that he would be there."[16]

"I hired Nadien," remembers Bob Ezrin. "I had worked with him in the past with Alice Cooper and he contracted that gig. So, he hired the orchestra."[17]

"One of the flutes was Julius Baker," says Macmillan. "He was principal flute in the New York Philharmonic at that time. I remember some of the musicians particularly acknowledging his presence, so they themselves knew that this was something that Julius would be on that session. But I guess Julius and David are no different than any other musician. We all need money from time to time."[18]

Stasiak: "The orchestra was comprised of session musicians, some of whom I worked with constantly. There were four first violins, five second violins, three violas, two cellos, an upright bass, plus woodwind horns and a percussionist. It was a forty or fifty piece orchestra, all told. They came in and smoked cigars, back in the days when you could still smoke in the studio; they read the *Wall Street Journal*; and they were always talking about the union when they weren't playing."[19]

Ezrin surprised his longtime friend and fellow arranger with a commemorative baton, encased dramatically in a long, glass-and-wood box with a silver plaque displaying the insignia "H. A. Macmillan Conductor in Residence of 'The KISS Grand Classical Orchestra & Chorale.'" Macmillan was so moved by the gesture that he made a point of noting its prominence in the proceedings during interviews for this book and promptly sent me photographs of the commemorative box and its contents: an ornately designed black baton with a white tip and a gold band atop it, just below the handle a beautifully inlayed gold treble clef.

Just as quickly as the chaos of a press event began, Ezrin made sure everyone got right down to business. The sudden appearance of bullpen guitarist Dick Wagner signaled that party time was indeed over, and an extremely important session was to begin. As mesmerized by it all as the green choir boys, the grizzled veteran, well acquainted with Bob Ezrin's Willie Wonka–like gift for exhibitionism, soon realized he had not exactly seen it all.

"I sat with my back to the orchestra facing the conductor," Wagner recalled. "That was the first and one of the few times in my career I got to play with an orchestra. It was fantastic. My memories of the day were all aural, just remembering how beautiful it sounded. I was amazed by how great it sounded, really, because I wasn't used to *that sound*. You're used to playing with a band onstage and all of sudden you have these violins and cellos and an entire orchestra behind you. It's pretty magnificent."[20]

"We set up the orchestra and choir all at once with Bob playing piano and everybody playing live," Jay Messina explains. "There was a conductor for the choir that all the boys were comfortable and familiar with and may have done a pass or two of the choir, but the orchestra and piano take that we chose for the record was recorded in one take. Brass or woodwind would be miked a little closer, not so much for brass, because there is always more miking needed for woodwind than brass or strings. There were more ambient mics for the strings. We didn't want the miking for the choir to be too close, otherwise you can hear individual voices. You had to mic from a fair distance to again allow the ambiance of the room to capture the voices. I think there were forty kids there, so you want to hear the bigger sound. We also used less mics for that size choir in such a big room to better capture that combination of presence."[21]

Macmillan: "We ran through the parts at least once, so that the musicians could check their bearings and any wrong notes that are there. You obviously want to pick those up before you start recording. I would run a take right through. I would not stop on my own volition. I'm taking directions from Bob and the engineers, and so if they want to stop, that's fine with me. We'll pick up wherever they want to hear it from, but it would've been only a couple of run-throughs before we were ready to record."[22]

"Near as I remember, the boys' choir sang along with the orchestra," Stasiak adds. "I think if we spent any more time than we did, they would have been hanging from the ceiling. But they were pretty well behaved for the recording. They knew they were going to be on a KISS record and were visibly excited about it."[23]

"Bob was pretty much in charge of or took control of the Brooklyn Choir," recalls Macmillan. "So I was not privy to what he and the director of the choir did, but they had obviously learned the part. They were going to sing on the actual recording, so they just took a cue when to enter from me, which they would've known anyway, but nonetheless, there would've been cues for their entries."[24]

Ezrin silenced the room, readying Macmillan, the orchestra, and the choir with a dramatic wave of his hand. Then, flipping back his tails to sit comfortably at the grand piano, he began to play the opening strains of the Beethoven piece he knew so well. Thrust back to his days of study and discipline, he became witness to the metaphysical transformation of KISS from underground hard-rock band into cinematic heroes.

Three years removed from playing in a cold, cramped loft, the four New York boys listened as their music was ornamented by some of the finest musicians in the world. A choir singing the refrain—"You've got great expectations!"—over and over, as if an ancient hymn; bells chiming on each beat; the orchestra enlivening the serenade. It was in every possible sense surreal, physically and emotionally transporting them from the three previously rushed studio experiences while single-handedly capturing the sound and fury of The Act.

"I'm standing up there at the stand, and they're all right in front of me," says Macmillan, who was photographed by Corky Stasiak with professorial brown-rimmed glasses proudly waving his commemorative baton toward the orchestra with the choir behind him. "There was nothing particularly difficult to play, but we wanted to get as much nuances into it as possible."[25]

The effect of *Alive!*'s success and the buzz surrounding the grit and extravagance of the *Destroyer* sessions paraded before them in a festive mélange of musical solemnity was profound. When asked about the occasion by *Circus* magazine's Frank Rose, Paul Stanley proudly exclaimed, "I felt that we put out the best albums we could under the circumstances, but I also knew what we were capable of. And I like to please myself, but if we attract an audience with the other stuff, wait until everybody hears what we can do."[26] In the same piece, a humbled Peter Criss effused, "I think this album made each one of us really have respect for one another as musicians."[27] Even Gene Simmons, still basking in the glow of hearing his introspective "ode to groupiedom" in this setting, waxed philosophic. "We've finally come to the point where we feel we can make personal statements. Until now we've been talking kind of generally about the road—your 'Stutter,' your 'Room Service,' where you ring up for room service and she goes down on her knees. Road life—the rigors of the road. Now we've come to the point where people know who KISS is, and we can kind of expand on our individual statements."[28] Stanley summed up the mood of the sessions:

"We're putting a conscious effort into the quality of our playing. Before we were more concerned with the feel. Now we think we can get the feel plus the quality. This album is no different from any of our others, except that it's ten times better."[29]

Macmillan remembers that after only a few takes, the choral and orchestral backing for "Great Expectations" was done. Neither he nor Ezrin nor either of the engineers recalls any serious overdubs. It was a clean and straightforward pass that would end up on the final mix of *Destroyer*.

Ezrin whisked into the control room for a playback with the original backing tracks (drums and bass against Ezrin's makeshift metronome), which was described by Frank Rose in his *Circus* piece. "The sound that emerged was enough to wipe the smirk off anyone's face. It's didn't sound like a KISS record at all. It sounded more like the Who, rich and lush and baroque, with thunderous power chords and measured majestic drums."[30] Rose described the young producer as "very pleased"—pleased enough to gleefully admit his nod to Ludwig van Beethoven. "If you're gonna steal from somebody," Ezrin told Rose, "you might as well steal from the masters."[31]

Of course, Ezrin knew of what he spoke. He had already successfully "stolen" from Rodgers & Hammerstein's "My Favorite Things" to enhance a verse for Alice Cooper's "Halo of Flies" on *Killer*, and later a memorable motif from Leonard Bernstein and Stephen Sondheim's *West Side Story* for the denouement of *School's Out*.

Out in the lobby, Simmons cornered Rose and continued to hammer home the importance of the work they were accomplishing. "Where we've changed direction is that with Bob Ezrin we've realized that an album is a separate entity," he said. "Recorded work doesn't necessarily have to really mirror what you do live. I mean it will, we'll be able to pull it all off live, but we've added a lot to it. It's just us going to a higher plane. It's still rock. It's not like we're gonna come out and try and give you a hidden message in the music. There's just more thought behind it. We've stopped being so straight ahead."[32]

After a short break and the extrication of the boys' choir it was time to record "Beth." The worth of Simmons and Stanley's bragging would be on full display now, for this song would require no backing from KISS: no drums, bass, or guitar licks. Ezrin summoned an enraptured Peter Criss to the center of the room, where he would lead the procession with a scratch vocal he and the young producer had worked out. "Peter sang with the orchestra, and it was just an orchestra," says Stasiak. "It wasn't anybody else, and he didn't play drums on that record, Gene didn't play bass, Paul didn't play guitar. We did the whole song in a couple of takes."[33]

Once again, Ezrin called for silence and cued Macmillan, who lifted his baton to ready the players. Nodding to Criss and his musician-in-residence, Dick Wagner, he once again flipped his tails and sat at the grand piano. Over the next two-minutes and forty-five seconds, Studio A1 was filled with the dramatic strains of an orchestra made up of some of the finest musicians in the world, the subtle power of which struck all who were present as much as any thunderous rock band. The music was in itself a statement, a concussive departure from the raucous attack of a KISS show, but far more theatrical than the band's most devoted fans could have ever expected.

The weight and breadth of the final recording of "Beth" resides in its elaborate musical subtext, which is firmly evident during Ezrin's stirring bridge section, superbly arranged by himself and Macmillan. Absent of guitar or any instrumental solo, the middle-eight section repeats the song's emotive intro/outro alongside the chorus/bridge into an orchestrated interlude before the dramatic tag line returns, this time brush-stroked with single-note violin and viola classically balanced by counter-melody cellos changing key from C major to A minor into a crescendo. Enter the horns (trumpets, trombones, tubas, French horns), which accentuate the hook line with an anguished flourish. It was, as everyone who was there to witness and hear it, a long way from the brain-rattling assault of a KISS standard. Yet "Beth" achieved the band and Ezrin's goals of playing with audience expectations—flirting with possibilities as if a magician or suspense-film director while placing more than whimsy beneath the clamor.

It was a poignant moment for an awestruck Criss, the street-tough Italian kid who once chased after Gene Krupa as if begging for musical scraps. Bizarrely incongruous in his signature KISS cat costume, Criss crooned along with his ballad in the very room where his idol, Frank Sinatra, had once channeled his own street roots with sultry vocals to create an urban soliloquy straight from the heart. Criss's wife Lydia, whom many at the time assumed was the inspiration for "Beth," openly wept as she sat listening. Given that it was such a tender ballad, however, Ezrin wanted the keeper vocal to be captured in a more controlled environment, and thus Criss's stirring guide vocal was lost to time. But as Corky Stasiak vividly recalls, "Peter's performance that day was really quite moving. There were tears in his eyes when he finished."[34]

"I was crying my eyes out, it was so beautiful," Criss writes, in *Makeup to Breakup*. "And the orchestra was clicking their bows and Bob stood up and called me up to take a bow as the writer. When I was bowing to the room, I never felt so proud in my life."[35]

Bob Ezrin's sense of creative satisfaction filled Manhattan. He had found the core of The Act—the scope, illusion, pathos, sentiment, musical theater—but most importantly he had added the key element he had planned from the start: to get the macho band to show its raw emotional side. He knew that ultimately, what would fully allow "Beth" to connect KISS fans to his turning a "joke song" into a lush, Sinatra-esque ballad, was a heartfelt vocal from its author. Criss's guide vocal at the A&R session convinced the young producer he could secure a stirring final take, and for that he decided to create a comfortable environment a few days later.

"I remember Peter's vocals for 'Beth' most of all," recalls Jay Messina. "It was in a different studio, Studio C on the tenth floor. It was a smaller studio and a more intimate setting for Bob to work with him. We turned the light way down in the studio and the control room; whatever would make Peter the most at ease to get that performance out of him, that's what we'd do."[36]

While effusive in his praise for Aucoin and Ezrin's support in including his first composition on a KISS album—especially one that was clearly becoming an epic project at a crucial time in the band's ascent—Criss clearly had mixed emotions about his memorable vocal performance. This was due in no small part to Simmons and Stanley's lack of enthusiasm.

"I went into the studio and Bob lowered the lights to get me in the mood," Criss recounts in his memoir. "Just then, Gene and Paul walked in, and they sat down on the couch in front of the board. I was shitting a brick, all alone in there about to sing KISS's first ballad. Meanwhile those two fuckfaces in the booth were stone-faced like they were in the zoo watching an animal through the glass." Criss goes on to describe his growing anxiety through each take, his legs shaking and his voice struggling not to tremble with emotion, as all the while he endure smirks and chuckles from Gene and Paul—until Ezrin shouted, "Hey, assholes, get your fucking asses out of the room!"[37]

"Bob had to record Peter singing the song probably a dozen times and cobbled together a single version from the passable parts of those takes," Stanley stingingly recounts. "Peter's chances of being able to sing a song off the cuff were about as good as my chances of throwing a penny and hitting the moon."[38]

After expunging the troublemakers, Ezrin once again took charge and focused Criss to simply sing the song to him, as if describing the teary story of his nomadic life on the road and missing the tender understanding of his lonely wife, Lydia. Criss gathered himself and performed take after take—this time in a far different approach than the browbeating he took from Ezrin during the drum tracks. He was coaxed to lift his voice into a more subtle register, abandoning his rocker growl for the smoky gravel of his streetwise voice to sweeten the lyric.

"It took him a little while to get it, and it wasn't because he wasn't capable," says Messina. "He may have been nervous about it or uptight about it for one reason or another, and that's what really kept him from singing it the right way. Peter was very happy and appreciative of Bob for getting him through the vocal take for 'Beth.' He did great. He was so proud of it. It was a bit of a chore for him to get it, but he got it."[39]

"It was a typical Bob Ezrin vocal session," says Stasiak. "He wanted it a certain way, and he wanted it perfect, and he got it. That's why it sounds so damn good. It had a lot of pathos in it. It wasn't your usual rock vocal. It was something much more personal that Bob got out of him, which was nice."[40]

Ezrin, in turn, was blown away. "I love it!" he shouted. "I fucking love it!"[41] But according to Criss, when Simmons and Stanley were called back into the room to listen to the playback, they displayed neither a positive or negative reaction. This may have been less an indictment of Criss's vocal talents—which the band appreciated enough to have insisted the drummer getting a vocal or two on each album—than it was Gene and Paul's continued reluctance to fully accept a ballad on The Act's decisive statement. Either way, Criss was hurt and predictably angry, and, as with Ace Frehley's retreat from the proceedings, it further severed the band into two competing camps that would become far more entrenched once *Destroyer* brought KISS greater fame and fortune.

Nevertheless, the First KISS Grand Orchestral and Choral Recording Session was a rousing success, not only for its opulent spectacle and giddy grandeur, but mostly because, from January 13, 1976, onward, *Destroyer* would emerge undaunted as the seminal KISS album.

18

The Cover

They had their act down; they had their stage show; they had everything set. They had the look. Now they wanted to project the look to the public, and it was fate. You can't say it any other way. It was fate.
—Ken Kelly[1]

During the months between the recording and mixing of *Destroyer*, Bill Aucoin once again went back to his partner in design, Dennis Woloch, to begin the process of building on the image-driven success of *Alive!* The packaging of the two-record set turned out to be an integral element—if not *the* integral element—of what separated it from the band's previous three records, and which resulted in its unprecedented chart presence. The breakout of *Alive!* triumphantly proved that KISS's success as a band, perhaps more than any other before or after it, relied on visual stimulation. And on record, unlike onstage or in photographs, it had previously failed to fully resonate with the public. Although the music on *Alive!*—faster, rougher, and more energetic versions of earlier songs, including, pointedly, "Rock and Roll All Nite"—attracted many new and old fans to previously recorded near-misses, it was Aucoin and Woloch's visual presentation of the four characters—the Star Child, Demon, Space Ace, and Cat Man—that finally realized The Act so expertly.

"Bill came to me for the next one, which was really a thrill, because I think that *Alive!* was desperation on their part," says Dennis Woloch. "They were not doing that great. I know Bill mentioned this in several interviews at the time, but the concept was a cheap way to get product out there. It was like a reality show where you point the cameras and go. That's essentially what a live album is—a quick way of getting it out there cheaply—and for *Alive!* I used parts that they gave me and tried to make it look good—*designed* it. So, a few months later, Bill comes in and says, 'We're doin' another album and I'd like you to design it, if you'd like.' I said, 'I'd love it.' This was the first time I would work on an album from scratch, as far as concept goes."[2]

With the fervor Ezrin and the band were putting into the new tracks, carefully crafting a cinematic rock novella steeped in themes of sex, power, lust, greed, speed, and youthful imagination, Aucoin knew that the album's cover had to match if not eclipse it. The visage of The Act must equal these elaborate soundscapes and herald its promise to fuel the aspirations not only of the band but its growing KISS Army. And although the time, money, and level of production that had gone into the *Destroyer* sessions would dwarf anything KISS had previously done in the studio, who would care if its aural imagery laid a visual egg?

As important as the design was the album's title. This was especially pertinent in the early months of 1976, when a record's title could make or break the density of its roll out. This was the height of prog and hard rock, when bands like Yes, Genesis, Black Sabbath, and countless others segued Bible quotes and mythic references into album titles. The primacy of cover art was also in its prime, becoming a cottage industry of fantasy, sexuality, and raw, shocking presentation. KISS needed to be in the game, if not leading it. But in its gestation period, the eventual title, *Destroyer*—as astutely memorable as one hundred admen could have deduced—was something of a crapshoot.

"Bill put the word out that if anybody could think of a good name for the new KISS record, for us to write 'em down and give 'em to him," says Woloch, who insists this democratic free-for-all was something of a regular practice in the KISS inner sanctum. "I'd usually have to start thinking of something and eventually a name would come out from somewhere."[3]

That "somewhere" was Woloch's assistant, a thirty-three-year-old graphic designer by the name of Vincent DiGerlando, who also happened to be a childhood friend of his from Newark. It was DiGerlando's job to come up with a list of around ten titles, and on that fateful list was "Destroyer." With a nonchalant chuckle, Woloch says today, "So, basically, Vinnie named *Destroyer*."[4]

"The way I remember it is Bill needed a name and nobody had one off hand, so my idea was to do a process like a flow of consciousness," says DiGerlando. "Write everything that comes to mind and that is where that list came from. I just sat down at my drawing board and wrote names that reflected the image and the whole idea behind it or what they were trying to project at the time. I remember some of the names: 'Conquer' or 'Conquerors,' 'Destroyer,' 'Demons of Rock.' I must have come up with a dozen names and then handed the list off to Bill, because at that time there was no real protocol. Bill would just walk in, and that's how the name came about."[5]

DiGerlando may officially go down in KISStory for having provided a title for the band's seminal studio work, but Woloch still had a major hurdle to mount. He had to consult with Aucoin, Howard Marks, and KISS on the all-important cover. In the initial meeting with the brain trust, Woloch concocted an idea on how to best get everyone excited about his unique proposal by slanting the pitch toward what he had come to know as the band's largest and most hands-on ego.

"Knowing that Gene was pretty much the alpha dog at that time within the group—he and Paul had a lot of say on the creative end, but Gene seemed to be a little stronger—I strongly considered his tastes as a comic book, science-fiction fan. As a kid, he accumulated a lot of knowledge of that stuff—collected it, what have you—and I said to the band, probably talking to Gene more than anybody, 'You know, fellas, your costumes, your faces lend itself to being presented in more of that style, so what do you think of getting Frank Frazetta to do your cover?'—knowing that Gene would know who that was. I was really pandering to his sensibilities, but I just knew it would work for the band. And he said, 'Oh, yeah, you kiddin' me?' So I said, 'Let me see if I can get him.'"[6]

To someone like Simmons, fully immersed since childhood in the gothic comic genre, Frank Frazetta was Pablo Picasso. There was simply no one better in his field in the mid-'70s than the forty-eight-year-old Brooklynite. His very name evoked fantasy, sexuality, and pathos in what had been, before him, a mostly juvenile discipline. Frazetta's pencil and brush were responsible for the brutish but noble visage of *Conan the Barbarian* and the voluptuously menacing *Vampirella*. His talents were also responsible for bringing to life Edgar Rice Burroughs's *Tarzan* series on paperback covers for the boomer generation.

Recognized as a prodigy at age eight, Frazetta attended the Brooklyn Academy of Fine Arts and by fifteen was already working professionally at the Bernard Baily studios. Baily had made his claim in the industry at DC Comics, among others, and held the distinction of having worked on the most famous comic book ever published, *Action Comics* #1, which introduced Superman to the world. By the 1950s, Frazetta was already becoming a hot commodity, producing covers for the famed *Buck Rogers* series, assisting Al Kapp on his classic *Lil' Abner*, and putting in time working with Dan Barry on the wildly popular *Flash Gordon*. By the 1960s, Frazetta was creating movie posters and salacious beauties for *Playboy*, while his paintings were gracing nearly every horror and fantasy comic magazine in the nation, culminating in his seminal work with the *Conan the Barbarian* and *Tarzan* renderings that made him arguably the most imitated artist of the period.

Merely dropping Frazetta's name meant Woloch would leave the *Destroyer* design meeting with Gene Simmons's full blessing. Assuming correctly that the other members of the band would simply dig the idea of being depicted as larger-than-life—and, under the guidance of Frazetta's pen, almost godlike—superheroes, and having closely observed the quirks of the young men he was working with during their long climb to stardom, he was certain that courting Simmons was his best bet.

Woloch: "Ace was a real character, usually drunk and wanting to kiss everybody, including me. He didn't care. He was out of it. 'Hey, Curly, give me a kiss!' He called everybody Curly. Peter seemed always troubled and pissed off about something, but he was okay. I ended up doing Peter's two solo albums after he left KISS. But Ace and Peter were more street guys. I mean, I'm from the northward of Newark, which was a pretty tough Italian neighborhood in those days, and it was a background probably similar to Ace and Peter's. Peter's from Brooklyn, Italian guy or half-Italian, whatever he is. I could kind of talk to those guys on a different level than Gene and Paul, two Jewish kids from Queens with completely different backgrounds—I mean, Gene being born in Israel and Paul being a very narcissistic guy. He never saw a mirror he didn't like. But when Gene walked into a room, it wasn't big enough for his ego and yours, believe me. You could feel it; it was tangible. It wasn't something you were making up in your head; you'd say to yourself, 'Holy crap, this guy . . . !' He almost tasted my knuckle sandwich. He doesn't know it, but I got close to boppin' him a couple of times. In private moments Gene was fine, but then he was an asshole, and then he was fine, and then he was an asshole."[7]

Woloch would now find himself caught between two massive egos: Simmons and Frazetta, the former imbued with the living spirit of The Act on the precipice of superstardom and the latter perched on his professional apex. The pressure was ratcheted up exponentially further by the mere fact that Woloch had no connections to the comic world nor any clue whether its most famous artist would be able to take on the project due to his immense workload—never mind if he would even deign to consider it.

Woloch: "So I look up Frazetta—I get his home number somehow, I don't know how—and call and wind up talking to his wife, who was his 'manager.' And she would never let me talk to Frank. She was going to filter and buffer all phone calls and make all the business deals and that was a big pain in the ass, because I had to explain everything to everybody three times; once to her, once to Frank, then back to the band. I finally said, 'Look, I'm working for a rock-and-roll group, they're really gonna be huge. They're on the verge, they're already starting to get big from their sales of their last album. The name is KISS, they paint their faces. They look like superheroes or monsters or demons, like fantasy characters with outlandish costumes and I think Frank would be perfect to do a painting. And she hemmed and hawed—'I don't know, who are they again?'—as if saying if they weren't famous he wouldn't want to do it. I kept going, 'They're gonna be famous, they're gonna be huge!'

"Finally, after two or three phone calls, she let me talk to Frank. I remember I was sitting on a little wooden folding chair late at night when I finally got him on the phone. I'm in the middle of my wrap trying to convince him that he's the perfect guy and we really need him to do it, and my chair breaks and I wind up on my ass on the floor with a big crash! But I never stopped talkin'. I had Frank Frazetta on the phone! I didn't want to say, 'Woops!' or none of that, and I just kept goin'. So he says, 'What was that noise?' I said, 'My chair collapsed. I'm sitting on the floor in a pile of sticks!' You should have heard him laugh. He had this uproarious laugh. He couldn't stop laughing. I told him, 'Frank, I had to keep goin', I had you on the line!' So I got him to agree to do it and he tells me it had to be $15,000 and he would have to keep the art and we could only use it for the album cover, nothing else. We'd have to make a separate deal if we wanted to use it for something else. I said, 'None of that's gonna work, Frank. They're gonna make underwear, lunch boxes—you name it, they're gonna put this image on it. I know it, 'cause we're at the beginning of this marketing thing.' And the money: I told him it was too much, maybe I could get a lot of that money, but do you have to own the art? We have to own it outright. Nobody wants to be a bookkeeper and say, 'We make T-shirts and we owe Frank 10 percent of T-shirt sales.' They want to take care of it now, give you the money, and that's the end of the story. He said no, and I wasn't sure we could get the money anyway. I mean, fifteen grand was a lot of money then—hell, it's a lot of money now. There's no arguing Frank was a god, he was the best of the best. He was *the man*, but there was no way."[8]

Frustrated but unbowed, Woloch imparted the bad news to Aucoin, who predictably told his designer to get back out there and find someone else—preferably a Frank Frazetta clone, since there were so many of them around. Leaving the meeting, Woloch took a lunchtime stroll along Fifty-Ninth Street between Third and Second Avenues where he came upon a large newsstand with dozens of comics. "I just stared at comic books for a long time and I found one that I really liked," remembers Woloch, in a tone that evokes the discovery of a rare jewel. "There was a painting of a robot on the cover of *Creepy* magazine, so I bought it and I still have it. So I took it back to the office, looked inside the front pages, got the publisher's number, and called them. I couldn't read the guy's name on the cover, the way he signed it. I could sort of read Ken or Elly, so I asked the publisher who the artist was and that I wanted to get in touch with him."[9]

The horror comic/magazine *Creepy* was, along with its companion periodical, *Eerie*, for Warren Publishing, one of the most popular of its genre. It was filled with more sophisticated storylines and creative art than its predecessors from the early days of horror comics, like *Tales from the Crypt* and *Vault of Horror*, whose popularity and influence among the youth of America in the 1950s sent shockwaves that reached the halls of the U.S. Congress, which all but shut down any violently provocative material under the tyrannical arm of the Comic Code Authority. *Creepy*'s founder, Jim Warren with his lead editor, Russ Jones, had—much like their publishing brethren Harvey Kurtzman and William Gaines over a decade earlier with the satirical *Mad*—exploited a loophole in the "code" by publishing their tales of the macabre under the guise of a magazine and not a comic, thus providing a new era of thrills for its vast audience.

By the 1970s, *Creepy* was churning out quality writers and artists, including Frank Frazetta, expanding into fantasy, science fiction, and even illustrated versions of classics written by Edgar Allen Poe. One of these entrenched professionals was a thirty-year-old struggling freelancer, Woloch's "Ken *Elly*."

Hired originally to work on *Creepy* covers by then managing editor Bill DuBay, Ken Kelly traveled into Manhattan weekly from his modest one-room walkup apartment in Long Island to choose what covers he could complete in a timely basis.

DuBay was one of the key figures in modernizing *Creepy* and *Eerie* in many areas, not the least of which was hiring foreign talent from Spain to provide a unique look to the design and covers. His keenly developed eye for a European look in his artists turned out to be Kelly's forte, as he struggled to gain a foothold on his talent in his early twenties while living in a house owned by his in-laws along the French Riviera in Cannes. It certainly did not hurt that Kelly was the great Frank Frazetta's nephew. Lucky for DuBay, and later for Dennis Woloch, Kelly had returned from a tour of duty in Vietnam with a talent to draw but little direction. He would speak on several occasions with the master, Frazetta, who challenged him to hone his skills with the promise of pointing him in the right direction professionally. When he returned after a year in France, Kelly showed Frazetta his work and, with his uncle's blessing, received an immediate commission to paint a cover for Warren Publications.

Interestingly, despite being a family member and having taken all of Frazetta's advice to heart, while also initially developing his talents to impress him, Kelly received very little in the way of tutoring or style secrets from his uncle. "He didn't actually say, 'This is how you do this, and this is how you do that,'" Kelly recalled, during an interview for this book. "He never did that. He would not give away his secrets. He took his secrets to his grave. There were occasions when I actually asked him, 'How do you do a bracelet like this? and

I got, 'I'm not telling you. You're on your own.' I don't blame him. I mean, without getting anything from him directly, just seeing his work, he was such a monumental talent that a lot of artists my age followed Frazetta during that era and their work ended up looking like his simply because he was such a tremendous talent, and it was harder and harder to pull away to make my stuff look more individual."[10]

Having been rejected by Frazetta, Dennis Woloch, who had already sold the idea of a classic comic-art style for the cover of *Destroyer* to Bill Aucoin and KISS, stood on the street holding Kelly's cover for *Creepy* #72, dated July 1975, and knew right away he had his man.

Before becoming a favorite of DuBay's, Kelly drove a truck full-time in New York while also somehow managing to work a second job in the toy department of a large chain and squeezing in freelance painting whenever he could. "DuBay said to me, 'If you quit your day job, I'll cover you. I'll make sure you make more than you did with both jobs,' which he did. God bless him. That was years before KISS, when I was still working as hard and fast as I possibly could and living in an apartment in Long Island with a little easel in the corner that I had made out of two-by-fours and, you know, nothing. I was a starving artist."[11]

It was during these times of relative poverty and high deadline pressure that Kelly recalls the opportunity to create the fateful cover for *Creepy* #72, which was based on a story titled "Vendetta," written by Rich Margopoulos and Gerry Boudreau and penned by Jose Gual (one of Warren's signature Spanish artists, full name Jose Gual Tutusaus). The young artist describes its creation: "He [DuBay] would have stuff ready for me when I'd come into the city from my day job, and he'd have either the storyboards half drawn, a particular illustration already there waiting for me, or sometimes nothing really, just an idea in his head over a fifteen-minute meeting, and I'd say, 'Okay, I could make a cover out of that, I could make a cover out of that, and I could make a cover out of that.' And he'd say, 'Okay, do that, do this, do this.' And it would be normally on a Thursday, but I'd have to get the painting done over the weekend and get it back to him by Monday. So most of the things I did for Warren, I did in four or five days. That cover was simply another one of the stories that some writer did and then a penciler did. There was this robot that was in this story, and I thought, 'Wow, I could see that in a room with nice lighting, it's very dramatic,' and he says, 'Yeah, go ahead. Whatever. Do it.' There could be no excuses, nothing. Monday, man—they got the presses rolling, and if you don't bring it in, you're fired. That's it. That's the end of your life."[12]

As usual, Kelly headed back to his cramped apartment and worked on the "Vendetta" cover over the weekend, as well as an additional cover painting in oils that he describes as being of "a red planet with a white spaceship and a spaceman, and he's kind of in a blue costume, floating out and he's fighting a robot."[13] He never dreamed of the impact his single dramatic robot creature would have on Woloch's eye.

Kelly: "I believe that the robot painting was part of a canvas pad, and the pad consisted of maybe ten sheets of canvas paper—eighteen by twenty-four, something like that, no larger than that—and you just simply peel off the canvas, tape it to a harder surface, and paint on it. Get it done, and then start the next one, and that's how I was delivering them. It's strictly oils on canvas, not even stretched linen. I was a starving artist, so I don't think I had the money for stretch wood."[14]

The solitary figure of the gray robot cast in eerie orange light and deep shadows, with a forlorn face echoing loneliness and suffering, is striking. The most engaging element, perhaps overlooked upon first inspection, is the eyes peering behind the metal, clearly visible and beseeching. This is a machine with the emotions of a damaged heart; the darker side of Frank L. Baum's weepy Tin Woodsman, long engrained in the national psyche by the actor Jack Haley's portrayal in the 1939 film epic *The Wizard of Oz*. The image evokes both science fiction and horror, underscored with tragedy. There is, as Bob Ezrin had pointed out to KISS months before, vulnerability behind the two-dimensional façade.

"I did both of those paintings in this four-day period and got them back to Warren," Kelly adds. "And it's just that my style looked like the Frazetta style—the heavy shadows and the deep lights. I was still very much under the influence of Frazetta's style, so the work looked similar, and I think that's what attracted Dennis."[15]

Clutching his copy of *Creepy* #72, Woloch hustled back to the Howard Marks Agency offices around the block to call the number he'd found on the masthead inside the magazine. The contact at Warren immediately gleaned that the person on the other end was excited about his artist and desperate to hire him for a fairly substantial sum of cash, so he cleverly told Woloch that he was Kelly's manager. Furiously pressed by Woloch, who had wasted enough precious time going a few rounds with Mrs. Frank Frazetta's hard line, the contact finally admitted to the ruse and coughed up Kelly's home number. "I call up Ken Kelly, I tell him what it's all about, he's *really* happy," says Woloch.[16]

"Imagine what it all comes down to: that cover of the horror comic was on the newsstand when Dennis walked by," effuses Kelly. "My whole life changed because that cover was sitting on the newsstand when Dennis walked down and looked. If it had been a day or two, maybe they would've taken it off and

Jay Messina, lead engineer at the board during the *Destroyer* sessions, is duly credited for giving the record its thunderous bottom end and raucous guitar attack, while providing Bob Ezrin a myriad of sound choices throughout. "Bob gave me a fair amount of rope to play with in the studio and the one thing I wasn't afraid to do is turn knobs all the way up." (From the private collection of Corky Stasiak)

The assistant engineer on *Destroyer*, Corky Stasiak, at the console with his ever-present studio journal. His energetic creative input and technical innovations rounded out the triumvirate that realized the majestic pomp of KISS's most compelling studio effort. "There was an air in the studio for me that we were making history with *Destroyer*." (From the private collection of Corky Stasiak)

The Invisible Virtuoso: Dick Wagner, guitar hero and studio free agent, would get the call from Bob Ezrin to play on four *Destroyer* tracks when Ace Frehley went AWOL. "When they just give you a spot and say, 'Go for it,' you got a chance to come up with something that will be lasting." (From the private collection of Dick Wagner)

Demonic Cherubs: The Ezrin boys, David (age ten) and Joshua (age eight), added their mischievously high-pitched voices to the ominous rumble of "God of Thunder." It was a tradition of the young producer to imbue darker themes with the voices of children, which he called "a phenomenal dramatic device," in almost all of his thematic productions. He remembers simply thinking, "Whoa, 'God of Thunder,' how cool would little monsters sound?" (From the private collection of Bob Ezrin)

White Tie and Tails: The *Destroyer* recording team in the master control room at A&R Studios before recording strings for "Beth" and the choir for "Great Expectations." *From left to right*: assistant engineer Corky Stasiak, lead engineer Jay Messina, unidentified, producer Bob Ezrin (cape, white gloves, and top hat in front of him), and Ace Frehley making his escape. Ezrin fondly remembers, "We were turning the album into an event, the whole thing was a little bit of the P. T. Barnum in me expressing itself." (© Bob Gruen/www.bobgruen.com)

The First KISS Grand Orchestral and Choral Recording Session: Conductor Alan Macmillan readies the orchestra at A&R Studio 1A as KISS mugs for the camera, January 13, 1976. Macmillan admits today, "It seemed a little overwhelming." (Fin Costello/Redferns/Getty Images)

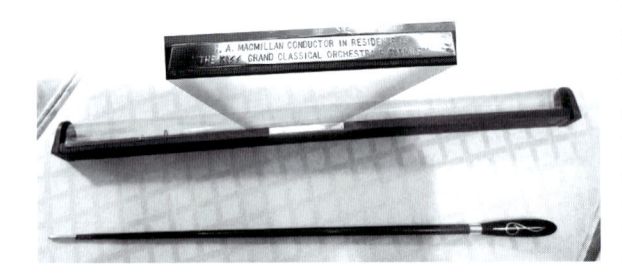

The official case and baton presented by Bob Ezrin to Allan Macmillan on the morning of January 13, 1976, before the recording of "Great Expectations" and "Beth." Macmillan: "I'm standing up there at the stand, and they're all right in front of me." (From the private collection of Allan Macmillan/Design by Roberto Tatis)

The forty-strong Brooklyn Boys Choir rambunctiously awaits its performance on "Great Expectations" as grizzled veteran classical musicians, led by the legendary concertmaster David Nadien, casually discuss union dues in the foreground. Corky Stasiak jokes today, "I think if we spent anymore time then we did, those kids would have been hanging from the ceiling." (From the private collection of Corky Stasiack)

Iconic Regalia: The first official photo shoot of KISS in brand new *Destroyer* costumes (not including the candid shots of the band's arrival a few weeks earlier at the orchestral sessions), which, along with Ken Kelly's cover painting, would complete the lasting aura of The Act. Paul Stanley recalls today, "Going into '76, we had no doubt we were going to be huge. The great rollercoaster ride we'd prayed for was about to start, and we knew we'd better hold on tight or we'd be thrown to certain death." (Fin Costello/Redferns/Getty Images)

Visual Guru: Creative/artistic director for Howard/Marks, Dennis Woloch, the man who devised the three-dimensional character of KISS with the career-defining *Alive!* rollout, would work his magic again, turning *Destroyer* into the band's metaphoric *tour de force*. Woloch recalls, "This was the first time I would work on an album from scratch, as far as concept goes." (David M. Spindel)

Vincent DiGerlando, the man who named *Destroyer* and designed the famed KISS Army chevron inspired by his time in the National Guard. "I just sat down at my drawing board and wrote names that reflected the image and the whole idea behind it or what they were trying to project at the time." (From the private collection of Vincent DiGerlando)

Spurned by renowned comic artist Frank Frazetta, creative designer Dennis Woloch was wandering despondently down Fifty-Ninth Street when the cover of horror comic *Creepy #72* caught his discerning eye. The solitary figure of the gray robot cast in eerie orange light and deep shadows with a forlorn face echoing loneliness and suffering, painted by Ken Kelly, would change both of their lives—and the fortunes of KISS and *Destroyer*—forever. Kelly says today, "My whole life changed because that cover was sitting on the newsstand when Dennis walked down and looked." (© New Comic Company LLC. Used by permission.)

Artist Ken Kelly in 1975. The epitome of the starving artist, Kelly would create one of the most iconic images in the history of American pop culture. Kelly remembers the crucial days of his creation: "The anxiety level is through the roof. If you're not a young man, you'll probably die from it because you don't know. You have no idea. You know it's huge, though." (From the private collection of Ken Kelly)

The Cover: Ken Kelly's image of four superhero figures in an ethereal glow, more champions against chaos than its perpetuators, forever etched KISS in the pantheon of rock mythology. Says the artist, "They planned it to be a painting, because they were not only comic heroes, but also living entities. You could actually touch them. It wasn't like Spider-Man and Batman that lived on this piece of paper. These guys *were* alive!" (Ken Kelly/Michael Ochs Archives/Getty Images)

Mark Ravitz, the man who would help design and create the greatest spectacle in the rock world: the Spirit of '76 Tour. "We were doing things in an arena setting that hadn't been seen before." (From the private collection of Mark Ravitz)

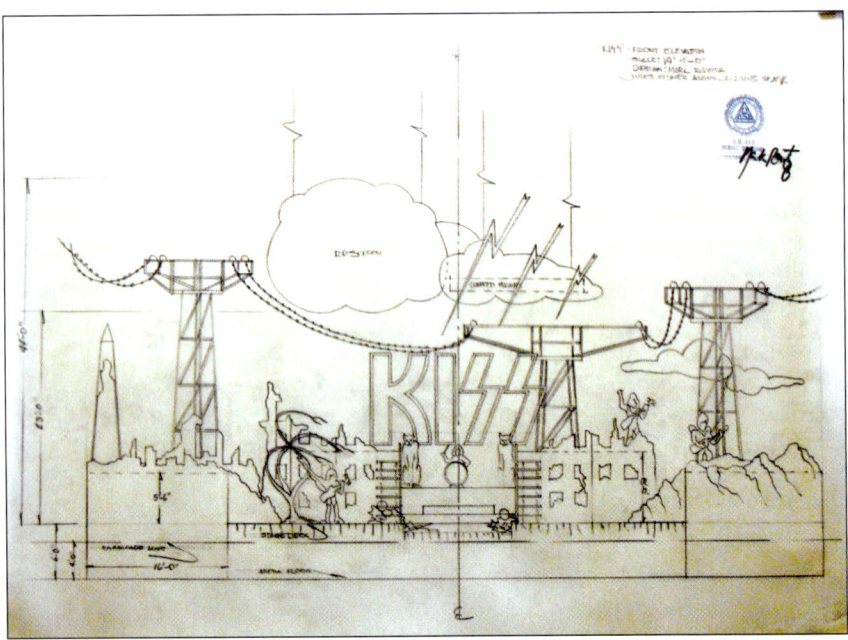

The original blueprint sketch for the Sprit of '76 stage set. Notice the individual environments devised for each character, reflecting the imagery of *Destroyer*. Much of it had to be revamped after the band, enraged at not being told of its construction while in Europe, tore it to pieces. Ravitz notes today, "Our stage dynamic for them was based on the idea that they were invading the space of the audience, coming down into their world in an assertive stance to begin the show." (From the private collection of Mark Ravitz)

The Stratosphere Team: Casablanca's minuscule but highly effective promotions department. *From left to right*: Chocolate City head Cecile Holmes, head of pop promotions Al Dinolble, vice president of promotions—and the man who broke "Beth"—Scott Shannon, and label president Neil Bogart. Shannon recalls his frantic grassroots push to make "Beth" a hit: "I knew the kid in the mail room—little guy with shoulder length hair, he now is an independent promotion guy in LA—and I said, 'I want you to do a Top 40 mailing, and I got like about 100 copies of the stock.' I took the stock copy and took a black magic marker and put X's on the side that had 'Beth.' I shipped it out to 100 people that I knew." (From the private collection of Scott Shannon)

Peter Criss performing "Beth" onstage in early 1977. Due to the overwhelming success of "Beth"—still the highest charting KISS single ever, after peaking at #7 late in 1976—*Destroyer* jumped back in and then up the charts, prompting Criss to sing it to the studio backup track on the band's ensuing tours. (Michael Ochs Archives/Getty Images)

sent it back to Warren, it would've been a whole different world for me. It's incredible."[17]

"I told him to come to the office and bring some of his original work, because I wanted to see what it looked like in person," says Woloch. "It was a big job. I couldn't give it to him on the basis of the one thing I saw. I told him to bring in pictures of *people*."[18]

When Kelly received Woloch's proposition he had never heard of KISS, but, unlike his mentor, Frazetta, he was in no position, professionally or financially, to begin spouting demands. "I had been working for five years in the horror industry, and here was an opportunity to work for a new company," says Kelly. "I didn't even know what KISS was. I had no idea. And luckily I don't believe Warren knew, either. But when I got there at the meetings, the Rolls Royces were down in the street—it was all the bankers that wanted to jump on the bandwagon with Howard Marks and Bill Aucoin. Everybody was on board in the right position, so you knew it was all happening. I immediately met the guys, too. Gene and Paul were there. Howard Marks was there. Bill Aucoin was there. And here they bring this artist upstairs and it's his first large assignment. It was just very overwhelming for me as a young artist to step into that world, and I had no idea really what was going on."[19]

So enthralled with the big time was Kelly, who recalls the impressive "black walls" of the offices with "giant billboards of KISS" everywhere, he remains sure, even today, that there must have been other artists considered.[20] But Woloch knew otherwise. He was up against a heavy deadline and had lost Frazetta. If the rest of Kelly's work was as beguiling as the "Vendetta" cover—and, of course, if he agreed to surrender full rights to his painting in return for a reasonable financial figure that Aucoin would accept—he was in.

"He brought his stuff in," says Woloch. "I thought it was great. I said, 'You got the job!'"[21]

"My God, here's my chance to expand and get out, wherever *out* was," remarks Kelly, on his sudden entry into the high-stakes rock-and-roll world, where he would take the significant financial leap from $175 a painting for Warren to a humbly undisclosed figure he says today was "astronomical." "Not that I didn't like horror, but you know, you want to expand, and Dennis was the vehicle that helped me. He was very kind and considerate and took care of me and guided me and talked to me about what they wanted, and of course I was going to jump on board. And we were versatile in our thinking patterns and our ideas and what he wanted and what I re-suggested. We got a rapport going right away."[22]

"I explained to him what I wanted, and that the album was called *Destroyer*," says Woloch. "I said, 'I don't know what it means. I don't know what we're referring to here, nothing—we're just going with the title. There'll be a scene of destruction behind them. Flames and smoke. It's in their act anyway.' But I wanted these guys to look like superheroes, larger than life, sort of like they'd always existed in that way. I gave him whatever photos we had and he used that for reference."[23]

Kelly: "Back in the '70s, we had these little portable slide machines that you held in your hand. You put the slide in and you pressed the button, the light went on, and you looked in there, and you could see this very small image. It must've been about an inch and a half by an inch and a half, and that's the photographic reference I had to work with, and when Dennis showed me these photos, that's when I discovered what this was all about. And I had no idea if I could do it. I did have five years' experience with Warren, which I guess paved the way, because I'd have to work with such speed."[24]

Excited, nervous, and determined, Kelly once again retreated to his Long Island apartment and began immediately sketching from the tiny slides of photographs taken by Fin Costello for the cover of *Alive!* along with other live action shots of the band. The first drafts would be in pencil during a stage in the process he calls "roughs." Completing these, which were usually twelve-by-fourteen-inch sketches, took up half of the thirty days he had been allotted by Woloch. He pained over getting the correct proportions, facial expressions, and body movements, basing them on the distant audience-perspective shots squeezed into a miniscule slide monitor.

Kelly: "I initially did exactly what I did with Warren. I went home, got some paper, a pad out, and drew the guys as basically as I could, and that took a while because I had gotten the feedback from Dennis in the office on what Ace was like and that Gene was very aggressive, and Paul is this and that, and now I had to work out a pose that met each emotion. So I acted out the character poses as my wife took pictures of me. I was on the ground floor apartment—there were two floors—and I would walk up four steps, turn around, and give a pose, and she'd snap a camera with a Polaroid. I probably did maybe fifty different shots and picked four, put them on the paper, drew them out, and got some oils, just picked some colors—'Okay, this is what I'm gonna do. I'm gonna make it very dusty on the ground, so it's going to be a beige-y color, and as you go higher, it's going to get darker to black at top, and then the fire's going to be right behind them.'

"For the different costumes, I had pictures from the slides. And that was the hardest part, because with the slide being so small and Fin Costello taking the pictures from being in the audience, the actual image that I had was probably a quarter of an inch or even an eighth of an inch—very small, small, small stuff. But thank God I was a young man and had good eyes and could tell what each costume was. I had never done anything like this. One of my anxieties was I could find no reference, and I never did. I had to create it myself: four men abreast, [in] perspective, how does that look? Technically they should be leaned, there should be a curvature, a little lean back so that Gene and Paul would be back a little and the other guys would be up front, and I didn't want that. I wanted it equal. For instance, there's a considerable difference in their heights. Peter's shorter than Gene and Paul, and all four were different sizes, but they wanted them to pretty much look equal, and that was another challenge. But it was a timeline, I had to do it, and so I did. I made the decisions. I didn't know how sound the decisions were at the time, but you make them, and they call you, and they say what do you think, and I said, 'I'm ready,' and they say, 'Well, come on in,' and you just come in, open it up, and show them. And there's your world: you win or lose, and they loved it. They loved it and said, 'Go home and paint it.'"[25]

Relieved, Kelly returned to his apartment and spent the next two weeks furiously painting the cover for *Destroyer*, first measuring the illustration board to the proper dimensions of a square album cover, which were quite different from his magazine parameters, and which would encompass both the front and back of the cover when eventually folded—each of the four figures meticulously sized and proportioned. "I had no equipment to do that like they have nowadays," he recalls. "You've got all of these things to help you today—projectors and slides and everything. I did it all manually. And painting, what are you going to? You're going to paint the white faces, you're going to paint the costumes, you're going to paint!"[26]

Kelly's portrait of KISS poised as superheroes leaping from the precipice of a desert netherworld with the flames of carnage nipping at their platform heels is powerful stuff. The four stark figures are adorned in their triumphant *Alive!* costumes: black leather and sequins with outrageously large silver and black boots. Paul Stanley is on the extreme left, taught and active, wrapped tightly in his star-bedazzled jumpsuit, arms spread like a majestic ringmaster, lips puckered, curls flowing. To his immediate right is the Cat Man, Peter Criss, muscular and distant, his gloved hands coiled in fists positioned as if shifting gears on an invisible motorcycle, a sparkling silver cross dangling from his neck. Next is Ace Frehley, whose contorted, almost gravity-challenged visage appears to be weightless, his fingers swirling about, looking for an instrument to best express his alien exploits. And finally, all the way to the right, is Gene Simmons, the Demon, adorned in bat wings and studs, his mouth agape, snarling with glee beneath a streak of pitch-black hair, kissing the sky as if flames, his raised fist a counterpoint to the frivolity of Stanley's long, slender, overtly feminine gesture.

With little background and no modern equipment, even by mid-'70s standards, and with Kelly having never even attempted an album cover before, it is a masterwork. In a single image, the first rendering of KISS as comic supermen—the very core and purpose of The Act—the young artist captured its aura. It is the reflection of what *Destroyer* was becoming, sonically, musically, and lyrically. It is what *Destroyer* would become to a generation of kids in the thrall of KISS. Yet when he returned to Manhattan to present his vision, Kelly was still nervous that he was in over his head and sure that he would be competing against other experienced artists.

"The anxiety level is through the roof," he says. "If you're not a young man, you'll probably die from it, because you don't know. You have no idea. You know it's huge, though. You can see the people walking around you, and they're not even talking to you, and you know they're loaded. You know there's big shit going on here, and I don't know what it is, but there's something really, really, really big going on here."[27]

Today it is known to KISS fans as "*Destroyer* Brown," since much of the colors, as Kelly recalls, resonate in browns and beiges. Before a desert motif with smoke billowing about, the band appears to be emerging as if warlocks out of a swirl of fire and brimstone. Dennis Woloch loved it, but there was suddenly an issue with the costumes—as in, KISS would be getting new ones before *Destroyer*'s release. And although Fin Costello was scheduled to take photos of the band in these proposed duds, all the design department had were sketches. Kelly, already jacked with adrenaline and paranoid he would be fired or replaced, was devastated.

"I thought my career was over," Kelly remembers. "I thought it was done. Oh, my God, I completely blew it. And they said, 'No, no, no, no, we're going to do another cover.' And I'm like, 'Oh, my God. Oh, my God.'"[28]

"It kind of got rejected, because we had to change costumes," explains Dennis Woloch. "I remember Bill saying something about doing it over because there was going to be different costumes and I wanted it to be up to date. Ken was okay with that. I guess we gave him a little extra money. I do know he made more money on this than on anything he had done up until that point by far."[29]

"Dennis kept it low key," says Kelly. "I mean, it was obvious it was big, but he kept saying, 'Let's just concentrate on the art, Ken. Let's concentrate on what our jobs are,' and I did. I took his advice and he walked me through it, and I knew exactly what I had to do and did it."[30]

Adding to the drama, the word from Casablanca was that the image of their supermen was too dark and far too violent. It appeared to the label as if KISS had literally "destroyed" the town engulfed in flames behind them. Of course, this is true. It was Woloch's and ultimately Kelly's vision to match the title with the environment of this hard rock, gothic outfit having burned down another town with its monster show. Kelly was, if nothing else, a suspense and horror artist. But what's most notable is that, while Dennis Woloch was well aware of Casablanca's refusal to consider Kelly's "*Destroyer* Brown" on the grounds of its excess violence, he informed the artist only of the need to change the costumes. He had another plan that he would share with Kelly before he went back for a second go-around.

Kelly: "Years later, I learned from Bill Aucoin just before he died that Casablanca rejected the cover because it was too violent. But at the time Dennis just stepped right up and gave me a new idea. 'Ken,' he said, 'we're going with the same thing, absolute same poses, same everything, but we're going to take the violence and put it way far back, and we're going to put them up on a mountain. So this way no one can say that they caused whatever was happening way back there, but there was still violence in the background.' And that's how '*Destroyer* Blue' was born."[31]

Woloch: "This time, though, I said, 'Since we're doing it again, the guys didn't look important enough.' So I stood on a desk and with Ken sitting down in front of me, looking up, I said, 'You see?' I was standing up there with my arms up over my head, flexing my muscles and I said, 'This is it! Come on, these guys are like gods come down from the heavens like Zeus!' So he said, 'Okay, I get it.' Somebody complained about the level of destruction in the background, so we minimized it a little bit. We tweaked it and it came out great. I told him on the back cover I want to see the scene of destruction without the guys, so I could put my type there, but I didn't want to have a blank back cover. I wanted it to be like a continual scene, a concept."[32]

"I left there with the absolute conviction that I was not going to fail, no matter what this was," says Kelly. "I still didn't know really anything about KISS—nothing—didn't know what they sang, never heard them, but you could've given me anything at that time and I would've made it work."[33]

Once again, Kelly headed back to his Long Island apartment, which he shared with his wife Rose and their young son Bobby, and literally took over the entirety of the front room, spreading the twenty-four-by-twenty-eight-inch canvas out before him. He first penciled out the figures, each between ten and twelve inches tall, allowing space for the KISS logo, which would appear centered on top. And, for a second time, Kelly began to paint, heeding Woloch's suggestions and pressing his imagination further.

Kelly: "The way I laid out that painting was the faces had to be the size of a quarter for me to get all the detail in the way I wanted. So, then extend that dimension out to their bodies and everything around them, you'll see just what the painting's going to be, and that's what it ended up being. And then you go out and buy the board, you do the drawing, put the drawing on it, and you start the painting. But that's all a blur now, thank God, because it was, you know ... scary."[34]

While the first painting was one long piece, front and back, this time, at Woloch's behest, Kelly created the front first. This was done so that it could quickly get approval from Aucoin, the band, and the label, before Kelly spent the last hours putting the finishing touches on what would be the back cover: a distant horizon of burning buildings.

"He painted a separate picture for the back," recalls Woloch. "It must have been a rush, because when he brought the job in, he never put the retouch—the final varnish—on it, and it was a pretty big panting. He brings me a jar of varnish and a paintbrush and said, 'If you don't mind Dennis, I didn't have time, but you should put a coat of varnish on this before you do anything with it.' So I sat there painting varnish onto the *Destroyer* painting for hours and protected it."[35]

"When I handed it in, it was a total blank," says Kelly. "It was probably so traumatic for me that I blocked it out, because I still don't recall when I handed in the final. I do remember when I was halfway through '*Destroyer* Blue,' Howard Marks called me up about five o'clock one night and said that he'd like to see it, and that was shocking because I was only like halfway through it. I guess he just wanted verification that it was being done. So I drove in and I went up the stairs and showed Howard, and he was alone in the office and as soon as he saw it, he just nodded his head and said, 'Okay, keep going.'"[36]

Soon the band and everyone at Rock Steady were raving. Woloch and Kelly had done it—they'd built the myth of KISS into supernatural idolatry. In every way, Kelly's painting was a visual microcosm of the music that would fill *Destroyer*. Its audacity, its playfulness, its imagination is all there in living color—not merely as the members of a New York City glam-rock band of leather-clad bohemians but as invincible comic book heroes. The Act had created an unequaled stage show, had worked for months laying down its musical manifesto, and now it would have its symbol.

Woloch would center the indelible KISS logo at the top-center of the painting, emblazoned in the azure sky above the four heads. Just below it, in a typeface that might today recall the Courier font, was the single word "Destroyer."

"I remember going around and sticking a piece of paper in every typewriter we had in the office and typing DESTROYER," remembers Woloch. "I wanted to get the worst typewriter, and I just picked one that I liked the characters of the letters, the way they came out, and I used that one. Then I sent it out for a Photostat, probably enlarged it slightly, and then just stuck it down on a mechanical. You know, this was all way before computers. So everything was Photostats and glue and razor blades."[37]

The final classic, indelible cover of *Destroyer* ("*Destroyer* Blue") would forever etch KISS into the pantheon of rock mythology. The azure blue surrounds the four figures, who now have an ethereal glow, more champions against chaos than perpetuators of it. The jagged stone at their feet evoking both a mountaintop—the band either ascending it or about to descend—or the ruins of some ancient temple, or perhaps the tumbled blocks of a once fortified castle torn down so that all may join in the conquest. Stanley, Criss, Frehley, and Simmons all strike the same poses as Kelly's impressive first painting, but now they seem to be literally dancing on hard rock in the heavens, basking in the zenith of their powers.

"Everything was so well planned," says Kelly, who would go on to buy his first house with his compensation for this propitious rendering. "They planned it to be a painting, because it was part of the comic industry, and they were the heroes of the comic world. But they were also living entities. You could actually touch them. It wasn't like *Spider-Man* and *Batman* that lived on this piece of paper. These guys *were* alive!"[38]

19

Finishing Touches

I'm there to help the artist realize their dreams, but also that their dream pleases an audience, because that's why we get to do what we do.
—Bob Ezrin[1]

Bob Ezrin decided to jumpstart the home stretch of the *Destroyer* sessions by pulling the entire band in to record the new anthem, "Shout It Out Loud," which he, Stanley, and Simmons had finished in his apartment only days before. There was still a buzz among the band and the engineers, following the A&R sessions for "Great Expectations" and "Beth," and, for one day at least, renewed vigor for Criss and Frehley. It would be the first time the band had all been in the studio together since the first grueling days of the sessions, and now, with the musicians fully indoctrinated in Ezrin's techniques for performance, the takes were swift and energetic. It would also be the last time KISS would appear together on the Studio A floor, working its hardcore magic for the crew, and when recording was completed, there were smiles everywhere. It was by far the most stress-free moment in the creation of *Destroyer*. There was even time to play a practical joke on Simmons, as Ezrin dramatically told him that they erroneously recorded over the backing orchestral and choral parts of "Great Expectations," and that his sweeping masterpiece for *Destroyer* had been lost to the ages. "I freaked," Simmons recalls, in the liner notes to *The Box Set*. "But as everyone broke into laughter, I realized it was a very effective joke at my expense."[2]

This was also an opportune time, as Corky Stasiak recalls, to pantomime the recording process for Neil Bogart and the Casablanca heads, Bill Aucoin, and the Howard Marks agency crew, in the kind of "VIP" ploy the Record Plant staff had seen many times before. The brass would stand up in the control booth and watch the band go through a faux recording or overdub, thus made to feel part of the experience. It was pretty standard procedure. Little did Stasiak realize it would end in minor disaster.

"So one day when the album was just about finished," he recalls, "Bill Aucoin brought his whole management people in, and brought Neil Bogart and all the dignitaries from Casablanca, and it was going to be a big day. Bobby says, 'We're going to leave them alone. We'll set them up, and show them where the play and stop button is, and we'll just let them go in there and talk, because they're doing their own business.' Bill Aucoin said, 'If we can keep this private, I'd really like it, because I want to schmooze Neil Bogart.'

"So they had this big meeting with the agency and the record company, and we started the tape, and the guys in the band, Gene and Paul were there, and they were, you know, really selling their stuff for the brass—doing a mock vocal, and Paul does a guitar overdub with his Gibson Firebird. It was this beautiful 1957, uniquely shaped model [the one Stanley is seen playing on the cover of *Alive!*]. But what I didn't know was that when they were done Paul had taken his headphones and put it through the guitar strap. Usually, you put the cord through the strap and into the guitar input jack, and now the guitar cord is out of your way, but more times than not, the headphone cord gets wrapped in there as well. I had warned Gene, Paul, and Ace about leaving the headphone cord tangled in there a few times during the sessions. You forget it's all tied together and you go to move and . . . well, we almost had one or two guitars hit the floor.

"So what happened was, after the mock recording, they were listening to the songs, and Bobby, Jay, and me went into the studio. And I went down and I picked up the headphones—pulling them, which, of course, are connected to the guitar that was teetering on the Anvil case. And the guitar starts to go and Bobby yells, 'Corky! Corky! The guitar!' And I just jumped in the air. My feet and my hands were on the same level in the air, and I jumped toward the guitar and the thing fell—BOOM! I heard *twaaang*, and I went, 'Oh, no,' just laying there with my face in the rug. Ezrin came over and says, 'You okay? You okay?' I said, 'Yeah, *I'm* okay, but it's broken.' And he goes, 'You broke your bone? Should we call a doctor?' I said, 'No. I know that sound.' He goes, 'What sound?' And Jay came over and gives me one of those, 'Hmmmm . . . hmmmm.'

"We all turn around and we look and nobody saw. They're all in the control room—we're looking through the glass, and they're in there with their eyes looking up at the speakers, and they're all bouncing and you can read Paul's lips: he's going, 'Yeah, now listen to this part! Oh, here comes the guitar break right here!' And everybody's rocking and grooving. Then Bob breaks the silence and says, 'You know, you gotta tell Paul.' Oh, God. It's a '57 Gibson! I mean, that was his signature guitar that he played. Jay and Bob could not contain themselves from laughing, the bastards.

"So I walk over to the door and I wait till the song fades out. I hear can hear the whole room clapping and, 'Oh, yeah! That's great! That's great!' And I open up the door and I go, 'Paul, can you come here for a second?' And he's all smiles and he goes, 'Later, later!' And I said, 'No, I gotta talk to you now.' The next song starts and he goes, 'What's so important, Cork?' And Jay and Bob are on the studio floor standing over the guitar like a dead body. They're kind of looking at it, blocking Paul's view as I'm walking over with him, and I say, 'Well, you know, we had a little accident here, and you know, what happened was, your guitar fell over.' So he says, 'Well, just pick it up . . . and . . . oh my God.'

"His face just dropped. And I immediately started apologizing and amazingly, he said, 'No, no. Don't worry about it, Corky. It's my fault. I should've put it in the case. You warned me.' He was being incredibly nice about the whole thing. 'Don't worry,' he said. 'Gibson's one of our sponsors. I'll just send it to Gibson and they'll fix it back up.' I said, 'You think they can do that?' And he assured me that they could fix anything.

"He runs back into the control room and I just breathe a sigh of relief, because at least I've put that off for a while, even though I know Gibson's going to come back to him and tell him it can't be done. It had happened to me once in my room when I was younger with the same guitar and it could not be saved. They tried everything, but they couldn't put Humpty Dumpty back together again. In the end, Gibson just made him another one. So, in essence, *Destroyer* was the last time anyone heard Paul Stanley play that particular guitar."[3]

During these final days of work, Dick Wagner returned for a separate mini-session to record an extended acoustic guitar accompaniment to "Beth." Although he played along with the orchestra on January 13, Ezrin had wanted the song to feature a full acoustic guitar track that may or may not be the one that ended up on the soundtrack for the 1978 television movie *KISS Meets the Phantom of the Park*. This take would remain in the original rough cut of "Beth" until the final mix, when, at the last moment, Ezrin decided only to use its descending coda. "I remember listening to it for the last time, and Bob making the decision to leave only the *glissando* ending," says Stasiak. Ezrin used the opportunity of remixing the record in 2012 to return Wagner's full overdub to the song, which significantly adds a softer texture beneath the track's grandiosity.

Soon the recording of lead vocals for eight of the nine songs would commence—the final, crucial ingredient that would fortify the personalities of the Star Child and the Demon. The months of meticulously crafting material to enhance the brand would be completed with the prominent voices in KISS— those that were, in essence, the spokesmen for The Act.

To heighten the mood and yield the best acoustics to match the density of the backing tracks, Messina and Stasiak set a vocal mic in the center of Studio A and dimmed the lights. "We set them up either on the wood or put the mic on the wood and had the singer stand on the area where the wood meets the rug and surrounded him with three large Gobos [portable sound baffles], which we'd wheel in and place one in the back and two on the sides," recalls Stasiak. "The advantage to that setup is you get the live-ness of the room bouncing off the floor when someone is shouting or singing coupled with the deadness behind them, so they can hear themselves, and it's more comfortable for some people to just sing in a lively environment. The Gobos were for sound, but also it's a more intimate setting than standing in the middle of a large studio. It's a psychological thing as well as a technical thing."[4]

Messina: "We'd put two speakers out there and put the mic in such a place that it was at the apex of where the sound of the speakers would converge and we would put the speakers out of phase, so the resulting leakage that you would get from the track in that mic would kind of cancel out and you would just get the clean vocal. It could have been a number of mics—a shotgun or a Sennheiser 405 or a 57 or 58. Some of the vocals we probably used headphones."[5]

As Stanley stepped up to the mic, Simmons joined the team in the control room to offer critique and encouragement, and vice versa. "Gene would produce Paul and Paul would produce Gene, and by 'produce' I mean they would ask each other for feedback, or if one heard something they liked or disliked they felt at ease expressing it," says Stasiak. "They had worked together closely for so long and knew each other's strengths and weaknesses and you could tell right away that they respected each other greatly. It was really a democratic society between those two guys. There was always a lot of back and forth between Gene and Paul. Of course, Ezrin, who was the high command, would have a say as well. In fact, his was the first and final say. They would work off of his direction and they saw the end result.

"They both liked to have the lights down low, but nothing special like burning incense or anything like that. It was wonderful to work with Gene because he would get into character: you could see him begin to turn into the character he created. Paul was a singer, so he would just sing the way you'd expect a rock singer to attack it. But Gene had that monster thing about him, and it was wonderful to see him get into that wheelhouse. Being in that room, I am a witness to the fact that that was Ezrin pulling that out of Gene and also Paul, guiding them in that cinematic view that Bobby was about. It's the first time I'd ever seen that kind of thing and the record shows it."[6]

Stanley and Simmons fully comprehended what was at stake. All that *Wild One* stuff and character identity and underlying pathos would have to come from these performances. The vocals on *Destroyer* were paramount, and both men delivered spectacularly. Stanley reached new ranges of emotion on "Detroit Rock City" and "King of the Night Time World," while maintaining his signature soulful pastiche. His balance between KISS bravado and sensitive longing on "Do You Love Me?" fulfilled Ezrin's image of an impenitent sex symbol kneeling before a throng of rabid girls in exposed splendor. Simmons unleashed his inner demon for the first time on "God of Thunder," an iconic translation of his stage persona. But it was his pass at "Great Expectations," a number closer to his songwriting heart—not quiet balladeer but crooner—that really stretched his talents and built on *Destroyer*'s musical depth. The two men worked diligently on the freshly recorded "Shout It Out Loud," trading lead lines and reveling in the Motown-esque call and response.

It began to dawn on Simmons and Stanley that for the past three years, an entire album's worth of vocal recording for *KISS*, *Hotter Than Hell*, and *Dressed to Kill* had been completed in the same time it took Bob Ezrin to accept a single, final performance. And it was during these waning days of the *Destroyer* sessions that the two men—who had begun their studio careers singing backups at Electric Lady for rent money and later recorded a sophistic one-off Wicked Lester project, which Epic Records shelved, and recently scrambled to re-record live tracks in a fury to satisfy a record contract—were receiving the attention to detail they always believed they deserved. And if their brethren, Criss and Frehley, found it mostly insipid and laborious, they reveled in the grind.

During this intense but rewarding end to months of sometimes tedious, other times exhilarating, but always challenging studio work, both vocalists found another technical oddity to chuckle about. "I had this cool little thing I would do for microphones that I picked up from somewhere that replaced the old-fashioned cushiony wind screens you'd put on mics to cut down on the plosives and protect them from spit," Corky Stasiak recounts. "Bob got a kick out of it. Gene and Paul got a kick out of it, because when you sang a word that had pressure it would flap, taking the brunt of the pops. It was the flapping that got Gene every time. He couldn't help himself from making X-rated connotations every time it would flip and flip back. But once the singer got over the oddness of it, it was probably the best pop filter anyone used at the time. It was a real utilitarian tool."[7]

Popping *p*'s, or "plosives," are the bane of the vocal mic engineer, whether it's a singer, a radio jock, or a voiceover pro at the mic. Wind screens were a staple of vocal recording since its inception, but were anything but failsafe. "All you want to do is stop the 'pops' you get from pronouncing a *p*," explains

Stasiak. "It crushes the mic's diaphragm and you hear this crushed sound, and if you're in the middle of a good take, it's devastating."

The plucky assistant engineer for *Destroyer* lent his own take on a standard device by removing the original foam wind screen from a Shure SM57 and taking a razor blade to cut a seam down the middle, opening it up as a butterfly. He then took two coffee stirrers and attached them, one on each side, to what was called at the time a "cage," which was suspended on a lockable cat's cradle, allowing the mic to float, so if a singer was tapping his foot or bouncing around it wouldn't budge, and put it about the distance of a Hawaiian shaka—a fist with an extended thumb and pinky finger—from the mic. This kept the singer at a safe distance but close enough to the mic to give it his all while still eliminating most, if not all, of the pops.

Stasiak: "Jay and I liked to use the Neumann U87 or U47 mic for vocals, switching between them depending on the guy or the girl's voice. You see, when you put the cover that came with the Neumann's over the mic it cut out much of the liveliness we were going for, you're kind of padding it down, dulling the sound. On occasion, I'd do a session and the producer would request it. It sounded so natural. Nowadays they have a round circular piece that they put a ladies' nylon on or a black mesh material to stop the pops, but that was much later after *Destroyer*. Jay showed me a trick once how to get around one that couldn't be handled during recording in the mix. We didn't want to lose a great take, so sometimes he would set it up, and during the mix, I would have cues, he would have cues and Bob would have cues—of course this was before computerized boards, back then everything was manual—so he would take a Pultec midrange equalizer and take the bottom and we'd make grease pencil marks on it, and when the offending *p* came I would quickly shut it on and shut it off, neutralizing the *p* if that pop came in a real good take in a part we had a problem with the singer to sing."[8]

There were no problems when the professional background duo of Tasha Thomas and Carl Hall were called in to provide soulful vocals for the refrain in "Sweet Pain." A Record Plant staple, the African American vocalists had just completed sessions for KISS heroes Slade during the past summer (produced by Chas Chandler, former bassist for the Animals and manager of Jimi Hendrix, also engineered by Corky Stasiak), to add to an already impressive list of recordings for Carly Simon, the Edgar Winter Group, B.B. King, Cat Stevens, and Bonnie Raitt.

The twenty-five-year-old Thomas, a singer/songwriter and vocalist, was enjoying a yearlong run on Broadway as Aunt Em in the original production of *The Wiz*, a funky urban musical based on *The Wizard of Oz*. A well-traveled musician, actor, and arranger, Hall had worked through the 1960s and early '70s with, among others, Quincy Jones and Jerry Ragovoy, always taking time to team up with Thomas to adorn a wide swatch of musical genres—probably the most bizarre of which took place in late January of 1976, for *Destroyer*.

Wrapping up the vocals late on January 23, KISS had finally completed the recording of its fifth album—the groundwork for what was shaping up as a make or break proposition for The Act. With some aplomb and reverence for the moment, Bob Ezrin bid adieu to the two men with whom he had become so close that he would enthusiastically call them "cousins" nearly forty years later. It was now time to get down to mixing the nine tracks that would change the course of KISStory.

According to Corky Stasiak's fastidious studio journal, the mixing of *Destroyer* took seven days, from January 27 to February 3, with Sunday, February 1, a scheduled off day.

The art of mixing the many tracks of a recording is the last and perhaps most crucial creative aspect of making an album, and in early 1976, even in a modern facility like the Record Plant, there was no escaping its disciplines: the fastidious millisecond balance of faders, the delicate separation of instruments, sounds, and vocals, and all the scientific minutia that dominates those agonizing minutes of taking a hodgepodge of musical parts and placing them as if a puzzle into song. It is an art Jay Messina had come to embrace on his way to being one of the most trusted mixers at the studio, which was not something Bob Ezrin took lightly.

"Bob usually let me go," Messina confidently recalls. "He might have an idea before the mix started and guide me in a certain direction, but he'd give me a fair amount of lead to possibly hear something that he wasn't thinking about. He liked that I could come up with a lot of different choices, both recording sounds and mixing, so he would let me go and only stop me if he didn't like the way it was sounding or he would ask for another choice or he would maybe come up with a new idea. But Bob had definite ideas about what he wanted the thing to sound like and he knew when he heard something he liked. If he liked something I was trying, he'd agree, and we'd go onto the next phase. We'd usually start with the drums then add the bass and then the guitars; get a good foundation before getting vocals in there."[9]

Messina notes that the main reason Ezrin never belabored a final mix was due to the fact that all of the main elements of a song—including effects like reverb, echo, distortion, and of course the Record Plant's state-of-the-art compression—had already been embedded into each track. And although Ezrin always instructed the engineers to leave a track or two open for the odd tambourine or handclaps, it was more the exception than the rule for *Destroyer*. The weeks of recording meant that it was all there on tape—something producer Jimmy Ienner and KISS staple Sean Delaney discovered a couple of years later, when they were tabbed by Casablanca to comb through the archives to put together the *Double Platinum* compilation. Despite the best efforts of studio magicians to try to match the disparate sounds from all the KISS tracks before and after *Destroyer*, there was no meddling with anything recorded in January of 1976. It was literally a permanent imprint.

"We were working with analog tape, so it's not like with Pro Tools today, where you can leave a lot of decisions until mix time," explains Messina. "With analog tape, you pretty much had to decide on what sounded good, and what I liked about working with Bob is he made a conscious effort to make it sound good every step of the way. And that's my philosophy of recording: not wishing or hoping for a sound once it's mixed and mastered. So when you're concentrating on mixing the record you're not also deciphering a bunch of different choices, you're just having fun painting a picture with all of the colors that you've amassed. The mix should be—and was, with Bob on *Destroyer*—the art of giving the already great-sounding tracks another dimension."[10]

Ezrin: "We had recorded it on sixteen-track, so I committed sounds to tape—effects, reverbs, delays, and all that stuff was already on the multitrack—combining them into single tracks or, at most, stereo pairs, including stereo pre-mixes of the drums, which meant little control over the relative balance of the snare to the tom-toms. All the guitars were mixed into one stereo pair, or sometimes two if there were acoustics on the tracks as well. Solos were separate, as were lead vocals. So mixing was really a matter of blending the sounds together in the most powerful way possible and making sure the balances were correct. When I remixed the record in 2012, I was surprised and gratified to push the faders up and hear the whole record. It was really quite something. You know, in this day of infinite possibilities and no one making commitments, it was really cool to see how clear in our vision and how committed we were. We made the record we wanted to make."[11]

Destroyer underlines the uniqueness of the Ezrin sound and imbues the record with a singular sonic template never duplicated by KISS. It is also fair to conclude that Ezrin himself never achieved this level of heavy, rich, raunchy power for the remainder of his stellar career, which still rolls on as this is written. Much of the accolades must go to Jay Messina and Corky Stasiak, who would work separately with both Ezrin and KISS after the January sessions, but oddly would never again share a studio. This lends gravitas and legend to the sound and fury of *Destroyer*, which is demonstrably evident on every note and syllable.

"Bob was Phil Spector on steroids," Stasiak concludes. "When you hear a Phil Spector record, you know it's Phil Spector. When you hear a Bob Ezrin record, he's got his fingerprints all over it. Some producers just want to be invisible. They want the group to shine through. But Bob puts his mark on a record, like Phil Spector. Listen to the end results. Those things are works of art. They could be hung in the Louvre."[12]

Much to Ezrin's surprise, this particular work of art fell a bit short, time-wise. In fact, it was way short. The nine musical tracks on *Destroyer* clock in at thirty-one minutes and change, barely meriting long-player status. With time running out on a hard deadline for spring release and the band already back on the road, the young producer quickly reasoned that the set list needed a prologue and epilogue to enhance the unfolding drama. Gathering his engineers together, a plan was hatched to execute a thematic touch to *Destroyer*—something to tie it all up while giving it a circular element that would wrap around the cinematic macrocosm. "It was necessary to round off the experience if you were listening to the album from top to bottom and that you really needed something to close the book," Ezrin told *KISS Online* in 2012.[13]

Messina and Stasiak readily provided solutions to bookend the theatrical arc with dramatic flair. "The ending sequence was my idea," Messina remembers. "It's not an original one. I had heard somebody do it once before."[14]

Messina recommended overlapping disparate tape loops of music (the choir from "Great Expectations") and sound (Paul Stanley's stage rap from *Alive!)* to provide a mysteriously cacophonous coda that might also be considered a non-linear introduction to "Detroit Rock City," if the record were ever to be played circuitously. To the lead engineer's amazement, Ezrin nodded approval, which set him off on reimagining a soundscape he had always wanted to try after being initially captivated by an eclectic musical piece by minimalist composer Steve Reich titled *It's Gonna Rain.*

Hailing from San Francisco by way of New York City, the improvisatory composer and Julliard alum Steve Reich created his groundbreaking dissident masterwork from multiple tape loops after being inspired by fellow minimalist pianist Terry Riley's *In C,* which author Will Hermes describes in *Love Goes to Buildings on Fire,* his comprehensive history of New York's '70s musical origins, as "a series of fifty-three melodic modules, each to be repeated by each group member as often as he or she liked, until moving on to the next, each at his or her own pace."[15] The 1965 experimental piece utilized the voice of Pentecostal preacher Brother Walter's sermon on Noah and the flood with intermittent sounds of a pigeon taking flight.

Messina: "It was a recording of a guy preaching, and he's outside, so you hear a lot of ambient sounds. Meanwhile, the preacher is talking, and he finally says, 'Unless we do this ... whatever,' he finishes with 'It's gonna rain, It's gonna rain, It's gonna rain!' And the recording loops there. The engineer did it with magstripes, and what he did is he let it loop on the first track. Then on the second track he looped the last phrase again, but just a little bit later. And then he did it on the third track, then on a fourth track and fifth track. Each time the voice comes in just a little bit later as you keep staggering it. When you get finished with 'It's gonna rain,' before you get [to] the end of 'rain,' the 'it's' is starting."[16]

Messina had already experimented with this process once before, when he directed a friend into a hall with a lot of ambiance and had him repeat, "Unless you change today, your future will be the same as your past," which the engineer then looped over twenty-four tracks. He discovered that by the time the phrase reached track eight or nine, the words began to naturally overlap. He continued to add the phrase again and again to create the desired effect.

"I reversed what we ended up doing with Paul's phrase for *Destroyer*," explains Messina. "When I had done mine I would add just a little delay to each track, and that added to the ambient sound. But what Bob wanted to do was to have it all on there first and then take one track away each time it went around. It winds up where you can actually hear what Paul's saying: 'We're gonna have ourselves a rock-and-roll party!' The ambiance of the background with him is what makes for that crazy effect."[17]

Later in the year, David Bowie, who reveled in Reich's work building percussive instruments in the same fashion, would create an instrumental homage to this minimalist approach in the form of "Weeping Wall," which rounds out his experimental *Low* album, recorded in France with eclectic sound master Brian Eno. Bowie had already paid tribute to Reich's art with "Chant of the Ever-Circling Skeletal Family," an unreleased track from his *Diamond Dogs* sessions in 1973, the same year Robert Fripp employed Reich's method for King Crimson's "Larks Tongue in Aspic (Part I)."

"It was a pastiche," Gene Simmons explained, in a 2001 interview with radio and television personality Eddie Trunk. "There is a German guy, who the Beatles listened to called [Karlheinz] Stockhausen, who was about creating symphonic noise, not necessarily based on music, but sounds put together. It's like when you'd go between radio stations—before digital radio and so on— you'd hear ten different radio stations talking at the same time."[18]

Although the track is unnamed and uncredited on the original album and all its subsequent reissues (cassette, eight-track, and later CD), including Ezrin's 2012 remaster, *Resurrected*, it has since become known to KISS fanatics and collectors as "Rock and Roll Demons." It would be unfair to leave out the exhaustive efforts of Julian Gill, who in his *KISS Album Focus* (originally part of the vast KISS FAQ web site but subsequently published in several print volumes) pointedly refers to the track as "Rock and Roll Party," a title also repeated among the most strident of underground KISS faithful.

"I honestly thought it was named 'Rock and Roll Demon' on the original album," its creator admits today.[19] This was apparently what the *Destroyer* team had titled it ("Demon," not "Demons"). When told the track was not listed on the album jacket, Messina was surprised and even argued that I might have a reissue, but that was not the case. Even if it were, there is still no version that lists the final singsong shouts of Paul Stanley over a cheering crowd from *Alive!* clearly backed by the Brooklyn Boys Choir singing, "You've got great expectations" from Simmons's folk song gone Beethoven. The swirling flange, Messina assures listeners, is the intriguing byproduct of Reich's original idea of creating one alien sound from a series of contrasting ones.

"That was Jay's baby," Corky Stasiak confirms. "We just filled up all the tracks with this stuff and kept doing it and doing and doing it. We looped it, as I remember it. But that was Jay and Bob's idea."[20]

Stasiak's idea was to casually show Bob Ezrin a copy of *dB Magazine* he had been reading during breaks in the marathon *Destroyer* sessions, specifically an article about modern binaural recording techniques and a brand new device that perfected its application. In layman's terms, a tech geek's wet dream.

"It was a recording apparatus worn like a stethoscope called binaural recording," he explains. "In the ears were microphones that were originally used down South in gospel shows. The technician would sit with a two-track tape machine and record these beautiful gospel singers in a church. It was easier than miking things up, but it was also better since there is a beautiful chamber in your ear to record in—you get the whole aural sound from the architecture of the church."[21]

Binaural recording techniques date back to late-nineteenth-century Paris and an opera house called the Palais Garnier, where carbon telephone microphones were installed along the front of the stage and broadcast to offsite subscribers in what was very much the origin of closed-circuit distribution. In 1920s America, exclusive listeners able to afford two radios would plug the two receivers into the left and right channels of their headphones, prefiguring the advent of stereo. Mainly, though, binaural techniques were featured in rare ambient or environmental recordings of nature or city sounds. It wasn't until the aural revolution of the 1970s, and the audiophile's preference for headphones, that a new and lasting generation of binaural interest bloomed. Hence the *dB Magazine* piece that had so captured the young assistant engineer.

Stasiak eagerly shared the article with Ezrin, whom he says was so "instantly fascinated with it"[22] that he wasted no time placing a call into the manufacturer. "The next thing I know, I had a box delivered from Sony at the studio, and when I opened it up there was a sculpture of a blank head with ear canals on both sides with the stethoscope microphones in them. And Bob walks in and says, 'Great, you got it! Let's try it out!'"[23]

Ezrin figured the binaural application would work beautifully on the front of his bookends concept of wrapping *Destroyer* in a cinematic milieu. Since "Detroit Rock City" had already been tapped for the album's opener, they would use the headset to prologue the youth's doomed joy ride, putting the listener into the automobile and thus into the fantasy realm of *Destroyer*. Building on that theme, Ezrin imagined a normal suburban kitchen scene: a table-top radio playing news of the accident, foreshadowing events, playing with time and space, much like Messina's "Rock and Roll Demon" concept of phrases intertwined to create a landscape of chaos.

"I think that the thought and the application were all part of the same thing," adds Ezrin, who would perform most of the sounds heard inside the car. "I was basically trying to do a thematic intro and had in mind a little play that would go before 'Detroit Rock City,' which I thought was a great way to start. And when I started thinking about that, I realized that the binaural mic would be perfect for the recording. It would be unbelievable for people listening on their headphones. They'd feel like they were right in the car."[24]

It's important that the sounds fade up. The listener is invited to eavesdrop. A radio is already playing as the news drones along with the morning chores (dishes being washed). It is pure *cinema verité*. Before a single note of *Destroyer* is played, there can be no doubt that this is not just any rock record, and certainly not just another KISS album. This will be a journey—with arcs and characters, villains and heroes. But this particular part of the journey has already played out. There has been a fatal car accident.

Suddenly there is surround sound, as in a film. It engulfs you. A car door slams shut, the gas pedal is pumped, a fumbling of the gearshift as the engine roars to life. This is a capsule, and in the capsule is a time shift. Through the speakers in the dashboard, KISS is onstage, ripping it up. The chorus of "Rock and Roll All Nite" from an album, and a band, that is still tearing through America. And we are about to chase them down.

"Bobby said, 'I don't want this to just be a song, I want to tell the story,'" remembers Stasiak. "He told me, 'My approach to making records is really making movies.' He writes and arranges first and foremost for the visual."[25]

Ezrin: "That came from growing up in the basement of my grandparents' house where my uncle lived. He was a bachelor until his middle/late fifties and lived with his parents the whole time, so that he could stay with his hi-fi collection in the basement of their house. He had the largest privately owned collection of jazz records in Canada and a sound system that was state of the art. It had various types of turntiles, depending upon what you were playing and different kinds of amps and all sorts of speakers. I was just a little kid and would go over there and stay overnight and go down to the basement with my uncle and listen to records. He was the first guy to have stereo in Canada.

"The first stereo record that I ever heard was in his basement in 1958 or '59: *Spike Jones and the Band That Plays for Fun* in '*spooktacular screaming sound.*' Basically it was a Spike Jones takeoff on a horror motif. It was an album of well-known songs that had been turned into horror songs sung by Boris Karloff and Peter Laurie, and of course they were imitating these people, but it was a really funny, great record with lots of effects and lots of sounds moving from left to right. It had a lot of theatrics to it. I think that imprinted on me. I was ten years old at the time, or not even, and I remember just listening to that in wonder. And putting on all these LPs and listening to them one at a time and really falling in love with the material. All of that informed the approach I took later on."[26]

"I don't know if you've ever listened to that beginning piece through headphones," says Stasiak. "It is eerie as all shit, because it sounds as if it is happening inside your head. You'll hear someone humming as if you're humming. It's Bobby humming."[27]

"At first, Bob asked Corky to go outside with a sign reading 'Honk Your Horn,'" recalls Messina. "He just went right out on Seventh Avenue to get sounds. We didn't use the sound effects library. We created all those sounds—the door opening, turning the radio on manually—all of it."[28]

Stasiak: "I parked my car right outside 321 [on] Forty-Fourth, down the street from Ninth Avenue, where the famous comedy club the Improv sat on the corner. There were a lot of people coming and going and I was worried we might not get a good sound, but I had these windows that opened to the side so we could feed the cables through it. It was my Toyota SR-5 stick shift and we ran wires from Studio B, which was right by the front door, all the way outside and into the street and into the car. The Record Plant was closer to Ninth Avenue than Eighth, so it wasn't that far. I remember it was in the middle of a cold winter night and there was ice and snow on the ground. I had a cassette copy of *Alive!* that KISS had just released and it was cued up and the car's in neutral and Bob's revving the engine, as you hear on the record."[29]

Ezrin: "Because I was on a mic and tethered to the studio, the car couldn't go anywhere, so I did all of the revving of the engine in neutral. The other interesting thing was that the Record Plant had a transmitter. It was a small illegal transmitter, the purpose of which was for people to pull their car up near the studio and to go out into their car to be able to do a mix. We actually pumped 'Rock and Roll All Nite' out through the transmitter, so what you hear is really the radio in the car playing 'Rock and Roll All Nite.'"[30]

"A day or so later, we did the other segment," recalls Stasiak. "Bob wrote some news-radio copy and read it. Jay recorded it in mono and took that mono player and put it through a filter so it sounded like it was on the radio, and we actually *sent* it through a radio. Occasionally, we did some jingles at the Record Plant, and if a client wanted to hear what it would actually sound like Roy Cicala had this radio set up that you could patch in whatever you had on the tape machine through the radio."[31]

For the sounds of the dishes being washed, there is general agreement on how and where it was recorded, but some discrepancy among the principals as to who actually was doing the dishwashing. "That was me," Bob Ezrin insisted to author Jeff Suhs in 2004. "All of the stuff done in the kitchen was actually in the first floor bathroom on the ground floor just outside of the reception area."[32]

In an interview for this book in 2012, however, Corky Stasiak was pretty specific. "So we set that up in one of the bathrooms and fed the sound through. We also got some dishes, filled up the sink with water, and we had the girlfriend of a guy named Andy Abrahams actually wash them. Her name was Ann, and she also worked at the studio. Ann put the binaural microphone in her ears and washed the dishes. So you can hear the dishes splashing around the water and the radio announcement in the far corner. That's the beauty of the binaural recording. It sounds like you are actually there, because it's being recorded from inside somebody's ear canal."[33]

Jay Messina too is sure that it was a woman who provided the dishwashing, and possibly the girlfriend of someone on the Record Plant staff. "If the guys say someone else did the dishes in 'Detroit Rock City,' then they're probably right," Ezrin told me in an email, after giving it further thought. "Though I have a vivid memory of standing at that sink and listening to my voice come over that little speaker, I'm probably wrong about it."

Although the mystery continues, all three men agree that the work was done in the final days after all the music for *Destroyer* had been mixed and in the can. "It was a moment of inspiration," says Ezrin. "The band wasn't there. We sort of constructed this thing and they came in and heard it at the mix."[34]

The final segments were then spliced together to form the vignette that famously ushers in the KISS novella. "The car crash at the end of 'Detroit Rock

City' was from a sound-effects record," recalls Stasiak. "We had a library of sound effects records, many of them produced in the '60s and the early '70s, and some of the other sound effects we used for *Destroyer* were taken from records. Not sure what the copyright was on those, like who could tell whose crash that was?"[35]

"A lot of the theatrics, if you will, was Bob's vision," concludes Messina. "He wanted more of a visual production, so having those sound effects in there just gives it another dimension. And that was done after the final mix of the song, not only to have control about when to put a particular sound effect in for dramatic purposes, but also the volume of it, how it plays inside the track, and of course you may mix the song with sound effects and the label doesn't want them there or suggest they be used a little differently. So instead of having to go back and mix the whole song again, we just return to the original two-track mix and adjust the sound effects over it."[36]

This proved problematic to Ezrin in 2012, when he was working from a digital copy of the original master tapes on *Destroyer Resurrected*, as he discovered that the dramatic opening and closing were not present. "Back then, we would 'cross fade' sections that included sound effects or where one song blended into another. To do that, we would have two separate stereo tapes—one for the mix and one for the sound effects—which were lined up and played back together and recorded onto a third tape, which was then edited into the stereo master of the album. Bottom line—they were gone."[37]

Back in 1976, Messina spliced the opening prologue and his chaotic tape loop to the beginning and end of the album, and *Destroyer* was complete. Nearly six months of writing, rehearsing, boot camp, recording, litigious interruptions, orchestral sessions, and finishing touches came to a close in a silent control booth on Forty-Fourth and Eighth in Hell's Kitchen. Ezrin exhaled and looked at Messina and Stasiak. There was nothing left to say or plan or cajole or create. Thus, on February 5, 1976, one very eventful month to the day since principal recording began, *Destroyer* was finished.

"Beth"

What can I do?

The piano opens tenderly, its notes guiding a solemn melody along a breath of supple violins. *What is this?* A forlorn, plaintive prelude that immediately touches the ear, as familiar as if crafted by Burt Bacharach, so languid and refined, broken only for the moment when a raspy new voice enters the scene.

Beth I hear you callin'
But I can't come home right now
Me and the boys are playin'
But we just can't find the sound

It is a requiem to pain: unrequited anguish of separation tinged with regret, draped mournfully across a bed of cellos. How did this humble beseeching sneak into this hardcore passion play? Only moments ago, there was a joyous call to the collective bellow—a charging brigade to live every moment without measure. We are barely able to exhale from its soaring crescendo, and suddenly this lonely ballad has drained the air. We are plummeting ...

Just a few more hours
And I'll be right home to you
I think I hear them callin'
Oh Beth, what can I do?

The preceding furor, which fueled the imagination through dreamscapes and netherworlds, relentless rebellious anthems to infinite youth, power, sex, and the demand for rock-and-roll justice, has left a trail of victims. There is the wild young motorist, a teen lost in fantasy, a virgin soul swallowed by growling demons, set alongside the lofty expectations of flag-waving solidarity, sexual freedom, and an invitation to serenade the hedonistic heavens. They have all borne a sacrificial font. There is always someone left standing beyond the dreamscapes and netherworlds, someone grounded and wondering if we will ever return home. But didn't we also leave that home undaunted, refusing to return unless victorious, or to die trying? We could not look back. Never. Yet the pull of immortality, stardom, and the draining of life's marrow has rendered those unable to cross over little recourse but to call out into the ether . . .

Beth what can I do?

The piano refrain is joined, *en masse*, by a full orchestra, led by searing cello and violin counter-melodies to this lone, desperate, pitiable voice pining, calling out, reaching out, but like Adam's outstretched hand to God under the dome of the Sistine Chapel, it will never quite get there.

You say you feel so empty
And a house just ain't a home
I'm always somewhere else
And you're always there alone

The pain has given way to empathy—a sense that the loss, the feeling of isolation, travels farthest. It follows the wandering troubadour to the ends of the earth, even when drowned out by youthful revelry. Love has made a place here—the cold studio, the stifling backstage, the cell of the dreary hotel room—if not on the surface, where the gruff exterior must meet the grinding challenges of men on the high wire of fortune, then it will settle in the dead of night. Love, even one separated not only by actual miles but by metaphysical eons, makes its home. For once again the voice, ravaged by these notions of distance, tells his love he must again break their bond to make *the sound*. Its call, the lights, the stage, the boys: *What can I do? Beth, what can I do?*

The opening chords play on, fully conjoined within the walls of heart-wrenching strings, give way to the choral response—a musical interlude reminding us of estranged lovers yearning for one last embrace to prove their survival. But the music does not offer much hope, even as the orchestral flourish resolves powerfully with a phalanx of triumphant horns. There is a sense that nothing can be done tonight, but that it shall never render the spiritual bond asunder.

A slight retard, the piano begins again, those moaning strings beside it.

"BETH"

> *Beth I know you're lonely*
> *And I hope you'll be all right*
> *'Cause me and the boys'll be playin'...*

Piano and the voice are now one, and the voice lets out two final notes, clinging hard to the harsh reality that love, in all its power, glory, and spiritual oneness, will have to wait.

> *... all night.*

One last piano coda is led to the altar of this tragic, unresolved emptiness by a willing orchestra that now, along with our resigned road warrior, has accepted its fate. The singer exhales a wistful *ah-haaaaaaa*, as if the evening's last breath is saved for her, for Beth.

20

Aftermath

Going into '76, we had no doubt we were going to be huge. The great rollercoaster ride we'd prayed for was about to start, and we knew we'd better hold on tight or we'd be thrown to certain death. Our attitude was that nobody was going to stand in our path, and we weren't going to take no for an answer.
—Paul Stanley[1]

With a new album in the can and the renewed sense of vigor that comes with the amped-up pressure of becoming the hot new band, KISS immediately did what it always did best: put the pedal down on The Act and hit the road.

The first KISS shows after the *Destroyer* sessions commenced when the band arrived in Detroit by way of a three-hour rehearsal back at "boot camp" headquarters, Carroll's Music in Manhattan, and a show in Eerie, Pennsylvania. The immediate influence of The Act's commitment to the new *Destroyer* gospel was felt in Bill Aucoin's video opening, which he put together for the express purpose of heralding the band onstage just prior to the tour. The shows would be accompanied the first ever KISS tour book, *In Concert 1976*, one of three initial pieces of merchandise sold by the newly acquired Boutwell Enterprises, which was brought on board during the *Destroyer* sessions in January to handle merchandising and the vastly expanding KISS Army.

Destroyer would be the first KISS album to promote what is now the legendary KISS Army, the rallying cry of a fanatic base of cult-crazed believers in the power and promise of The Act, whose official shield was boldly displayed on the record's inner sleeve opposite the lyrics to "Detroit Rock City" (ironically a song that depicts the death of a KISS fan speeding to a concert in the ultimate sacrifice for the cause). The exploitation of the KISS Army was fairly new, but the concept was, like KISS itself, a wholly grassroots, spitfire, blood, sweat, and tears operation.

Begun as a vocal petition by two Indiana teenagers in January 1975 to force local radio station WVTS to play KISS records—initially met with bemused neglect by program director Rich Dickerson—the very idea of the KISS Army was imbued with the forces of The Act. Bill Starkey and Jay Evans, who hailed from Terre Haute, a small river town in the southwest corner of the state located about seventy-five miles outside of Indianapolis, decided to stop *begging* and begin *demanding* their favorite band be added to the playlist. They identified themselves with each badgering phone call as members of the KISS Army. This was followed by officially worded letters signed "Bill Starkey—President of the KISS Army," and "Jay Evans—Field Marshall." Seven long months later, the relentless efforts of Starkey and Evans would pay off as KISS was regularly featured on the station. Jockeys playfully introduced the cuts as appearing "courtesy of the KISS Army," and soon fans started calling the station to request where they could sign up.

Dickerson, hardly unaware of the publicity this kind of obsessive behavior could garnish a small rock station, enlisted the help of Starkey and Evans to promote an upcoming KISS show at the Hulman Civic University Center in Terre Haute. With the band plowing through the *Alive!* tour, the KISS camp unleashed publicity man Alan Miller on the scene to co-ordinate a recruitment effort on the air. The show was a sellout (the only other one at that venue was Elvis Presley's on October 5, 1974) and Starkey was given the honor of receiving an official plaque from the band onstage.

Once the KISS Army was funneled through the KISS machine back on Madison Avenue, there would be an official, military-style shield logo, designed by Howard Marks Agency art director/creative director Dennis Woloch, who once again called on his friend and compatriot Vinnie DeGerlando to assist. "Bill came in, as usual, and said he wanted me to work off an army logo that someone, maybe Bill Starkey, might have put together earlier," remembers DeGerlando. "He wanted to establish it more as a design concept—more, I think, attractive. He said, 'Instead of a fan club, I want it more like an army thing or related to that.' So, being that I was in the National Guard at the time—you know, chevrons and different emblems and patches that they had—I thought that would be perfect to use all the graphics and the stripes. So, I just put that together and that was the main thing that came about."[2]

"I remember doing the mechanical—the design—with my own two hands, the whole thing," says Woloch. "That lettering that says 'Army,' I remember doing that with my T-square and triangle and my Rapidograph pen, doing the best I could. I would've really liked to have farmed that out to get somebody to do it better, somebody like Michael Doret, who wound up doing *Rock and Roll Over* for us, because he's great at lettering. But, you know, you don't always have money to be throwing around, so they said, 'Why don't you do it?' So I did."[3]

"Bill sent it to the guys and they all loved it," concludes DeGerlando. "So things took off like that, and nobody really paid a lot of attention to the idea that this might be something that was going to be an iconic thing. At the time you're just solving a design problem and then later on you realize how it picks up momentum. These things just grow out of it, like the album cover. Dennis got this idea that they like comics and he puts it together, and then before you know it, it works, and then it achieves its own fame."[4]

In a combined effort to pool all the promotional resources for *Destroyer*—including effectively utilizing the Ken Kelly painting on all posters, billboards, merchandising, and overall presentation of the massive rollout—the KISS Army became the band's official fan club, which at its peak Boutwell estimated was earning five grand a day from its 100,000 members.

Soon the KISS Army would be treated to the living embodiment of Kelly's efforts. Before the first post-*Destroyer* week was out, well-known rock photographer Fin Costello—a KISS favorite since his off-the-cuff photographs of the band's inaugural headlining show in New York City and his striking photos for the *Alive!* cover—photographed all four members in their new *Destroyer* costumes officially for the first time. Fashioned as the cover painting was being completed, and debuted at A&R Studios on January 13 during the orchestral sessions for "Great Expectations" and "Beth," these images were mostly kept under wraps until the summer's Spirit of '76 tour kicked off on July 3, one day before the nation's bicentennial.

With a headwind behind them, KISS exhaled and prepared to conquer the world, just as Simmons, Stanley, Criss, and Frehley had designed it three years before in a cramped loft. They had never wavered from their mission statement of fame and fortune by any means necessary, and now it was finally happening. These were high times for KISS, and they merely had to brace for the accolades and riches. Then, almost inexplicably, the bottom fell out.

The relentless critical flagellation of *Destroyer* began immediately, *en masse*.

In the June 1976 edition of *Rolling Stone*, John Milward wrote, "There's no doubt that *Destroyer* is KISS's best album yet or that Bob Ezrin, Alice Cooper's heavy-handed wizard of heavy-metal production who helped write seven of the nine tunes here, has made the difference. Unfortunately, KISS entirely lacks the satiric distance that often made Cooper's use of such conceits genuinely funny, and worse yet, such gimmickry is the best *Destroyer* has to offer. The songs, save for two bloated ballads, are relentless riff rockers rooted in patently pedestrian drumming. Although constructed with professional aplomb, making use of a wide array of heavy-metal conventions, there's nothing new here. Even when an effective melody, such as the rabble-rousing 'Shout It Out Loud' is presented, the lackluster performances dampen the effect. The vocals are undistinguished and emotionally empty; the lyrics—about partying and the rock scene, with plenty of campy S&M allusions—trite. Worse yet, there's not a memorable guitar solo on the album."[5]

Harry Doherty registered his summation of *Destroyer* in the April 17 issue of *Melody Maker*, stating that KISS "cling to the tried and tested formula" of "driving riffs, hysterical vocals and predictable chorus lines" whose "contribution to rock is negligible." He notes that, on the one hand, the band was "continuing to tread a path that will very soon be wearisomely familiar if they don't become a little more adventurous," before almost immediately contradicting this assessment by admitting, "There are two tracks on this album which could change that. 'Great Expectations' and 'Beth' both show intelligent and sensitive use of orchestra and choir."[6]

United Press International checked in with "decidedly uneven album" as "all of KISS's recorded songs are simple, riff-laden, and unburdened with 'meaningful' lyrics," and declared the band's mostly ignored first record to be "still the best."[7]

Max Bell's review in the *New Musical Express* raked the band and the record over the coals, concluding that Ezrin's touch moved an image already "gratuitously gimmick ridden, ham-fisted dose of fall-out entirely bereft of humour or excitement" from "contrivance to downright self-parody." He finished the assault by emphatically deciding, "Musically, it sucks."[8]

A great deal more media outlets than ever before made it a point to weight in, doubtless due to the immediate, and to some stunning, explosion of *Alive!* up the charts, catapulting KISS into the mainstream mere months before the release of *Destroyer*. KISS—battered, bruised, exhausted, and dead broke only four months earlier, dangling precariously between a debt-addled manager and a sinking record company, unable to collect a dime for its recording efforts and spending hundreds of thousands of dollars no one had on a spectacular stage show—were suddenly seen as an overnight sensation. And now here comes *Destroyer*, the blistering new commodity, with its hotshot producer and slick design and rollout. It was a setup for backlash. And backlash it received.

The singular reaction in the KISS camp was, *What the hell happened?*

The stars were all aligned. The band had broken through in the winter with *Alive!* and was poised to set a significantly expanded audience on its ear with its most creative, intricate, and all-consuming effort imaginable. The songs were meticulously structured, rehearsed until fingers bled and patience expired, and were sifted through an exploration of musical calisthenics. The master of theatrical rock had taken the reins and ushered the band through a whirlwind soundscape—and for what? To be lectured on how KISS was dumping its hard rock integrity?

What may have stung the most was the alarm and evisceration that sprung from an underground rock press that had solely touted the band's efforts to shed the joke tag during three years of struggles. *Creem* magazine's Rick Johnson peppered his review with backhanded compliments of the KISS canon, before bemoaning the Ezrin factor: "His influence while not altogether dippy, is still unfortunate, having deprived them of much of their rusty coat-hanger appeal while filling the album with cute Cooper-ish touches like giggle children effects, female back-up singers, and, worst of all: *strings*!" Calling the ballads "ludicrous" and criticizing the use of "random atrocities" he sarcastically whined, "This ain't the skuzzy KISS we all came to love (and hate) so well." He completed his screed by warning that, though sales of the record may boom, it was a "big mistake in the long run."[9]

In *Circus*, Robert Duncan facetiously framed KISS as "spokesmonsters for a generation" while accusing the band of "pretending." He began his cruel dissection with cliché vignettes of a dying New York milieu halted by choirs of youth angels singing "OY WANNA ROCK UN ROLL AWL NOYT UN PWTY EV-VARY DEH!" who are suddenly squashed with the graying loom of *Destroyer*'s arrival. "Somewhere—perhaps in a listening booth at Sam Goody's—the street-corner angels stand glassy-eyed and silent. An ugly world sneers in their faces. Today, they offer no salvation. The new KISS album stinks." Quick to pounce on the producer by blaming Ezrin for neutering Alice Cooper, he was appalled by the presence of a piano. "KISS don't do it no more," he coolly dismissed, using his worst Lester Bangs-style street cred, wrapping up his review up with "It's a sad day."[10]

This dog-piling was followed by first whispers and then shouts from the fan base, the majority of which initially viewed the whole thing as a sellout, from the shiny coat of classical strings to the boys' choir, never mind the pretentious guitar symphonies, weird sound effects, and finally, almost insultingly, for the love of God, a ballad!

Ignoring the national press and the nose-thumbing establishment was business as usual for KISS, but when its core press support group (*Creem*, *Circus*), along with what Gene Simmons considered "our bosses" (the fans), began to bristle, the band reached out to Bill Aucoin to halt proceedings. Calls for *Destroyer* to be shelved—or even, ironically, "destroyed"—began to be heard.

Long before the laborious joy of pushing through to new heights in the studio, surviving a "boot camp," and putting together a proud set of highly charged dutifully arranged songs into a cohesive narrative, the rough-and-ready streetwise KISS paranoia was palpable. Now, in the face of so much unexpected derision, it had apparently come home to roost; cracks, long-since lengthening over the past year, began to spread. Ace Frehley's dissatisfaction with his talents being ignored and eventually replaced on several tracks; Peter Criss's constant battles against being reined in like a common session drummer; Paul Stanley's worries about not staying true to the rock roots he worshipped; Gene Simmons's abject fear of losing the one fulcrum against the entire operation tumbling down: the unwavering faith of the fan base. It all built to a collective rage aimed at one man: Bob Ezrin.

"There was so much bad press from the beginning," recalls Ezrin. "Scathing stuff, like one guy writes he wants to go up to Toronto and punch me in the nose on behalf of KISS fans everywhere. They said I put Ann-Margret horns on everything and that I had destroyed the band and it was all my fault. And I think what really happened was all those fifteen-year-old pimply boys who were part of that crowd that I had seen in Michigan that made me want to work with KISS in the first place were up in arms, and much of the reaction came from that. There was a resistance to having the band go from these two-dimensional cartoon characters to the three dimensions we were striving for. And once this negativity seeped into the band's entourage and eventually up to Bill, they simply lost confidence in the record and specifically me."[11]

"The first thing we did was contact Jack Douglas, who had produced Aerosmith's three most recent albums, *Get Your Wings*, *Toys in the Attic*, and *Rocks*," writes Paul Stanley, in *Face the Music*. "The problem was Jack was friends with Bob, and he turned around and told Bob we had asked him. It wasn't tactful on Bill's part not to tell Bob first—the whole thing blew up, like we'd been caught hitting on a friend's girlfriend."[12]

Ezrin: "In the days before cell phones or answering machines, I had this answering service made up of little old ladies who took a maternal interest in me and my well being. They used to lecture me when I'd get in late at night: 'Where have you been?' 'I was working!' 'You should not work that late!' That sort of thing. So I get back from vacation and one of the ladies said, 'You need to call Mr. Douglas, he's very upset. He must have called here twenty-five times!' So I call Jack thinking something dreadful has happened and he tells me he had been approached by KISS to do the next album and that he would never even think about it if that would bother me. Jack was like my protégé. I trained Jack. I started him in the business. I brought him Aerosmith."[13]

Jay Messina's partner in sound, Jack Douglas was hired in 1973 by Bob Ezrin to work with Nimbus 9 and would assist in the seminal Sha Na Na sessions that brought Messina and Corky Stasiak together for the first time.

After Ezrin—courted by Aerosmith's management in the manner his mentor, Jack Richardson, was by Alice Cooper's manager, Shep Gordon, a few years earlier—passed the band on to Douglas, Aerosmith would develop both in the studio and onstage as a major force in rock. By the spring of 1976, Douglas was to Aerosmith what Ezrin had been to Alice Cooper, and he felt as much of an obligation to the band as he did to Ezrin. "I could have done KISS and made a lot of money," he said, in 1997's *Walk This Way: The Autobiography of Aerosmith*. "But that would've been unfair to Aerosmith because KISS was their only competition, at least among American rock bands."[14]

"I was so taken aback by hearing all this I just told Jack to go ahead and do it," says Ezrin. "I said, 'Fuck those guys!' I didn't know what I had done to deserve that. I thought we made a really great record and it was going to be a big record for them."[15]

Perhaps a little too late to smooth over a glaring professional *faux pas*, Bill Aucoin drafted a letter to Ezrin explaining why he needed to be replaced on the next album, the crux of which was the young producer had failed to produce "the KISS sound." Ezrin's recollection of this, nearly forty years later, still comes with a measure of incredulity and a tinge of sadness. "Basically, Bill said he was disappointed that I failed to capture the essence of the band and that they were moving on."[16]

The pressure was mounting.

Corky Stasiak, effusive in his dismay at how quickly the band ran from its triumph, is still irked today. "They were unfortunately privy to all the reviews and critics, and they concentrated only on the bad ones from guys who had their heads up their asses: writers whose meat-and-potatoes come from writing a bad review. It's like being an actor who has more fun playing the bad guy than playing the good guy. The media role is always the 'bad guy' role. KISS was haunted by the critics. They were shaken by the amount of blowback they received from the rock press wondering why the hell they put a piano on a KISS record, you know, 'More guitars! More bass! More drums! Rock! Rock! Rock!' They could not rise above this deluge of criticism after *Destroyer*. The fact that they had just made a brilliant album seemed lost on them, at least at first."[17]

Amid the fear, trepidation, and gnashing of teeth, Casablanca released "Shout It Out Loud" (backed by "Sweet Pain") as a single on March 1. It spent ten solid weeks on the charts, eventually reaching a reputable #31 in *Billboard* and topping the Canadian charts, making it the first #1 KISS single anywhere. It may not have held the same impact of "Rock and Roll All Nite," but it acted as a fine forerunner to the album's release, two weeks later, on March 15.

Ignoring the panic from the KISS camp, Casablanca went all out on promotion for the first time, taking out full-page ads in every major rock publication and a huge billboard on the Sunset Strip. Time and again, the Kelly painting was prominently displayed (proving the worth of Dennis Woloch's prediction to artist Frank Frazetta), branding KISS as the superheroes the band and Bob Ezrin had imagined over the grueling weeks of recording.

"The last time I saw the original painting was when I handed it off to them, and the next time I saw it was months later in the window of the Roosevelt Long Island mall," remembers Ken Kelly. "It's a huge mall, a couple of miles from our apartment, and we drove down one night, and we had the child holding our hand, and I looked over, and I'm like, 'Oh, my God!' From floor to ceiling in the front window of this glass store was three twenty-foot panels of glass, and the store owners had filled it—filled it—with *Destroyer*! There must've been 500 copies of *Destroyer* on this one wall. As you walk in the mall entrance and you go past the first store and look to your left and oh my God Jesus there is just KISS as far as the eye can see. And from then on, the work was coming in. I did *Rainbow Rising* for Deep Purple and I almost did *Bat Out of Hell* with Meatloaf, but I had no time!"[18]

Stasiak: "When *Destroyer* came out I was blown away. Wow, this is energy, this is color, this is cinematic; this is big and in your face. This is how a rock record should sound. It sounded so good on my stereo, man. I knew we had a hit. There was never any question for me. When you're working on something like when I was working with John Lennon and we did 'Whatever Gets You Through the Night,' I thought that that song was okay. Never in my wildest imagination did I think that it would sell better than 'Imagine,' but it did! And that threw me for a loop. But when I was working on *Destroyer*, I knew that record was gonna kill. It was going to nail the listener to the floor squealing. Before *Destroyer*, records never sounded that big—even the Alice Cooper stuff Bob Ezrin produced. *Destroyer* shits on them when it comes to a sonic experience. *Destroyer* is three steps and a hop beyond anything else that was out there at the time, specifically for the hard rock genre. For me, *Back in Black* by AC/DC, which came much later, was on the same level as *Destroyer*. Of course, the technology was more modern for that record, but back then, the three producers that made records that really stood out were Bob Ezrin Mutt Lange, and Roy Thomas Baker. When those guys made records, you had to sit up and listen."[19]

Despite the eviscerating reviews and the shock and dismay from fans, *Destroyer* surpassed any previous KISS album in the immediacy of its chart ascent, reaching gold status by April 22 while selling an estimated 850,000 copies. Upon hearing the news, Casablanca quickly released "Flaming Youth," backed with "God of Thunder," as the second single at the end of April, complete with a rare picture sleeve of the record's iconic cover. Although the single only reached #72 in *Billboard*, it did not halt the album's rise up the charts into early May, when it peaked at #11. Onstage in Ontario, Canada, the band was informed that the bottom had in fact not dropped out: they had indeed built on the momentum of *Alive!* and had a legitimate hit on their hands. Gene Simmons once again lit his hair on fire. Normalcy had returned.

Meanwhile, KISS continued its seemingly endless touring, traversing much of the South and Midwestern United States, followed by an eight-city tour of Canada beginning April 18, before embarking on the band's first ever turn through Europe from May 13 to June 6. It would be the first time the band performed overseas. Yet despite the fact that KISS had already worked the new *Destroyer* material into its set list, including "God of Thunder," "Flaming Youth," "Shout It Out Loud" and "Detroit Rock City," it wasn't until July that the band unveiled its new costumes and the immense staging that would remain a staple for the rest of its history, even as it jettisoned original members, shed the makeup, and later reconciled for the 1996 Reunion Tour.

An influx of two million dollars funneled from the new Casablanca deal was allocated for the next phase of The Act, described in *KISS Alive Forever* as "the most radical staging change in KISS's history."[20] In May, Bill Aucoin proudly announced to *Billboard* and *Performance* magazines that he was expanding Rock Steady into a separate enterprise called Aucoin Management Incorporated (AMI) and moving his operations to a palatial office suite at 645 Madison Avenue, the epicenter of modern American marketing. Glickman/Marks would remain as hands-on business managers for KISS and, as authors Gooch and Suhs describe, forever divide the "energetic, mad improvisation of '74 and '75 and the calculated extravaganza that was to follow."[21] The account goes on to illustrate physical and psychological changes to the way The Act would fulfill its mission statement. The entire original KISS touring crew was replaced, including cherished road manager J. R. Smalling, a charter member and voice of the fanfare opening, "You wanted the best, you got the best!" Longtime lighting director Mike Campise, also sent packing, believed Aucoin was building upon the KISS mystique by eliminating those who had grown too close over the lean years. Although after *Destroyer* it is well documented that Aucoin's dream of maintaining a lofty status for his charges meant that nobody but Gene, Paul, Ace, and Peter be allowed access to the beating heart of The Act, when accounting for the enormity of the new staging, the personnel needed to maintain and run it called for seasoned professionals used to working with Broadway spectaculars, not mere rock tours.

Casablanca vice president Larry Harris offered a different take when interviewed for this book. "Bill lost some power to Carl Glickman, but he had to. Bill was very close to he and Howard Marks and they kind of saved his ass a few times even before KISS. They used to let Bill use their offices in New York before he even got involved with KISS. Bill was like Neil [Bogart]. They were both gamblers on a high level. But Bill had no choice financially. It was all or nothing."[22]

"Basically when I got into the advertising at Howard Marks it was more low-key, like a studio," Vinnie DeGerlando, assistant to Dennis Woloch at Howard Marks, recalls. "It was like an eclectic thing, where you could do different kind of work, that's how KISS came into that. They didn't come to an advertising agency; they came to a small studio in an interesting building that was dubbed 'the music building.' Todd Rundgren was there, also Bob Dylan or Janice Joplin. I would meet them in the elevator going up to their managers. It was all in that music building on Fifty-Fifth Street before we moved to Madison Avenue. When we got to Madison that is when everyone joined together. That's when the money was coming in so they had a big office at that time. The one on Fifty-Fifth was very different than the original small room with three people working in it. The new one has this huge art department where sometimes people would open the door and look in and think, 'Okay, these are the crazy guys!' and then the door would close and they would go around to the other offices. Dennis and I suddenly had this huge office we would work out of, a lot of space."[23]

What was to come both on- and offstage was beyond the scope of anything the KISS inner sanctum had previously attempted. As Gooch and Suhs conclude, "Gone were the days when a wide-eyed band and a small, loyal road crew crisscrossed the country on nothing but naiveté, ambition and attitude; there was no mistaking that KISS was now a business."[24]

The stage show—once an ingenious hodgepodge of crude hydraulics, safety-challenged pyrotechnics, raw costuming, and choreographed play-acting controlled and operated by half-soused roadies and performed by experimenting neophytes—would now be a full-scale showcase worthy of any Las Vegas spectacular. Aucoin and Sean Delaney agreed to once again employ the services of the Jules Fischer Organization, which had tapped Mark Ravitz to design the now famous KISS stage sign, as well as key, if not crude, special effects for KISS's industry debut in late 1973. Fischer and Ravitz's extensive resume of Broadway sets had also included the design of David Bowie's elaborate 1974 *Diamond Dogs* show, with its towering buildings and catwalks, and a sudden foray into outlandish prop theater by the Rolling Stones, trying desperately to keep up with the joneses on its 1975 tour.

Ravitz, partnering with Mark Krueger, took the entirety of the *Destroyer* concept—its comic book superhero, fantasy cover, and the thunderously conceptual music—to draft blueprints for nothing short of a rock landscape of demonological, intergalactic, and superstar proportions. It was to be an imposing atmospheric expanse that would solidify the living myth of The Act while similarly lending portions of its enormity to the individual personas that made up KISS, a prevalent thesis initially realized in Sean Delaney's stage directions, made manifest in Dennis Woloch's *Alive!* booklet, and finally set down on vinyl in Bob Ezrin's insistence on infusing personality, narrative, and pathos into the music. As Gooch and Suhs expound in *KISS Alive Forever*, "Two emerald-eyed cats flanked Peter's drum platform. The area where Frehley did portions of his solo was distinctly lunar in theme, and Simmons, in turn, would ascend to a crumbling gothic castle for his solo."[25] If *Destroyer* provided The Act its irrefutable sonic canvas, Fischer, Ravtiz, and Krueger realized its colossal potential.

The original staging was so massive and intricate that many of the ideas didn't make it out of the development stage, most strikingly an opening that featured an actual car being hoisted above the stage before crashing to the floor to accentuate the "Detroit Rock City" epilogue. Also not making it out of rehearsals was the razed city set design of foam rubber brick and mortar that was to crumble at the show's climax, but was eventually considered too hard to clean up prior to encores—not to mention incredibly time-consuming to place about the stage in the first place. Stage props that came and went as the tour progressed include a God of Thunder Machine (a prototype of the original 1931 *Frankenstein* film designed by Ken Strickfadden that was too large and heavy and wholly unreliable to maintain), Tentacle Tree (originally designed as an animated prop to whip around menacingly, but which allegedly never got to that stage), and Bloody Stake (a red-soaked phallic device that would rise as Simmons spat blood, which had something to do with flames bursting out, but was abandoned).

What remained intact was a fifty-two-by-forty-foot monolith that literally changed theatrical staging for rock concerts forever, and would rarely be stripped down by KISS until well into the band's post-makeup days, only to once again ceremoniously return for the reunion tours. Highlights included the first ever dual-staircase platforms, flanking the spacious stage set that rose and lowered at the prelude and finale of each show. The band, along with Criss in his drum rig (featuring a vintage black cat unfurled on an ebony curtain) ascended high in the air in a highly intricate riser; Simmons, Stanley, and Frehley would then descend upon the floorboards toward the audience, as if emerging triumphantly from Mount Olympus. "Our stage dynamic for them was based on the idea that they were invading the space of the audience, coming down into their world in an assertive stance to begin the show," Mark Ravitz explains.[26]

Lighting trees designed as high-tension steel utility towers not only added to the "city within a city" motif but also flooded the stage with magnificent lighting effects. Giant clouds decorated with patriotic red, white, and blue lightning bolts surrounded the still imposing, fully-lit KISS logo, which was originally to be used as a rear-projection screen for video images, but which according to Ravitz was a concept too far behind today's digital technology to work effectively. Long strings of colored lights—not unlike Christmas tree lighting—were strung from the towers along the back of the stage and all around the arena, bathing the audience in an effervescent glow, projecting The Act's precious connection to its fans. This was accentuated by two enormous unfurled KISS Army shields that fell from the top of the lighting towers during the final numbers, holding the band within its grasp and illustrating the solidarity of The Act as an all-inclusive cult of personality.

The entire rig was assembled for two months and eventually displayed at the Stewart Airbase in Newburgh, New York, a Hudson River suburb of New York City. From concept to construction, all of Ravitz and Krueger's designs were completed without the knowledge of the band, which was touring in Europe—something Aucoin failed to mention to either party until it was too late.

Ravitz: "It's all built and ready and Bill brings the band up to Newburg to take a look at everything and they were very unhappy, to say the least, that they weren't consulted about any of this. So they commenced to literally break up the set. It was just disgusting. This was top-of-the-line Broadway craftsmanship: most of the people that worked on that set worked with the Metropolitan Opera. And Bill just sat back and watched them do it. I guess he wanted them to blow off some steam, but it ended up costing them a lot of money. People put a lot of time and effort and talent into that set and they came in and just ripped it apart."[27]

Frehley infamously called the set "a fucking fruit salad." Criss writes in his memoir that it looked more like Disneyland than a rock-and-roll stage. Even Simmons and Stanley were dubious. Soon after the outburst, Aucoin held several meetings with the band and the scenic shop, as well as the Jules Fischer people, and, with some tweaking, the work continued.

"In a couple of days, all the feelings were assuaged and revisions were undertaken, but really it was a *fait accompli*," says Ravitz. "They could certainly put their own stamp on it, but they could never argue that most of the staging was very good. There were minor changes here or there. If they wanted something, then they bought it. The design and building costs were anywhere from thirty-five to fifty thousand [upward of $208,000 in 2015], but I don't remember anyone haggling over cost. We provided them with whatever they needed in the end."[28]

On July 3, 1976, the eve of America's bicentennial celebration, the enormous rolling carnival known as the Spirit of '76 tour embarked on its assault of the U.S., the breadth and width of which Ravitz recalls took roughly a day and a half to break down, load out, ship, and rebuild again in each city. This led to some in the KISS Camp, specifically the money voices, expressing alarm.

Business analyst Robert Brown was hired by Glickman/Marks to make heads or tails of a roadshow that Ravitz points out "had never been attempted in the rock field before."[29] Brown observed four of the early shows, from July 13 at the Baltimore Civic Center to the now famous Anaheim Stadium concert on July 20, and sent his report back to the agency, as printed in Dale Sherman's *Black Diamond*. It details ill-conceived scheduling and haphazard marketing schemes "lacking a viable game plan," with "expenses way out of line." Brown concluded: "Too many trucks. Too many people traveling and of course, too much time between gigs."[30] However, in a prescient upside, Brown also pinpointed where KISS merchandising was cleaning up (tour books, T-shirts, hats, bumper stickers, et cetera), but how it could do even better with strategic selling points and locations at the shows, expanding on the idea of using the superhero images of *Destroyer*'s cover was systematically turning KISS from rock band to icon.

For the remainder of America's bicentennial summer, the Spirit of '76 tour became the story. The absurd enormity and pure arrogance of such a traveling spectacle was news. No one—not Alice Cooper or Pink Floyd or any '70s showbiz rock operation for that matter—had dared attempted anything approaching its magnitude. It was the talk of the entertainment industry.

"Several giant confetti machines and sixty-foot flames exploding toward the ceiling at show's end; the equivalent of five sticks of dynamite are detonated," Kathi Stein extolled, in the September 28, 1976, issue of *Circus* magazine. "It was more than a rock & roll tour. It was more than a carnival. It was more than an election primary. It was KISS on the road—forty cities in two months, more than half a million people flocking to the largest stadiums available. It was $250,000 in special effects alone, tons and tons of equipment demanding the rental of seven forty-five-foot semi-tractor trailers to cart it from city to city and the trucks were preceded by two custom scenic cruisers with toilets, the KISS jet, and a road crew of over forty."[31]

Although *Alive!* had indeed altered the narrative, putting KISS in the conversation of notable headlining rock acts, it was *Destroyer* and its ensuing monster tour that cemented the myth of KISS—a myth its members have perpetuated to the tune of millions of dollars for nearly forty years. *Destroyer*, the Spirit of '76 road show, and the marketing machine it unleashed had taken The Act, once an illusionary force within the band and later embraced by its rabid fans, into a living, breathing business model.

The show's set list, now committed to featuring half of the *Destroyer* album, bumped staples such as "Deuce" and "Strutter" from their previous positions as show openers—a role they had served well for three years. The furious charge of "Detroit Rock City" followed by the rousing "King of the Night Time World" opened every show with ostentatious revelry. They would remain as KISS's opening live salvo for nearly the entirety of the shows involving the original members of the band for most of the next three years. Gene Simmons's bass solo and blood spitting ritual, once the domain of "100,000 Years," settled neatly within his new theme, "God of Thunder," replete with voice effects to capture the demonic reading on record. Peter Criss's drum solo, more of a plodding tank assault than the rhythmic jamboree of *Alive!* days, would eventually take refuge there. "Shout It Out Loud" became a staple in the KISS stage repertoire in perpetuity, while "Sweet Pain" would make its only appearance on the tour's initial show in Norfolk, Virginia, and "Flaming Youth," with its difficult time signatures, would soon be phased out.

On July 10, KISS headlined its first stadium show at Jersey City's Roosevelt Stadium, complete with an elaborately catered pre- and post-show party staged by ATI and Glickman/Marks attended by celebrities, industry insiders, and the rock elite. A black-and-white video of a feed originally broadcast via closed-circuit TV to revelers in the backstage tent is one of the few artifacts from the early staging of the Spirit of '76 tour. Its ambitious set and the brand new costumes designed by Larry LeGaspi, which utilized to great effect the iconic images of the Ken Kelly painting, are a definitive flourish to the ear-splitting volume, lighting, and explosions. The band is lean, mean, and in its prime, each member pristinely comfortable in his new roles as a megastar. Stanley twists and sashays about invincibly, a blonde streak interrupting a now wildly tall mane of curly black hair. Frehley gyrates lithely across the huge stage, swinging his favorite Gibson Les Paul as if it's a loaded weapon. Criss is beatific upon his throne of drums, pounding away in a controlled rage. And Simmons, a monstrous figure, is in his element, clad in faux battle metal. Guitars burst into flames, blood splatters, fire is breathed, and the smoke from dozens of explosions fills the air.

When it was over, the spacious tent backstage was packed in with hundreds of VIP's playing arcade games and making merry on an endless stream of food and drink. KISS had hit the big time.

Yet this was only a prelude. Nothing compared to the strange tale of how the little "joke song" turned lavish ballad transformed *Destroyer* into a juggernaut. The song Ezrin had painstakingly coerced from Peter Criss; the track that caused the band to battle internally over whether to even include it on the album; and most certainly the emissary for dozens of critics from across rock journalism to pummel KISS as softening sell-outs, was about to blow up.

21

Stratosphere

I went to Larry Harris and said, "Larry, you hired me to break this group into the Top 40—THIS is the Top 40 single!"
—Scott Shannon[1]

Months before the Spirit of '76 tour ripped through thirty-two cities over the span of two months, selling out arenas and moving merchandise at a record pace, *Destroyer* peaked at #11 on the *Billboard* charts. It was May 15: the band members were sky high, having attended Ace Frehley's wedding to longtime girlfriend Jeanette Trerotola on May 1, where they jammed onstage sans makeup for the first time at any public venue, albeit only for close friends and family. The band embarked on a quick run through Bob Ezrin's home country of Canada and then headed to Europe for the first time, taping a television special for the BBC and mostly complaining about the antiquated accommodations, lousy food, and limited television entertainment. Upon its return, however, *Destroyer* began to tank. Casablanca's release of the first three mostly non-selling KISS albums in a collection called *KISS: The Originals* on July 21 did little to curtail its rapid descent all the way to #192. It was nearly out of the charts altogether by early August.

As Peter Criss told Ken Sharp in 1993, "The album was failing. It was falling off the charts. It wasn't making it. It was like, 'What happened?' We were really sweating it like crazy. We were going, is this going to work? Did we do the right thing? We used Bob Ezrin, and no one is better than that. So we had so much on it. We spent a fortune to do it and we were really sweating when we saw the bullet drop and we saw it going down in *Billboard* and we started going, 'Oh, no, Jesus Christ!' After all the primal therapy I went through, I said, 'This can't happen.'"[2]

A week after *The Originals* hit the stands, Casablanca released "Detroit Rock City" as a single, absent of the entire symphonic guitar interlude, the vignette intro, and the horrific concluding car crash. The label was banking on KISS's connection to Detroit and the powerfully influential 50,000-watt CKLW, which had pumped the best American rock music out of Ontario, Canada, to Michigan, Ohio, Indiana, Illinois, and Pennsylvania for over a decade. "The Big 8," as it would come to be known, also helped the original Detroit bands gain greater audiences north of the border, including Alice Cooper, who had decamped to the Motor City from Los Angeles prior to meeting up with Bob Ezrin. Detroit had earned KISS's title of "Rock City" thanks to its embracing of the Midwest's heaviest acts, from the MC5 to Iggy and the Stooges, Ted Nugent and the Amboy Dukes, and its support for the early purveyors of English heavy metal, most notably Black Sabbath, whose working-class grit loudly spoke the city's language. Detroit, the home of *Creem* magazine, KISS's journalistic champions, had been one of the first cities to take the band under its wing, most notably the tiny suburban town of Cadillac, Michigan, which declared a KISS Day when the local football team had achieved a winning season blasting KISS music at practice and before games. The mayor of the town even dressed in KISS makeup for the occasion. And, of course, Cobo Hall had been KISS's touchstone long before it stood as the home office for the visual banner that heralded *Alive!* to a willing rock nation.

CKLW's program director, Rosalie Trombley, who had held her job since 1968 and would maintain it until 1984, had been a fan of KISS from the beginning—something Aucoin, Bogart, and the band did not take lightly, as they had wined, dined, and limo'd her right through the *Alive!* experiment, to lucrative results. This was the kind of special treatment Trombley was used to; as the "Girl with the Golden Ear," she excelled at taking alternative or hard-rock records and creating a crossover effect. She provided the AM audience a way to discover acts usually reserved for concert halls and FM headphones, and those acts then gained the type of exposure reserved for pop's elite. Trombley was also renowned in the industry for picking hits from relative unknowns, as she had successfully prognosticated for Elton John, Earth, Wind & Fire, Chicago, the Stylistics, and Detroit stalwart Bob Seger, among many others. (Seger immortalized her chart prescience in his 1973 song "Rosalie," in which he sings, "She's got the power / She's got the tower.") Trombley also had a serendipitous connection to Nimbus 9 and Jack Richardson, as she is credited with helping launch the chart success of the Guess Who's first single, "These Eyes," as well as Alice Cooper's "Eighteen."

According to Casablanca vice president Larry Harris, it was Trombley who the label's newly hired director of promotions Scott Shannon visited upon the release of the new KISS single. Unexpectedly, Trombley told Shannon that she did not care for "Detroit Rock City," or at least the butchered single version. In fact, she actually preferred its flipside, the tender ballad "Beth." Rumor had it that Trombley's nine-year-old daughter had nagged her about "Beth" prior to Shannon's visit and greatly influenced her opinion of the song. Shannon, a savvy radio veteran, understood Trombley's power and track record and was immediately faced with a rare opportunity to push "Beth," a song he had already predicted would be KISS's first hit. "Now, there are other people who worked for the company at the time who tell me different stories," says Harris. "But that's the story I remember."[3]

Scott Shannon, a radio giant and industry insider for nearly six decades, remembers things far differently. "Dorothy had already told them she would break 'Detroit Rock City' wide open, so there was no way 'Beth,' which was stuck on the B-side, was going to be the single," he argued, during an interview for this book.[4] He also makes it clear that while Trombley's "golden ear" may have given the song a boost in Detroit, it ultimately failed her, as the song never charted, prompting Shannon to make a bold move—something he was already well known for in the music business.

Casablanca had wooed Shannon during his short stint at *Radio & Records*, an influential industry publication. Before that, his streak of success in radio, both as a personality and a program director, was staggering. By 1976, Shannon had already made a name for himself (most notably as "Big Shan") across the South in Columbus, Georgia; Mobile, Alabama; Nashville, Tennessee; and finally running what would become under his guidance the top radio station in Atlanta, WQXI.

"I became kind of a media darling," says Shannon, who appeared to possess the same knack for hit songs as Rosalie Trombley. "I was colorful and began to gain a reputation for having pretty good ears. I would discover album cuts to be the next single and talk them up to the A&R guys. When Ringo Starr came out with 'Good Night Vienna,' I wanted to play the other side, which was the 'No No Song.' No one at the label thought it was viable."[5] The almost forgotten B-side became a smash for the former Beatle, who summarily gave Shannon a gold record for his prescience.

For a year and a half, Shannon used the 28,000-watt WQXI—"Quixie in Dixie"—to break several hits, including Jim Croce's "Time in a Bottle," Olivia Newton John's "I Honestly Love You," and Andy Kim's "Rock Me Gently," before parlaying his influence into a regular feature he penned for *Radio & Records* called "Street Talk," which was, as he puts it, "a glorified radio gossip column."[6] It was then that Shannon grabbed Neil Bogart's attention. Casablanca's president remembered him from two years earlier, when Shannon had ably assisted with the odd but fairly successful kissing contest that helped KISS get a modicum of media attention and a spot on *The Mike Douglas Show*, despite moans from the band. "Those guys hated me for that," chuckles Shannon today. "They blamed me for that mess. It was my idea, but they really didn't care much about doing it when they did it."[7]

Suddenly flush with money from *Alive!* and a colossal hit called "Love to Love You Baby," on which an unknown Donna Summer moaned with sexual delight over a disco beat for seventeen minutes, Bogart offered Shannon $70,000 a year (around $300,000 in 2015), supplied him with an unlimited expense account, and threw in a Mercedes convertible for good measure. It turned out, for Casablanca and KISS, to be the bargain of bargains.

Larry Harris knew what he was getting in Shannon, as illustrated in his summation of the hire in *And Party Every Day*. "Scott had solid relationships with PDs [program directors] nationwide. He'd been in radio for a long time, mostly in the South. He'd had great success in places like Mobile, Memphis, Nashville, and Atlanta, often increasing ratings for his stations. The name Scott Shannon carried some weight in radio circles and beyond. The other program directors in Top 40 radio knew him by reputation, if not personally, and they took his calls, which was not always the case when I rang them. It was a great hire for us and for Scott, and within a matter of months, he would pay an integral role in cementing KISS's superstar status."[8]

Shannon: "When I got to Casablanca, I found out there had been no such thing as A&R director. Neil [Bogart] handled all A&R. I mean, I was vice president of promotion and A&R, but mostly promotion. What he told me was he wanted me to break KISS in the pop-music stations. That was my number-one mission; even though I had to promote people like Parliament, Donna Summer, Larry Santos, and the Village People, my number-one priority was getting KISS on Top 40 radio stations, which was difficult, because they hated them. They thought they were just a loud heavy-metal group with no hit potential whatsoever."[9]

Bogart immediately handed Shannon a test pressing of *Destroyer* and told him to give his honest opinion as to which songs had hit potential. "I came back and I told him the only hit on the album I heard was 'Beth.' He said, 'Forget that, what's the next one?' I said, 'Why do we have to forget that?' He said, 'Scott, they just put that on as a favor to Peter Criss.' When I pressed him further, he said that since neither Gene nor Paul wrote the song and it didn't reflect the spirit of KISS, that they wanted to be known for and it was still no. Plus he insisted he had Rosalie Trombley and her guarantee to break 'Detroit Rock City.'"[10]

Frustrated, Shannon took his case to Larry Harris, who informed him of the real reason why: Casablanca's founder and president had declared that "Beth" would never be a hit for KISS. After listening to an acetate of *Destroyer* with Harris a few months earlier, Bogart, still smarting from being sued by Aucoin, snapped. "Neil was going through a pretty miserable divorce," explains Harris. "His first wife's name was Beth, and because we were having contractual problems with KISS and there was animosity there, Neil thought, when he heard 'Beth' the first time—and he heard it without listening to the words real closely—that it was a put-down of him getting a divorce. So I called Peter, and I said, 'What the fuck is this?' And he said, 'What do you mean?' And I said, 'Well, why would you do this to Neil?' And he goes, 'It's not about Neil!'"[11]

Bogart didn't buy it. Before leaving for a vacation in Acapulco, he set down an edict to the entire Casablanca staff that no way "Beth" would ever be a hit, going as far as demanding it end up as a B-side to bury it.

Shannon: "The B-side would always be a song that has no chance of being a single, because they didn't want to waste it. The kids would already have purchased it. So, I said to Larry, 'Do you think you can get this put on the B-side of what we call the stock copy?' He said, 'I can get that done for you.'

"Fast forward a couple weeks, I had the entire promotion staff working their butts off on 'Detroit Rock City,' but it was just considered too hard for many of the Top 40 stations, and on top of that it didn't seem to be doing so well in Detroit. Once it stalled on the charts, I went to the mail room, because I knew the kid in the mail room—little guy with shoulder-length hair, he now is an independent promotion guy in LA—and I said, 'I want you to do a Top 40 mailing, and I got like about one hundred copies of the stock.' I took the stock copy and took a black magic marker and put X's on the side that had 'Beth.' I shipped it out to one hundred people that I knew and then I called around to some people that owed me favors. If people took 'Beth' I did a promotion for them or KISS would do a free show in the lounge or whatever. I said, 'Will you test this record at night, will you play it at night? That's all I'm asking.' The first station that agreed to do that was in Columbus, Georgia. The guy called me after a week of playing it and said, 'It's our #1 requested record on the radio station.' That's all we needed—a little reassurance that my ears weren't fooling me.

"The next thing I did was call my number-one promotion guy, the best promotion guy in the country, a guy named Brian Interland. I said, 'Brian, can we get this played?' And he said, 'If you come in, we'll get it played.' So I flew in there. We took some of the people from the #1 Top 40 station in Boston, WRKO, and we went up to the radio station and we talked to the night jock and then we talked to the program director and he said, 'I'd love to play this.' They had a 'Make It or Break It' battle of the new sounds. We got them to play

'Beth' that night. Within a week, it was the #1 requested song at WRKO, which showed the country that we had a hit. Finally, we went back, and I convinced Neil this is the hit; we have to go for it, forget all the excuses. From then on, he put all the force of Casablanca behind 'Beth.'"[12]

Larry Harris: "Scott was scared, because he had just started working for us not too much before, and he was afraid Neil would be pissed off at him. Neil was not there to say anything, because he was away, and of course we didn't have cell phones in those days, so I just said, 'Fuck it.' I told him I would take the heat from Neil. And from that point forward, 'Beth' was the single's A-side and 'Detroit Rock City' was its B-side."[13]

Quite suddenly, in a classic story of mid-'70s wild freelance grassroots momentum, "Beth" worked its way through the pertinent channels that broke records into legitimate hits—radio add-lists, breakouts, and most importantly hot lists in the trade publications. "There still was a lot of resistance to KISS," Shannon admits. "I said, 'Don't say who it is, just play it.' A lot of stations did that. Don't identify it, just play 'Beth.'"[14]

Upon Bogart's return from Mexico, Harris had to break the news to him. Perhaps because he was tanned and rested, or maybe because his sharp pop sensibilities were telling him that a syrupy ballad was just the kind of KISS single he had been waiting for, Casablanca's president took it in stride. "Neil was the consummate record man," says Harris. "If it was a hit, it was a hit. If it could generate dollars, that's all he really gave a shit about. He just sucked it up and said, 'Let's go!'"[15]

Casablanca officially released "Beth" as a single in early August, and by Labor Day it had begun making its steady accent up the *Billboard* charts, entering the Top 100 on September 4. Then, over the ensuing weeks, it went from #57 to #44 to #30 to #24, hitting the Top 20 with a bullet on October 9.

"Once the record started selling, it started getting other stations jumping on it," recalls Harris. "It was getting phone calls from listeners saying they loved the song or 'Who is this artist?' Nobody knew it was KISS from first hearing it, obviously. I mean, how would you know? It certainly didn't sound like anything else they ever did. So yeah, now Neil embraced it."[16]

Scott Shannon: "The one that helped break it was John Parker, who ran our Southern region, and Brian Interland, who was definitely responsible for it getting on RKO in Boston, which was a major market. But more importantly it was part of the Drake chain. Drake controlled airplay around the country—Los Angeles and KFRC in San Francisco and other big stations—so when people saw it working at RKO, it was legitimate. By that time we had ten other what I call 'cockroach stations' all through the South that had it at #1."[17]

The song no one seemed to want on *Destroyer*, beyond a motivated Bob Ezrin and an insistent Bill Aucoin, and that was held in contempt by scores of fans and rock journalists, was now rescuing KISS's seminal record and fast becoming the unlikeliest hit of 1976. "One day I was channel surfing and 'Beth' was playing on three different stations simultaneously," Peter Criss proudly writes in his memoir. "I was on cloud nine. Not just for a personal accomplishment but because my song propelled the album back onto the charts. *Destroyer* was our *White Album*, the best album we ever did in our lives, and it was nice to see Bob Ezrin get the credit he richly deserved. He may have been a hard taskmaster, but the result was more than worth it."[18]

One evening soon after the breaking of "Beth," Bill Aucoin showed up at Criss's Manhattan brownstone with a bottle of Dom Perignon to congratulate the always volatile and mostly insecure drummer for his achievement. Criss remembers Aucoin saying, "The irony is that you saved the album, Peter, and they're going to hate you for it."[19] "They," of course, meant Simmons and Stanley, who come across in much of Criss's storytelling as jealous and petty, but not without some validation. Over the years, both of KISS's main songwriters would admit their trepidation over having "Beth" define their breakout studio achievement—something Bogart made plain to Scott Shannon when he pitched the ballad as the band's first potential chart hope.

"When 'Beth' started to hit, you have to remember the guys in the band, besides Peter Criss, really didn't support it that much," says Shannon. "They didn't want it, because it didn't sound like KISS. They wanted to stick to the macho, 'I'm going to bang her all night long,' kinda sound. The minute it started to hit, credit to Gene and Paul that they accepted it as a KISS record and they went for it."[20]

Decades later, in their memoirs, Stanley and Simmons would handle the import and legacy of "Beth" differently. Stanley is mostly dismissive, broaching its crucial breakthrough with one line about "Beth" being "a chart hit and crossed over to AM radio."[21] Simmons points out that the single's success cemented the breakout of *Alive!*—which could have been seen as a fluke—and that "Beth" and the resurgence of *Destroyer* created a new distinction for KISS. "Now rather than having a hit with a live record then sinking back down, we were riding the crest of two massive hit records," he writes. "In pop music this has been the way to create superstars from stars, and sure enough, we were superstars."[22] However, in both depictions, the two men who tried to scuttle the "Beth" experiment at several intervals from its recording, its inclusion on the album, and its representation of the KISS brand, go straight on to cite the enormity of the band's first sold-out arena show at Anaheim Stadium on

August 20 (to a crowd of more than 40,000 people), a couple of weeks after "Beth" hit the airwaves, as the moment when KISS was transformed.

Even Bill Aucoin, the song's greatest proponent outside the creative team, who had warned Criss that it would cause friction in the band while sipping celebratory champagne with him, would express reservations about the single. Two decades later, he told KISS's biographers, "'Beth' was so much of a departure that the fans didn't know quite what to make of it. They were shocked. For us, that was an experimental period, and it was an odd situation at first. We had to let the fans know that everything was all right, that we were just trying some new things."[23]

By Thanksgiving, "Beth" was firmly in the Top 10 at #9. It ended up at #7 the first week of December, certifying it as a gold record and making it the biggest-selling single in the band's history—a feat that would never be topped. Nearly a full nine months after *Destroyer* hit the streets, the former "joke song" took KISS into the stratosphere, crossing the band into untapped markets, and, as Bob Ezrin envisioned, expanding its appeal to a variety of listeners—including, most pointedly, engaging women for the first time.

When pressed during interviews for this book as to whether the success of *Destroyer* and ultimately the unprecedented chart explosion of the song he crafted almost entirely alone had given him a measure of vindication, the now sixty-five-year-old Ezrin was quite adamant.

"I knew I was right about *Destroyer* before we started, during its creation, and when it was mixed, mastered, and released. It was obviously a great record, and I wasn't the only one who thought so. The guys loved it. Bill loved it. All the guys at the Record Plant loved it. Those were heady days at the Record Plant, man. There was some really good shit going on there, and some amazing musicians were making their best work there all at the same time. And everyone who heard what we were doing in there knew it was pretty magical stuff. If anything, I was shocked when I got the blowback that I did—shocked and a little hurt and offended by the notion that this was anything other than really great. I really believed in it. The fact that *Destroyer* panned out and proved itself to be historical for them and contained some their most beloved material was never a surprise to me, and so I didn't sit back and say, 'Yeah, I was right all along.' But we eventually got past all that. Believe me, I understand when it's your career on the line and you do something very brave and very different and put your nuts on the line you hope that the world accepts and appreciates what you do, but then there's always that little voice in the back of your head that says [he sings], 'Do you love me?'"[24]

"'Beth' gave KISS credibility with a whole new audience that they would've never hit just getting played on AOR progressive radio, which is what they were getting played on, which was my purview," says Larry Harris. "I got them tons of airplay on rock stations around the country like WNEW in New York or KLOS in L.A. I mean, they were all over the place. We did the Kiss-Off and that made national news, but *Destroyer* solidified the fact that this was really a legitimate band that could have hits, not just a live band that did well on the road."[25]

The stunning success of "Beth" coincided with the band's October 29 appearance on *The Paul Lynde Halloween Special* on ABC, the nation's highest-rated network, which had a jarring effect on the audience demographic at KISS shows. Stanley told a Memphis reporter on December 2, at the absolute apex of the song's ramble up the charts, that he was beginning to see parents bringing their four-year-olds. Frehley writes in his memoir that he suddenly felt strange doing anything remotely sexual with the guitar due to the increased influx of prepubescent fans.

Subsequently, merchandise sales at shows and in stores skyrocketed. Aucoin had secured the rights to mass-produce Ken Kelly's *Destroyer* painting on T-shirts, posters, lunchboxes, bumper stickers, and more. Halfway through the Spirit of '76 tour, Simmons, Stanley, Frehley, and Criss were notified that they were now millionaires. Each member began buying cars and property and setting up parents and friends with a brand new this and that. *Destroyer*, given up for dead on August 21 when it fell off the charts, reentered *Billboard* at #133—already fifty-nine places higher than before. The album remained on the charts for twenty-seven consecutive weeks from late '76 into '77 (peaking at #37 on February 5 and exiting the charts on April 2, over a year after its release), long after KISS had already released its follow-up, *Rock and Roll Over*, and embarked on a tour to promote it. On November 11, 1976, *Destroyer* officially became KISS's second platinum album (marking sales of over one million copies), and appeared to have a life of its own.

"That's what really makes an album sell, when it has a song that really lasts a long time," says Scott Shannon. "'Beth' is what we call a perpetual recurrent. It never burned out."[26]

On February 10, 1977, "Beth" won the People's Choice Award for Best Song of 1976, edging out a pair "joke songs" about animals, "Disco Duck" and "Muskrat Love." Introduced by 1950s television icon Dick Van Dyke, dressed nattily in a tux and calling KISS a "musical revolution," the band performed the song in a live taping in Chicago. Adding "Beth" to the band's shows was something that had become unavoidable once the song dominated the airwaves. Peter Criss would sit alone on a stool at center stage, a single spotlight on him, singing to a backing track of the orchestral recording of January 13—Bob Ezrin's piano accompanied by the conducting of Allan Macmillan blaring over the deafening P.A. After that, another 1960s television icon, Goldie Hawn, joined the stage and called the music of 1976 "frenetic, dissident, and cacophonous," playfully butchering her pronunciation of the last word. She then presented the award, giggling as if completely baffled by the absurdity of this harlequin freak show winning an award for a lovelorn ballad. Lydia Criss, looking quite "Hollywood" in a black dress but conspicuous by her thick Noo Yawk accent, accepted the award for the band and her husband by nervously stating that her love of the song was not only due to it expressing how Peter felt about her, "but how every man feels when he's away from the woman he loves." Somewhere Bob Ezrin, now estranged from the KISS inner sanctum, smiled triumphantly, his job accomplished.

And as KISS became the superstar rock group it had formed, and traversed countless hardships, to be, much of it due to the incredible creation, marketing, and success of *Destroyer*, it became impossible for the mainstream media to ignore. *Destroyer* not only obliterated the passé notion proffered by naysayers in the press that KISS was a fad but set forth a new phenomenon that demanded to be addressed. Predictably, those who would never embrace the idea of KISS as a tangible force were quick to explain it away as something akin to the mass hallucination of the great unwashed, or, worse yet—and flying in the face of how KISS had been ignored for four years—a media creation.

Articles began to appear in national magazines as discussions sparked on news shows, while fringe petitions wielded by religious groups asked, "What sort of nonsense have our innocent children been suckered into now?" It is not a coincidence that, shortly after *Destroyer*, evangelical protesters began hounding KISS shows with signs containing the dubious acronym, "Knights in Service of Satan." On a grander scale, there appeared to be—as with most art forms that mythically explode out of nowhere overnight—a serious deconstruction of KISS's popularity as a calculated brainwashing by insatiable capitalists perpetuated upon a gullible populace. The first part of the equation is unquestionably true, but the second is highly suspect. KISS, in its dedication to the airtight parameters of The Act and ultimately *Destroyer*, was as transparent a statement as an artist could make as to its defining principles. Deriding the tenets of something built to be just what it has professed—whether artistic, political, religious, or consumer-based—is laughably naïve.

Beyond the glut of overhyped press—both scathing and curious—KISS faced in the weeks and months following the release of *Destroyer* and on the Spirit of '76 tour, a theme recurred throughout the ensuing wildly successful years at the top of not only the rock world but the entire entertainment/celebrity culture, and which culminated in an NBC report hosted by crusty journalist Edwin Newman titled *In the Land of Hype and Glory*, which aired on January 10, 1978. The one-hour "news" special begins at a traveling carnival beneath the glowing lights of a gaudy Ferris wheel, as a barker promises "wonders, freaks, curiosities," which cues Newman, in his best cynical façade, to muse about "suckers being born every minute" and "more to the point, now there's a consumer born every ten seconds." He then proposes that, for the next forty minutes, the National Broadcast Company, itself propped up by entertainment and advertising, would dissect the effects of using mass communication or "routine exaggeration we've become accustomed to"—a more condescending chunk of hypocritical drivel is hard to imagine—on the American consumer, which he describes as "intense and desperate." Less than two minutes in, and directly following the words "deceptive and outrageous," comes a shot of Paul Stanley onstage, shouting his famous "Hit it!" from "Black Diamond," and the screen is awash with the pomp and dazzle of a full-blown KISS show.

NBC's hatchet job on The Act, now fully realized and seemingly unstoppable, ruminates on subjects covered extensively in this book: "style over substance," "gimmicks," "sold and packaged," "controlling public reaction," "superhero portrayal," "projecting the notion of power," all phrases used in the piece. However, the most ambiguous invective thrown around in Newman's report is "exploitation," which again presumes that there is a victim in this scenario—as if the mighty news organization is going to save a generation from its enslaved torpor.

Newman takes time out from his screed for a group interview in which he reads a *SoHo Weekly News* editorial describing rock and roll as being "bludgeoned to death" by "insidious and boring" trappings that had been previously covered in the extended opening. After some philosophizing by Stanley and a monosyllabic defense by Frehley, Simmons asks the question that was answered the minute KISS was formed: "Why are you looking for meaning when there is none?"

Of course, this wasn't entirely true either. *Destroyer* had meaning—a deeper meaning than KISS had ever attempted before—and that would become the cognitive thread to what forced NBC to dedicate an hour of precious network primetime to psychoanalyzing it. Like so many in the industry that had pegged KISS as a goof, a heavy-metal sideshow, Newman and his incredulous staff scrambled to understand the sudden cultural impact, the almost cult-like status, of KISS, because it *was* real—emotionally, thematically, and now financially. Consequently, the band and its camp would also struggle with taming this thing they had unleashed. It was stardom or bust for each and every one of them, and now it was exploding in all directions at once.

After the Spirit of '76 juggernaut, the obscenely expensive tours would continue to crisscross the U.S., each one becoming bigger and badder and ever more absurd, selling out the largest arenas and eventually the legendary Madison Square Garden (the Mecca of rock shows and the promised land for four NYC boys). KISS would head to Japan, where the band would be received as all-conquering superheroes.

"We had now entered the era of institutional KISS where KISS's influence would emanate like rays into every aspect of pop culture," writes C. K. Lendt, then vice president of Glickman/Marks Management, in *KISS and Sell*. "KISS could do everything and anything; they were omnipotent and omniscient. It was pretty heady stuff. This was no longer an ordinary job working for a rock group, if such a job was ordinary. I was connected to something on a cosmic scale. Everything about the show of shows now fell into place. This show would travel the countryside and bring KISS in all their glory to their devoted followers. It would be a shrine that would be transported across the land, stopping all the way for committed believers to pay homage to KISS and for KISS to perform their ritual. And the followers would flock to this traveling shrine to bear witness at their own version of Lourdes. It was intoxicating."[27]

Along the way, as *Destroyer* faded in the rearview mirror, the creative presentation began to display less of an undercurrent of mystique. This was due in large part to the absence of Bob Ezrin in the studio. Much of the subject matter for songs shifted back to the cock-rock that dominated the band's pre-*Destroyer* work. "I was shocked that they went with Eddie Kramer on the next record," recalls Corky Stasiak, who would stay on as engineer. "After *Destroyer* I thought this was a match made in heaven, Bob Ezrin and KISS, because these guys were a lot better than they even thought and were willing to take direction and giving Bob what he needed, trusting he had their best interests at heart, and if they couldn't give it to him, trust that he'd get the right people to make it the best KISS album possible."[28]

Yet a hint of what Ezrin introduced to KISS still resonated: Simmons continued to find material to support his sexually charged Demon persona, such as "Calling Dr. Love," "Almost Human," and "Larger Than Life." Stanley made attempts to build on the wounded ego of "Do You Love Me?" in such personal songs as "I Want You," "I Stole Your Love," and "I Still Love You," passing along another slow pop tune, "Hard Luck Woman," which he originally penned for rock crooner Rod Stewart, to Peter Criss to keep up the momentum of "Beth."

Unfortunately, what would also resonate is the backlash from the initial response from fans to *Destroyer* and the band's paranoid reaction to it, which eventually severed the once seemingly impenetrable bond of The Act. With Frehley and Criss carping about wanting to leave the band, Stanley and Simmons agreed to bring in Eddie Kramer for the follow-up records, *Rock and Roll Over* and *Love Gun*, both of which were smash hits. "Bringing in Eddie was probably to keep harmony in the band," says Stasiak. "I am sure Ace and Peter, having heard the cheers of thousands of KISS fans, had a few things to say night after night, touring that record, away from the confines of the studio and the demands of Bob and the aims for perfection, and listening to fans and hangers-on ask them why they had choirs and ballads and calliopes on their record. What did they need that for?"[29]

"The truth is the change scared us, too," Paul Stanley admits in his memoir. "Maybe we didn't want to have a nanny this time around, either—someone telling us how to do everything and blowing a whistle in our faces. We figured we'd done our apprenticeship. And Peter and Ace certainly had no desire to work with Bob again. We decided to try a more meat-and-potatoes approach, go back to basics."[30]

"From the very beginning, the hardest thing about working with KISS is those guys didn't like to be told what to do you," Stasiak concludes. "Remember: rock musicians are generally immature when it comes to a controlled environment. They don't want to be reprimanded. They want you to kiss their asses and 'yes' them to death. Eddie Kramer was more in line with being charitable in the studio to the guys. He was English—really South African, but with an English demeanor to get along to go along. Very rarely did Kramer come up with musical ideas for the guys during *Rock and Roll Over*. One of the jobs of a producer is to make the artist feel at home and comfortable with you, so you can pull what you need from them, and for the most part an artist doesn't want a producer's fingerprints on a record—they want it to be *all them*. So when they go out and promote it and tour it, they are on the hook for it, good or bad. Even the positive feedback they got for *Destroyer* had a lot to do with Bob's influence, and that was written, too—'Bob Ezrin did this and Bob Ezrin did that'—and they found themselves having to say, 'Hey, we played on the record, these are our songs, it's a KISS record!' *Rock and Roll Over* is a great record, but it's not *Destroyer*."[31]

Attempting to reach for the creativity or the perfection attempted on *Destroyer* mattered little in the new superstar world for KISS. Follow-ups forged by the success of *Destroyer* meant the band was entering an era in which it could release just about anything and it would sell, including what turned out to be a haphazard attempt to recapture *Alive!* with *Alive II*. KISS was a brand with an image that now, instead of hindering popularity, seemed to precede it. There didn't appear to be any overt signs the wheels would come off.

However, bristling at being treated like underlings by Stanley and Simmons, feeling uncomfortable with the "selling of KISS" as a marketing scheme for a mass audience, and suffering from increased drug and alcohol abuse, Criss and Frehley would force the band's management to try and smooth things over by convincing Casablanca to release separate solo albums by all four members, to be launched on the same day in September of 1978—an unprecedented and never-repeated event in popular music. Although an excellent publicity stunt, and something that kept The Act steamrolling for another year, the KISS solo albums were mostly a bust, due to Casablanca pre-shipping far too many in an attempt to achieve platinum status for all four records. Ace Frehley initially outsold the other three, thanks to the hit "New York Groove," while Gene Simmons's effort would continue to sell over time, thanks in part to his singular celebrity as the Demon and more so to his tabloid life dating Cher.

None of this helped to protect The Act from its own demons: the flipside of ego, brashness, and the relentless pursuit of fame and fortune—jealousy, paranoia, and excess.

Peter Criss was the first to go. By his own admission, he was done, physically and mentally, by 1979, so much so that the band hastened his exit, replacing him on all but one track on the band's seventh studio album, *Dynasty*, the penultimate KISS record with all four members pictured on the cover, and the last with all of the original members contributing something. The follow-up, *Unmasked*, was completed entirely without Criss, despite his likeness appearing in yet another post-*Destroyer*, comic book–style cover.

The next off the gravy train was Ace Frehley. His solo record's success, and an increased confidence to pen and sing his own songs (from *Love Gun* on, he would contribute at least one song and would actually sing it), would lead him to finally demand his walking papers in 1982. The final straw for Frehley came in the considerable shadow of Bob Ezrin's return to the producer's chair, as the band feared it had completely lost its rock credibility and hoped to appease critics by cobbling a half-baked concept into a project called *Music from 'The Elder'*. Ezrin—by both his own admission and the band members' recollections—was compromised by years of cocaine and alcohol abuse and, having barely survived the harrowing experience of realizing the brilliant Pink Floyd opus *The Wall*, burned out. Frehley only received backing tracks to record his parts at his Connecticut home, and some of those were shortened or replaced, as trust issues from the *Destroyer* sessions sealed his fate.

By 1983, with new members installed, KISS would decide to remove the makeup and thus the original mystique and legend of The Act. And although the band, which continued to be led by Simmons and Stanley, would remarkably secure a place alongside the 1980s "hair band" craze, it would never again capture the pomp and glory of its '70s heyday, when for four years KISS was everything it was formed to achieve: total domination of a vast array of mediums beyond that of any rock band before or since.

22

Legacy

KISS was my first favorite band. It was my first concert. It was the band that made me love rock and roll. They were our generation's Beatles, our generation's Elvis, our generation's Rolling Stones. They made everyone who loved that band want to pick up an instrument.... And the first song that ignited my KISS engine was "Detroit Rock City." It's the song I tried to learn on guitar, semi-successfully, as a twelve-year-old. It made an impression on me later in my career.
—Guitarist, Tom Morello, Rage Against the Machine/
Bruce Springsteen's E. Street Band, during the press
conference for KISS's induction into the
Rock and Roll Hall of Fame, 2014[1]

The morning I began to write this final chapter, I was driving in my car, listening to ESPN Radio's popular morning show *Mike & Mike*, broadcast live from Detroit, Michigan, the site of the 2014 NFL season's opening *Monday Night Football* game between the NY Giants and the hometown Lions. Coming out of a commercial break, piercing through the speakers, was Motown's unofficial anthem, "Detroit Rock City." Later in the day, while working with the TV tuned to AMC—the network home to some of television's most popular and highly acclaimed shows, including *Mad Men* and *Breaking Bad*, both pop-culture touchstones inspiring scores of merchandising—I hear "Shout It Out Loud" and quickly crook my neck to see a promo for a reality show called *4th and Loud* starring Gene and Paul and their foray in founding the Arena Football League's newest and most outlandishly promoted team, the L.A. KISS. Still later that day, reading a story on Yahoo's home page, I see a Gene Simmons quote from *Esquire* magazine: "Rock did not die of old age. It was murdered." The tweeted response from Foo Fighters lead man Dave Grohl to Simmons begins "Not so fast, Mr. God of Thunder."

Twenty-eight years after the release of *Destroyer*, three of its most prominent songs are front-and-center in the mainstream of pop culture (radio, TV,

Internet, and social media). The album that changed everything for KISS remains ingrained in our social consciousness, further proving how wide the chasm gapes between rock star and cultural icon. The most notable evidence of this may be that in *Billboard*'s Top 100 Albums of 1976, *Destroyer* settled in at #55, right in the middle of the pack. Not stellar, but not putrid either. For KISS, this was a gargantuan leap forward, but that is not the point. How many albums that finished ahead of it still resonate in pop culture? Rod Stewart's *A Night on the Town* (#6)? Neil Diamond's *A Beautiful Noise* (#9)? Whoever the heck Boney M is (#17)? Manfred Mann's Earth Band (#30)? Sure, we all loved the Eagles' *Hotel California* (#1), or maybe most of us did, or some of us . . . well, someone must have loved that record, or certainly we dug Stevie Wonder's *Songs in the Key of Life* right behind it, or the Abba record at #3, but none of the artists before or after #55 would appear in a 2014 animated Google Start television commercial, as KISS did.

Speaking of the search engine giant, Google lists *Destroyer* as "the most frequently mentioned KISS album on the web." Today the record that took its share of critical hits appears in most of the major "top album" lists. Although it barely makes the cut at #489, it is the only KISS studio effort in *Rolling Stone*'s official Top 500 Albums of All-Time (*Alive!* comes in at 159). Yet upon the band's long-overdue induction into the Rock and Roll Hall of Fame in March of 2014, the magazine's Top Ten KISS Albums ranks *Destroyer* third, behind *Alive!* and *KISS*. For what it's worth, the Best Ever Albums web site—a composite of fan sites and critics lists—puts *Destroyer* as the #1 KISS album, just ahead of *Alive!* Digital Dream Door, which boasts the most rock lists online, also finds room for *Destroyer* in its Top 200 Albums list, at #199. It's the only KISS record mentioned, just as it is the only one to make author Robert Dimery's enjoyable 2005 book *1001 Albums You Must Hear Before You Die*.

But beyond revisionist accolades, *Destroyer* provided KISS that elusive vehicle to leave its peers in the rock world to become part of Americana, as it once absorbed and then fully realized in the creation of The Act. In fact, it was *Destroyer* that finally fused KISS and The Act to form a singular entity only achieved by American musical acts that truly reflect their times, putting them in the company of Al Jolson (the teens and '20s), Frank Sinatra (the '40s and '50s), Elvis Presley (the '50s and '60s), Madonna (the '80s and '90s), and Jay Z (the '90s to the early 2000s). Many American acts of the 1970s sold more records than KISS or had a string of bigger hits—to name a few, there's Billy Joel, the aforementioned Stevie Wonder, and the Eagles; even the godfather of shock rock, Alice Cooper, who in his own right became something of a beloved American icon. But through its characterization and later merchandising and expansion into film, television, and comic books, which were amazingly perpetuated through KISS conventions and expos that for decades drew thousands of fans to trade memorabilia and celebrate the band like no other save the Beatles, it was as if KISS literally became a brand, like Coke and EXXON, the NFL, Nike, and Apple. Right before the bottom fell out in late 1979, there were plans for a KISS theme park, which would seem laughable for any other star save for, apparently, Dolly Parton. Twenty years later, during the hype and nostalgia of the reunion tours—wherein Gene, Paul, Ace, and Peter found themselves once again gracing magazine covers, making guest appearances on sitcoms, and hawking ever more merchandise—New Line Cinema released a period piece called, of course, *Detroit Rock City*, about the KISS fan phenomena of the '70s—the brand still alive and kicking.

Moreover, the KISS era resonates among the Gen X musicians that KISS inspired—not just musically but spiritually, psychologically, and passionately—and in almost all cases, like yours truly, it trends toward the prepubescent, when we were all so young and impressionable but ready to burst out and express ourselves, in deep need of a vehicle to, well, shout it out . . . *loud*.

In 1994, twenty years after the band's first album, Mercury records released a KISS tribute collection titled *Kiss My Ass: Classic KISS Regrooved*. The eclectic assembly of artists taking turns with the band's '70s material speaks to the impressive reach of its influence over my generation, which by the early 1990s had emerged in the dying groans of the previous decade's MTV crossover explosion. Among the list was Lenny Kravitz (throwback analog-embracing funk/rock performer), Garth Brooks (modern country-music star), Anthrax (one of the celebrated "Big Four" of speed metal), Yoshiki Hayashi (Japanese heavy-metal star credited with pioneering the culture's *visual kei* movement), Die Ärzte (German punk-rock band), the Mighty Mighty Bosstones (ska band), and Toad the Wet Sprocket (alternative rock band).

On the celebratory occasion of the original lineup's 1996 reunion for a highly rated *MTV Unplugged* session, wherein Ace and Peter joined Gene and Paul for, among other KISS classics, a version of "Beth," which roused a standing ovation from the rapturous studio audience—a moment the song's composer said was "like that old feeling never went away"[2]—the once hidden guilty-pleasure of KISS poured from the woodwork. Joey Ramone of the punk pioneer Ramones, a fellow Queens resident, told reporters on several occasions of having attended the band's very first shows. The Ramones had done a reverse of The Act, dressing as punk teenagers, in ripped jeans and leather jackets, all sporting the same hair length and each member taking on the last name of the band—a mash-up of the Alice Cooper concept with the indisputable uniformity of KISS. Paul Westerberg, the leader of alternative stalwarts the Replacements, whose seminal album *Let It Be* (1984) included a stirring version of "Black Diamond," admitted to KISS's biographers that although he may have been ashamed to openly admit to his devotion to KISS, he spent hours in his room poring over the cinematic intricacies of *Destroyer*. This is something Joe Elliott of Def Leopard also admitted in Robert Dimery's record guide. "I bought it purely for the sleeve," he said.[3] Motley Crew, which led the next wave of hard rock during the late-'80s heavy-metal resurgence—which itself may have been the closest to the original KISS presentation of makeup, leather, street-tough enthusiasm—paid overdue homage to their mentors. Even the offspring of an all-mighty Beatle, Julian Lennon, who by the early 1980s had carved out a modest music career of his own, proudly told the world his first album was *Alive II*.

Two of grunge rock's most influential and successful bands, Nirvana and Pearl Jam, may have discovered their musical roots in punk and the ballsy din of Neil Young's Crazy Horse period, but they were awakened as kids by the mesmerizing force of The Act. The doomed and later deified Kurt Cobain led Nirvana through a pretty representative version of *Destroyer*'s "Do You Love Me?" during sessions for its first album, *Bleach*—a recording that ended up on a KISS covers compilation in 1992. Cobain moves between a mock-Stanley preen into his trademark anguished screeches, bringing to life Bob Ezrin, Paul Stanley, and Kim Fowley's query as to where stardom and passion collide, eerily presaging the troubled singer's suicide two years later. Pearl Jam's Mike McCready, who is pictured as a preteen in the April 2014 issue of *Rolling Stone* dressed as Peter Criss on Halloween of 1976, the week KISS performed "King of the Night Time World" and "Beth" on national television, wrote for the magazine, "They were the Beatles to me. They are the reason I started playing music." In fact, on the band's 1991 debut album, *Ten*, on a song ironically titled "Alive," McCready had nicked Ace's lead from "She" (which Frehley admitted he'd nicked from the Doors' Robbie Krieger on "Five to One"). The band has also occasionally unfurled its own version of "Black Diamond" onstage, even once with Ace in tow.

Chad Smith, drummer for the funk/rock fusion Red Hot Chili Peppers, has spent most of his public life retelling a story of sitting in the twelfth row for the famous Fin Costello shot for the back of *Alive!* "I was there! I saw it happening!"[4] In 2012, he serendipitously appeared with Bob Ezrin in a symposium called the Mentor Sessions for the Nimbus School of Recording Arts in Toronto.

Amid all this generational revelry, KISS launched a reunion tour, conceived after the band reappeared in makeup together for the first time during the 38th Annual Grammy Awards with rap icon Tupac Shakur. The announcement was emceed by late-night television icon Conan O'Brien on the USS *Intrepid* (a U.S. Navy icon). Forty thousand tickets for the first show sold out in less than an hour. The tour, which was the band's highest grossing ever, lasted for 192 shows over 11 months and earned $43.6 million, cementing KISS, exactly twenty years after the summer of *Destroyer*, as the top-drawing concert act of 1996. Six of the twenty-two songs played as part of these historic shows, including a live version of "Shout It Out Loud" chosen for the official reunion video to promote the tour, were taken from *Destroyer*—more than any other KISS album.

In fact, *Destroyer* holds the distinction of having had all of its songs played live at some point in the band's career. The final number to grace the stage, "Great Expectations," was recorded with the Melbourne Symphony Orchestra, arranged by famed composer/conductor David Campbell and accompanied by the Australian Children's Choir, in 2003. Seven of the fifteen songs performed for the one-off session with both the full orchestra and the Melbourne Symphony Ensemble hailed from *Destroyer*, allowing Peter Criss to finally sing "Beth" live in all its grandeur without a canned backing track. The show would be released on CD and DVD later that year as *Alive IV*.

Destroyer is well represented on each of the thirteen KISS compilations released to date, and in most cases songs from the album outnumber those of any other KISS record, almost without exception including "Detroit Rock City," "Shout It Out Loud," and "Beth" (which was curiously released with a vocal by Peter Criss replacement, Eric Carr, on 1988's *Smashes, Trashes & Hits*). The songs—all of which were conceived as part of a singular package—have indeed stood the test of time.

A few years after I interviewed Counting Crows front man Adam Duritz for a 2008 *Aquarian Weekly* cover story in which we reveled in '70s music and pop culture, I happened to see a recording of him performing live from Town Hall in NYC wearing a *Destroyer* T-shirt. Years earlier, Duritz had begun wearing shirts depicting the albums nearest and dearest to his heart, so I pressed him in 2014 on what the album may have meant to him. "Oh yeah, I got *Destroyer* when I was in my very first band," the fifty-year-old Duritz told me excitedly. "I really loved that record. In fact, quite honestly, that's my first experience with singing songs out behind school. Singing 'Beth' to a bunch of girls and saying, 'Oh, I see. This is kind of a good reaction! I should probably be in a band, that's a good idea.' I remember that, at thirteen or twelve—I don't know how old I was when that came out, but I was in a band right after that. Your thirteen-year-old motivation of being in a band is entirely different from later. It's really simple. It's like, 'Oh, girls like this.' So, yeah KISS had a big, big effect on me back then. That's a great record, ya know?"[5]

Another professional life altered by *Destroyer* is that of multimedia talent Eddie Trunk, who has written a two-volume history of heavy metal, *Essential Hard Rock and Heavy Metal*, hosts a nationally syndicated rock radio show on New York's Q104.3 as well as two SiriusXM satellite radio shows, and co-hosts the popular VH1 show *That Metal Show*, all of which have featured members of KISS, most notably Ace Frehley and Peter Criss. As vice president of the influential Megaforce Records at the tender age of twenty-five, Trunk would sign Ace Frehley to record his first post-KISS solo effort, *Frehley's Comet*. Criss and Frehley even invited Trunk to KISS's induction into the Rock and Roll Hall of Fame in 2014, the details of which he described hilariously the next day on his SiriusXM show.

It all started for the now fifty-year-old in the spring of 1976. "*Destroyer* was my first KISS album and my first real exposure to hard rock," he wrote to me, upon my completion of this book. "It was truly the gateway album and band for me that made me consumed with hard rock and set me on the path I have been on for the last thirty-one years. I vividly recall getting it at my local record store, dropping the needle on the vinyl, hearing the open to 'Detroit Rock City,' and staring at the album cover. From that point forward, for a long time, KISS was the only thing that mattered, and the album still holds up today."[6]

"I got *Destroyer* the day it came out," recalled fifty-one-year-old Scott Ian, guitarist and founder of Anthrax, in an interview for this book. "I was completely blown away by the Ken Kelly art when I saw it in a magazine. KISS already owned my life by that point. When I got it, I remember being obsessed with the intro to 'Detroit Rock City'; with the news report and the guy getting ready to go and he's singing 'Rock and Roll All Nite' along with the radio. I would listen to that over and over—remember I had it on vinyl, so you would have to keep moving the needle back. It was weird; kinda created this world. I was this twelve-year-old kid listening to the record and I felt like there was some guy in Detroit and I was listening in on his life or something. I just remember being fascinated by that whole record. I mean, great, great songs on that album. I loved it."[7]

Destroyer, which was certified multi-platinum (signifying more than two million units sold) by the Recording Industry of America in September 2011, ushered KISS unto the lofty perch it was designed to reach, and in many ways remains on today—beyond music or mere celebrity into what Gene Simmons today unapologetically calls KISStianity. (Not bad for an Israeli immigrant.) His success story is only one of many born in the saga of *Destroyer*, forged during those crucial four months when KISS was staggering, as if courageously holding on like Rocky Balboa in the 1976 underdog escapist (in very KISS-like fashion) hit film *Rocky*, which would go on to beat out the ultra-realist reflection of the times, *All the President's Men*, for Best Picture at the 1977 Academy Awards.

In KISS's corner was Bill Aucoin, who, in the wake of *Destroyer*, would build a mini-empire of his own before drugs and overzealous spending sank Aucoin Management. He and the band parted ways in 1982, just as KISS was planning on ditching the makeup and thus the image he'd exploited so brilliantly. The break was partly due, according to sources at the time, to his partnering with Howard/Marks, as the agency had completely taken over the KISS machine—something many interviewed for this book predicted would happen once Aucoin shared business interest in the KISS enterprise. Paul Stanley states in his memoir that the once guiding light of KISS had succumbed to the excesses of the rock world and was simply unable to maintain the pace and control that once led the spiritual charge of The Act. Although he stayed in touch with the band while working on several side projects in the ensuing years, Aucoin would fail to achieve the heights he did while managing KISS. No one would ever again be as influential within The Act's inner sanctum. He died of complications due to prostate cancer in 2010 at the age of sixty-six.

Aucoin's one-time lover and protégé, Sean Delaney, would parlay his many years developing the KISS stage image into co-writing songs with the band on the follow-ups to *Destroyer*, co-producing Gene Simmons and assisting with Peter Criss's 1978 solo albums, and later releasing a forgotten one of his own, *Highway*. Many of those interviewed for this book agree that Delaney was "always around" the band until the early '80s, breaking off just when KISS abandoned the makeup and costumes, which he helped to develop into three-dimensional characters on and off the stage. He would die in 2003 at age fifty-three from heart failure after battling advanced diabetes.

On the momentum of *Destroyer*, Neil Bogart's Casablanca Records became the height of excess in the late '70s, gathering a cadre of disco acts and producing monster hits until the genre's inevitable fall from grace. By decade's end, his rabid spending and drug abuse had, like that of his friend and partner in wild abandon, Bill Aucoin, tanked the label, which sent the KISS recording contract into chaos, since all agreements between the band and the label constituted Bogart being in charge. This led to a lucrative six-album deal negotiated by the Howard Marks Agency with its new parent label, Polygram, allowing Simmons and Stanley to resurrect KISS during the 1980s hair-band era. Bogart, ever the gambler and fearless entrepreneur, rallied within months of Casablanca's demise with Boardwalk Records, boasting hits by Joan Jett ("I Love Rock 'n' Roll") and launching '80s power-band Night Ranger. He died of lymphoma in May of 1982 at the age of thirty-nine.

Burned-out and disillusioned by the pomp and excess of Casablanca, executive vice president Larry Harris abandoned ship in 1979. He would return to work in music again as a consultant or in management while hosting numerous syndicated radio shows, and went on to publish the wildly entertaining *And Party Every Day—The Inside Story of Casablanca Records*, which he revealed during our discussion for this book was to be the primary source for an upcoming movie project called *Spinning Gold*, co-produced by Justin Timberlake, who would play Bogart, and directed by Spike Lee. (At the time of this writing, he is working on a baby-boomer magazine project.)

Scott Shannon, the man who broke "Beth," which turned *Destroyer* from hit album to a seminal piece of KISStory, left Casablanca and the music business altogether in the early '80s to return to his first love, radio, where he would become one of the most recognized voices in the industry. Beginning a peripatetic ride through the dial from Washington, D.C., through Tampa, Florida, where he developed the craze known as "The Morning Zoo," he eventually landed in New York City to launch Z100 radio and helm the *Z Morning Zoo* with partner Ross Brittain. Within seventy-four days the station went from the bottom of the ratings to #1. After a short stint in Los Angeles, Shannon returned to put a jolt into New York's WPLJ's ratings as host of *The Big Show*, a role he held for twenty-three years before decamping to WCBS oldies radio, where today he is the morning man after nearly forty years in the business. Shannon would eventually be inducted into the National Association of Broadcasters Hall of Fame and the National Radio Hall of Fame, as well as joining several prominent disc jockeys responsible for the evolution of pop music in the Rock and Roll Hall of Fame.

Marks/Glickman and KISS parted ways toward the end of the 1980s when, in a scene that's all too familiar in the entertainment world, Simmons and Stanley became apoplectic that they had no real financial nest egg for their "retirement." The agency claimed, as did Casablanca in those critical months of legal tension that nearly derailed *Destroyer*, that keeping KISS's notorious professional extravagance afloat in the leaner years had sapped any reserves. The obligatory lawsuits followed, and soon anyone who had much to do with KISS during *Destroyer* was fired, including C. K. Lendt, who as vice president had always had a hands-on role with the band. He writes forlornly in his book, *KISS and Sell*, of the final somber happenstance meetings with Gene and Paul after the deluge, in which neither seemed the slightest bit moved by any of it.

Dennis Woloch, the art/creative director at Howard Marks Advertising, continued the wild ride with KISS well into the 1980s, designing seven more KISS albums and the four joint solo records, until he too was a victim of the band's split with the agency. His talents have since spread out to creating logos for products and companies, as well as designs in the entertainment and corporate world. At the time of this writing, he lives in New York City, and his Dennis Woloch Design company is still going strong. "You look at the stuff we designed for *Destroyer* and it's so visual and visceral," he says proudly, looking back. "It just was a perfect marriage of a client and an art style. It *had* to happen."[8]

"Dennis's idea of creating a cartoon around KISS, like Superman, that had not yet existed before in the rock world, is what made them so huge," says his partner, Vinnie DeGerlando, the man who named *Destroyer* and gave a military feel to the fabled KISS Army.[9] He would also continue to work on designs for KISS albums and tour rollouts until the eventual split with the agency. Today he lives what he describes as a "simple artist's life" in a small Jersey Shore town.[10] Having published three books of his photography and taken commissions for his paintings, he is currently working on his first children's book. "I have a three-year-old grandson who saw a painting I did it for the Mexican Day of the Dead featuring Superman with the iconic mask. I asked him, 'Who's this?' and he knew right away that it was Superman. KISS lives on today because they picked up that iconic image through the heroic cartoon Dennis envisioned for *Destroyer*."[11]

After Mark Ravitz set the concert world on its ear with the groundbreaking Spirit of '76 tour, he found himself and his work in heavy demand, leading to him designing sets for both ends of the pop spectrum, from Frank Sinatra to the Backstreet Boys, while also realizing the sets for two of David Bowie's largest and most lucrative tours, Serious Moonlight (1983) and Glass Spider (1987). In 1981, there was talk of bringing Ravitz back into the KISS camp for a conceptual tour for the *Music from 'The Elder'* project, which was to present a stage show that would illustrate the album's arcane storyline, but due to the album's poor sales numbers and the critical rebuke it received the tour never materialized. In the end, it was Ravitz's Herculean work on the bombastic design of the Spirit of '76 tour that broke the mold for extravagant rock shows worthy of the pomp and fantasy of *Destroyer*. "I was real happy with the *Destroyer* tour," he told me confidently. "We were doing things in an arena setting that hadn't been seen before, especially with the light that went up toward the balconies that connected the arena to the stage and the dynamic shape of the lighting towers. All the elements of that stage were custom designed."[12] At the time of this writing, his company, Ravitz Design, works its magic with corporations all over the U.S.

Bob Gruen, whose relationship with KISS was severed when the famed photographer began immersing himself into the burgeoning NYC punk scene of the mid-to-late '70s, where he became the movement's chief visual archivist, taking some of the first published photographs of the Ramones, Television, Blondie, and most of the CBGB's underground revolution. Soon he would be capturing the most recognizable images of the era while touring with the Sex Pistols and the Clash all the way into the 1990s, with pseudo-punk offspring Green Day. His intimate photographs of John and Yoko as their son Sean was being born are some of the most moving in his canon. Shortly after our time discussing his singular place as the man who snapped the photos of the famed First KISS Grand Orchestral and Choral Recording Session came the premiere of a documentary on his life's work, *Rock 'N Roll Exposed: The Photography of Bob Gruen*. You can still find Bob out there shooting rock photographs, as ever, working out of the same cramped but cozy office in the Westbeth Artists Community building on Manhattan's Lower West Side and continuing to sell prints of his work online.

Kim Fowley, a man for whom my three-hour interview would have itself made a hell of a book, possessed more grit and energy than that of ten men two-thirds his age. His immense contribution to the shaping and expanse of *Destroyer*'s songwriting and its imagery helped build his already legendary status in the history of rock and roll. "Suddenly Kim Fowley is consistent," he colorfully intoned to me, during our late-night, one-way discussion. "I had hits before and I had hits since and hits during the *Destroyer* time, but KISS was about to be the biggest band in the world, and to land two songs on *Destroyer* would be like today in sales some guy getting two songs on a Lady Gaga record. Like *wow*, because she's gigantic now. Now, will she have the career that KISS had? Probably not. That's thirty-five years of success, non-stop. It was just very significant, and I enjoyed all the money. I collected every dime due me. I always got paid and continue to get paid, thank you Gene and Paul, and it's been a tremendous credit. I got laid a lot with a lot of girls who couldn't fuck KISS, but got to at least fuck the guy who co-wrote two songs on *Destroyer*. I still get fucked today because of KISS."[13] A week after this book was presented to the publisher, Fowley succumbed to bladder cancer at the age of seventy-five.

Fowley astutely pointed out that in the only photograph ever taken of him and KISS together—taken, incidentally, by Bob Gruen backstage at the Anaheim Stadium show, at the very height of the Spirit of '76 tour—he is as tall as KISS *without* the heels. At that event, Gene Simmons introduced him to Japanese photojournalist Ginger Suzuki—the woman Fowley credited with breaking his band the Runaways for the first time. It was, in the end, the success of the Runaways, forever captured in proper Hollywood fashion in the 2010 film *The Runaways* (in which Michael Shannon masterfully portrays Fowley) that forevermore cemented the status of this pop raconteur, and the man who co-wrote "King of the Night Time World" and "Do You Love Me?" "I am a four-time cancer survivor," he boasted to me. "Survivor of pneumonia nine times, polio twice, positional vertigo, currently suffering from post-radical-cancer-surgery depression recall—I walk with a cane, and I have a girlfriend who's a model who is half my age and we're touring."[14] At the time of our conversation, he still hosted a show on SiriusXM and had recently published the first volume of his memoirs, *Lord of Garbage*.

The visual impact of *Destroyer* on the pop-art world immediately catapulted the man who painted its cover into the big time. From the shadow of the great Frank Frazetta, Ken Kelly emerged as a hot commodity. The money he earned for the project alone, for which he was paid twice due to the old costumes and violent imagery of "*Destroyer* Brown" being replaced with the final, stunning superhero splash of the now classic "*Destroyer* Blue," which transformed KISS for an entire generation, helped him put a down-payment on his first home. Kelly moved out of his one-room walkup and into the mainstream, displaying his talents for various toy lines, Dark Horse Comics' *Star Wars* series, and album covers for several bands, most noticeably Rainbow's *Rising*, which came out later in 1976. KISS would rush back to him to paint the medieval fantasy–based cover for 1978's *Love Gun*, which in a very real way reflected the idol-worship The Act had received since it came powering off that mountain on *Destroyer*.

"Every aspect of my life changed because of *Destroyer*," Kelly told me, as we wrapped up our time together. "It was monumental. Still is. And I thank God KISS has been an active part of my life. It's not like it dies. George Lucas owns eighteen originals of mine in his office in his home and I've had other parts of my career that have gone through the roof too, yet it's 'You're the KISS guy! You're the KISS guy!' and I don't mind it, I love it. I mean, it's just, 'Yup, yup. Those are mine.' And now it's forty-something years ago and KISS has gone through the roof with so many different albums, but it all started with *Destroyer*. Yes, they had done *Alive!*, but they really went through the stratosphere with *Destroyer*, and I played a role."[15]

Today, Kelly sells oil paintings, lithographs, and prints of original drawings of his most famous pieces on his web site and speaks at various functions and schools. His generous gift of an original pencil drawing of the *Destroyer* cover, which he sent to me a few months after our discussion, came with a signed note: "Good luck with the book." It hangs today in a prominent place in my home and will always remind me of the first time I laid eyes on the LP at the age of thirteen, and of these past few years I spent putting the *Destroyer* story on paper. He still works with Gene Simmons on designing his basses, and his appearances at KISS conventions and fan expos are among the most popular.

So, where is the original fate-altering, mind-blowing *Destroyer* painting today? "The story I got from the doctor who treated Bill [Aucoin] while he was dying, which he told me at his wake in Manhattan, was that Bill, while he was cleaning out one of his mansions—because he fell into financial troubles later in his life—and he had a stack of stuff he was throwing out in one corner and a stack of stuff he was keeping in one corner, accidentally put *Destroyer* in the throw-out pile and it actually was tossed in the garbage. That's the story I got from the doctor. I believe it, because I have never ever heard anyone say they had it. I actually met the guy who bought the original *Love Gun* painting recently, but never *Destroyer*. So I think it went into the back of a New York City garbage truck and got crushed up and it's, as the doctor put it, part of the ages now."[16]

One of the great thrills of doing research and conducting interviews for this book was the friendship I forged with Dick Wagner. The "Invisible Virtuoso"—a name I bestowed upon him that he loved—lived the rock-and-roll life to the hilt, putting it all down in a stirring 2011 autobiography titled after perhaps his biggest and finest song, *Not Only Women Bleed*, to which I was honored to provide a blurb on the back cover alongside his musical brethren, Alice Cooper and Bob Ezrin. Wagner's songwriting talents leaped to the fore after his work on *Destroyer*, as he and Cooper penned the star's biggest hits of the late '70s, "I Never Cry" (#12), "You and Me" (#9), and "How You Gonna See Me Now?" (#12). After working with Nils Lofgren and later on Air Supply's 1985 hit "Just as I Am," Wagner continued playing, even after a massive heart attack in 2007 that led to him being in a coma for two weeks before awakening with paralysis in his left arm. In 2009, he reunited with Cooper and Ezrin for an unlikely sequel, *Welcome 2 My Nightmare*, having in the interim miraculously survived two brain surgeries. In late 2013, he wrote and produced a song called "If I Had the Time (I Could Change the World)" in support of St. Jude's Children's Research Hospital in Memphis, backed by some of his veteran rocker friends, including Mark Farner of Grand Funk, Trini Lopez, and Elliott Easton of the Cars. He tragically died of heart failure seven months later at the age of seventy-one. I miss him every day.

At the hearty age of eighty-six, Allan Macmillan is retired and relaxing in his hometown of Toronto, Canada. After conducting the First KISS Grand

Orchestral and Choral Recording Session—likely his most visible moment in a long and distinguished music career—he moved on to work extensively with famed producer Ron Nevison through the 1980s on records by Flo & Eddy, UFO, the Babys, and Dave Mason. Later in 1976, Macmillan would reunite with Bob Ezrin and Alice Cooper to play piano, arrange strings, and conduct orchestrations for *Goes to Hell* and its 1977 follow-up, *Lace and Whiskey*.

"It was fun to be part of *Destroyer*," Macmillan concludes, before we part ways. "But you know, there's a lot of other good stuff happening on there aside from the two songs I worked on. I didn't spend a lot of time listening to work I'd done. Whether that's psychological or artistic gravitas, I don't know, but I did listen to *Destroyer* and formed my impression of Bob's level of success with it, which was almost entirely, Wow! It is pretty amazing what he turned out over those years."[17]

Corky Stasiak's career, which was on an upward trajectory from the minute he stepped into a studio, expanded further after his stint as assistant engineer for *Destroyer*. He would go on to work with Lou Reed and the Clash, among others, and would engineer KISS's three follow-ups to *Destroyer*: *Rock and Roll Over*, *Love Gun*, and *Alive! II*. He later returned to sit in with Bob Ezrin for the ill-fated *Music from 'The Elder'*, while also working the board for Ace Frehley's post-KISS solo debut, 1985's *Frehley's Comet*.

"There was an air in the studio for me that we were making history with *Destroyer*," Stasiak says, as we were finishing up our weeks of discussions from his winter home in Puerto Rico. He is living out his retirement on Long Island and Puerto Rico with his wife Trina, whom he married later in that fateful year of 1976—a wedding Gene Simmons attended. "Listening back to the tracks when they were finished, I had a premonition it would be a lasting achievement for KISS. I've done 200 albums, but I always go back to *Born to Run* and *Walls and Bridges* or *Toy in the Attic* and *Destroyer*, and not because those albums sold millions, they did well, and they are classic albums, but for me they were enjoyable professional and personal experiences. I walked away from those sessions thinking that not only had I done my best but that the artists really brought it. There were times I'd leave a project and think the band could have played better or if we only had more time we could have done better or maybe I was disappointed with the mastering, but those records stand out. *Destroyer*, I think, is the best record of KISS's catalogue."[18]

One of the main reasons for Stasiak's claim that *Destroyer* is "the best record of KISS's catalogue" was Jay Messina, who, by 1976, in his crucial position as lead engineer for the sessions, was at the top of his game. Already one of the finest sound engineers of his or any time, Messina's star would go on to shine ever brighter. He would emerge from the studio that February straight into another project and on and on until today, where he is still plying his trade at the highest level around the world and in his own studio, West End Sound. Messina's run through the history of popular music is as impressive as his noted "bottom end," from Cheap Trick to Supertramp to Aerosmith in the '70s to John Lennon to Miles Davis to Hanoi Rocks in the '80s to Sara Lovell to Patti Smith to Aerosmith's comeback in the '90s to Slash's Snakepit to the Roots to Krishna Das in the 2000's and on into this decade, where in 2014 his work garnered two Grammy nominations, for Big Band Jazz Ensemble (Vanguard Jazz Orchestra) and Latin Jazz Album (Pedrito Martinez Group). But as with many who were integral to the making of *Destroyer*, the album has followed him everywhere he goes.

"I'm glad I was part of *Destroyer*, because I truly believe it's a great record and a classic and I'm proud of it," Messina said, at the end of many weeks of discussions. "I grew up playing in a jazz band, so that's my background, so without being disrespectful, in those terms, I would put the experience of working with Miles Davis as more satisfying from a musical standpoint. I also worked with John Lennon too, which strictly from the musicality sense was just as satisfying, but one thing I'll tell you about working on *Destroyer* and the Aerosmith records, and I recently spoke with the Aerosmith guys and thanked them for all the joy those records have brought me over the years—and I put *Destroyer* in this category—I'll work with new assistant engineers that I hadn't met before treat me a like a god because I recorded *Destroyer* or 'Walk This Way' and that makes you feel good. To have younger guys look up to you because you affected their lives and how much they appreciate those recordings has brought me a special kind of enjoyment that really touches me. In that way, *Destroyer* is right up there with anything I've done. I never had a chance to thank Paul and Gene and the guys for that the way I did with Aerosmith, but if I could I'd tell them the same thing. I mean, I get young jazz enthusiasts who come up to me and talk about Miles Davis, but way, way more want to talk about *Destroyer*, because of its lasting popularity. To this day, someone will come up to me and say, 'You recorded, *Destroyer*? Wow!' And that always touches me."[19]

For Bob Ezrin, *Destroyer* would become "one of the most important and formative albums I ever worked on."[20] For the man who would author one of the most impressive runs in rock history, those momentous months in late 1975 through early 1976 seemed at the time to be the culmination of his youthful exuberance and an incredibly vibrant experimentation period, which began with transforming Alice Cooper from ragtag miscreants to the most powerful band in America. It was with that sense of adventure and determination that the young producer saw something in KISS that his creative sensibilities simply could not ignore.

"You know, what's interesting about the entire *Destroyer* experience for me," he says today. "This is more a marketing thing, and I'm not really a marketing guy, I'm a creative guy, but for me it was *the guys*. The guys in KISS are such interesting people. If you spent any time with them, they're so bright and creative and interesting and funny and at the same time crazy on certain levels. You know, they're complete people. They have many sides and personalities, yet they're wearing the costumes of one-dimensional superheroes. So I just thought, if we could get all of that other stuff in there in spite of the costumes and the makeup, we could actually make it work. We can achieve very human moments."[21]

Ezrin would go on to produce two more KISS albums and five more Alice Cooper records (including the extensive *Old School* boxed set in 2012) during the ensuing forty years after *Destroyer*. His work with Pink Floyd became legendary, most specifically *The Wall* in 1979 but also the comeback albums *A Monetary Lapse of Reason* (1987) and *The Division Bell* (1994). And the list continues: Peter Gabriel, Kansas, Berlin, Rod Stewart, Nine Inch Nails, Phish, and Taylor Swift, to name just a few. When we held the interviews for this book, Ezrin was hard at work in the studio with Deep Purple for the band's first studio album in eight years. In 2006, he'd helped produce a concert to reopen the New Orleans Superdome, following the damage caused by Hurricane Katrina, featuring U2 and Green Day, and then in 2009 he co-produced the Clearwater Concert for Pete Seeger at Madison Square Garden with acts that included, among others, Bruce Springsteen, Joan Baez, Dave Matthews, and Emmylou Harris. He has gone on to win numerous Canadian lifetime-achievement awards, develop educational and entertainment software, and today works extensively with his Nimbus School of Recording Arts between his unbelievably crowded producing schedule.

This was his final observation on *Destroyer*, which he would revisit in 2012 with the remix/remaster *Resurrected*, sending the record back onto the *Billboard* chart: "Most of my records are kind of like *Destroyer* in the sense that I visualize the stage when we're doing this stuff. I see everything as the stage. I feel like the listener is watching the show with their ears, so to speak. We only have sound, and specifically, we only have sound in the home, which is smaller than the P.A. that you get at the live gig, and also, it's lacking the visual experience, the social experience; the energy in the air generated by thousands of people being together. So you have to enhance what comes out sonically, so it creates the same level of excitement without those elements. So you have a larger than life soundscape and you try and make it as powerful sounding and emotionally moving as you possibly can. You want it bigger than real. So when people close their eyes and listen to it they get the feeling they got when they went to see the whole thing. That's always been my general underlying philosophy. Obviously, certain things have to be treated in different ways, and we did a couple of those things on the record, but for most part that's what I was going for."[22]

Destroyer's content, aim, creation, and finally its legacy are a microcosm of KISS. It broke personal barriers, expanded the brand, caused controversy among the rock press and the fan base, and even managed in a backward way to spawn a hit song. Most importantly, The Act in all its hope and glory was fully crystallized. What was at first an illusionary concept—in many ways a charade for three solid years of overcoming a myriad of professional obstacles—had by 1976 become reality. That year, KISS was indeed bigger than life. The four boys from the outer boroughs of New York City were bona-fide superstars with a signature sound to go alongside their incredible ambition. *Destroyer* and the ensuing tour would mark the end of the fringe days for KISS. For the remainder of the "Me" Decade, KISS would command center stage and explore the loftiest heights of fame and fortune above and beyond even its members' wildest imaginations. The Act would take a rock band where only the mighty Beatles had gone before, into the realms of complete saturation of markets and avenues for revenues around the globe. After *Destroyer*, mediums no longer had parameters for KISS. Within a year of its release and marketing, contracts were offered and production started on a feature film: the 1978 Hanna-Barbera television movie *KISS Meets the Phantom of the Park*, which became the second-highest-rated show of the year. Predictably, a comic book produced by the largest most influential publishers of the genre, Marvel, would appear in two hugely successful volumes, the first of which boasted real KISS blood poured into the ink. In October of '76, KISS's appearance on *The Paul Lynde Halloween Special*, wherein they lip-synched to "Detroit Rock City," "King of the Night Time World," and "Beth," solidified its costumed personnel as a holiday staple for years to come. A 1976 Gallup poll listed KISS as America's Favorite Rock Group, soon after the four makeup designs were officially registered with the government as commercial trademarks. Henceforth, every consumable item known to modern technology and manufacturing bore the likeness of its members and the logo of its name. From 1977 to 1979, the height of KISS-mania, the brand's merchandise—expanded to toys (Mego action figures, guitars, and board games), Donruss trading cards (with bubble gum) and a Bally pinball machine (a very popular high-school pastime of your humble author)—topped $100 million.

What *Destroyer* accomplished most of all for KISS is to create fantasy figures of Gene, Paul, Ace, and Peter. The masked faces—kept hidden from the paparazzi when no one seemed to care—now gave them free rein on anonymity that would be viewed by the public as a four-headed behemoth. A seminal KISS cover for *Creem* magazine during the band's 1977 Japanese tour had a cartoon rendering of a giant four-headed reptilian creature conquering Tokyo à la Godzilla. Mere rock bands contained human subjects; the KISS characters now had a vehicle to absorb their humanity and present something far more invincible. Thus *Destroyer* turned a previously mocked "gimmick act" into iconic gold. And, to varying degrees of discomfort, the band became willing slaves to its seduction.

The post-*Destroyer* KISS transformation is best exemplified by the covers of the band's next two albums, *Rock and Roll Over* and *Love Gun*, which display KISS as a cartoon in the case of the former and as gothic royalty in a second Ken Kelly painting in the latter. When the band members miraculously released four solo albums on the same label on the same day in 1978, images of their alabaster faces adorned each cover in painted form. Only *KISS Alive! II* and *Dynasty* would feature photographs of the band members, but in both cases only the painted faces were displayed, appearing as if their very faces were the canvas. The final KISS album covers featuring both Peter Criss, who would officially resign his post following *Unmasked*, and Ace Frehley, who exited after *Creatures of the Night*, share one key element: they are both cartoon renderings (although, in the case of *Creatures*, in the form of a doctored photograph). Twenty years later, when the original lineup reunited for *Psycho Circus*, there was indeed a comic book–style cartoon depiction of the Star Child, the Demon, the Space Ace, and the Cat Man on the album cover and promotional material.

Destroyer also corrected the key mistake the band had made with its first three studio efforts and began to amend in the *Alive!* packaging by featuring individual notes from each member and distinctly posed portraits in the accompanying booklet. *Alive!* may have effectively used imagery to usher home the individual characters and their strengths to the fore, but *Destroyer* put a sonic stamp on that claim. More than any KISS album that followed, *Destroyer* strikes closest at depicting the band's live assault—and, most importantly, its grandiosity. *Destroyer*'s colossal production and noir-esque songs, strengthened by their lyrical imagery, amply provide a core foundation for a distinct voice and an unveiling of the caricatures needed to complete The Act's ultimate fantasy experience.

Paul Stanley, already considered the effeminately sensitive face of KISS, is made manifest during his empathetic Hamlet moment in "Detroit Rock City," while his rousing call for endless party power on "King of the Night Time World" and "Flaming Youth" underscores the bravado of his pied-piper testifying. His vocal plea in "Do You Love Me?," which perfectly closes *Destroyer*, brings his arc full circle: the indomitable rock spirit haunted by vulnerability. His insecurity over whether fame and fortune has rendered him truly unlovable is irony personified. What KISS song prior could have hinted at such depth?

Gene Simmons is clearly and forevermore the Demon on *Destroyer*. His first lead vocal has him in a growling pique in "God of Thunder," a song that altered his stage and overall public persona from weirdly contorted bat-thing to axe-wielding dark lord. His "Great Expectations" is both seductive and eerie, allowing a glimpse into the man behind a velvet curtain that all worshipers of rock pray to experience. He is skillfully surrounded by choirs and strings and hailed as the thunder god he had foretold. And then there is "Sweet Pain," the cock-rock tour de force that hides nothing. It is the groupie maven unleashed without restraint or censor, funky, delicious and forbidden—a hedonistic sex fiend worthy of the Marque de Sade.

Peter Criss, the Cat Man, pent up from the mean streets and made to fight for song scraps, bellows from behind his kit to be noticed in the three-ring circus of bombs and blood. His moment of sweet respite arrives with "Beth," on which he is the lone voice intoning the shared sacrifice of the highlife. For the lovelorn, the spotlight isn't what it's cracked up to be. There is loneliness behind the cheers and an emptiness that comes with the accolade, and sometimes the victim is true love. A gruff exterior is fully exposed in a true romantic tragedy, his vocal a gravely plea to never forget what truly matters when it is all-but lost.

Ace Frehley, without a lead vocal—which was his wish until the appearance of his signature "Shock Me" from *Love Gun* and later the biggest hit off the KISS solo albums, "New York Groove" put him front and center—has his moments on *Destroyer*, albeit some of them are manufactured. But his underlying alien presence is there. It glides above the fray, feeling his measure, following one face-melting lead after another on *Alive!*, which is ever present in *Destroyer*'s opening on the car radio, crooned along with the doomed driver on "Detroit Rock City," and in the distended voice of Paul Stanley imploring the audience forever and ever to have themselves a "rock and roll party!" in the cacophony of the final, looping echo of "Rock and Roll Demons."

Most assuredly for the band itself, *Destroyer*'s first single, "Shout it Out Loud," may be its greatest rallying cry. It reflects The Act so acutely that it is hard to imagine another band besides KISS penning it or singing it. There are, of course, gang vocals galore and one singular message: pour the desires of an entire generation into a voluminous rant of orgasmic merriment and "Shout it out loud!" at every turn. Be louder, be bolder, be immovable, be defiant, be alive—this is KISS and The Act and *Destroyer*'s gospel for all time.

KISS would indeed go forth from this time on as an entity far beyond music or theatrics into living myth—an impregnable masquerade that both Simmons and Stanley to this day speak of as separate from their careers. Stanley wraps up his memoir, *Face the Music*, by exclaiming that when he is gone—retired or dead—KISS will still be rolling along, making albums, putting on shows. "Causes go on. Political parties go on without their founders. I think someone could come along who would be capable of carrying the flag just as well if not better—someone who can build on the foundation. I look forward to the day that I'm replaced in KISS. Not because I want to leave, but because it will prove I'm right: *KISS is bigger than any of its members.*"[23]

KISS could—as postulated by several observers quoted in this book—be everything to all comers: heroes, villains, sex symbols, horror icons, science-fiction warriors, and youth ministers. With mere pop culture conquered throughout the wonderfully wild 1970s, KISS would go on to challenge the realm of American culture.

"Do You Love Me?"

I wantcha to . . . I needja to . . .

Boom-bop-boom-boom-bop, Boom-bop-boom-boom-bop . . .
  The tribal sounds of the beating heart; the pounding, rolling thunder; the thumping canons and relentless fist-pumping hordes.
  Boom-bop-boom-boom-bop, Boom-bop-boom-boom-bop . . .

> *You really like my limousine*
> *You like the way the wheels roll*
> *You like my seven-inch leather heels*
> *And going to all of the shows*

> *But . . .*

Guitars ring out, two by two, as if ushering the march . . .

> *Do you love me?*
> *Do you love me?*
> *Do you love me?*

  Now the band kicks in: bass, drums, and riffing guitar. They take us there, the place where it all goes down: the stage, the sky, the fashion, the chime of rock and roll. Our voice from the opening number—our wild road victim, our teenage dreamer, our defiant clarion of flaming youth, our commanding order to "Shout it out loud!" has one more message:

> *You like the credit cards and private planes*
> *Money can really take you far*
> *You like the hotels and fancy clothes*
> *And the sound of electric guitars*

But . . .

Back to the pounding of the drums and those guitars that usher in the grand query:

Do you love me?
Do you love me?
Do you love me?

You really like rock and roll
All of the fame and the masquerade
You like the concerts and studios
And all the money, honey that I make

But . . .

Do you love me?
Do you love me?
Do you love me?

Harmonious notes ring out, signaling a truce; a search for tenderness beneath the insatiable lust for money and fame and power and endless youth. The voice is now shunted, put back inside that radio transistor from our novella's opening. The voice of the past *and* the voice of the future, he is no longer demanding an answer but wandering through his two-dimensional affections to discover a fleeting grope for love . . .

Your backstage pass and my sunglasses
Make you look just like a queen

The distant sound of chiming bells accentuate the mood, reaching perhaps for a higher calling, a spiritual awakening from the music—not the business or the star system or the money-honey, or the intoxicating invincibility of mass worship . . .

Even the fans they know your face
From all of the magazines

Our voice cries out in an echo chamber, trapped but not forgotten . . .

But...

Do you love me?

An angelic choir echoes...

Do you love me?

Repeats again, as if a mantra...

Do you love me?

A whispered *I wanna know* inches beneath it; our voice, humbled, wanting, asks again, *I mean like do ya...?*

Do you love me?

This time he screams, *I wanna know!* and the bells chime forth like haunting embraces, shooting stars and ephemeral wishes.

Do you love me?

The voice is now yearning, beseeching, crying out to the heavens, beyond the lover, beyond the fans, beyond the silent deity, beyond the inner turmoil in his head: *I wantcha to... I needja to... And you know, I'm so tired of everybody sayin' it... and you know, I just gotta know... if you really, really, really, REALLY love me!*

Do you love me?

The echoes, the chimes, the power-chunk guitars, the drums pounding, pounding, pounding away into the fade. Yet still the voice calls out from the ether: *I needja to... I wantcha to... I need ya... I wanna know... do ya, do ya?*

He is fading.
The music is fading.
The story is fading...

I just gotta have some love! I just got to have some love!

The ether gathers its own momentum, absorbing the shouts, the guitars, the drums, the chimes, and infinite sound of the band hammering away, as if it will never end, it cannot end, as long as you keep the record spinning, as long as you keep the concerts full and wear your badge—the army shield of defiance for the eternal fusion of youth and boundless strength and blessed, naïve hubris.

I just got to have some love, love, love, love, love . . .

Afterword

It is the autumn of my fifty-second year. I am holed up in the tiny microfiche room of the State Heritage Library in downtown Raleigh, North Carolina, chasing a ghost: an apparition that has haunted the pages of this book for week after week and year after year as I busied myself with uncovering the details of one seminal mystery behind the album that captured my imagination four decades ago. It is as relentless a haunting as it is glaring, and it echoes inside a gnawing question: who was the young KISS fan who died on that infamous evening so many years ago? The one whose alleged fatal car crash was immortalized by Paul Stanley in words and music, set to operatic heights in "Detroit Rock City" by Bob Ezrin in the grooves of *Destroyer*, and written out conspicuously (the only lyrics that are) in the inner jacket of the album that I first opened on that steamy summer day in 1976?

At first, this random if not inspired vehicular misadventure seemed an afterthought, trapped as it was beneath volumes of source material, research, and interviews that make up the cluttered life of an author. When the spirit moves me enough, I figured, I would merely have to go on the Internet and someone, somewhere—after so much time—will have written about it. But alas, this was not to be, and knowing that a book of this size and scope about one album in one corner of time must provide the reader this nugget, I found it suddenly became an imperative.

Months before I found myself in this hall of records in the municipal section of the state capital, I simply worked my way backward from the original Paul Stanley quote about the inspiration of "Detroit Rock City," as first discussed during interviews around the release of *Destroyer* and later reiterated in the booklet accompanying 2001's *The Box Set*. Long before deciding to take on this project, I asked Stanley about it, while wrapping up a phone interview in 2006 for a cover story on his solo album *Live to Win*.

During our conversation then, he pretty much repeated the same thing. "At the time I was writing the lyric, I remember we had played somewhere in the South—and I'm not sure if it was Charlotte, but someone had been killed outside the arena in a car accident and I thought, how strange to want to come out to an event that's such a celebration of life and you lose yours going to it."

This was not unusual for Paul. He and Gene Simmons, keepers of KISS myths for decades, have made an art form of turning bits and pieces of truth into other things entirely. This is not to say that Stanley's tale could not be factual, but, then again, fact continued to be elusive.

A review of the band's itinerary in the incredibly detailed *KISS Alive Forever* by Curt Gooch and Jeff Suhs produced a date: April 29, 1975. Beneath it is the following: "Charlotte, North Carolina/Charlotte Park Center Auditorium/ Opening Acts: Rush, Heavy Metal Kids/Attendance: Sold Out/Promoter: Kaleidoscope Productions—A fan on his way to see KISS in Charlotte was killed in a car accident. The event provided the back-story for the narrative in 'Detroit Rock City' in which a young person is killed in a collision on the way to a rock concert."

The book also reveals that the Charlotte show was smack-dab in the middle of an extended Southern swing of the *Dressed to Kill* tour that would later provide the basic tracks for the career-shifting *Alive!* album. From April 21 through 27, KISS played Louisville, Kentucky, Indianapolis, and Indiana (just a little north); then Charlotte and Fayetteville, North Carolina; and finally Richmond, Virginia. Outside of a quick stop on May 10 in Landover, Maryland, these were the only shows "down South" to which Stanley could have been referring.

So, beginning with the Charlotte lead, I phoned the county police of Mecklenberg, North Carolina, where the city resides, and had several conversations with bemused officers who informed me in several fairly amiable ways that digging up that information nearly forty years gone was near impossible, specifically without a name attached. I also got the sense, or the hint, that they had much more important things to tend to, like protecting the populace, upholding the law, and catching bad guys. A KISS book? Let's just say they were not as intrigued as I was. However, one officer, whose name I regrettably cannot recall, referred me to the archives of the *Charlotte Observer*, the 128-year-old paper of record for the area.

The people at the *Observer* were far more "intrigued" than the cops. One thing is for certain: writers of nonfiction and those who have chosen the life in the library sciences and/or toil in historical archives are of like mind. This came in handy when I spoke to one Marie David, who began to dig through the paper's stories from the days following the KISS show at the Charlotte Park Center Auditorium (a defunct facility well known for hosting professional wrestling cards, as well as rock shows). Despite Ms. David's kindness and welcomed sympathy, there were no reported accidents of any kind on the day of

AFTERWORD

April 25 or the ensuing days afterward. Just to be sure, I did a quick check of the city-data web site and its list of vehicular fatalities dating back to 1975—no names or details, just the number of deaths—but this too came up empty.

Figuring the newspaper route might be a good way to stay on the case, and frankly because Ms. David suggested it, I moved onto the state capital's newspaper of record, the 149-year-old *News & Observer*. Once again, and despite the enthused efforts of a Mr. David Raynor, nothing concrete emerged. He did, however, find one reported accident in which a nineteen-year-old kid named Ricky Franklin Gadd from the little town of Biscoe was killed in Spring Lake, North Carolina, in a single-car wreck when the "sports car he was driving at a high speed ran off the road and over-turned." Almost word for word it could have come from the dramatic opening to *Destroyer*. The only problem was that the accident was reported to have happened at 5:00 p.m., two days after the KISS show. Still, Spring Lake is only 122 miles due east of Charlotte, and just outside of Fayetteville, where the band would play the very next day.

Fayetteville is a town that seemed to pop up more than once during my agonizingly unsuccessful rambles through the Internet. KISS blogs, fan web zines, chat rooms, and tribute web sites from around the world provided no answers, except one: the Facebook page of Joe Bonamassa, from which a few small but captivating clues surfaced. On a thread below Mr. Bonamassa's post of a list of songs about Detroit, there was a lively discussion involving the song's mysterious origin. Some argued the more literal: it was a KISS fan from Detroit that died on the way to a show there, just as the song describes. Some veered off and said they had heard the kid was from Ann Arbor (forty-six miles due west of Detroit) and still another said Pontiac (thirty-one miles due north). Then, after the expected calls of "Who gives a shit?," the thread swung to the Charlotte story and a few mentions of the town of Greenville, NC. This seemed the unlikeliest of locations, seeing that Greenville is some 248 miles east of Charlotte—and, more pointedly, that KISS did not play there in 1975. But then the musically named Salvatore-Lomonico-Jones added this: "Lived in Fayetteville, and you can't be a kids fan there without knowing that tidbit" (my guess is he meant "KISS fan").

That got my wheels rolling: either the doomed youth in question hailed from Fayetteville, and/or that the purported accident occurred not at the Charlotte show that Stanley vaguely recalled (April 25) but the following day in Fayetteville (April 26).

So I made a call to the daily periodical of record in Fayetteville, the *Fayetteville Observer*, a small, family-owner newspaper founded in 1816, but found it had no archive department. In order to search through their records I had to . . .

you guessed it . . . visit the State Heritage Library in downtown Raleigh, North Carolina, where a wonderfully cheerful woman by the name of Carla Morris set aside the materials I needed to peruse. So I booked a mid-November flight to head down and face the music, so to speak.

My parents have been living in nearby Cary by way of Raleigh since 1986 and knew exactly where this building was, enabling me to save lodging expenses and hitch a ride to boot. And so here I sit for three solid hours poring over daily records of the *Observer*—and, just to be safe, the *Asheville Citizen Times*, since KISS played there on November 28. The results are paltry and vague at best. One article, dated April 27, described two accidents: one involving an automobile running off the road into a tree, killing twenty-year-old Steven Lane Stilwell and fifteen-year-old Anne Garinger; and another when eighteen-year-old Gary Edwards Blue was killed while another unidentified youth was seriously injured when "a small foreign car hit a train in Asheboro and caught fire." Asheboro is eighty-three miles north of Charlotte.

I figure that, while I'm here, I may as well check the dates for when the band revisited Fayetteville and Charlotte following the November 28 Ashville show, but I get nowhere. Not to mention that since Paul Stanley demoed "Detroit Rock City" in July of 1975 before presenting it to Bob Ezrin, who began to work out its intricacies during the infamous "boot camp" in August into September of that year—two full months before these dates—this is becoming an exercise in futility.

I'm defeated.

I leave the place stunned that there is no mention at all of any accidents anywhere in North Carolina during any part of the *Dressed to Kill* tour. Despondency gives way to anger. Did Paul make this goddamn story up? Tons of rock bands, and surely KISS, make stuff up. Why not? Good press. Great story. Gives "Detroit Rock City" some depth, and certainly the pathos Bob Ezrin had demanded. Classic showbiz.

But wait a minute. If Stanley made it up, then why not just say it happened in Detroit? The song is about Detroit. If you are going to lie, *lie big*. That's the KISS model, right? Why mention the South, or even specifically Charlotte? Why Charlotte of all places? "Charlotte Rock City"? This place must have meant something to him. I decide the story has to be real, and that maybe I'm just failing to uncover it. Just because I've harbored high hopes for finding the actual newspaper account that Paul may have read lounging in his hotel room a day or so after the show, which would go on to inspire this rock-and-roll tale, does not mean it didn't happen.

So I head back to the drawing board—where by now even my poor parents have caught the detective bug—and get to work. But to what end? I had exhausted the Southern dates of the *Dressed to Kill* tour. Am I supposed to check every town KISS played for the entire tour?

Yup.

So now I'm back home, helplessly trudging through the city-data site once again and rummaging around the net and making calls. It's beginning to dawn on me that I may have to come clean and admit this car accident story is a hoax, or if not a hoax a pretty fair piece of folklore—a Paul Bunyan and the Ox kind of thing. And then, just as I'm on the cusp of giving up, a fellow scribe comes to the rescue.

When I started this project, I contacted the co-author of the aforementioned *KISS Alive Forever*, Jeff Suhs. He and his partner, Curt Gooch, wrote a piece on the making of *Destroyer* for *KISS Magazine* in 2006, and he had worked with Larry Harris on his entertaining and informative Casablanca book, *And Party Every Day*, making Suhs a valuable contact. Kind enough to grant me some encouragement along the way, as well as some background of his own, Suhs also prompted me to send him the manuscript once the project was complete.

In so doing, I mention that although the book is pretty much done, I'm still vexed by this question: what the hell happened in 1975 to inspire Paul Stanley to write "Detroit Rock City"? I am happy to report that this also befuddles Suhs, who, if we recall, is partially responsible for sending me on this wild goose chase with his blurb on the April 25, 1975, Charlotte show.

To Suhs's credit, he emails me the following missive a couple of days later: "Here's some interesting info for you. I asked some of the road crew guys if they remembered this. Moose said he definitely remembered hearing about this back in the day. Now, he left the road on 12/30/74 due to his accident in Springfield, so it had to have happened before that."

The "accident" Suhs is referencing occurred when original KISS crewmember Peter "Moose" Oreckinto was messing with one of KISS's always-dangerous pyrotechnics before a gig when it went off in his hand. In Suhs's account, road manager J. R. Smalling describes "Moose" as screaming while clutching his damaged appendage, while Peter Criss is quoted as saying he had never seen so much blood. A Vietnam veteran who had seen it all asked the surgeons at the nearby hospital to sew the hand back on, and they did, successfully.

Okay, so Moose, having sustained this horrific injury, left his post at the bitter end of 1974. And, as Suhs states in a follow-up email, this renders the April 1975 shows I had been boarding airplanes and bugging poor archive personnel to dissect obsolete. He then mentions that I should consider the November 1974 Carolina appearances: Greenville, November 27; Charlotte,

November 28; Fayetteville, November 30; and Ashville, December 1. Any of them would have included the services of "Moose," and, if his memory serves me, then there is still a chance.

Suddenly . . . renewed vigor.

So, back to the *Charlotte Observer* and the *Fayetteville Observer* I go, bugging Ms. David and Mr. Raynor, but neither uncovers anything new. It is time to test the considerable patience of Ms. Morris at the Historical Library, who had informed me that they could transfer materials to my local library upon request, saving me a second trip to NC. Up against a deadline to submit the manuscript, she goes above and beyond by volunteering to begin her own search. This proves lucrative.

The first story to catch Ms. Morris's keen eye is from a small daily, the *Burlington Day Times*. A sixteen-year-old Cummings High School student by the name of Gail Renee Crisp was killed when her twenty-year-old boyfriend, Keith Baker, drove his 1968 Pontiac due west at high speed and "ran off the right side of the road, struck several mailboxes and snapped off a utility pole" before careening 120 feet into an overturned heap. Ms. Crisp sustained severe head injuries and was pronounced dead at the nearby Alamance Hospital. Baker was later charged with driving under the influence, driving without a license, and manslaughter.

The story is riveting for more than one reason; the biggest, for yours truly, is that it is the closest I have come to something relevant to my search. More to the point, although nothing is mentioned about where exactly Mr. Baker was driving, it was at least noted as due west—Charlotte is 110 miles southwest of Burlington, where KISS played the night before. Without knowing the time of the accident, since the date of the report is September 29, 1974, I wonder if perhaps Baker was ushering the young Ms. Crisp back from the Charlotte show during the black of night, high from the proceedings and exhausted from the long ride. He was stoned, reckless, and without a license—something of a signature for Stanley's metaphor of the invincible naiveté of youth. The only drawback to this find is that KISS was playing in Charleston, South Carolina, that evening, which is 301 long miles south of Burlington. So it is unlikely that this is where the doomed couple was headed, if they were headed to or returning from a KISS concert at all, since once again there is no mention as such. Although one would be right to ask: why would any news organization report what kind of adolescent activity these kids were going to or coming from, especially if it wasn't taking place directly in town? Not to mention, despite the heady affectations of The Act, KISS was still not well known almost anywhere. And this was the South. It's not like they were going to see Elvis.

The second striking find is a blurb in the Sunday, December 1 edition of the *Fayetteville Observer* covering a spate of fatal accidents occurring over the Thanksgiving weekend across North Carolina—fifteen in all. One is particularly intriguing, if only for the young gentleman's age and town of residence. Dwayne Kevin McGlaughlin, a Charlotte native, who was eighteen when he was struck by a car.

Another notice of nine deaths occurring over the Thanksgiving holiday appears in the *Daily Reflector*, established in 1882, and located in Greenville (mentioned earlier in the search by a Facebooker), where KISS would play on November 27, 1974, the day before the band headed to Charlotte. Since the paper is smaller than some and covers all of Eastern Carolina, its archive resides on the sprawling campus of Eastern Carolina University and is manned by one Arthur Carlson. Upon receiving my harried request during the dwindling days of my research, he sprung into action, discovering several possible traffic-related fatalities.

Of the nine victims reported (perhaps some of them overlapping those mentioned in the *Fayetteville Observer*), only two fit the profile of a probable rock concert attendee. The first is twenty-seven-year-old Robert Bradford Midgett of Pine Hill, North Carolina, a town located approximately ninety-one miles north of Charlotte, although there is no mention of where the accident occurred or when; the other is twenty-year-old John Alexander Mearas of Fair Bluff, who was killed in Florence, South Carolina, when his car struck a tree early in the morning hours of November 28. This story is also corroborated in the Greenwood, South Carolina, newspaper the *Index Journal*, and a day later in North Carolina's *High Point Enterprise*. Fair Bluff is 137 miles southeast of Charlotte and 166 miles south of Greenville, but only 134 miles north of Charleston, South Carolina. But the Mearas lead becomes less likely when considering the location of the tree he hit—Florence—and his accident happened on the morning of November 28, hours after KISS played in Greenville, North Carolina, on the 27th, simply because he died some 191 miles from there.

Enter my assistant, Kathy McCormick, who informs me of a cousin on the police force, who may be able to get past the otherwise incompliant cops down there. However, despite having some names this time, he comes up with nada, but he does recommend we contact the DMV for the areas in question. According to Kathy, DMV personnel, well documented in the annals of American comedy for typically being recalcitrant, radiate with excitement over the prospect of hunting down this mystery. One woman spends an inordinate amount of time pointing out major thoroughfares in and out of Charlotte and

Fayetteville on which the accident must have occurred, if it occurred at all. However, all of this back and forth gets us no closer to our answer.

With the North Carolina archives exhausted, I turn to the last vestige of possible information to mine, and that is Charleston, South Carolina, where KISS played at the Charleston Municipal Auditorium on November 29, 1974, the day after Charlotte and the evening before Fayetteville. This time it would be Ms. Liz Foster from the city's *Post and Courier*, established at the turn of the nineteenth century and known as one of the longest running dailies in the United States. Once again, Ms. Foster finds that although Mr. Mearas's accident is prominent in the November 28 issue of the paper, there is nothing binding by way of a name attached to an accident before, during, or after a KISS concert.

And that, in the end, is the mystery. If, as Moose remembers it, they all recall "hearing" something about a fatal car crash resulting in a young KISS fan dying outside an arena in the South—most likely North Carolina, and more specifically Charlotte—then it was just that: "hearing." There is no newspaper report about it. And unless there was a radio blurb—dramatized by Bob Ezrin, as the opening of *Destroyer* portends—or a brief mention on the evening's local television news, then the inspiration for "Detroit Rock City" is lost to time, and in its place lives the myth. In an ironic but predictable twist, this is the very essence of KISS, the underlying force of The Act, and ultimately *Destroyer*, an album that tore the top of my head off and unleashed parts of my imagination that would never again be contained. Almost forty years have passed since the summer of 1976, and maybe somewhere in that imagination resides a fatal car crash. The time and date and name may elude us, like so much of our imagination, yet it remains alive in our spirit, as it will in song *and* story.

Acknowledgments

First off, I must thank the patience, love, and support of my family: my beautiful wife, Erin, who had to listen to hours of fits and the inevitable rallies that come with the long process of research and interviews with KISS music blaring from all corners of the house. My daughter, Scarlet, who grew from a rock-and-roll toddler (her beloved AC/DC cranking) to a super-cool kid with eclectic musical tastes throughout the writing of this book, for keeping relatively quiet during the long interview process and occasionally popping in with whispered encouragements. No one sings "Shout It Out Loud" with more gusto anywhere.

Next, I have to thank my dear friends Chris Barrera, the first pal from childhood who boarded the KISS bandwagon in the summer of '76 with me and shouted Gene Simmons-like *oohhh-yeahs* of support whenever I sent him half-finished chapters, and Peter Blasevick, a classically trained musician and sometimes songwriting partner, who, upon hearing of this project, asked, "Isn't there something more meaningful you could be doing with your talents?" Even though he later admitted that *Destroyer* was "the first record I bought with my own money in fourth grade." Chris kept me on the straight and narrow, reminding me of certain elements from the time and the band I may have irreparably strayed from, and Peter's hours of listening to, deconstructing, and explaining much of Bob Ezrin's incredible contributions to the writing of and recording of this seminal album were essential.

Much love to my two assistants during the duration of this work (and it took long enough to span both): Jessica Perrin, for her constant but tender haranguing to keep me in line, and Kathy McCormick, who jumped in and did a yeoman's job on the remaining interview transcriptions and the circuitous search for the mystery behind "Detroit Rock City." And to my current assistant Stephen Rakeckas, I thank you for jumping into the social media deep end to help promote the book. Oh, and lest I forget the woman who plowed through hours upon hours of discussions that helped fill this book, Diane Genender of Proto Type Transcripts. I did that gig for too long and I know how difficult it can be.

It is important to acknowledge three principals that helped get Backbeat Books in the picture: the talented and hilarious Adam Busch (actor, musician, gad about town) for suggesting I review his cousin Mike Segretto's *The Who FAQ*, which led me to several pertinent emails with the author, and finally to Bernadette Malavarca, Associate Editor of Backbeat Books, who facilitated my relationship with Backbeat during a four-month series of detailed correspondence which led to this book seeing the light of day. Thanks also to John Cerullo (the Publisher), Tom Seabrook (copyeditor), and Wes Seeley (the marketing and publicity manager).

Professional gratitude must be paid to fellow KISS authors, Jeff Suhs and Ken Sharp, both of whom lent their time and encouragement when needed. It was a boon to have these talented gentlemen on my side all the way.

Next up are the principals in this immense tale who lent their memories and expertise to these pages, not the least of which are lead engineer Jay Messina and his assistant, Corky Stasiak. These men, both consummate pros, not only gave me ridiculous swaths of their precious time, poring over the minutest details of these sessions, but also helped me contact other participants and offered cherished advice and much-needed words of support. Jay was my first interviewee and Corky led me to him after, thank goodness, he answered his phone in Puerto Rico and gave me the hope that I could get a foothold on this monster. I made sure this book was the best it could be to honor them.

Much praise to all the Record Plant NYC guys who came in at the eleventh hour of the project to fill in some important details about the studio and Bob Ezrin and the wild and wooly *Destroyer* sessions. The late Roy Cicala, whose contribution to my descriptions of the renowned but since retired Studio A of his Record Plant was paramount to my reconstruction for readers. Same goes to Grammy-winning producer David Thoener, whose insights into the Plant were a boon, and who got me in contact with Gray Russell, whose Friends of the Record Plant Studio NYC Facebook page is a treasure trove of memorabilia. Also much gratitude to Rod O'Brien, who gave of his time and memories to help me make those long days in the nation's coolest studio come alive.

Thanks must also go to the delightfully eccentric Kim Fowley, who was quite simply a human encyclopedia about all things rock and roll and, of course, his myriad of achievements.

Appreciation goes to Dennis Woloch for his stark honesty and enviable memory for specifics. His friend and compatriot, "the guy who named *Destroyer*," Vincent De Gerlando, deserves props as well.

The master, the late Dick Wagner, really came through with new info on his extensive behind-the-scenes contribution to *Destroyer*, and after our interview became a dear friend. Also a cherished friend, his assistant Susan Michelson, who sent me intimate photos of Dick to be used in the published work. I was thrilled that Dick chose my "Invisible Virtuoso" tag for him as a moniker and ecstatic that he asked me to write a jacket blurb for his intense autobiography, *Not Only Women Bleed*, in 2012. He is sorely missed.

And what a thrill it was to visit the legendary photographer Bob Gruen at his studio in the West Village. His insights were instrumental in my getting a grasp on the KISS mystique, while his photos have leant a gravitas to this project that cannot be overstated. And to his assistant, Sarah Field, who patiently waited for me to confirm the purchase of Bob's incredible photo of the studio team for my collection, and helped me choose the best of his work to grace these pages, I say, thank you.

Thanks also goes to another grand rock-and-roll photographer, Fin Costello, who never failed to answer an email and send me so many of his cool photos of the band.

I could not have done without Larry Harris's wonderfully colorful stories inside Casablanca Records and for his providing crucial perspective on a difficult time between his label and KISS.

The same goes out to the über-talented Allan Macmillan, for taking me inside the process of composing and arranging strings with the great Bob Ezrin, and for generously providing a personal photo of the official baton used on the First KISS Grand Orchestral and Choral Recording Session.

Thanks also to imaginative Karl Ravtiz, for providing extensive descriptions of his designs for the Spirit of '76 tour and later the photos of his blueprints.

And gratitude to radio giant Scott Shannon, for setting the record straight on the breaking of "Beth," his sharing of a photograph of the mighty Casablanca promotion team, and mostly for his hilarious phone message about being a standing member of the KISS Army.

Perhaps the greatest reward for these many years of work came from painter extraordinaire Ken Kelly, who not only played a mean game of phone tag that went on for months but also gave of his time and shared incredibly moving stories of his exploits as an artist—and, in one hard-to-fathom gesture, sent me an originally penned *Destroyer* cover, which hangs with honor on my living room wall.

Plaudits and appreciation goes out to Marie David of the *Charlotte Observer*, David Raynor of the *News & Observer*, Jakon Hayes of the *Virginian Pilot*, Arthur Carlson of East Carolina University, and Liz Foster of the Charleston *Post and Courier*, all of whom work tirelessly at the research libraries of their respective publications, and Carla Morris from the State Heritage Library in

Raleigh, North Carolina, for their assistance in trying to track down the name and details behind the subject of "Detroit Rock City." Our emails and phone calls had the flair of a detective novel.

Of course, infinite thanks to my hero, Alice Cooper, whose inexhaustible spirit was always in these pages, and who has been my favorite interview for several publications over the years, some of which made its way into this work. The weight and breadth of his legendary name alone helped me gain access to Dick Wagner and eventually Bob Ezrin.

Speaking of Bob, there will always be a special place in my heart for Kim Markovchick, Mr. Ezrin's assistant, who went above and beyond any call to any duty known to an author. If you ever attempt to get to someone that means everything to what you are paining to achieve, especially someone who is busier than humanly plausible, I wish you someone like Kim: kind, supportive, communicative, and an empathetic soul. She is quite simply the unsung hero of this work.

And there is no way for me to ever express my immense gratitude to the genius that is Bob Ezrin, who gave of his time on several occasions, answering questions about the most mundane of minutia with aplomb and humor. His enthusiastic flair for ushering you back into his time inside the studio and inside the heads of enormous talents, as if you were there, was nothing less than a godsend. This work could not have been completed without my time with Bob, and certainly the idea of its origins lies in his imagination and creativity, which inspired a kid all those years ago to dream so big he eventually had to write this book.

To KISS—Gene, Paul, Ace, and Peter—the four guys from my hometown of New York City, I say congratulations for spawning lunatics like myself who would take years off his life trying to track down all the stories behind the stories to produce this work. What can I say, I am a KISS fan, but no more crazed than those millions who share my blessed obsession. I did this ultimately for them.

Finally, thanks to my parents for getting me my first KISS records, not the least of which was *Destroyer*, and for all the equipment on which I listened to them incessantly throughout my greasy teen years. You, along with my little brother, PJ, had to endure quite a bit of volume and madness emanating from my room upstairs. Hope this book can begin to show my appreciation for your supporting my love of rock and roll, writing, and, most of all, life.

Notes

Chapter 1
1. Scott Cohen, Raves, 1976
2. David Leaf and Ken Sharp, *KISS: Behind the Mask* (New York: Warner Books, 2003), 48
3. Leaf and Sharp, *Behind the Mask*, 49
4. Leaf and Sharp, *Behind the Mask*, 47
5. Author interview, May 16, 2012
6. Author interview, April 3, 2012
7. Author interview, May 16, 2012
8. Frank Rose, "Invasion of the Glitter Goths," *Circus*, April 8, 1975, 29
9. Rose, "Invasion of the Glitter Goths," 29
10. Curt Gooch and Jeff Suhs, *KISS Alive Forever* (New York: Billboard Books, 2002), 18
11. Jeff Stein, *The Kids Are Alright* (London: New World Pictures, 1979)
12. Paul Stanley, *Face the Music—A Life Exposed* (New York: Harper One, 2014), 19
13. Leaf and Sharp, *Behind the Makeup*, 56
14. Peter Criss, *Makeup to Breakup* (New York: Scribner, 2012), 78–9
15. Author interview, April 11, 2012
16. Author interview, October 22, 2012
17. Larry Harris, *And Party Every Day* (Milwaukee: Backbeat Books, 2009), 37
18. C. K. Lendt, *KISS and Sell* (New York: Billboard Books, 1997), 39
19. Author interview, November 13, 2013

Chapter 2
1. Rose, "Invasion of the Glitter Goths," 28
2. Leaf and Sharp, *Behind the Mask*, 67
3. Leaf and Sharp, *Behind the Mask*, 67
4. Leaf and Sharp, *Behind the Mask*, 67

5   Tony Horkins, "Tin Machine: Bowie & Gabrels," *International Musician*, December 1991
6   Dana Polan, *Pulp Fiction* (London: British Film Institute, 2000), 77
7   Dave Schulps, "Product Report: KISS Inc." *Trouser Press*, December 1978, 32
8   Richard Creamer, "Diary of a KISS Photographer," *Punk Rock*, Summer 1978
9   Ace Frehley, *No Regrets* (New York: Gallery Books, 2011), 180
10 Kathi Stein, "KISS Tour '76: The Ooze of the Greasepaint, the Roar of the Crowd," *Circus*, September 28, 1976, 34–5
11 Lendt, *KISS and Sell*, 69
12 Lendt, *KISS and Sell*, 38
13 Roy Carr, *New Musical Express*, September 1974
14 Gene Simmons, *Kiss and Make-Up* (New York: Three Rivers Press, 2001), 65
15 Cameron Crowe, "Playboy Magazine Interview," *Playboy*, September 1976
16 Lester Bangs, "Detroit's Rock Culture," *Phonograph Record*, December 1972
17 Jessica Joy Wise, *Metal: A Headbanger's Journey*, 2005
18 Author interview, April 28, 2014
19 Criss, *Makeup to Breakup*, 80
20 Frehley, *No Regrets*, 102
21 Paul Stanley, Gene Simmons, and Ken Sharp, *Nothin' to Lose: The Making of KISS 1972–1975* (New York: It Books, 2013), 162
22 Stanley, Simmons, and Ken Sharp, *Nothin' to Lose*, 162
23 Stanley, Simmons, and Sharp, *Nothin' to Lose*, 162–3
24 *Billboard*, February 23, 1974
25 *Circus* Magazine, 1974
26 Gordon Fletcher, *Rolling Stone*, April 1974
27 Leaf and Sharp, *Behind the Mask*, 66

Chapter 3
1   Jaan Uhelszki, "I Dreamed I Was Onstage with KISS in My Maidenform Bra," *CREEM*, August 1975
2   Gooch and Suhs, *KISS Alive Forever*, 27
3   Jaan Uhelski, "When KISS Was Cool—The *CREEM* Magazine Unmasking," Dogmatic web site
4   Author interview, May 16, 2012
5   Harris, *And Party Every Day*, 68

6   Leaf and Sharp, *Behind the Mask*, 224–5
7   Frank Rose, "Stanley Struts—KISS Tapes, Part III," *Circus*, August 24, 1976, 42
8   Stanley, Simmons, and Sharp *Nothin' to Lose*, 354–5
9   Leaf and Sharp, *Behind the Mask*, 222
10 Frehley, *No Regrets*, 122
11 Leaf and Sharp, *Behind the Mask*, 222
12 Leaf and Sharp, *Behind the Mask*, 223
13 Ed Naha, *Rolling Stone*, January 30, 1975
14 Harris, *And Party Every Day*, 76
15 Author interview, December 10, 2013
16 Author interview, December 10, 2013
17 Gordon Fletcher, *Rolling Stone*, July, 17, 1975
18 *Billboard*, April 5, 1975
19 Leaf and Sharp, *Behind the Mask*, 64
20 Rose, "KISS: Invasion of the Glitter Goths," 27
21 Lendt, *KISS and Sell*, 15
22 Rose, "KISS: Invasion of the Glitter Goths," 27
23 www.blabbermouth.net, September, 11, 2005
24 Leaf and Sharp, *Behind the Mask*, 65
25 Stephen Davis, *Walk This Way* (New York: Harper Collins, 1997), 222
26 Harris, *And Party Every Day*, 3
27 Author interview, December 10, 2013
28 Dale Sherman, *Black Diamond* (London: CG Publishing, 1997), 63

Chapter 4

1   Jane Stevenson, "Ezrin's Day Has Come," *JAM! Showbiz Music* on www.canoe.ca, November 30, 2004
2   James Campion, "The Indestructible Three-Dimensional Cabaret Villain," *East Coast Rocker*, September 23, 2009
3   Demorest, *Alice Cooper* (New York: Gerald Rothberg Publications, Inc., 1974), 34
4   Danny Goldberg, "Love Them to Death," *Circus*, June 1971
5   Greg Pederson, "Bob Ezrin—I Was a Teenage Record Producer," *Electronic Musician*, August 1996
6   Author interview, March 10, 2012
7   Mitch Lafon, "Bob Ezrin's Favorite 'Ghost' Allan Schwartzberg Talks About Working with KISS, Alice Cooper, Cheap Trick, Jimi Hendrix," www.bravewords.com, October 22, 2010

8   Author interview, October 30, 2014
9   Greg Kenton, "Kiss or Miss? Bob Ezrin Made Sure They Didn't," *Circus*, June 1, 1976, 36
10 Nick Sahakian, *Welcome to My Nightmare*, DVD Audio, 2001
11 Larry LeBlanc, "Industry Profile," *Celebrity Access Mediawire*, May, 24, 2009
12 Author interview, April 4, 2012
13 Author interview, July 17, 2013
14 Author interview, July 17, 2013
15 Author interview, July 17, 2013
16 Author interview, July 2, 2013
17 Author interview, July 17, 2013
18 Greg Kenton "Kiss or Miss? Bob Ezrin Made Sure They Didn't," 34
19 Alice Cooper, Nimbus School of Recording Arts
20 Michael Butler, *Rock N' Roll Geek Show*, 2006
21 Greg Pederson, "Bob Ezrin—I Was a Teenage Record Producer," *Electronic Musician*, August, 1996
22 www.vinyl.com
23 Nick Kent, "The Square and the Faggots," *New Musical Express*, August 18, 1973
24 Nimbus School of Recording Arts

Chapter 5

1   Dave Thompson, *Alice Cooper: Welcome to My Nightmare*, (London: Omnibus Press, 2012), 92
2   Thompson, *Alice Cooper: Welcome to My Nightmare*, 91
3   Greg Kenton, "KISS or Miss? Bob Ezrin Made Sure They Didn't," 36
4   Nimbus School of Recording Arts
5   Author interview, July 2, 2013
6   Author interview, September, 30, 2013
7   Author interview, July 3, 2013
8   Rose, "KISS: Invasion of the Glitter Goths," 24
9   Thompson, *Alice Cooper: Welcome to My Nightmare*, 167
10 Thompson, *Alice Cooper: Welcome to My Nightmare*, 167
11 Author interview, April 9, 2013
12 David McGee, "Success—It's Just a Kiss Away, Kiss Away," *Rolling Stone*, March 25, 1976, 9
13 James Campion, "Alice Cooper: American Treasure," *Aquarian Weekly*, June, 20, 2012

14 Author interview, April 9, 2013
15 Campion, "Alice Cooper: American Treasure," June 20, 2012

Chapter 6

1. Simmons, *KISS and Make-Up*, 112
2. Author interview, April 9, 2013
3. Author interview, April 9, 2013
4. McGee, "Success—It's Just a Kiss Away, Kiss Away," 9
5. Author interview, April 9, 2013
6. Author interview, April 9, 2013
7. David McGree, "The Mask Is for Real," *Wilmington Star News*, NC, February 29, 1976, 14A
8. Kenton, "KISS or Miss? Bob Ezrin Made Sure They Didn't," 34
9. Leaf and Sharp, *Behind the Mask*, 252
10. Leaf and Sharp, *Behind the Mask*, 252
11. Kenton, "KISS or MISS?—Bob Ezrin Made Sure They Didn't," 34
12. Robert Hilburn, "Kiss to Build a Dream On," *Los Angeles Times*, August 30, 1977
13. KISS online
14. Author interview, April 9, 2013
15. Author interview, April 9, 2013
16. George Nobbe, "Fonzie Is My Fantasy," *Circus*, 48–50
17. Author interview, April 9, 2013
18. Criss, *Makeup to Breakup*, 126
19. *KISStory*
20. Simmons, *KISS and Make-Up*, 112
21. KISS online
22. Stanley, *Face the Music*, 188
23. Rose, "Invasion of the Glitter Goths," 24–25
24. Stanley, *Face the Music*, 187
25. Rose, "Invasion of the Glitter Goths," 24

Chapter 7

1. Criss, *Makeup to Breakup*, 250
2. Author interview, April 9, 2013
3. Author interview, April 9, 2013
4. Author interview, April 9, 2013
5. Author interview, July 2, 2013
6. Stanley, *Face the Music*, 189

7. *The Box Set* (London: Mercury Universal, 2001), 46
8. Suhs interview, November, 2004
9. Leaf and Sharp, *Behind the Mask*, 254
10. Kenton, "Kiss or Miss? Bob Ezrin Made Sure They Didn't," 34
11. Jeff Suhs interview, November 2004
12. Simmons, *KISS and Make-Up*, 112–13
13. Robyn Flans, *Modern Drummer*, February 1999
14. Author interview, April 19, 2013
15. Stanley, *Face the Music*, 188
16. Frehley, *No Regrets*, 148–9
17. Leaf and Sharp, *Behind the Mask*, 252
18. Criss, *Makeup to Breakup*, 127
19. Author interview, April 9, 2013
20. Bob Ezrin, *Destroyer Resurrected* liner notes
21. Author interview, April 9, 2013
22. Author interview, April 9, 2013
23. Author interview, March 24, 2011
24. Peter Crescenti, "KISS ALIVE!—Sing While You Die," *Circus*, January 20, 1976, 37
25. Crescenti, "KISS ALIVE!—Sing While You Die," 37
26. Rose, "Invasion of the Glitter Goths," 27–28
27. Author interview, March 24, 2011
28. Author interview, December 10, 2013
29. Author interview, November 20, 2013
30. Stanley, Simmons, Sharp, *Nothin' to Lose*, 394–5
31. Author interview, December 10, 2013
32. Author interview, December 10, 2013
33. Harris, *And Party Every Day*, 140
34. Harris, *And Party Every Day*, 105
35. Harris, *And Party Every Day*, 114
36. Curt Gooch and Jeff Suhs, "Destroyer: Recording and Marketing a Rock and Roll Classic," *KISS Magazine*, Spring 2005, 17
37. Curt Gooch and Jeff Suhs, "Destroyer: Recording and Marketing a Rock and Roll Classic," *KISS Magazine*, Spring 2005, 17
38. Supreme Court of the State New York, County of New York Affidavit, Index no. 16385
39. "Bill Aucoin Q & A Session at Atlanta KISS Expo," *Kissaholics* #20, September 1997

40 Supreme Court of the State New York, County of New York Affidavit, Index no. 17433, Page 2
41 Supreme Court of the State New York, County of New York Affidavit, Index no. 17433, Page 2
42 Supreme Court of the State New York, County of New York Affidavit, Index no. 17433, Page 3
43 Author interview, December 10, 2013
44 Supreme Court of the State New York, County of New York Affidavit, Index no. 17433, Page 4
45 Author interview, April 9, 2013

Chapter 8
1 Susan Whithall, "Bat Lizard Rocks the Boat," *CREEM*, April, 1979
2 Author interview, December 10, 2013
3 Author interview, May 30, 2012
4 Author interview, May 30, 2012
5 Lendt, *Kiss and Sell*, 40–41
6 Author interview, May 30, 2012
7 Author interview, December 10, 2013
8 Author interview, December 10, 2013
9 Author interview, December 10, 2013
10 Sherman, *Black Diamond*, 71
11 Author interview, December 10, 2013
12 "Bill Aucoin Q&A Session at Atlanta KISS Expo," *Kissaholics* #20, September 1997
13 Alan Niester, *Alive!* review, January 1, 1976
14 Devon Powers, *Writing the Record*, (Amherst/Boston: University of Massachusetts Press, 2013), 92
15 *KISSOLOGY Volume I* DVD set (New York City: VH1 Classic Records, 2006)
16 Leaf and Sharp, *Behind the Mask*, 252

Chapter 9
1 Author interview, July 17, 2013
2 James Campion, "The Purpose-Driven Life—Paul Stanley on Life After KISS and His Solo Album *Live to Win*," *Aquarian Weekly*, October 18, 2006
3 *The Box Set*, 60
4 *The Box Set*, 60

5   Author interview, April 9, 2013
6   Author interview, April 9, 2013
7   *The Box Set*, 60
8   Ken Sharp, *Goldmine*, November 20, 1998
9   Author interview, April 9, 2013
10 Author interview, April 9, 2013
11 *The Box Set*, 60
12 Ken Sharp, *Goldmine*, November 20, 1998
13 Author interview, April 9, 2013
14 Frehley, *No Regrets*, 153
15 *The Box Set*, 60
16 Author interview, April 9, 2013
17 Author interview, July 2, 2013
18 Leaf and Sharp, *Behind the Mask*, 262
19 Leaf and Sharp, *Behind the Mask*, 262
20 Leaf and Sharp, *Behind the Mask*, 262
21 Leaf and Sharp, *Behind the Mask*, 262
22 Campion "The Purpose-Driven Life—Paul Stanley on Life After KISS and His Solo Album *Live to Win*," October 18, 2006
23 Leaf and Sharp, *Behind the Mask*, 265
24 Leaf and Sharp, *Behind the Mask*, 265
25 Leaf and Sharp, *Behind the Mask*, 265
26 Rose, "KISS: Invasion of the Glitter Goths," 29
27 Leaf and Sharp, *Behind the Mask*, 262
28 Leaf and Sharp, *Behind the Mask*, 262
29 *The Box Set*, 48
30 *The Box Set*, 48
31 Leaf and Sharp, *Behind the Mask*, 262
32 Leaf and Sharp, *Behind the Mask*, 262
33 Author interview, July 2, 2013
34 Author interview, July 17, 2013

Chapter 10
1   Bob Ezrin at the Midtem Net Forum, 2008
2   Author interview, April 9, 2013
3   Author interview, July 2, 2013
4   Author interview, April 9, 2013
5   Stanley, *Face the Music*, 213
6   Author interview, July 2, 2013

7   Leaf and Sharp, *Behind the Mask*, 266
8   Rose, "KISS: Invasion of the Glitter Goths," 29
9   Leaf and Sharp, *Behind the Mask*, 266–7
10 Leaf and Sharp, *Behind the Mask*, 266
11 Leaf and Sharp, *Behind the Mask*, 267
12 Author interview, July 2, 2013
13 Kim Fowley, "Into the Sinister '70s," *Rock's Back Pages*, 1999
14 Author interview, April 5, 2012
15 Author interview, April 5, 2012
16 Author interview, April 5, 2012
17 Author interview, April 5, 2012
18 Author interview, April 5, 2012
19 Author interview, December 12, 2014
20 Ken Sharp, *Goldmine*, November 11, 1998
21 Author interview, April 5, 2012
22 Author interview, July 2, 2013
23 Robyn Flans, "Peter Criss Interview," *Modern Drummer*, February 1999
24 Author interview, July 2, 2013
25 Author interview, July 2, 2013
26 Author interview, April 5, 2012
27 Author interview December 12, 2014
28 Author interview, April 5, 2012
29 Leaf and Sharp, *Behind the Mask*, 269
30 *The Box Set*, 50
31 Author interview, July 2, 2013

Chapter 11

1   Criss, *Breakup to Makeup*, 129
2   Julien Gill, *The Other Side of the Coin*, (San Francisco: KISSFAQ.com, 2007), 22
3   Gill, *The Other Side of the Coin*, 22
4   *The Box Set*, 48
5   *Rock 101 on the Record*, 2010
6   Criss, *Makeup to Breakup*, 129
7   Criss, *Makeup to Breakup*, 129
8   Author interview, July 2, 2013
9   Leaf and Sharp, *Behind the Mask*, 268
10 Author interview, April 12, 2012
11 Author interview, July 2, 2013

12   Author interview, July 17, 2013
 13   Author interview, July 17, 2013
 14   Author interview, July 17, 2013
 15   Author interview, July 17, 2013
 16   Author interview, July 17, 2013

Chapter 12
  1   Author interview, March 11, 2012
  2   Author interview, July 2, 2013
  3   Author interview, October 30, 2014
  4   Author interview, July 2, 2013
  5   Author interview, July 2, 2013
  6   Author interview, July 2, 2013
  7   Author interview, July 2, 2013
  8   Author interview, July 2, 2013
  9   Bob Margouleff, *New Times*, 1977
 10   Author interview, July 2, 2013
 11   Author interview, March 10, 2012
 12   Author interview, March 10, 2012
 13   Author interview, March 10, 2012
 14   Author interview, March 10, 2012
 15   Author interview, April 18, 2012
 16   Author interview, March 10, 2012
 17   Author interview, March 10, 2012
 18   Author interview, March 10, 2012
 19   Author interview, July 2, 2013
 20   Author interview, July 2, 2013
 21   Author interview, March 10, 2012
 22   Author interview, July 2, 2013
 23   Author interview, July 2, 2013
 24   Author interview, March 30, 2012
 25   Author interview, March 30, 2012
 26   Author interview, March 30, 2012
 27   Author interview, March 30, 2012
 28   Author interview, March 30, 2012
 29   Author interview, March 30, 2012
 30   Author interview, March 30, 2012
 31   Author interview, March 30, 2012
 32   Author interview, March 30, 2012

33　Author interview, March 30, 2012
34　Author interview, March 30, 2012
35　Author interview, March 30, 2012
36　Author interview, March 30, 2012
37　Author interview, July 2, 2013
38　Author interview, March 30, 2012
39　Author interview, March 30, 2012
40　Author interview, March 10, 2012
41　Author interview, March 30, 2012

Chapter 13
1　Author interview, July 2, 2013
2　Author interview, March 30,
3　Author interview, March 11, 2012
4　Author interview, March 10, 2012
5　Author interview, July 2, 2013
6　Author interview, March 10, 2012
7　Author interview, April 12, 2012
8　Author interview, March 10, 2012
9　Author interview, July 2, 2013
10　Stanley, Simmons, and Sharp, *Nothin' to Lose*, 401
11　Author interview, July 2, 2013
12　Criss, *Makeup to Breakup*, 126
13　Frehley, *No Regrets*, 144
14　Author interview, July 2, 2013
15　Author interview, April 18, 2012
16　Author interview, April 19, 2012
17　Author interview, April 19, 2012
18　Author interview, July 2, 2013
19　Criss, *Makeup to Breakup*, 126
20　Stanley, *Face the Music*, 209–10
21　Author interview, April 19, 2012
22　Leaf and Sharp, *Behind the Mask*, 252
23　Author interview, July 2, 2013
24　Author interview, April 12, 2012
25　Author interview, July 2, 2013
26　Author interview, April 12, 2012
27　Leaf and Sharp, *Behind the Mask*, 252
28　Author interview, July 2, 2013

29 Author interview, April 5, 2012
30 Criss, *Makeup to Breakup*, 125
31 Author interview, April 12, 2012
32 Simmons, *KISS and Make-Up*, 113
33 Author interview, April 12, 2012
34 Stanley, Simmons, and Sharp, *Nothin' to Lose*, 400–1
35 Jeff Suhs interview, April, 2004
36 Author interview, April 12, 2012
37 Author interview, March 10, 2012
38 Author interview, March 10, 2012

Chapter 14
1 Author interview, April 12, 2012
2 Author interview, July 2, 2013
3 Author interview, March 11, 2012
4 Author interview, April 12, 2012
5 Author interview, April 18, 2012
6 Author interview, March 11, 2012
7 Author interview, April 12, 2012
8 Author interview, March 11, 2012
9 Author interview, April 12, 2012
10 Author interview, April 18, 2012
11 Author interview, April 12, 2012
12 Author interview, April 18, 2012
13 Author interview, April 12, 2012
14 Author interview, March 11, 2012
15 Author interview, March 11, 2012
16 Author interview, March 11, 2012
17 Author interview, April 12, 2012
18 Author interview, March 10, 2012
19 Ezrin, *Destroyer Resurrected* liner notes
20 Author interview, March 10, 2012
21 Author interview, April 18, 2012
22 Author interview, March 10, 2012
23 Author interview, July 2, 2013
24 Author interview, April 12, 2012
25 Flans, "Peter Criss Interview," *Modern Drummer*, February 1999
26 Flans, "Peter Criss Interview," *Modern Drummer*, February 1999
27 Ken Sharp, *Goldmine*, November, 20, 1998

28   Author interview, April 18, 2012
29   Author interview, April 12, 2012
30   Criss, *Makeup to Breakup*, 127
31   Author interview, July 2, 2013
32   Author interview, April 12, 2012
33   Criss, *Makeup to Breakup*, 126
34   Joe Degraffenreid, *KISS Hell Online*, 1998
35   Author interview, April 12, 2012
36   Author interview, March 10, 2012
37   Criss, *Makeup to Breakup*, 126
38   Joe Degraffenreid, *KISS Hell Online*, 1998
39   Criss, *Makeup to Breakup*, 126
40   Author interview, July 2, 2013
41   Criss, *Makeup to Breakup*, 128

Chapter 15
  1   Author interview, April 12, 2012
  2   Author interview, July 2, 2013
  3   Author interview, April 19, 2012
  4   Author interview, April 19, 2012
  5   Author interview, March 10, 2012
  6   Author interview, October 30, 2014
  7   Author interview, April 12, 2012
  8   Suhs interview, April 2004
  9   Stanley, *Face the Music*, 191
 10   Author interview, April 9, 2013
 11   Author interview, April 5, 2013
 12   Author interview, October 30, 2014
 13   Author interview, April 5, 2013
 14   Author interview, October 30, 2014
 15   Author interview, April 5, 2013
 16   Stanley, *Face the Music*, 191–2
 17   Author interview, April 5, 2013
 18   *The Box Set*, 61
 19   Simmons, *KISS and Make-Up*, 114–15
 20   Stanley, *Face the Music*, 191
 21   "Ace & Paul Talk to Vintage Guitar," *Vintage Guitar*, March 1997
 22   Author interview, April 19, 2012
 23   Author interview, April 19, 2012

24 Suhs interview, Novembe, 2004
25 Ezrin, *Destroyer Resurrected* liner notes
26 Ezrin, *Destroyer Resurrected* liner notes, Suhs interview, November 2004
27 Author interview, March 11, 2012
28 Author interview, April 5, 2013
29 Suhs interview, November 2004
30 Author interview, October 21, 2014
31 Author interview, October 30, 2014
32 Author interview, July 2, 2013
33 Author interview, October 30, 2014
34 Author interview, October 30, 2014
35 Author interview, October 30, 2014
36 Author interview, October 21, 2014
37 Author interview, July 2, 2013
38 Author interview, October 21, 2014
39 Author interview, July 2, 2013
40 Author interview, October 21, 2014
41 Author interview, October 30, 2014
42 Author interview, November 4, 2014
43 Author interview December 18, 2014
44 Author interview, April 19, 2012
45 Author interview, April 19, 2012
46 Author interview, December 12, 2014
47 Author interview, April 18, 2012
48 Author interview, December 12, 2014
49 Author interview, April 19, 2012
50 Author interview, April 18, 2012

Chapter 16
1 Author interview, April 28, 2012
2 Author interview, July 2, 2013
3 Joe Degraffenreid, *KISS Hell Online*, 1998
4 Author interview, July 2, 2013
5 Leaf and Sharp, *Behind the Mask*, 252
6 Criss, *Makeup to Breakup*, 128
7 Author interview, April 5, 2013
8 Author interview, July 2, 2013
9 Frehley, *No Regrets*, 148
10 Author interview, April 19, 2012

11 Author interview, December 12, 2014
12 Author interview, April 28, 2012
13 Alice Cooper, Foreword, *Not Only Women Bleed*
14 Author interview, April 28, 2012
15 Author interview, April 28, 2012
16 Author interview, July 2, 2013
17 Frehley, *No Regrets*, 148
18 Simmons, *KISS and Make-Up*, 115
19 Author interview, December 12, 2014
20 Author interview, April 28, 2012
21 Author interview, April 19, 2012
22 Leaf and Sharp, *Behind the Mask*, 266
23 Author interview, April 28, 2012
24 Author interview, April 28, 2012
25 Author interview, December 12, 2014
26 Author interview, April 19, 2012
27 Author interview, April 28, 2012
28 Author interview, April 28, 2012
29 Greg Pederson, "Bob Ezrin—I Was a Teenage Record Producer," April 18, 2007
30 Author interview, April 28, 2012
31 Author interview, April 28, 2012
32 Author interview, December 12, 2014
33 Leaf and Sharp, *Behind the Mask*, 266
34 Author interview, April 5, 2013
35 Author interview, March 20, 2012
36 Author interview, July 2, 2013
37 Author interview, March 20, 2012
38 Author interview, July 2, 2013
39 Author interview, July 2, 2013
40 Author interview, July 2, 2013
41 Author interview, July 2, 2013
42 Author interview, April 12, 2012

Chapter 17
1 Rose, "KISS: Invasion of the Glitter Goths," 24
2 Simmons, *KISS and Make-Up*, 116
3 Sherman, *Black Diamond*, 75
4 Leaf and Sharp, *Behind the Mask*, 268

5   Rose, "KISS: Invasion of the Glitter Goths," 27
6   Author interview, July 2, 2013
7   Email from Jay Messina, December 26, 2013
8   Phil Ramone, *Making Records* (New York: Hyperion, 2007), 137
9   Author interview, July 17, 2013
10 Author interview, May 16, 2012
11 Author interview, May 16, 2012
12 Author interview, July 2, 2013
13 Author interview, April 12, 2012
14 Author interview, April 12, 2012
15 Author interview, April 12, 2012
16 Author interview, July 17, 2013
17 Author interview, December 12, 2014
18 Author interview, July 17, 2013
19 Gooch and Suhs, "Destroyer: Recording and Marketing a Rock and Roll Classic," 18–19
20 Author interview, April 28, 2012
21 Author interview, April 18, 2012
22 Author interview, July 17, 2013
23 Author interview, April 19, 2012
24 Author interview, July 17, 2013
25 Author interview, July 17, 2013
26 Rose, "KISS: Invasion of the Glitter Goths," 24
27 Rose, "KISS: Invasion of the Glitter Goths," 29
28 Rose, "KISS: Invasion of the Glitter Goths," 29
29 Rose, "KISS: Invasion of the Glitter Goths," 29
30 Rose, "KISS: Invasion of the Glitter Goths," 24
31 Rose, "KISS: Invasion of the Glitter Goths," 24
32 Rose, "KISS: Invasion of the Glitter Goths," 29
33 Author interview, April 12, 2012
34 Author interview, April 12, 2012
35 Criss, *Makeup to Breakup*, 130
36 Author interview, April 18, 2012
37 Criss, *Makeup to Breakup*, 130
38 Stanley, *Face the Music*, 190
39 Author interview, April 18, 2012
40 Author interview, April 12, 2012
41 Criss, *Makeup to Breakup*, 131

Chapter 18

1. Author interview, September 30, 2013
2. Author interview, April 11, 2012
3. Author interview, April 11, 2012
4. Author interview, April 11, 2012
5. Author interview, October 24, 2014
6. Author interview, April 11, 2012
7. Author interview, April 11, 2012
8. Author interview, April 11, 2012
9. Author interview, April 11, 2012
10. Author interview, September 30, 2013
11. Author interview, September 30, 2013
12. Author interview, September 30, 2013
13. Author interview, September 30, 2013
14. Author interview, September 30, 2013
15. Author interview, September 30, 2013
16. Author interview, April 11, 2012
17. Author interview, September 30, 2013
18. Author interview, April 11, 2012
19. Author interview, September 30, 2013
20. Author interview, September 30, 2013
21. Author interview, April 11, 2012
22. Author interview, September 30, 2013
23. Author interview, April 11, 2012
24. Author interview, September 30, 2013
25. Author interview, September 30, 2013
26. Author interview, September 30, 2013
27. Author interview, September 30, 2013
28. Author interview, September 30, 2013
29. Author interview, April 11, 2012
30. Author interview, September 30, 2013
31. Author interview, September 30, 2013
32. Author interview, April 11, 2012
33. Author interview, September 30, 2013
34. Author interview, September 30, 2013
35. Author interview, April 11, 2012
36. Author interview, September 30, 2013
37. Author interview, April 11, 2012
38. Author interview, September 30, 2013

Chapter 19
1. Ralph Simon, *Music Matters*, 2012
2. *The Box Set*, 48
3. Author interview, April 19, 2012
4. Author interview, April 19, 2012
5. Author interview, April 18, 2012
6. Author interview, April 19, 2012
7. Author interview, April 19, 2012
8. Author interview, April 19, 2012
9. Author interview, April 18, 2012
10. Author interview, April 18, 2012
11. Author interview, December 12, 2014
12. Author interview, April 19, 2012
13. *KISS Online*, 2012
14. Author interview, April 18, 2012
15. Will Hermes, *Love Goes to Buildings on Fire: Five Years in New York That Changed Music Forever* (New York: Faber and Faber, 2011), 42
16. Author interview, April 18, 2012
17. Author interview, April 18, 2012
18. Eddie Trunk interview, December 8, 2001
19. Author interview, April 18, 2012
20. Author interview, April 19, 2012
21. Author interview, April 5, 2012
22. Author interview, April 5, 2012
23. Author interview, April 5, 2012
24. Suhs interview, November 2004
25. Author interview, April 5, 2012
26. Author interview, July 2, 2013
27. Author interview, April 5, 2012
28. Author interview, April 18, 2012
29. Author interview, April 5, 2012
30. Suhs interview, November 2004
31. Author interview, April 5, 2012
32. Suhs interview, November 2004
33. Author interview, April 5, 2012
34. Author interview, April 9, 2013
35. Author interview, April 19, 2012
36. Author interview, April 18, 2012
37. Ezrin, *Destroyer Resurrected* liner notes

Chapter 20

1. *Uncut*, February 6, 2006
2. Author interview, October 24, 2014
3. Author interview, May 30, 2012
4. Author interview, October 24, 2014
5. John Milward, *Rolling Stone*, June 1976
6. Harry Doherty, *Melody Maker*, April 17, 1976
7. United Press International, 1976
8. Max Bell, *Melody Maker*, April 24, 1976
9. Rick Johnson, *CREEM*, July 1976, 66
10. Robert Duncan, *Circus*, August 24, 1976, 10
11. Author interview, December 12, 2014
12. Stanley, *Face the Music*, 206
13. Author interview, December 12, 2014
14. Davis, *Walk This Way*, 292
15. Author interview, December 12, 2014
16. Author interview, December 12, 2014
17. Author interview, April 19, 2012
18. Author interview, September 30, 2013
19. Author interview, April 19, 2012
20. Gooch and/Suhs, *KISS Alive Forever*, 68
21. Gooch and/Suhs, *KISS Alive Forever*, 67–8
22. Author interview, December 10, 2013
23. Author interview, October 24, 2014
24. Gooch and Suhs, *KISS Alive Forever*, 67–8
25. Gooch and Suhs, *KISS Alive Forever*, 69
26. Author interview, October, 22, 2012
27. Author interview, October, 22, 2012
28. Author interview, October, 22, 2012
29. Author interview, October, 22, 2012
30. Sherman, *Black Diamond*, 80
31. Stein, "KISS Tour '76: The Ooze of the Greasepaint. The Roar of the Crowd," 34

Chapter 21

1. Author interview, April 17, 2014
2. Ken Sharp interview, 1993
3. Author interview, December 10, 2013
4. Author interview, April 17, 2014

5   Author interview, April 17, 2014
6   Author interview, April 17, 2014
7   Author interview, April 17, 2014
8   Harris, *And Party Every Day*, 136
9   Author interview, April 17, 2014
10 Author interview, April 17, 2014
11 Author interview, December 10, 2013
12 Author interview, April 17, 2014
13 Author interview, December 10, 2013
14 Author interview, April 17, 2014
15 Author interview, December 10, 2013
16 Author interview, December 10, 2013
17 Author interview, April 17, 2014
18 Criss, *Makeup to Breakup*, 131
19 Criss, *Makeup to Breakup*, 131
20 Author interview, April 17, 2014
21 Stanley, *Face the Music*, 204
22 Simmons, *KISS and Make-Up*, 117
23 Sharp and Leaf, *Behind the Mask*, 69
24 Author interview, December 12, 2014
25 Author interview, December 10, 2013
26 Author interview, April 17, 2014
27 Lendt, *KISS and Sell*, 100
28 Author interview, April 19, 2012
29 Author interview, April 19, 2012
30 Stanley, *Face the Music*, 206
31 Author interview, April 19, 2012

Chapter 22
1   Tom Morello, Rock and Roll Hall of Fame press conference, 2014
2   Criss, *Makeup to Breakup*, 273
3   Robert Dimery, *1001 Albums You Must Hear Before You Die*, (Milan: Universe Publishing, 2005), 360
4   Adam Budofsky, "RHCP's Brad Smith," *Modern Drummer*, August 17, 2011
5   Author interview, August 12, 2014
6   Eddie Trunk to author, September 26, 2014
7   Author interview, October 21, 2014
8   Author interview, April 11, 2012

9   Author interview, October 24, 2014
10 Author interview, October 24, 2014
11 Author interview, October 24, 2014
12 Author interview, October 22, 2012
13 Author interview, April 5, 2012
14 Author interview, April 5, 2012
15 Author interview, September 30, 2013
16 Author interview, September 30, 2013
17 Author interview, July 17, 2013
18 Author interview, April 19, 2012
19 Author interview, April 18, 2012
20 Ezrin, *Resurrected* liner notes
21 Author interview, April 9, 2013
22 Author interview, July 2, 2013
23 Stanley, *Face the Music*, 456

Selected Bibliography

Criss, Peter. *Makeup to Breakup*. New York: Scribner, 2012.
Davis, Stephen. *Walk This Way*. New York: HarperCollins, 1997.
Demorest, Steve. *Alice Cooper*. New York: Gerald Rothberg Publications, Inc., 1974.
Dimery, Robert. *1001 Albums You Must Hear Before You Die*. Milan: Universe Publishing, 2005.
Frehley, Ace. *No Regrets*. New York: Gallery Books, 2011.
Gill, Julien. *The KISS Album Focus (3rd Edition)*. San Francisco: KISSFAQ.com, 2008.
Gill, Julien. *The Other Side of the Coin*. San Francisco: KISSFAQ.com, 2007.
Gooch, Curt, and Jeff Suhs. *KISS Alive Forever*. New York: Billboard Books, 2002.
Harris, Larry. *And Party Every Day*. Montclair: Backbeat Books, 2009.
Hermes, Will. *Love Goes to Buildings on Fire—Five Years in New York That Changed Music Forever*. New York: Faber and Faber, 2007.
Leaf, David, and Ken Sharp. *KISS: Behind the Mask: The Official Authorized Biography*. New York: Grand Central Publishing, 2003.
Lendt, C. K. *KISS and Sell*. New York: Billboard Books, 1997.
Polan, Dana. *Pulp Fiction*. London: British Film Institute, 2000.
Powers, Devon. *Writing the Record*. Amherst/Boson: University of Massachusetts Press, 2013.
Ramone, Phil. *Making Records: The Scenes Behind the Music*. New York: Hyperion, 2007.
Sherman, Dale. *Black Diamond*. London: CG Publishing, 1997.
Simmons, Gene. *Kiss and Make-Up*. New York: Crown Books, 2001.
Stanley, Paul. *Face the Music—A Life Exposed*. New York: HarperOne, 2014.
Stanley, Paul, Gene Simmons, and Ken Sharp. *Nothin' to Lose: The Making of KISS 1972–1975*. New York: HarperCollins, 2013.
Thompson, Dave. *Alice Cooper: Welcome to My Nightmare*. London: Omnibus Press, 2012.

Index

acoustic instruments. *See also* guitar(s)
  on "Beth," 249
  Ezrin recordings of, 136, 143, 155, 187, 254
  in "Great Expectations," 91
  on "Rock Bottom," 35
  in "Sweet Pain," 117–19, 155
The Act
  adding depth to, 72–73, 187
  changes in, 74–75, 104
  concept of, 17
  during *Destroyer*, xiv–xv
  early development of, 7–8
  Ezrin changing, 74–75
  first public display of, 223
  formation of, xiv
  four pieces of, 97–98
  money models of, 20–21
  paintings of, 242
  post-*Destroyer*, 295–96
  promotion of, 12
  at Studio A, 160–61
  theme songs defining, 116–17, 123–24
  vulnerable side of, 131, 140
Action Comics, 233
Adagio, 120
advertising. *See also* marketing
  at Casablanca Records, 273–74
  early band, 86–87
  Howard Marks agency, 13, 98, 100, 237–39, 305
  of KISS Army, 267–68
  marketing themes in, 296
  music in, 51
  publicity as, 7–8, 25–26
Aerosmith
  Ezrin and, 148
  guitar playing in, 205
  Messina with, 312
  success of, 273
  Wagner appreciating, 201–2
Alamance Hospital, 328
album cover art
  back themes of, 244
  Casablanca Records opinions about, x, 243
  colors for, 242–45
  designer of, 235–36
  after *Destroyer*, 315
  for *Destroyer*, 240–43
  Frazetta attempt at, 235
  logo as, 268
  paintings for, 241–44
  Woloch concept of, 233
the Alice Cooper Group
  child's sounds recordings for, 210
  circus themes of, 47
  Ezrin relationship with, 52–53, 167–68

formation of, 45
image of, 46–47
shows of, 46
songs of, 47–48
Alive!
  Aucoin during, 99
  Casablanca Records during, 101–2
  charting of, 101
  criticism of, x, 75, 104
  famous back cover shot on, 39, 99
  finances during, 87, 97–102
  marketing of, 98–100
  photo shoot for, 96, 98–99
  Rolling Stone reviews of, 103
  sales of, 95
  sounds on, 163–64
  tour for, 97
Alive II, 302
ambient sound, 177–78, 256
American Graffiti, 127
AMI. *See* Aucoin Management Incorporated
Ampeg B-15, 171–72
Anaheim Stadium, 279
analog tape, 254
And Party Every Day, 30, 286
Animal House, 124
Ann Arbor, 325
"Another Brick in the Wall," 210
Anthony, Mark
  Fowley relationship with, 126–27
  history of, 127
Anthrax, 304
Argent, 37
Arista Records, 127
A&R Studios
  engineers at, 142, 247
  environment of, 145, 147
  orchestra recording at, 219

Asheville Citizen Times, 326
Aucoin, Bill
  at A1 Studio, 220–21
  in *Alive!* years, 99
  during "Beth," 290
  Bogart battles with, 89
  career of, 12–14, 305
  in *Circus* magazine, 74, 218
  Ezrin relationship with, 70–71
  finances of, 85, 100
  Harris critique of, 85–87
  at Howard Marks, 239
  legal troubles of, 88–89
  management career of, 14
  reputation of, 221
Aucoin Management Incorporated (AMI), 275, 305

babies
  recording sounds of, 210
Bach, Johann Sebastian, 155
Baker, Julius, 223
Baker, Keith, 328
ballad(s)
  "The Ballad of Dwight Frye," 137
  "Beth" as, 137, 288–89, 292
  circus themes in, 78
  on *Destroyer*, 217–18
  "Great Expectations" as, 79, 135
  "Only Women Bleed" as, 62, 131
  standards of, 62
  writing "Flaming Youth" as, 80, 121
Baltimore Civic Center, 279
Bangs, Lester, 23
bass
  compressor, 172
  on *Destroyer*, 112–13, 171–72
  tuning down, 189
bathrooms

recording sounds in, 260
the Beach Boys, 43
Beacon Theater, 36
the Beatles
    era of, 21–22
    four pieces of, 97–98
    Ringo, 285
Beck, Jeff, 135
Beethoven, Ludwig van, 81–83, 91–93, 119–20, 139, 225–26
Bell, Max, 270
Bell Sound studio, 98, 134
Berlin
    children recorded on, 211
    Macmillan on, 138
"Beth"
    acoustic instruments on, 249
    analysis of, 263–65
    argument during, 218–19
    Brand influence on, 134
    changes to, 137
    chords of, 136–37
    conception of, 217–18
    credibility of, 290–91
    Criss influence on, 133, 135–37, 227–28, 289–90
    as epic ballad, 137, 288–89, 292
    Ezrin influences on, 135–36
    Ezrin/Macmillan collaboration on, 138–40
    final recording of, 227
    as a hit, 286–89
    instrumentation on, 140
    orchestra on, 136–37, 217–18, 227, 264–65
    Penridge guitar on, 133
    piano on, 137–38, 264–65
    success of, 291
    themes of, 140
    writing of, 133–34
"The Big 8," 284
"big room sound," 160
"Big Shan," 285
The Big Show, 306
Billboard chart, 274–75, 283, 300
Billion Dollar Babies
    drums on, 178
    writing of, 47
binaural techniques, 258
Black Diamond, (Sherman), 38
"Black Diamond," 95, 293
    Replacements' version of, 302
Black Sabbath, 37, 284
Bloody Stake, 277
blowing fire, 13
Bogart, Neil, 14
    Aucoin battles with, 89
    as cheerleader, 169
    after *Destroyer*, 305–6
    divorce of, 287
    finances of, 87
    legal trouble with, 88–89
    recordings of, 35–36
    Shannon relationship with, 26
Bonamassa, Joe, 325
boot camp
    creative process during, 82–83
    song writing during, 79–81
    tension during, 75–76
    timing during, 81
Born to Run, 150
Boston, 287
Boutwell Enterprises, 267
Bowie, David
    Diamond Dogs, 256, 276
    in early 1970s, 7
    personas of, 18
    Ziggy days of, 22

The Box Set, 111
Bradford, Robert, 329
Brand, Michael, 133–34
Brando, Marlon, 72–73
bridges, 122
Briggs, David, 53
Brooklyn Academy of Fine Arts, 233
Brooklyn Boys Choir
   costumes of, 222
   engineers at, 224
   Ezrin directing of, 225
   first meetings with, xvi, 217
   orchestral style of, 224–25
   at Studio A1, 220–21
Brooks, Mel, 149
Brown, Robert, 279
Buck Rogers, 233
Buddah Records, 14
Burroughs, Edgar Rice, 233
Buxton, Glen, 55

calliope, 196–97
car crash
   in "Detroit Rock City," 260–61, 326–30
   in "King of the Night Time World," 41
Carlin, George, x
Carlson, Arthur, 329
Carroll's Music, 267
Carroll's Rehearsal Studios, 77
Casablanca Records
   Alive! influence on, 101–2
   cover art opinions of, x, 243
   going under, 305
   after KISS, 305–6
   KISS at, x, 14, 85–89
   lawsuits, 84–86, 88–89, 219
   promoting KISS, 273–74

Cat Box, 180
the Cat Man
   analysis of, ix
   comic book style depiction of, 315
   role of, 316
Caucasian blues, xiv
CBGB's, 308
Chaney, Lon, 9
Charleston Municipal Auditorium, 330
Charlotte, North Carolina, 323–24
Charlotte Observer, 324
Cheetah Club, 46
Chelsea
   "Beth" written in, 134
   Criss in, 11, 134
Cher, 296
chicken incident, 47
children
   the Alice Cooper Group recording of, 210
   in *Berlin*, 211
   book written for, 307
   Ezrin's recording of, 209–12
   innocence of, 210
   in *The Wall*, 211
Chocolate City, 26
choral voices. *See also* vocal(s)
   in Brooklyn Boys Choir, 224–25
   on "Shout It Out Loud," 213–14
church recordings, 257
Cicala, Roy, 145, 150
Circus magazine
   Alice Cooper Group in, 47
   Aucoin in, 74, 218
   on comic books, 20
   cover story, 8
   Duncan in, 271

INDEX

early recording sessions
    documented by, 84
early reviews by, 27, 31
Ezrin in, 49, 51, 55, 71
the Fonz's interview in, 73
Frehley interview in, 81
Rose interview in, 74, 221, 225
Simmons interview in, 124
Stanley interview in, 75
circus themes/performances
    in ballads, 78
    extravaganza, xvi
    Ezrin's, 78
    in "Flaming Youth," 107–8, 196–97
    imagery of, 107–8
    jokes about, 30
    lessons in, 13
    in recording, 196–97
citizens band radio, 161
CKLW, 284
classical music
    Bach, 155
    Beethoven, 81–83, 91–93, 119–20, 139, 225–26
    influencing Ezrin, 206
Clayton, Peter, 51
Cobo Hall, 284
cocaine
    during *Destroyer* album, 163–66, 182, 192, 199, 200, 296
Columbus, 287
comic books
    Action Comics, 233
    Circus magazine on, 20
    culture of, 233
    DC, 233
    influence of, 20
    about KISS, 314–15
compression, 172–74, 188

Conan the Barbarian, 233
confetti machines, 279
Cooper, Alice, 7
    chicken incident, 47
    Circus interview, 47
    Ezrin relationship with, 52–53, 167–68
    Fowley influence on, 125
    group, 45–46
    manager of, 46, 51, 59
    recording sessions for, 55
    recording studios for, 142
    as rock-and-roll villain, 45
Costello, Fin
    book contributions of, 333
    Destroyer photo shoot by, 269
    famous *Alive!* cover shot by, 39, 99
    first KISS show for, 36
    photos, sketches of, 240
costumes
    of Brooklyn Boys Choir, 222
    character development with, 9–10
    dashikis, 222
    drawings of, 240–41
    Frehley's, 10–11
    Simmons', 10
    S&M, 12
    tuxedo t-shirt, 222
Counting Crows, 303
covers compilation, 302
Creem magazine, 30, 221, 271, 284, 315, 336, 342
Creepy #72, 235–37
Criscuola, Lydia, 227, 292
Crisp, Gail Renee, 328
Criss, Peter (Criscuola), xiii
    anger of, 182–83
    on "Beth," 133, 135–37, 227–28, 289–90

changes in, xiii, 104
in Chelsea, 11, 134
drug use of, 164–65
drum kit of, 171
drumming process of, 179
early history of, 10
Ezrin relationship with, 181–82
influences on, 11
on "King of the Night Time World," 128
leaving band, 296
life history of, 234
moods of, 180–81
role of, 316
songwriting of, 80
stress of, 190–91

Daisy Club, 111
"Dance of the Hippos," 119
dashikis, 222
David, Marie, 324
dB Magazine, 257
DC Comics, 233
Decca Records, 133
DeGerlando, Vincent, 232, 276
Delaney, Sean, 12–13
career of, 305
the Demon
analysis of, ix, 10
comic book style depiction of, 315
growl of, 115
role of, 316
songs about, 119
theme, 93
"Demons of Rock," 232
Derringer, Rick, 201
Destroyer
The Act during, xiv–xv
backup vocals on, 252–53
ballads on, 217–18
bass on, 112–13
"Blue," 243, 245, 309
Bogart after, 305–6
bookend to, 255
"Brown," 242–43, 309
cocaine use during, 163–66, 182, 192, 199, 200, 296
cover art themes for, 240–43
defining KISS's sound, 169
early sessions for, 84
engineers, adding thematic touch to, 311–12
Ezrin drug use during, 165–66
Ezrin influence on, 71–72, 113–15, 140, 312–13
final cuts of, 253–54, 260–61
finishing touches on, 261
first public display of, 223
Fowley influence on, 8
funding of, 84–85
going multi-platinum, 304
importance of, xiii–xiv, 290–91
influences on, xvi–xvii
instruments on, 171–73
KISS post-, 315
legal trouble during, 88–89
live sound of, 177
longevity of, 303, 304
at Magna Graphic Studios, 112, 117
making of, 83–84, 109–10, 173–74
meaning on, 293–94
media after, 292
Messina on, 312
mixing of, 253
myths around, 208–9
orchestral influence on, 139–40
paintings for, 310

photo shoot for, 269
production of, xv, 75, 186–89
recording final days of, 250–61
recording sessions for, 185–86
recording street sounds for, 173–74
reviews of, 269–70
Rolling Stone reviews of, 69, 269
Rose during, 84–85
Stanley views of, 75–76
technological tricks on, 189
theme songs on, 116–17
time signatures on, 121–22, 179–80
title of, 232
tour for, 275, 279–80
vocals on, 250–51
Woloch packaging of, 98, 231
writing of, 121–22
Destroyer Resurrected
  making of, 83
  original master tapes of, 261
  songs of, 111
Detroit 1970s
  KISS's connection to, 284
  musical influence from, x, 23–24
  songs written for, 96, 110
"Detroit Rock City"
  analysis of, 3–6
  car crash related to, 260–61, 326–30
  chords of, 112–13
  first plays of, ix
  guitars on, 3–6
  inspiration for, 323, 330
  layering on, 190
  as Morello's favorite, 299
  release of, 283–84
  song structure/themes of, 110–11
  vocals on, 3–6
  writing of, 80, 111–12
"Deuce," 95

Diamond Dogs, 256, 276
Dickens, Charles, 118
Dickerson, Rich, 268
Digital Dream Door, 300
Dimery, Robert, 300
Disney, 119
Doherty, Harry, 270
Dolby machines, 187
Don Elliott Production studio, 146
the Doors, 27
Doret, Michael, 268
Double Platinum, 111
Douglas, Jack, 148, 272
"Do You Love Me?"
  analysis of, 319–22
  drums on, 319–22
  Fowley on, 309
  guitars on, 319–22
  influences on, 130
  Nirvana cover of, 302
  orchestral bells on, 187–88
  time signatures on, 131
  vocals on, 319–22
  writing of, 129–30
Drake, 288
drawings, 240–41
Dressed to Kill, 324, 326–27
  Destroyer compared to, 84
  Ezrin working on, 71
  recording of, 34
  reviews of, 35–36
  songs of, 34
drug use
  during *Destroyer* album, 163–66, 182, 192, 199, 200, 296
  Ezrin's, 165–66, 182, 199, 296
drum(s)
  on *Billion Dollar Babies*, 178
  Criss's signature, 179

on "Do You Love Me?," 319–22
engineer recordings of, 49
on "God of Thunder," 65–67, 207
on "King of the Night Time World," 41–43, 128
kit, 171
recording of, 176, 178
-riser, 160
on "Shout It Loud," 213, 215
DuBay, Bill, 236
Dunaway, Dennis, 55
Duncan, Robert, 271
Duritz, Adam, 303
Dust, 26
Dylan, Bob, 21, 220

East Coast Rocker, 45
Eastern Carolina University, 329
East Village's Electric Circus, 134
Easy Action, 53
Edgar Winter Group, 118
Eerie, 235–36
Electric Lady Studios, 11
Electronic Musician, 48, 52
EMT echo chambers, 188
engineers
    at A&R Studios, 142, 247
    assistant/new, 312
    at boys choir, 224
    buzz of, 247
    Destroyer final cuts by, 253–54, 260–61
    Ezrin reputation as, 49
    looping by, 256
    Messina reputation as, 311–12
    Ramone influence on, 219
    recording drums, 49
    at Record Plant, 145, 254
    straightforwardness of, 226

thematic touches added by, 255, 311–12
Eno, Brian, 256
Epic Records, 124
Essential Hard Rock and Heavy Metal, 304
Evans, Jay, 268
Eventide digital tape delay, 188
Ezrin, Bob
    with Aerosmith, 148
    Alice Cooper relationship with, 52–53, 167–68
    answering service of, 272
    artistic views of, 71
    with Aucoin, 70–71
    being replaced, 273
    during "Beth," 135–36, 138–40
    as bridge-maker, 122
    career of, 48, 312–13
    changes made by, 74–75
    in *Circus* magazine, 49, 51, 55, 71
    circus of, 78
    classical music influence on, 206
    collaborations of, 123–24
    Criss relationship with, 181–82
    on *Destroyer*, 71–72, 113–15, 140, 312–13
    directing Brooklyn Boys Choir, 225
    disciplinary tendencies of, 167–68
    dramatizations of, 330
    on *Dressed to Kill*, 71
    drug use of, 165–66, 182, 199, 296
    as engineer, 49
    on "Flaming Youth," 122–23
    Fowley relationship with, 126–28
    impact of, 50, 55
    influencing KISS, 81–83, 294
    KISS tension with, 77–78
    KISS writing with, 79–80

as "knowing" music, 50–51
Macmillan relationship with,
   50–51, 139–40
Messina relationship with, 48,
   148–49, 162
musical influences of, 50
O'Brien relationship with, 49, 141
philosophy of, 314
pranks of, 193
quotes of, xv, 45
Ramone relationship with, 219
recording, knowledge of, 189–90
recording, of acoustic instruments,
   136, 143, 155, 187, 254
recording, of children, 209–12
recording, of street sounds, 259
at Record Plant, 142–43
reputation of, 49, 151–52
Roger Waters relationship with,
   210–11
Stasiak relationship with, 152–53
uncle's influence on, 258–59
unique visual sound of, 254–55,
   260–61
vision of, 168, 261
Wagner relationship with, 202–3
whistle of, 166–67

Face the Music, 74, 316–17
Fantasia, 115
"Fantasy Sound," 119
Fayetteville Observer, 325
Fender Tweed twin-reverb amp, 172
finances
   during *Alive!*, 87, 97–102
   Aucoin influence on, 85, 100
   Bogart influence on, 87
   at Casablanca Records, 85–86
"Firehouse," 95

First KISS Grand Orchestral and
   Choral Recording Session,
   218–19, 223–24, 228–29, 308
"Flaming Youth"
   analysis of, 107–8
   circus themes in, 107–8, 196–97
   Ezrin coaching on, 122–23
   lyrics of, 107–8
   music of, 122
   release of, 274–75
   themes of, 140
   time signatures in, 122–23
   vocals on, 107–8
   writing of, 80, 121
Flash Gordon, 233
Flickinger, Peter, 142
Flickinger bass compressor, 172
Flipside, 12
flutes, 223
the Fonz, 73
Foo Fighters, 299
Foster, Ms. Liz, 330
4/4 time
   during boot camp, 81
   during *Destroyer*, 122
Four Tops, 125
Fowley, Kim
   Anthony relationship with, 126–27
   career of, 308
   during *Destroyer* sessions, 8
   on "Do You Love Me?," 309
   Ezrin relationship with, 126–28
   influencing Alice Cooper, 125
   on "King of the Night Time
      World," 309
   KISS collaborations with, 128–29,
      308
Frazetta, Frank
   career of, 233

INDEX

cover art attempts by, 235
ego of, 234
nephew of, 236
"Free Ride," 118
Frehley, Ace (Paul)
  changes in, xiii, 104
  in *Circus* magazine, 81
  costume development of, 10–11
  drug use of, 164–65, 199–200
  guitars of, 172
  history of, 10–11, 234
  leaving band, 296
  No Regrets, 19
  precision of, 169
  recording attitude of, 190–91
  replacement of, 208–9
  role of, 316
  self confidence/fears of, 200–201, 203
  Wagner stepping in for, 203–4
  wedding of, 283
  writing *Destroyer*, 121
  on writing solos, 191
Frehley's Comet, 304
Frey, Don, 220
Furnier, Vincent, 45

Garinger, Anne, 326
Garnier, Palais, 257
Germano, Ed, 150
Get Your Wings, 201
Gibson guitars. *See also* guitar(s)
  nine1957, 248
  custom, 249
  Explorer, 172
  Firebird, 248
  Les Paul, 206
  Ripper LS-9, 171–72
Glantz, Steve, 36

Glickman, Carl, 99
Glickman/Marks
  business management team, 99, 275, 279–80, 294
Gloria Gaynor, 49
"God of Thunder"
  analysis of, 65–67
  drums on, 65–67, 207
  guitar on, 65–67, 207–8
  influences on, 209
  machine, 277
  release of, 274–75
  vocals on, 65–67
  writing of, 115
Goes To Hell, 49
Gooch, Curt, 29, 277, 324
"Good Night Vienna," 285
Google Start television commercial, 300
Gordon, Shep
  as Cooper's manager, 46, 51, 59
gospel recordings, 257
Great Expectations (Dickens)
  in songwriting, 118, 120, 139
  theme of, 92–93
"Great Expectations"
  acoustic instruments in, 91
  analysis of, 81–83
  Beethoven influence on, 81–83
  as folksy ballad, 79, 135
  piano on, 81, 187
  recording of, 225–26
  vocals on, 81–83, 251
Greene, David, 142
Gruen, Bob, 221–22, 308
guitar(s). *See also* acoustic instruments, Gibson guitars
  Aerosmith's, 205
  on "Beth," 133

on "Detroit Rock City," 3–6
on "Do You Love Me?," 319–22
Frehley's, 172
Gibson, 171–72, 206, 248, 249
on "God of Thunder," 65–67, 207–8
on "King of the Night Time World," 190
Les Paul, 146, 171–72, 187
Simmons', 171–72
on "Sweet Pain," 206, 208
tuning down, 189
Wagner's favorite, 206

"hair band" craze, 297
Hall, Carl, 252–53
handcuff prank, 195–96
Happy Days, 73
Harris, Larry
    on Aucoin's abilities, 85–87
    after Casablanca, 306
    hiring of, 26
    on running label, 30, 33–34, 38
Hawn, Goldie, 292
headphones, 56
heavy metal
    Detroit influences on, 24
    Japanese, 301
    KISS influences on, 23
Hit Factory, 150, 222
"Hit it!," 95
Hitler-rock, 36
the Hollies, 124
Hollywood Stars, 125–27
hookers, 191
Hotel Diplomat, 98
Hotter Than Hell
    photo shoot, 96, 98–99
    recording of, 31
    reviews of, 33, 103

    Rolling Stone review of, 33
    tour for, 34
    writing of, 32
Howard Marks advertising agency, 13
    Aucoin at, 239
    Kelly at, 237
    scene at, 237–39
    taking over KISS, 305
    Woloch at, 98, 100
Hulman Civic University Center, 268

Ian, Scott, 304
Ienner, Jimmy, 194
"I Love It Loud," 115
In Concert 1976, 267
Index Journal, 329
Interland, Brian, 287–88
In the Land of Hype and Glory, 293
"Invasion of the Glitter Goths," 8
Iovine, Jimmy, 145, 150–51
Isley Brothers, 124
It's Gonna Rain, 255
"I Wanna Shout," 124

Jagger, Mick, 21
Japanese heavy metal, 301
Japanese kabuki, 8, 25
Japanese photojournalist, 308
Japanese tour, 294, 315
Jett, Joan, 305–6
jingles, 50, 51
Johnson, Rick, 271
Jones, Spike, 259
Jules Fischer Organization, 13, 276

Karloff, Boris, 259
Kellgren, Gary, 144

Kelly, Ken
    album back created by, 244
    artistic process of, 237–38, 240
    current career of, 309–10
    discovery of, 236
    first album cover done by, 242
    history of, 237
    at Howard Marks advertising
        agency, 237
    impact of, 309
    meeting KISS, 239–40
    merchandise design of, 291
    painting billboard, 274
    personality of, 236
Kerner, Kenny, 26, 143
KFRC, 288
Killer, 47
King Crimson, 256
"King of the Night Time World"
    analysis of, 41–43
    car crash in, 41
    Criss drumming on, 128
    drums on, 41–43
    Fowley on, 309
    guitars on, 190
    time signature on, 128–29
    versions of, 128
    writing collaborations on, 125–27
KISS
    band bonding moments of, 225–26
    boot camp for, 75–76
    branding of, xvi
    at Casablanca Records, x, 14, 85–89
    Casablanca Records after, 305–6
    Casablanca Records promoting,
        273–74
    changes in, 75–76
    comic books about, 314–15
    concepts of, 18
    Costello's first show of, 36
    covers compilation's of, 302
    crew, 37
    Day, 284
    debts of, 37–40
    depth of, 72–73, 187
    Destroyer tour, 275, 279–80
    in Detroit 1970s, 284
    drawings of, 240–41
    drug use in, 164–66
    early *Circus* magazine reviews of,
        27, 36
    Ezrin influence on, 81–83, 294
    Ezrin tension with, 77–78
    Ezrin writing with, 79–80
    fan, who died, 323–28
    first gigs, 28–29
    First KISS Grand Orchestral and
        Choral Recording Session,
        218–19, 223–24, 228–29
    four pieces of, 97–98
    Fowley collaborations with, 128–29,
        308
    heavy metal influences from, 23
    history of, xiii, 7
    humor of, 183
    Kelly meetings with, 239–40
    live recordings of, 169
    logo of, 268
    longevity of, 304
    in Los Angeles, early days, 30–32
    marketing ethos of, 20–21, 296
    Marks/Glickman after, 306
    at Max's, 8–9
    media about, 292
    memorabilia, 301, 314
    merchandise for, 279, 291
    as millionaires, 291
    modern influence of, 301

Motown influence on, 124–25
music theory of, 82–83
myths surrounding, 324, 330
new members of, 297
New York Dolls influence on, 8–9
in NYC, early days, 8–9
paintings of, 241–44
personality clashes in, 165–67
in pop culture, 294
post-*Destroyer*, 315
pranks of, 193–96
production of, 186–89
publicity of, 7–8, 25–26
recording sessions of, 175–76, 185–86
at Record Plant, 163–64, 185–86
rock-star attitudes of, 295–96
set design for, 13, 278–79
sound of, 169
stage design for, 276–77
Stanley on, 317
theme songs of, 116–17, 123–24
total domination of, 297
trading cards of, 314
tv movie about, 314
vulnerable side of, 131
KISS Album Focus, 257
KISS Alive! Forever, 9, 29, 324
KISS Army, 123
   logo, 268
   publicity by, 267–68
   shields, 278
"Kissin' Time," 25
KISS Magazine, 327
KISS Meets the Phantom of the Park, 249, 314
Kiss My Ass: Classic KISS Regrooved, 301
KISS Online, 255

KISStianity, 304
Klein, Gene, xii
Klosterman, Chuck, 23–24
Kramer, Eddie, 11, 73, 294–95
   piano playing of, 168
Krueger, Mark, 277

Lace & Whiskey, 49
"Larger Than Life," 115
"Larks Tongue in Aspic (Part I)," 256
Laurie, Peter, 259
lawsuits, 84–86, 88–89, 219
Lendt, C.K., 14, 180, 294, 306
Lennon, John
   photographer for, 221
   recording *Walls and Bridges*, 151
Lennon, Julian, 302
Les Paul
   custom guitars from, 146, 171–72, 206
   recording theory of, 187
   Triumph, 171–72
Let It Be (1984), 302
Line 6 Pocket POD, 173
Linet, Lew, 9
looping, 256
Lord of Garbage, 309
Los Angeles, 288
   early KISS in, 30–32
Love Goes to Buildings on Fire, 255
Love Gun, 295, 310, 315
Love It to Death, 47
"Love to Love You Baby," 286
Low, 256
Lucas, George, 127, 309

Macmillan, Allan
   on *Berlin*, 138
   during "Beth," 138–40

career of, 310–11
early Ezrin connection with, 50–51
Ezrin collaboration with, 139–40
history of, 138
musical influences of, 51
"Mad Dog," 122
Madison Square Garden, 294
Magna Graphic Studios
　boot camp at, 79–80
　Destroyer at, 112, 117
Manhattan's Academy of Music, 13
manslaughter, 328
marketing. *See also* advertising
　in advertising, 296
　during *Alive!*, 98–100
　ethos, 20–21
　ethos, of KISS, 20–21, 296
Marks, Howard, 99–100
Marks/Glickman
　after KISS, 306
Marshall amps, 175
Martha & the Vandellas, 124
Martin, George, 50
Marvel, 314
Max's Kansas City, 8–9
Mayer, Mike, 88
Mayer, Roger, 142
McCormick, Kathy, 329
McCready, Mike, 302
McCue, David, 142
McGlaughlin, Dwayne Kevin, 329
McPeek, Ben, 51
Mearas, John Alexander, 329
Mecklenburg, North Carolina, 324
"Me" Decade, xiv, 19
Melissa Manchester, 49
Melody Maker magazine, 21, 270

memorabilia, 301, 314
Mentor Sessions for the Nimbus School of Recording Arts, 302
merchandise, 279, 291
Messina, Jay
　at A1, 220–21
　with Aerosmith, 312
　career of, 311–12
　on compressing, 174
　on *Destroyer*, 312
　engineering reputation of, 311–12
　Ezrin relationship with, 48, 148–49, 162
　history of, 146–47
　on mixing, 253
　recording philosophies of, 175
　at Record Plant, 147–48, 159–60
　resume of, 146
　Stasiak meeting with, 150
Metropolitan Opera, 279
microphones
　binaural, 258
　on EMT chambers, 188
　for live sound, 176–77
　types of, 173
　for vocals, 252
The Mike Douglas Show, 286
Mike & Mike, 299
Miller, Alan, 268
Milward, John, 269
mixing, 253
Monday Night Football, 299
Moon Rentals, 172
"Moose," 327
Morello, Tom, 299
"The Morning Zoo," 306
Motown, 124–25
Mott the Hoople, 128, 130
Mount Olympus, 278

movie soundtracks, 149
MTV Unplugged, 301
multi-platinum, 304
"My Favorite Things," 226

Nadien, David, 223
National Association of Broadcasters Hall of Fame, 306
National Broadcast Company, 293
National Radio Hall of Fame, 306
National Recording Studios, 149
Nazis, 36
Neumann U87, 252
Newman, Edwin, 293
New Musical Express, 21, 53, 270
News & Observer, 325
news-radio, 260
New York City
  KISS early experience in, 8–9
  West Coast, 127
New York Dolls, 8–9, 127
"New York Groove," 296
New York Philharmonic Orchestra, 223
New York School of Music, 134
Nietzsche, 42
Night Ranger, 305–6
Nimbus 9, 302
  hiring of, 273
  starting of, 51
Nimbus School of Recording Arts, 52, 313
1960s existentialism, 18, 22
Nirvana, 302
Nixon, Dick, 96
"No No Song," 285
No Regrets, 19
Nothin' to Lose—The Making of KISS 1972–1975, (Sharp), 14, 26

O'Brien, Rod
  Ezrin relationship with, 49, 141
  history of, 141
  pranks of, 194–95
"oldies," 124
"Only Women Bleed," 62, 78, 131
On the Record, 135
orchestra
  at A&R, 219
  on "Beth," 136–37, 217–18, 227, 264–65
  in Brooklyn Boys choir, 224–25
  on *Destroyer*, 139–40
  on "Do You Love Me?," 187–88
  KISS grand, 218–19, 223–24, 228–29
  New York Philharmonic, 223
  photo shoot of, 221
  session musicians in, 223
  at Studio A1, 219–20
Oreckinto, Peter "Moose," 327
The Originals, 283
ostinato, 111–12
The Other Side of the Coin, 134
overdubbing, 187

paintings
  for billboard, 274
  for cover art, 241–44
  Destroyer, 310
  robot, 237–38
Parker, John, 288
Pearl Jam, 302
Penridge, Stan, 133
People's Choice Award, 291
Perry, Joe, 205
Phonograph Record, 23
photo shoot
  for *Alive!*, 96, 98–99

of Costello, 36, 221, 240, 269
  for *Destroyer*, 269
  for *Hotter Than Hell*, 96, 98–99
  of orchestra, 221
Photostats, 245
piano
  on "Beth," 137–38, 264–65
  on "Detroit Rock City," 186–87
  on "Great Expectations," 81, 187
  Kramer playing, 168
  Steinway grand, 160
pie fight, 194
Polygram, 305–6
Post and Courier, 330
power chords, 189
Powers, Devon, 103
Power Station, 222
pranks
  Ezrin's, 193
  handcuff, 195–96
  KISS's, 193–96
  O'Brien's, 194–95
  at Record Plant, 193–96
Presley, Elvis, 21
Pretties for You, 53
primal scream therapy, 200
The Producers, 149
Pro Tools, 254
Psycho Circus, 315
Pulp Fiction, 18
Pultec equalizer, 252
Punk Rock magazine, 19

Q104.3, 304
"Queen for a Day," 80

Radio & Records, 285
Raleigh, 323

Ramone, Phil
  Ezrin relationship with, 219
  influence of, 219
The Ramones, 301
"rattly clankings," 23, 37, 98
Ravitz, Mark, 276, 307
Raynor, Mr. David, 325
RCA Studios, 142
Record Plant
  amenities at, 143
  bands recorded at, 141, 144, 159
  drum-riser at, 160
  engineers at, 145, 254
  environment/layout of, 147, 159–60
  Ezrin days at, 142–43
  formation of, 144
  gear at, 142, 159–60, 171–72
  illegal transmitter at, 260
  KISS at, 163–64, 185–86
  Los Angeles edition, 145
  Messina at, 147–48, 159–60
  pranks at, 193–96
  sound/recording at, 162, 173–78, 186–89
  Stasiak at, 149–50
  weed at, 164
Red Hot Chili Peppers, 302
Reed, Lou
  recording *Berlin*, 138, 211
Reich, Steve, 255
Reingold, Buck, 26
the Replacements, 302
reunion tours, 301, 303
Revlon, 144
Richardson, Jack, 51, 148
Riley, Terry, 255
RKO, 288
robot painting, 237–38
"Rock and Roll All Nite," 74, 95

"Rock and Roll Demons," 256–57
Rock and Roll Hall of Fame, 300, 304
rock and roll lineage, 215
rock and roll manifesto, 42
Rock and Roll Over, 295, 315
"Rock and Roll Party," 257
"Rock Bottom," 35
Rock N' Roll Geek Show, 52
Rock Steady
    lawsuits of, 84–85, 88–89, 219
Rolling Stone reviews
    of *Alive!*, 103
    of *Destroyer*, 69, 269
    of *Hotter Than Hell*, 33
    of *KISS*, 27
    top 500 albums, 300
the Rolling Stones, 47, 100, 150, 276
Roosevelt Stadium, 36, 280
Rose, Frank, 8, 84
    during Brooklyn Boys Choir
        recordings, 221
    in *Circus* magazine, 74, 221, 225
    during *Destroyer* sessions, 84–85
the Runaways, 126, 309
Rundgren, Todd, 276

sadomasochism, xv–xvi
San Francisco, 288
Savoy Brown, 37
School's Out, 47, 142
Schulps, Dave, 19
Schwartzberg, Allan, 48–49
Sennheiser 405, 250
Sennheiser 421, 17, 173
session musicians, 223
set design, 13, 278–79, 307
7/4 time
    during boot camp, 81
    on *Destroyer*, 122

Sgt. Pepper's Lonely Hearts Club Band, 103
Shaffer, Paul, 50
shaman, 92
Shankar, Ravi, 146
Shannon, Scott
    Bogart relationship with, 26
    career of, 283–86
    in radio, 306
Sharp, Ken, 14–15, 283
"shavers," 177
"She"
    guitar parts in, 302
    writing of, 95
Sherman, Dale, 38
"Shout It Out Loud"
    analysis of, 213–15
    choral voices on, 213–14
    collaborations on, 123–24
    drums on, 213, 215
    as first single, 316–17
    reviews of, 273
    writing of, 124
The Show, 45, 62
Shure 57, 173, 180
Simmons, Gene
    anti-drug behavior of, 165
    artistic taste of, 233
    on "Beth," 289
    blowing fire, 13
    changes in, 104
    characters of, 250
    in *Circus* magazine, 124
    costumes of, 10
    early history of, 9–10
    early publicity of, 7–8, 25–26
    ego of, 234
    as front man, 10
    guitars of, 171–72

lighting hair, 27, 102, 275
name transformation of, xiii
role of, 315–16
songwriting of, 79–80, 115–16
Stanley relationship with, 125, 191
tongue, 10
womanizing of, 191–92
writing *Destroyer*, 121
Simon & Garfunkel, 220
Sinatra, Frank, 220
SiriusXM satellite radio shows, 304
sixteen-track, 254
slide machines, 240
SM57s, 177
Smalling, J.R., 80, 117
S&M fashion scene, 12
Smith, Chad, 302
Smith, Neal, 53
SoHo Weekly News, 293
Sonata No. 8 (Beethoven)
    chords of, 120
    in "Great Expectations," 81–83
    history of, 119–20
    influence of, 92–93, 119, 139, 225–26
    structure of, 91
Sony microphone, 173
sound effects, 260–61
South Africa, 295
Soviet Union, 96
the Space Age
    analysis of, ix
    comic book style depiction of, 315
Spector, Phil, 254–55
Spector bass, 171–72
Spectra-sonic console, 159
Spinning Gold, 306
Spirit of '76 tour, 208, 280
Springsteen, Bruce, 150

stage design, 276–77
stage props, 277
Stanley, Paul
    on "Beth," 289
    changes in, 104
    in *Circus* magazine, 75
    collaborations of, 123–24
    demos of, 79–80
    on *Destroyer*, 75–76
    ear condition of, 116
    in early 1970s, 7
    Ezrin influence on, 74
    history of, 10
    inspiration of, 323–24
    on KISS legacy, 317
    name change of, xiii
    role of, 315–16
    Simmons relationship with, 125, 191
    singing style of, 250–51
    songwriting of, 109–10, 115–16
Star Child, 115–16
    analysis of, ix
    comic book style depiction of, 315
Starkey, Bill, 268
Starr, Ringo, 285
Stasiak, Corky, 50
    career of, 311
    on compressing, 174
    diaries of, 159
    Ezrin relationship with, 152–53
    at Hit Factory, 150
    Messina meeting with, 150
    photographic record by, 222
    recording street sounds, 259
    at Record Plant, 149–50
State Heritage Library, 323
Stein, Kathi, 20, 279
Steinway grand piano, 160

Stewart Airbase, 268
Stilwell, Steven Lane, 326
Stone, Chris, 144
street sounds, 260
Streisand, Barbara, 220
Studio 54, 165, 192
Studio A
   the Act at, 160–61
   albums recorded at, 141
   final session at, 247–48
   gear at, 143
   layout of, 160
   recording process at, 162, 173–78
   rivalries of, 193–95
Studio A1
   Aucoin at, 220–21
   aura at, 220
   Brooklyn Boys Choir at, 220–21
   producers at, 220–21
   recording orchestra at, 219–20
Studio B, 194–95
studio vocals, 251–52
Suhs, Jeff, 29, 277, 324, 327
Summer, Donna, 86
Superman, 42, 233, 307
Suzuki, Ginger, 309
"Sweet Pain"
   acoustic instruments in, 117–19, 155
   analysis of, 155–57
   Bach influence on, 155
   guitar playing on, 206, 208
   lyrics of, 155–56
   recording of, 178
   writing of, 117–18

Tales from the Crypts, 236
Tarantino, Quentin, 18
Tarzan, 233
Taxi Driver, 8
Tentacle Tree, 277
Terre Haute, 268
That Metal Show, 304
Thoener, David, 195–96
Thomas, Tasha
   vocals of, 252–53
Time Is Money, 167
time signatures
   on *Destroyer*, 121–22, 179–80
   on "Do You Love Me?," 131
   in "Flaming Youth," 122–23
   4/4, 81, 122, 131
   on "King of the Night Time World," 128–29
   7/4 time, 81, 122
Tony Orlando & Dawn, 49
"Too Young," 111
Top 40, 286–87, 290
Toronto's Spring Thaw, 137–38
tours
   Alive!, 97
   band members on, 280–81
   costs of, 279–80
   Destroyer, 275, 279–80
   Dressed to Kill, 326–27
   expanse of, 294
   for *Hotter Than Hell*, 34
   in Japan, 294, 315
   merchandise sales during, 279
   reunion, 301, 303
   songs on, 280
   Spirit of '76, 208, 280
   stress during, 190–91
Townshend, Pete, 9
trading cards, 314
Trerotola, Jeannette, 283
Troggs', 118
Trombley, Rosalie, 284

Trouser Press, 19
Trunk, Eddie, 256, 304
tuxedo T-shirts, 222

United Press International, 270
Unmasked, 296
Ursa Major, 201

Vampirella, 233
Van Dyke, Dick, 291
Vault of Horror, 236
vehicular accidents, 260–61, 326–30
vehicular tragedy songs, 6
"Vendetta," 237
VH1, 304
Village Recorder Studios, 30
villains, 45
vocal(s). *See also* choral voices
  booth, 160
  in Brooklyn Boys Choir, 224–25
  on *Destroyer*, 250–53
  on "Detroit Rock City," 3–6
  on "Do You Love Me?," 319–22
  on "Flaming Youth," 107–8
  on "God of Thunder," 65–67
  on "Great Expectations," 81–83, 251
  of Hall, 252–53
  microphones for, 252
  recording of, 250
  on "Shout It Out Loud," 213–14
  studio, 251–52
  of Thomas, 252–53

Wagner, Dick
  appreciating Aerosmith, 201–2
  author relationship with, 310–11
  career of, 310

Ezrin relationship with, 202–3
favorite guitar of, 206
history of, 201–2
philosophy of, 204
at the Plaza Hotel, 203
songwriting of, 205
taking Ace's parts, 203–4
The Wall, 210–11
Walls and Bridges, 151
"War Machine," 115
Warren Publishing, 236
Waters, Roger, 210–11
WCBS, 306
weed, 164
Welcome to My Nightmare, 55, 138
West End Sound, 311–12
Westerberg, Paul, 302
Westlake Audio, 150, 159
"Whatever Gets You Through the Night," 151
whistle, Ezrin's, 166–67
Whitford, Brad, 205
Wicked Lester, 124
The Wild One, 72–73, 131
"Wild Thing," 118
Wilson, Brian, 43
Winkler, Henry, 73
Wise, Kenny, 32
Wise, Richie, 26
The Wiz, 252
The Wizard of Oz, 237–38
WNEW, 291
Woloch, Dennis
  assistant to, 232
  creativity of, 99–100
  Dennis Woloch Design company, 307
  design career of, 307
  on designing cover art, 233

designing logo, 268
history of, 13, 98
at Howard Marks advertising
  agency, 98, 100
packaging *Destroyer*, 98,
  231
Woodstock, xiv, 21
WPLJ, 306
WQXI, 285
Writing the Record, 103

WRKO, 287–88

Yakus, Shelly, 145
"You've Got Nothing to Live For"
  inspiration for, 118
  music for, 119

Z100 radio, 306
Zappa, Frank, 53
Ziggy Stardust, 22

Permissions

TEXT PERMISSIONS
Excerpts from *And Party Every Day: The Inside Story of Casablanca Records* by Larry Harris, with Curt Gooch and Jeff Suhs. Copyright © 2009 by Larry Harris. Reprinted by permission of Backbeat Books, an imprint of Hal Leonard Corporation.

Excerpts from pp. 19, 187, 188, 190, 191, 204, 209–210, 213, and 456 from Face the Music by Paul Stanley. Copyright © 2014 by Paul Stanley. Reprinted by permission of HarperCollins Publishers.

Excerpts from *Kiss Behind the Mask: The Official Unauthorized Biography* by David Leaf and Ken Sharp. Copyright © 2003 by David Leaf, Ken Sharp, and KISS Catalog Ltd. Used by permission of Grand Central Publishing. All rights reserved.

Excerpts from *Kiss and Make-Up* by Gene Simmons, copyright © 2001 by Gene Simmons Company. Used by permission of Crown Books, an imprint of the Crown Publishing Group, a division of Random House LLC. All rights reserved.

Reprinted with the permission of Scribner, a Division of Simon & Schuster, Inc., [excerpts] from *Makeup to Breakup: My Life in and Out of Kiss* by Peter Criss, with Larry "Ratso" Sloman. Copyright © 2012 by Catapult Enterprises, Inc. All rights reserved.

Reprinted with permission of Gallery, a Division of Simon & Schuster, Inc., [excerpts] from *No Regrets* by Ace Frehley, with Joe Layden and John Ostrosky. Copyright © 2011 by Ace Frehley. All rights reserved.

Excerpts from *Nothin' to Lose: The Making of Kiss 1972–1975* by Ken Sharp and Paul Stanley and Gene Simmons. Copyright © by Paul Stanley, Gene Simmons, and Ken Sharp. Reprinted by permission of HarperCollins Publishers.

LYRIC PERMISSIONS
Beth
Words and Music by Bob Ezrin, Stanley Penridge and Peter Criss
Copyright © 1976 ROCK STEADY MUSIC, ALL BY MYSELF PUBLISHING CO., CAFE AMERICANA and PETER CRISS PUBLISHING
Copyright Renewed
All Rights for ROCK STEADY MUSIC Controlled and Administered by UNIVERSAL-POLYGRAM INTERNATIONAL PUBLISHING, INC.
All Rights for ALL BY MYSELF MUSIC PUBLISHING CO. Controlled and Administered by IRVING MUSIC, INC.
All Rights for CAFE AMERICANA Controlled and Administered by CHAPPELL & CO.
All Rights Reserved. Used by Permission.
Reprinted with Permission of Hal Leonard Corporation

Detroit Rock City
Words and Music by Paul Stanley and Bob Ezrin
Copyright © 1976 HORI PRODUCTIONS AMERICA, INC., ALL BY MYSELF MUSIC, and CAFE AMERICANA, INC.
Copyright Renewed
All Rights for HORI PRODUCTIONS AMERICA, INC. and ALL BY MYSELF MUSIC Controlled and Administered by UNIVERSAL-POLYGRAM INTERNATIONAL PUBLISHING, INC.
All Rights for CAFE AMERICANA, INC. in the U.S. Administered by INTERSONG-USA, INC.
All Rights outside the U.S. excluding Japan Controlled and Administered by UNIVERSAL-POLYGRAM INTERNATIONAL PUBLISHING, INC.
All Rights Reserved. Used by Permission.
Reprinted with Permission of Hal Leonard Corporation

Do You Love Me
Word and Music by Paul Stanley, Bob Ezrin and Kim Fowley
Copyright © 1976 HORI PRODUCTIONS AMERICA, INC., ALL BY MYSELF MUSIC, CAFE AMERICANA and PEERMUSIC LTD.
Copyright Renewed
All Rights for HORI PRODUCTIONS AMERICA, INC. and ALL BY MYSELF MUSIC Controlled and Administered by UNIVERSAL-POLYGRAM INTERNATIONAL PUBLISHING, INC.
All Rights for CAFE AMERICANA in the U.S. Administered by INTERSONG U.S.A., INC.
All Rights Reserved. Used by Permission.
Reprinted with Permission of Hal Leonard Corporation

Flaming Youth
Words and Music by Gene Simmons, Paul Stanley, Ace Frehley and Bob Ezrin
Copyright © 1976 HORI PRODUCTIONS AMERICA, INC., ALL BY MYSELF MUSIC and CAFE AMERICANA
Copyright Renewed
All Rights for HORI PRODUCTIONS AMERICA, INC. and ALL BY MYSELF MUSIC Controlled and Administered by

UNIVERSAL-POLYGRAM INTERNATIONAL PUBLISHING, INC.
All Rights for CAFE AMERICANA in the U.S. Administered by INTERSONG U.S.A., INC.
All Rights outside the U.S. excluding Japan Controlled and Administered by UNIVERSAL-POLYGRAM INTERNATIONAL PUBLISHING, INC.
All Rights Reserved. Used by Permission.
Reprinted with Permission of Hal Leonard Corporation

God of Thunder
Words and Music by Paul Stanley
Copyright © 1976 HORI PRODUCTIONS AMERICA, INC. and CAFE AMERICANA, INC.
Copyright renewed.
All Rights for HORI PRODUCTIONS AMERICA, INC. Controlled and Administered by UNIVERSAL-POLYGRAM INTERNATIONAL PUBLISHING, INC.
All Rights for CAFE AMERICANA, INC. in the U.S. Administered by INTERSONG U.S.A., INC.
All Rights outside the U.S. excluding Japan Controlled and Administered by UNIVERSAL-POLYGRAM INTERNATIONAL PUBLISHING, INC.
All Rights Reserved. Used by Permission.
Reprinted with Permission of Hal Leonard Corporation

Great Expectations
Words and Music by Gene Simmons and Bob Ezrin
Copyright © 1976 HORI PRODUCTIONS AMERICA, INC., ALL BY MYSELF MUSIC and CAFE AMERICANA
Copyright Renewed
All Rights for HORI PRODUCTIONS AMERICA, INC. and ALL BY MYSELF MUSIC Controlled and Administered by UNIVERSAL-POLYGRAM INTERNATIONAL PUBLISHING, INC.
All Rights for CAFE AMERICANA in the U.S. Administered by INTERSONG U.S.A., INC.
All Rights outside the U.S. excluding Japan Controlled and Administered by UNIVERSAL-POLYGRAM INTERNATIONAL PUBLISHING, INC.
All Rights Reserved. Used by Permission.
Reprinted with Permission of Hal Leonard Corporation

King Of The Night Time World
Words and Music by Paul Stanley, Bob Ezrin, Kim Fowley and Mark Anthony
Copyright © 1976 HORI PRODUCTIONS AMERICA, INC., ALL BY MYSELF MUSIC, CAFE AMERICANA, PEERMUSIC LTD., SCREEN GEMS-EMI MUSIC INC. and 8TH POWER MUSIC
Copyright Renewed
All Rights for HORI PRODUCTIONS AMERICA, INC. and ALL BY MYSELF MUSIC Controlled and Administered by UNIVERSAL-POLYGRAM INTERNATIONAL PUBLISHING, INC.
All Rights for CAFE AMERICANA in the U.S. Administered by INTERSONG U.S.A., INC.
All Rights for 8TH POWER MUSIC Controlled and Administered by SCREEN GEMS-EMI MUSIC INC.
All Rights Reserved. Used by Permission.
Reprinted with Permission of Hal Leonard Corporation

Shout It Out Loud
Words and Music by Paul Stanley, Gene Simmons and Bob Ezrin
Copyright © 1976 HORI PRODUCTIONS AMERICA, INC., ALL BY MYSELF MUSIC and CAFE AMERICANA
Copyright Renewed
All Rights for HORI PRODUCTIONS AMERICA, INC. and ALL BY MYSELF MUSIC Controlled and Administered by UNIVERSAL-POLYGRAM INTERNATIONAL PUBLISHING, INC.
All Rights for CAFE AMERICANA in the U.S. Administered by INTERSONG U.S.A., INC.
All Rights outside the U.S. excluding Japan Controlled and Administered by UNIVERSAL-POLYRGAM INTERNATIONAL PUBLISHING, INC.
All Rights Reserved. Used by Permission.
Reprinted with Permission of Hal Leonard Corporation

Sweet Pain
Words and Music by Gene Simmons
Copyright © 1976 HORI PRODUCTIONS AMERICA, INC. and CAFE AMERICANA
Copyright Renewed
All Rights for HORI PRODUCTIONS AMERICA, INC. Controlled and Administered by UNIVERSAL-POLYGRAM INTERNATIONAL PUBLISHING, INC.
All Rights for CAFE AMERICANA in the U.S. Administered by INTERSONG U.S.A., INC.
All Rights outside the U.S. excluding Japan Controlled and Administered by UNIVERSAL-POLYGRAM INTERNATIONAL PUBLISHING, INC.
All Rights Reserved. Used by Permission.
Reprinted with Permission of Hal Leonard Corporation